Marianne Wetzel

Real Estate Damages
An Analysis of Detrimental Conditions

Readers of this text may be interested in these related texts available from the Appraisal Institute:
- *The Appraisal of Real Estate,* 11th edition
- *Appraising Residential Properties,* 2d edition
- *The Valuation of Wetlands,* by David M. Keating, MAI
- *Property Inspection: An Appraiser's Guide,* by John A. Simpson, MAI
- *Appraising the Tough Ones: Creative Ways to Value Complex Residential Properties,* by Frank E. Harrison, MAI, SRA
- *Real Estate Valuation in Litigation,* 2d edition, by J.D. Eaton, MAI, SRA
- *Environmental Site Assessments and their Impact on Property Value: The Appraiser's Role,* by Robert V. Colangelo, CPG, and Ronald D. Miller, Esq.
- *The Dictionary of Real Estate Appraisal,* 3d edtion

Real Estate Damages
An Analysis of Detrimental Conditions

APPRAISAL INSTITUTE®

875 North Michigan Avenue, Suite 2400
Chicago, IL 60611-1980

http://www.appraisalinstitute.org

By Randall Bell, MAI

Vice President, Educational Programs and Publications:	Sean Hutchinson	Reviewers Diane Gilbert, MAI, SRA
Director, Content Development and Quality Assurance:	Margo Wright	Frank E. Harrison, MAI, SRA Michael MaRous, MAI, SRA
Manager, Book Development:	Stephanie Shea-Joyce	
Cover Designer:	Amy Reichard	
Editor:	Michael McKinley	
Production Specialist:	Michael P. Landis	

For Educational Purposes Only

The material presented in this text has been reviewed by members of the Appraisal Institute, but the opinions and procedures set forth by the author are not necessarily endorsed as the only methodology consistent with proper appraisal practice. While a great deal of care has been taken to provide accurate and current information, neither the Appraisal Institute nor its editors and staff assume responsibility for the accuracy of the data contained herein. Further, the general principles and conclusions presented in this text are subject to local, state, and federal laws and regulations, court cases, and any revisions of the same. This publication is sold for educational purposes with the understanding that the publisher is not engaged in rendering legal, accounting, or other professional service.

Important Notice Regarding Permissions

Portions of this book were quoted or paraphrased from *Bell's Guide: The Real Estate Encyclopedia,* second edition, by Randall Bell, MAI. Mr. Bell retains the copyright for this material, including the charts and models presented. Below is a list identifying the quoted or paraphrased material in this book and the corresponding pages from *Bell's Guide.*

Pages from *Real Estate Damages*	Pages from *Bell's Guide*
268–272	136–145
15	253–255
16–17	256–258
47, 51, 57, 69, 80	257
107, 111, 123, 156, 193	259
18, 20, 23	261
263–267	262–268
138	269–272
113, 116–117	274–277
132	278–280
134	281–289
273–321	290–292
336–349	298–305

Nondiscrimination Policy

The Appraisal Institute advocates equal opportunity and nondiscrimination in the appraisal profession and conducts its activities in accordance with applicable federal, state, and local laws.

© 1999 by the Appraisal Institute, an Illinois not for profit corporation. All rights reserved. No part of this publication may be reproduced, modified, rewritten, or distributed, either electronically or by any other means, without the express written permission of the Appraisal Institute.

Printed in the United States of America

Library of Congress Cataloging-in-Publication data

Bell, Randall.
    Real estate damages: an analysis of detrimental conditions / by Randall Bell.
        p.   cm.
    Includes bibliographical references and index.
    ISBN 0-922154-55-4
        1. Real property—Valuation—United States.   2. Damages—United States.   3. Real property—Valuation—United States—Case studies.
    I. Title
    HD1389.5.U6B45   1999
    333.33'2—dc21
                                                                                                        98-52196
                                                                                                              CIP

Table of Contents

Foreword		vii
About the Author		ix
Acknowledgments		xi
Introduction	Detrimental Conditions and Property Values	1
Chapter 1	No Detrimental Conditions or Benign Condition	46
Case Study:	Bruce McNall House – Randall Bell, MAI	48
Chapter 2	Nonmarket Motivations	49
Case Study:	Feng Shui – Orell C. Anderson, MAI	52
Chapter 3	Market Conditions	55
Case Study:	Weatherby Pointe – Orell C. Anderson, MAI	61
Chapter 4	Temporary Conditions	68
Case Study:	Davis Building – Mark W. Smith, MAI	75
Chapter 5	Imposed Conditions	79
Case Study:	Sea-Tac International Airport Hellmuth, Obata + Kassabaum, Inc. Raytheon Infrastructure Services, Inc. Thomas Lane & Associates, Inc. Michael J. McCormick, AICPA	98
Chapter 6	Building Construction Conditions	105
Case Study:	Fine Mountain Condominiums – Richard A. Neustein, MAI, SRA	108
Chapter 7	Soil and Geotechnical Construction Conditions	110
Case Study:	California Condominiums – Michael V. Sanders, MAI, SRA	119
Chapter 8	Environmental Conditions	122
Case Study:	Ashby Building – Randall Bell, MAI	152
Chapter 9	Natural Conditions	155
Case Study:	Alaskan Good Friday Earthquake – Randall Bell, MAI	187
Chapter 10	Incurable Conditions	190
Case Study:	Benedict Canyon Landslide – Randall Bell, MAI	194

Additional Case Studies

1	Hill View Development – Joe Haeussler, MAI	199
2	Durham Woods – Randall Bell, MAI	203
3	Simpson Condominium – Randall Bell, MAI	204
4	Luby's Cafeteria – Randall Bell, MAI, and Orell C. Anderson, MAI	205
5	Pacific Motel – Orell C. Anderson, MAI	206
6	Airport Noise Impact Study – Randall Bell, MAI	213
7	Hollywood Boulevard Sinkhole and Subsidence – Orell C. Anderson, MAI	216

8	Desert Resort Subdivision – Mark W. Smith, MAI	218
9	Beverly Hills Estate – Randall Bell, MAI	221
10	Krantz House – Joseph Haeussler, MAI	225
11	Kangaroo Hill Slope Instability – Randall Bell, MAI	228
12	Geotechnical Issues – Michael V. Sanders, MAI, SRA	229
13	Degrees of Indemnification – Richard A. Neustein, MAI, SRA	231
14	Three Brownfield Case Studies – Gregory D. Trimanche and Craig A. Moyer	234
15	Exxon Valdez Oil Spill – Randall Bell, MAI	237
16	Love Canal – Randall Bell, MAI	238
17	Three Mile Island – Randall Bell, MAI	242
18	Yuba River Floods – Burrell E. Montz and Graham A. Tobin	245
19	Oklahoma Federal Building – Randall Bell, MAI	257
20	Sinkholes – Sandra Laudone, MAI, SRA	258
21	Dahmer Apartment Building – Orell C. Anderson, MAI	260

Appendixes

1	Detrimental Conditions and Typical Classification	263
2	Americans with Disabilities Act (ADA) Overview	268
3	Federal Agencies and State Agencies	273
4	Associations and Periodicals	322

Glossary	366
Bibliography	350
Index	355

Foreword

The cost of all natural disasters in the United States has doubled in the last decade, from roughly $25 billion to $50 billion a year. Research has yet to reveal clear reasons for this phenomenon, though many experts point not to climatic changes but to the growing concentration of wealth and population in coastal areas of the country, which are most at risk from natural disasters. The publication of *Real Estate Damages* comes at a fortunate time, with property damage increasing at a geometric rate and appraisers looking for practical solutions to a variety of new valuation problems.

Under normal circumstances, estimating property value poses a set of logistical challenges. The specific issues arising from soil subsidence problems, earthquake damage, environmental contamination, and other detrimental conditions complicate the process further. With the publication of this book, the Appraisal Institute hopes to take the guesswork out of appraising property affected by a variety of detrimental conditions, from crime scene stigma to environmental contamination, and to help practitioners develop the skills they need to analyze these tragic and often emotional situations effectively. Ten classifications of detrimental conditions are discussed in depth, each in its own chapter. With case studies and examples of actual detrimental conditions as well as listings of reference works and government contacts on the state and federal levels, *Real Estate Damages* is the most complete resource on the subject available.

Bert L. Thornton, MAI
1999 President
Appraisal Institute

About the Author

Randall Bell, MAI, is a world-renowned expert in property damage issues and is credited with developing the study of detrimental conditions. He has traveled extensively in his research of detrimental conditions and the impact they have on real estate values. Founded upon this research, he has written various specialized methodologies, which were the basis for the Detrimental Conditions Seminar developed by the Appraisal Institute

Mr. Bell is the author of *Bell's Guide: The Real Estate Encyclopedia,* as well as numerous articles that have been published in various professional journals. He has lectured internationally on the topic of property damages and mitigation strategies.

Often quoted in the national and international media, Mr. Bell's career has been profiled on many occasions, including in the *Wall Street Journal,* the *San Francisco Chronicle, People Magazine, Today's Realtor, Chicago Tribune, New York Times, Los Angeles Times*, all major television networks, and CNN. Additionally, his career has been profiled by the media in Europe, Asia, and Australia.

Mr. Bell has an MBA in real estate from UCLA and a BS in finance and accounting from BYU. He is a native of Southern California, where he resides with his wife, Melanie, and their three children, Michael, Steven, and Britten.

Acknowledgments

In the early 1990s, a rash of problems hit southern California. They included the Malibu floods and fires, the Los Angeles riots, the contamination of much of the city of Avila Beach, the Laguna Niguel landslides, the O.J. Simpson murder trial, the Laguna Canyon floods and firestorms, and the Northridge earthquake. Of course, these situations damaged many properties, and like other appraisers in the area, I received many assignments to determine the impact that these events had on property values. Aside from these issues, my family had just moved to a new house. While I knew that it was nearby a small sewage treatment plant, I was not aware that the plant was soon to be expanded. On top of that, the area had expansive soils, slope creep, and would be in an area near the flight path for a proposed international airport. Shortly after moving, an earthquake cracked our swimming pool. Both my business and home life were now filled with situations that I came to call *detrimental conditions*.

Faced with this, I researched volumes for a central source to deal with the valuation of these situations. I found that many outstanding articles have been written on specific topics of environmental contamination, airport noise, crime scene stigma, geotechnical issues, and so forth; however, I could not find anything that addressed all these situations collectively, and a universal valuation methodology was nowhere to be found.

Consequently, I listed all the situations that I was dealing with and started categorizing them. Eventually a chart evolved that I started using in my practice. One day I showed the chart to my friend and colleague, Joanne Cheynne, SRA, a leading residential appraiser. Joanne then told me that she was responsible for organizing 10 seminars for the Summer Seminar Spectacular in Anaheim, California, that she only had found nine, and that I would be the tenth. Her faith in me prompted an amazing journey.

After the Anaheim seminar, a woman by the name of Misa Zane, MAI, approached me. Misa asked me if I would like to teach the seminar in Hawaii. After considering her offer for about half a second, I agreed. That seminar led to others, and eventually the detrimental conditions seminar was approved and sponsored nationally by the Appraisal Institute. From there, I traveled extensively around the country and around the world conducting research and lecturing.

Having had this amazing experience, there were many important people that unselfishly contributed their support, time, and talents in this book effort, and I wish to thank them.

First, I wish to acknowledge the authors of the many articles and papers written on various property damage-related topics. Many of them were very helpful in developing a detrimental condition valuation methodology, and they are referenced at the end of each chapter. Next, my great friend and colleague, Orell C. Anderson, MAI, assisted me greatly along the way. He received many late night phone calls and faxes and always provided invaluable insight and feedback as I obsessed with refining the detrimental condition matrix, models, and charts. Along with Orell, I surrounded myself with technical advisors whom I consider to be some of the brightest minds in the profession. They are Michael Sanders, MAI, SRA, Richard Neustein, MAI, SRA, and Valeo Schultz. I greatly thank them.

Ted Whitmer, MAI is probably the nation's best-known and most-liked appraiser. In spite of his busy schedule, he provided invaluable encouragement and insight in the earliest stages regarding the dynamics of the appraisal community, as well as considerable technical insight. My good friend (and Spanish interpreter) Neil Balholm provided an outstanding tour of the earthquake damage in Mexico City. Duane King and Jon Wilcox, also great friends and well-known Los Angeles bankers, provided extensive tours of fire-damaged properties in Malibu.

One night I watched a documentary on television about the great Alaskan earthquake of 1964. A woman relayed her ordeal when, as a young girl, along with her family she clung to the roof of her home as tidal waves continuously pounded them throughout the night. Wanting to study the long-term effects on real estate, I called the only person I knew in Alaska, a prominent appraiser by the name of Steve MacSwain, MAI, who I had met when I lectured at the national conference of the Appraisal Institute in Washington, D.C. Steve graciously offered to show me around Alaska. When I arrived there I learned, in an amazing coincidence, that it was his wife, Linda, whom I had seen on TV. On top of this, Steve had done much of the appraisal work on the Exxon Valdez oil spill. Together they provided one of the most amazing tours in my professional life.

I also had the honor of meeting a group of prominent appraisers in Hawaii, who provided invaluable insight as I visited some of the most spectacular natural disasters in the world, ranging from landslides, rockslides, volcanoes, and tidal waves. They are Misa Zane, MAI, Cary Murakami, John Tuquero, Walter Jung, SRA, J. Michael Chun, SRA, Harlin S.K.Y. Young, MAI, SRA, and Tom Miyata.

Jim Eaton, MAI, a well-known appraiser and author, patiently answered many questions about the Mount St. Helens volcano eruptions and the residual effects on real estate. Also, John Van Vlear, attorney at law, provided significant data on environmental contamination. Steve Yoblanzki, the attorney who successfully defended Occidental Chemical in the Love Canal litigation provided many interesting and useful documents surrounding the most famous environmental contamination case in the world. Joe Haeussler, MAI, a friend and former colleague at Bell & Associates, Inc., conducted considerable research. I also wish to thank Nick Tillema, MAI, SRA, Rudy Robinson, MAI, Wayne Hunsperger, MAI, SRA, Joe Campanella, MAI, and Mike Hedden, MAI. Each of these individuals work extensively in the field of property damages and provided important insights.

Ted Slack, MAI, one of the best known instructors for the Appraisal Institute, along with his wife, Sue Slack, MAI, and Diane Gilbert, MAI, and Chris Moore, MAI, all provided considerable information, including a tour of Miami. Edward N. Parker, MAI, got up early one Saturday morning to provide a tour of properties damaged by Hurricane Andrew on the east coast of Florida. Ronald A. Oppedisano, MAI, did research of the Gray home in suburban Chicago, and provided photographs and data. Dan Jalber, MAI, provided various items of research he conducted into recent legislation on disclosure issues for Massachusetts.

Maureen Kanka, the mother of Megan Kanka shared many difficult and incomprehensible experiences with me about the tragic loss of her daughter, and recounted to me the events that occurred within her neighborhood. Her activism resulted in federal legislation of "Megan's Law." Louis Brown, the father of Nicole Brown Simpson, shared many of his experiences with me, as did Sam Kouthesfahani, PhD, the owner of the Heaven's Gate mansion in Rancho Santa Fe, California. These conversations provided invaluable insight into the dynamics and profound impact of market resistance, or "stigma."

I had written this book by the time that I joined Price Waterhouse in 1997 and founded the Real Estate Damages practice there. Nonetheless, two of the firm's partners, Robert Knudsen and George Strong, encouraged me to use the resources of the firm to make further enhancements. As a result, my research team at Price Waterhouse provided details that I added to the book. At what would become the world's largest consulting firm of PricewaterhouseCoopers after a landmark merger, Jim Chalmers, PhD, provided a review of the manuscript that prompted some refinements.

The people of Appraisal Institute have been incredible, and I have a tremendous respect for the organization, the staff, and many of its members. John Ross and Sean Hutchinson have been very supportive. Their leadership has not only been helpful in this project but also has fundamentally altered the course of the Appraisal Institute and put it onto a new and dynamic path. I believe that all members of the Appraisal Institute owe them a great measure of thanks, as their vision and work have had profound consequences. Chris Bettin, Francine Rosenstein, and Donna O'Loughlin have been very helpful and supportive. Without question, the detrimental conditions seminar was a major factor that contributed to this book. I wish to thank Diane Gilbert, MAI, SRA, the project coordinator for the seminar, and William Christensen, MAI, SRA, Brooke Leer, MAI, George Ryon, MAI, John D. Dorchester, Jr., MAI, and Bill Mundy, PhD, MAI, who all contributed to the review process. Also essential in the seminar were the efforts of Cecilia Merino, Margo T. Wright, Linda Willet, and Christopher Freeborn. Also, I wish to thank William Kinnard, PhD, MAI, for allowing me to use his compilation of articles which are the basis for the "further reading" sections of this book. Diane Gilbert, MAI, and Frank Harrison, MAI, spent countless hours reviewing the manuscript and provided invaluable feedback, and Michael McKinley did an outstanding job editing the barrage of revisions to the manuscript.

Of course, I believe that the book is greatly enhanced by the many case studies that were contributed, and my thanks goes to each of those authors: Orell C. Anderson, MAI, Joseph Haeussler, MAI, Sandra Laudone, MAI, SRA, Richard A. Neustein, MAI, SRA, Michael V. Sanders, MAI, SRA, Mark W. Smith, MAI, Burrell E. Montz, and Graham A. Tobin. I appreciate Peter Bernstein providing the aerial photographs. I must also thank all the people responsible for research and other contributions who haven't yet been mentioned: Barry J. Alperin, MAI, ASA, Stephanie Cochran, Brandon Dickens, John Ellis, MAI, Steve Johnson, Gary Justiss, James Kerns, Daniel Kim, Jeff Leedom, Kelly Mellahan, Bryan Merica, Craig A. Moyer, Rebecka Nevarez, Ken Rugeti, Michael Terry, and Gregory D. Trimarche.

As I have lectured and taught the seminar around the country, I had the benefit of receiving considerable comments, letters, and feedback from hundreds of very intelligent people, many of who are members of the Appraisal Institute, and I thank them. My invitation to lecture in South America, at an international conference sponsored by UPAV, was a great honor. There I addressed real estate experts from many countries. From that conference and others, I gained considerable insight into detrimental conditions all over the world, including Russia, Japan, Chile, Germany, China, and others, which I hope to write about in the future.

Finally, this book involved a period of considerable travel and many nights and weekends of exhaustive research and writing. Though all of this my beautiful wife, Melanie, kept our three great kids, Michael, Steven, and Britten, happy and smiling. Her job as a mom is far more work and far more important than anything that I have done in business. She gave the greatest support of all, and I give her my greatest thanks.

INTRODUCTION

Detrimental Conditions and Property Values

The events that grab newspaper headlines and lead the news updates at the top of the hour often involve death and destruction—floods, earthquakes, tornadoes, neighborhood nuisances, environmental contamination, crime, economic downturns, bankruptcies, public work projects, catastrophic disasters, and the list goes on and on. In the aftermath of a damaging event, firefighters put out the fires and rescue the victims, paramedics treat the survivors, police arrest the criminals, lawyers have trials, and reporters tell the story. Many of these events involve very emotional issues for the participants, yet every one of these situations also has a practical consideration, specifically the impact that the event had on property values.

An old and simplistic real estate adage states that real estate values are driven by "location location location." Clearly, there are many important issues other than location. One way to view the concept of "value" is to consider that the needs, tastes, fears, sensitivities, desires, and anticipations of sellers and buyers are being translated into a number, i.e., a price. To accurately analyze real estate, one must be able to monitor and interpret the actions of the participants within the market because properties do not deal with one another, people do. When carefully considered, all the factors that have an influence on a property's desirability, and therefore its value, are traced back to the market's perceptions. To truly understand real estate valuation, one must conscientiously focus upon and measure these perceptions. In fact, a more accurate real estate adage may be "perception perception perception."

Real estate values are estimated through the application of the three traditional approaches to value, and volumes have been written on the many facets of real estate economics, principles of value, and the appraisal process. However, when real estate is damaged or impaired, an additional and often more complex analysis is required. At this point the assignment makes a transition from an appraisal to a damage analysis. Although these studies of property damages can be very involved, they are, in fact, based upon these same fundamental economic and valuation principles. The traditional appraisal techniques provide the foundation upon which the analysis of real estate damages and detrimental conditions may be made.

The term *unimpaired value* refers to the value of a property as if no detrimental condition exists, while the term *impaired value* reflects the value of the property with the influence of a detrimental condition. An estimate of the unimpaired value is almost always part of a detrimental conditions assignment because it is the effect of the detrimental condition that is usually at issue, and furthermore the measure of the effect, or damages, is the difference between the unimpaired and the impaired values. Sometimes, however, if a market transaction has established the value of the property as impaired, then the essence of the assignment is to estimate the unimpaired value. Other times the unimpaired market value is known and not at issue, and the task that remains is to estimate the impaired value. More commonly, neither is known and so the analysis requires estimation of both values.

Estimation of the unimpaired value does not differ from a traditional appraisal assignment except that the value estimate often refers to some retrospective date—i.e., the date of the damage or the date of discovery of the damage. As this starting point, the unimpaired value is derived by the application of several fundamental appraisal concepts and one or more of the three traditional approaches to value.

Ownership Rights

Understanding ownership rights is essential in any valuation assignment including damaged real estate. The most complete ownership of real estate is the *fee simple estate*, which is the complete and total *bundle of rights*, as shown in Exhibit 0.1. This is subject only to taxes (i.e., property taxes), police power (i.e., zoning and other land use regulations), eminent domain (the sovereign right of the government to take property for the public good and pay just compensation to the owner), and escheat (governmental intervention if the owner dies with no will).

Portions of the bundle of rights may in turn be broken off, given away, or sold. For example, the right to occupy the property may be given to another party in return for a rental or lease payment. In this case, the fee simple owner becomes the owner of a leased fee estate, or lessor, and the tenant or lessee has a leasehold estate.

Principles of Conformity and Regression

Other important concepts in the valuation of real estate are the principles of conformity and regression, which are illustrated on pages 4 and 5. Property values are negatively impacted when surrounding properties are of a lesser value. Conversely, a property of lesser value is enhanced when the adjoining property values are high. For example, a run-down house in an expensive beach community tend to be worth much more than the same house in a community where all the houses are run down. On the other hand, in terms of optimal value, it is generally not a good idea to buy or build the biggest and best house in the neighborhood. Optimal property values are experienced when the properties within a neighborhood conform to one another.

The appraisal process involves three main categories, as shown in Exhibit 0.4 on page 6:

1. Defining the appraisal problem
2. Describing the subject property
3. Analyzing the property and reconciling its value

Defining the appraisal problem involves identifying the subject property by legal description—i.e., assessors' parcel map and address. The rights involved must also be discussed, along with the conditions of the appraisal. An appraisal also includes a general description of the area, a market analysis, a description of the site, as well as any improvements.

Next, a study of the property's highest and best use must be completed, as if vacant and as improved. Under such an analysis, the physically possible, legally permissible, financially feasible, and maximally productive uses are considered. This study considers these four issues, which like a funnel narrow the options to a final conclusion as to the maximally productive use of the property, as is shown in Exhibit 0.5 on page 7.

Once the highest and best use is determined, the property may be valued by employing the three approaches to value: the cost approach, the sales comparison approach, and the income capitalization approach. Each approach represents a technique by which market data may be processed into an indication of value. All three approaches to value are, in essence, market data approaches because the data inputs are market-derived.

The cost approach in appraisal analysis is based on the proposition that an informed buyer will pay no more than the cost of producing a substitute property with the same utility as the subject property. This approach is particularly appropriate when the property being appraised includes relatively new improvements that represent the highest and best use of the land, when relatively unique or specialized improvements are located on the subject site, or when market data of similar properties cannot be obtained. Simply stated, an indication of value is estimated by adding the land value to the depreciated value of the improvements. A simple cost approach valuation may include the following type of calculations:

Exhibit 0.1   The Bundle of Rights

The Complete "Bundle of Rights"
Fee Simple Estate

Improvement value new	$500,000
Less physical depreciation	− 100,000
Depreciated value of the improvements	400,000
Plus land value	+ 600,000
Indicated value (cost approach)	$1,000,000

Exhibit 0.2 Principle of Regression

A property's value is negatively impacted when surrounded by properties of lesser value.

A property of lesser value tends to be enhanced when the adjoining property values are high.

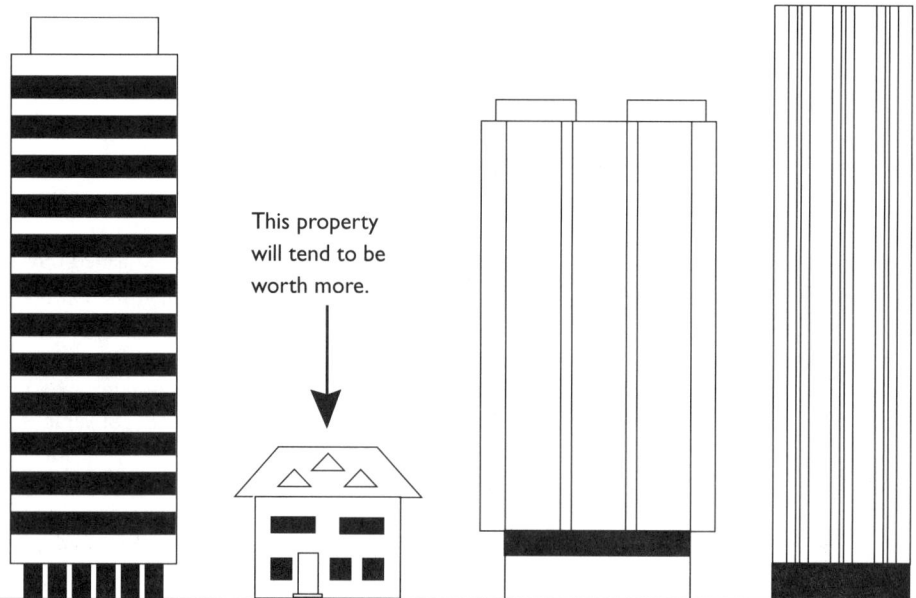

Real Estate Damages: An Analysis of Detrimental Conditions

Exhibit 0.3 Principle of Conformity

Property values are optimal and are maximized when a property generally conforms to the surrounding properties and are negatively impacted when the property does not.

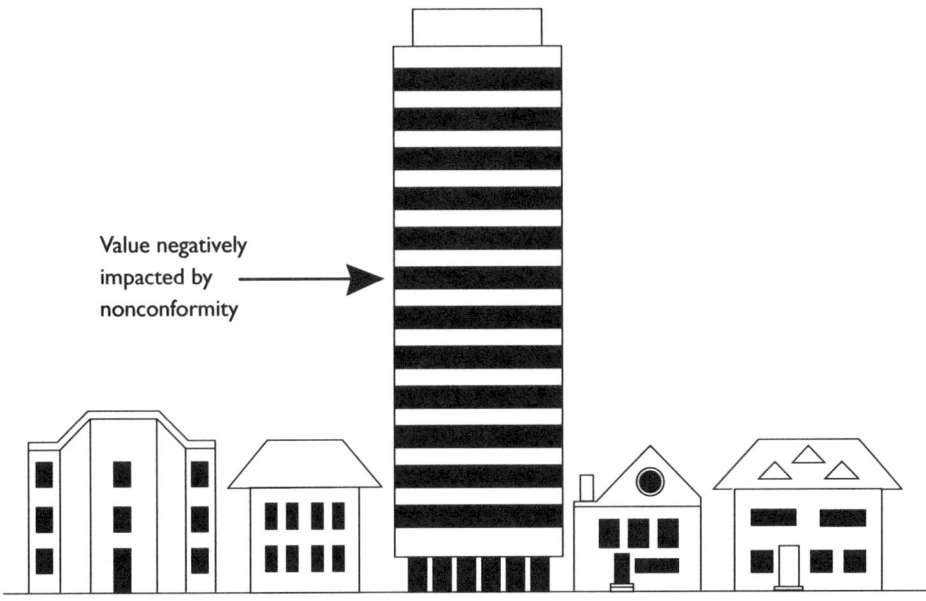

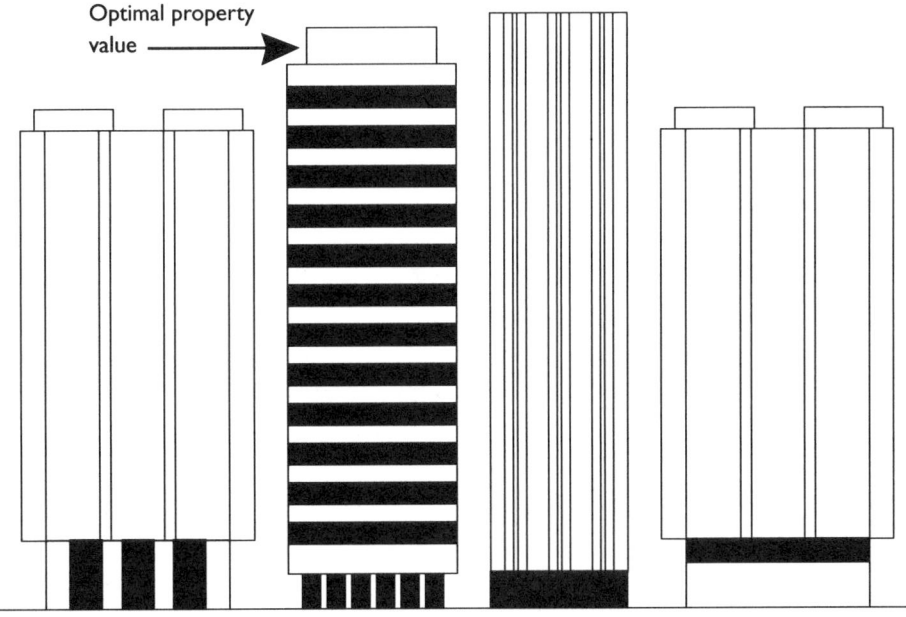

Detrimental Conditions and Property Values

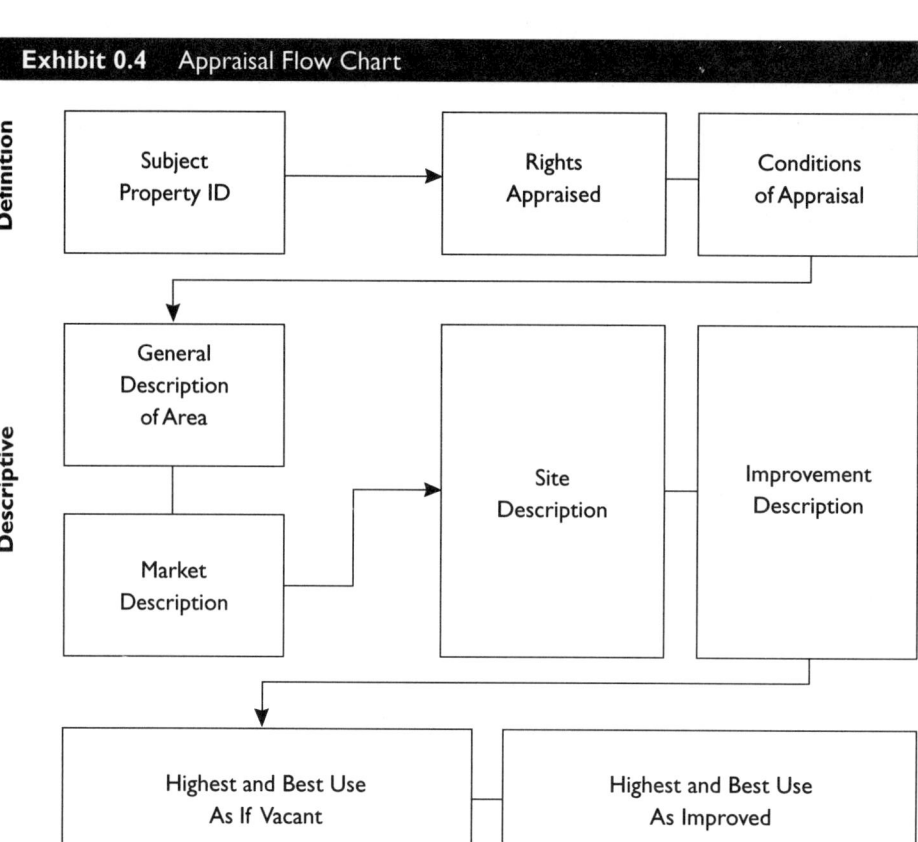

Real Estate Damages: An Analysis of Detrimental Conditions

In the sales comparison approach, the market value estimate is predicated upon prices paid in actual market transactions and reflected in current listings. This approach involves a process of analyzing sales of similar properties with relevant sale dates to derive an indication of the most probable sales price of the property being appraised. For single-family residences, the price of each sales comparable may be analyzed, with adjustments made for physical and perceptual locational differences between the sales comparable and the subject property. The adjustment process can also be applied to commercial and industrial properties, which are often compared on a price per square foot basis or price per unit. An illustration of the final indication from the sales comparison approach might be:

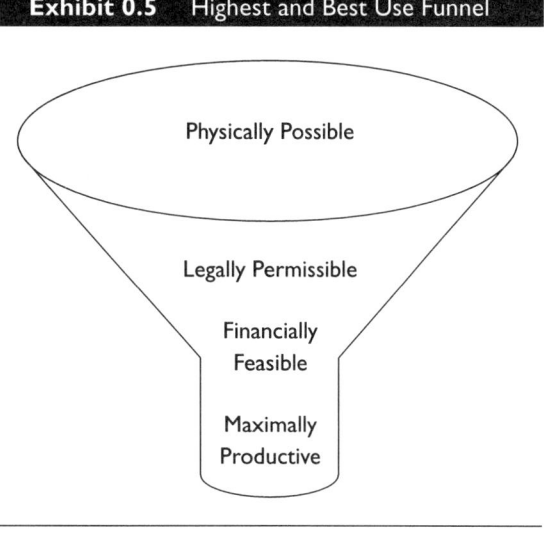

Exhibit 0.5 Highest and Best Use Funnel

10,000 square feet @ $100 per square foot = $1,000,000

The income capitalization approach converts anticipated income to be derived from the ownership of the property into a value estimate. This approach is widely applied in appraising income-producing properties. Anticipated future income and/or reversions are discounted to a present value through a capitalization process. The most common process is based upon a relationship that exists between value, income, and rate. The net operating income (I) divided by the rate (capitalization rate, or R) results in an indication of value.

$$V = I/R$$

A means of extracting the capitalization rate from the market is to divide the income by the sale price (V) of relevant market sales data. A simple example of such an indication of value from the income capitalization approach would begin by calculating the net operating income and then dividing it by the capitalization rate:

Potential gross income		$150,000
Less vacancy and collections loss		− 15,000
Effective gross income		135,000
Less expenses		
Taxes	10,000	
Insurance	6,000	
Management	7,000	
Maintenance	5,000	
Utilities	5,000	
Reserves	+ 2,000	
Total expenses		− 35,000
Net operating income		100,000

By using a market-derived capitalization rate, the net income can then be capitalized into an indication of value.

$100,000 (net operating income) ÷ 10% (capitalization rate) = $1,000,000 (value)

The income capitalization approach can also include a discounted cash flow analysis, whereby the cash flow, before taxes and mortgage payments, is projected for a certain period and then discounted to a present value based upon a selected yield rate (Y).

By utilizing one or more of the three approaches to value, and by ignoring the effects of the detrimental conditions, a value as if no detrimental condition exists, or unimpaired value, may be derived. This generates a benchmark for the following studies that establish the effect, if any, on the value of the property caused by the detrimental condition.

Detrimental Conditions

During the career of virtually any real estate professional, he or she will be confronted with a situation involving a property that has been impacted by a detrimental condition. As set forth within Appendix One, there are literally hundreds of such situations that impact property values, and many of them create a valuation challenge that goes well beyond the scope of the three traditional approaches to value. To add to the complexity, a property may be impacted by two or more detrimental conditions.

A framework must be established to study the vast number of detrimental conditions and the issues surrounding them. Although identifying, categorizing, and analyzing the numerous conditions may seem overwhelming, the task becomes manageable when the fundamental stages and value effects are considered in a logical sequence. The basic tools for detrimental condition analysis are the following:

1. The Detrimental Condition Matrix
2. The Detrimental Condition Model
3. The Bell Chart
4. Three Detrimental Condition Approaches to Value.

The Detrimental Conditions Matrix

Detrimental conditions follow a logical sequence of events, and identifying and organizing these issues can facilitate a useful study. The first step is to recognize that real property affected by a detrimental condition has a lifecycle that involves three potential stages. Exhibit 0.6 outlines a matrix of the three stages of analysis and related issues that should be considered for every detrimental condition: the assessment stage, the repair stage, and the ongoing stage, along with the cost, use, and risk value issues. The legal, physical, and financial perspectives should be considered in each of the nine quadrants, just as they are in the highest and best use section of a typical appraisal

Not every stage is necessarily relevant to every detrimental condition. For example, if an airport is developed near a residential neighborhood, there may be no assessment or repair stage, only an ongoing stage. The value is driven not only by the inclusion or exclusion of these stages but also by three fundamental issues that may occur within each relevant stage:

Exhibit 0.6 Detrimental Condition Matrix

		Detrimental Condition Stages		
		Assessment	**Repair**	**Ongoing**
Detrimental Condition Issues	**Cost**	Cost to assess and responsibility Engineering Phase I, II, III studies	Repair costs and responsibility Repairs Remediation Contingencies	Ongoing costs and responsibility Operations and maintenance (O&M) monitoring
	Use	All loss of utility while assessed Disruptions Safety concerns Use restrictions	All loss of utility while repaired Income loss Expense increase Use restrictions	Ongoing use disruptions Alterations to highest and best use
	Risk	Uncertainty factor Discount, if any, where extent of damage is unknown	Project incentive Financial incentive, if any, to complete repairs	Market resistance Residual resistance, if any, due to situation

Source: Bell's Guide: The Real Estate Encyclopedia

1. Costs and responsibility for payment of those costs
2. Use and any restrictions on use
3. Risks

While all valuation assignments depend critically on the date of valuation, a property impacted by a detrimental condition has an even more important issue in this regard because the property's value can vary considerably over these potential stages.

Assessment Stage

If applicable, the assessment stage is when the damage is assessed, usually by engineers, contractors, or other qualified experts, and includes all the costs, use issues, and risks associated with monitoring and assessing the detrimental condition before any repairs are made.

If the problem is self-evident, there may not be an assessment stage at all. For example, if a tornado destroys a tool shed, there is no question as to what the damage is; the only question is what will be the cost to repair or replace it. With other detrimental conditions, the assessment stage may be very involved, as the extent of the problem may not be self-evident and requires the expertise of qualified engineers or other professionals. This could include environmental studies, engineering studies, contractor estimates, soils and geotechnical studies, well monitoring, laboratory analysis, and other assessment costs. The contractors or engineering firms that do such studies would normally provide cost estimates for repairs. Just as an owner or prospective buyer would do, the appraiser should review the estimates for reasonableness.

Repair Stage

If repairs are required, they take place during this stage and could involve remediation, reconstruction, preventative construction, the actual repairs, cleanup and correction of the condition, and contingencies. This could include a vast spectrum of costs depending upon the remediation method chosen. The costs would also include any agency oversight, engineering, legal review, permits, sampling, improvement demolition, improvement reconstruction, scientific analysis, backfill, and so forth.

Ongoing Stage

There may be continuing issues or aftermath issues associated with the detrimental condition. If so, this stage reflects those factors. Sometimes a detrimental condition will cause ongoing costs to be incurred even after repairs are completed. These might involve ongoing responsibility for monitoring and reporting on groundwater or soil conditions or some continuing maintenance costs to repairs made to a foundation due to a geotechnical condition. Such a situation could also involve operations and maintenance (O&M) programs to monitor asbestos air fibers or to maintain drainage systems installed in the aftermath of a problem.

The Value Issues

Within each applicable stage, any costs, use restrictions, and risks must be considered as they relate to the subject property at the specific date of value. While these headings are the same for each stage, the issues may have different perspectives depending on the stage being considered.

Cost

This value issue must be considered for each stage, and it includes all the direct costs, related costs, and contingencies. In addition, the party responsible for the payment of those costs should be considered as it relates to the impact on value. These cost estimates are often provided by the engineers of the firm contracted to conduct the remediation; however, special care should be taken to review the completeness of such estimates, as it is not uncommon to greatly exceed original cost estimates for remediation involving environmental, geotechnical, or other complex problems. The firm providing the estimates should clearly set forth whether the costs are best case, expected case, or worst case scenarios. Exhibit 0.7 illustrates an actual compilation of a relatively small environmental cleanup with estimates from four environmental contractors.

As the table illustrates, a wide range of estimates can be presented for the same situation. In fact, some unscrupulous contractors will purposely submit low initial quotes

Exhibit 0.7 Comparison of Environmental Remediation and Cost Benefits

Contractor A		Contractor B		Contractor C		Contractor D	
Asbestos removal/disposal	$46,080	Asbestos removal/disposal	$18,500	Asbestos removal/disposal	$34,135	Asbestos removal/disposal	$18,500
Lead-based paint removal/disposal	22,500	Lead-based paint removal/disposal	22,500	Lead-based paint removal/disposal	35,000	Lead-based paint removal/disposal	22,500
Demolition	704,160	Demolition	289,000	Demolition	509,625	Demolition	289,000
UST removal/closure	34,560	UST removal/closure	Included in Demolition	UST removal/closure	21,000	UST removal/closure	34,258
Remediation of hazardous waste and site closure	27,099	Remediation of hazardous waste and site closure	22,850	Remediation of hazardous waste and site closure	94,000	Remediation of hazardous waste and site closure	7,900–11,800
Total	$834,399	Total	$352,850	Total	$693,760	Total	$364,258–376,058

Comments:
1. Prices for "budget" purposes only and are subject to change.
2. All permits and below ground demolition included in bid.

Comments:
1. Add $50,000 to remove crushed concrete from site for a total of $402,850.
2. Includes removal of structures below grade.

Comments:
1. Demolition budget includes below ground demo with off-site removal of concrete.
2. Bid does not include security, water and power, permits, finishing grading, removal of lead-based paint (if required), and fill.
3. Bid assumes removal of lead-based paint will not require additional payment given demolition of site.
4. Demolition bid includes removal of structures to 5 feet below surface, off-site concrete crushing, and $60,000 for oversight of demolition.

to get the contract, yet fully expect that as the job progresses more costs and contingencies will be added. An expression that is often heard in the environmental cleanup industry—"the hole always gets bigger"—means that the initial site assessments often do not characterize all of the contaminants and the required remediation sometimes goes beyond what is originally expected.

Because remediation costs can exceed their original estimates, contingencies are sometimes required to adjust remediation costs to reflect the full range of possible outcomes. Informed potential buyers must have the reasonable assurance that they have a clear indication of their total exposure and potential cash liability, so it is essential that the total remediation costs accurately reflect the total reasonable repair costs, not just a cursory and optimistic estimate.

For example, there may be $150,000 of environmental testing and analysis together with $50,000 of attorneys fees just to define the nature and extent of the contamination and to understand what kind of remediation is going to be required by the regulators. This activity culminates in an approved remediation plan as part of the assessment stage. Next, during the repair stage, implementation of the remediation plan could involve any number of actions and might cost $700,000. Finally, even after the remediation is complete and a no further action (NFA) letter has been issued, there may be ongoing costs of $15,000 per year for 10 years to monitor environmental conditions at the site.

Understanding the magnitude of each of these costs and how they relate to each stage is a critical task in assessing damages. Of course, the estimation of these costs is not the responsibility of the appraiser or analyst. Rather, qualified environmental engineers and scientists must provide the foundational estimates on which the appraiser's analysis is built. These must be reviewed for reasonableness, internal consistency, and so forth, but ultimately the credibility of these numbers lies with the experts who generate them.

Along with the issue of costs is the question of who is responsible for the payment of those costs. Relevant statutes are important here as are contractual obligations such as representations, warranties, and indemnities. In the illustration above there were assessment plus remediation costs of $900,000, as well as ongoing costs of $15,000 per year for 10 years, although responsibility for those charges remains unclear. This is particularly true if the detrimental condition is an externality. Possibly an up-gradient neighbor or a previous owner aware of the detrimental condition has assumed full responsibility for the condition and therefore the value of the subject property is not affected by these repair costs.

Such situations often occur where a seller indemnifies a buyer against the detrimental condition in question. In environmental contamination cases, a responsible party (other than the property owner) will often assume full responsibility for the cleanup. If the responsibility for repair falls to someone other than the owner of the subject property and the responsible party is solvent, the value of the subject property may not be affected by the cost of repair. As another example, if a building material manufacturer has assumed all responsibility for replacing defective materials, the owner may have no liability for repair costs. Other cases may involve the owner bearing some of the costs, while a responsible party bears the rest.

In interpreting the responsibility for repair or remediation, an appraiser will often need professional legal input on liability issues driven by various statutory or contractual considerations. Further, these issues will often be very much in dispute between the parties. In fact, disagreement over cleanup liability or repairs is at the heart of many detrimental condition disputes. The appraiser or analyst does not have a responsibility to resolve the issue, which ultimately is a question of law settled in court, but the assumptions made in developing the impaired value estimate must be addressed clearly.

Finally, insurance recoveries and other mitigating factors should be considered. Although insurance recoveries may mitigate the losses associated with a detrimental condition, it may not be appropriate to incorporate them into an analysis because insurance may not be relevant to the real property—i.e., it is often an attribute of the business or individual that owns the policy. As such, its incorporation may be more relevant to investment value than market value. Consequently, the significance of a particular detrimental condition to a particular individual with a particular set of insurance policies may not be interpreted as typical of the market.

On the other hand, other mitigating factors may be considered and even offset the damages. For example, if certain insurance proceeds are held in an escrow account and are specifically earmarked for property repairs, this amount could offset damages because it is assured that the real estate, and not an individual, will directly benefit from the proceeds. Additionally, if a property can generate some rental income while being repaired, or if property taxes can be appealed, these factors, along with any other benefits, should be considered as an offset to any damages.

Use

Detrimental conditions may impact or restrict the use of a property. During each stage, the use or utility of the property should be considered as compared to the use during the unimpaired stage.

In the context of income-producing properties, *use* has specific consequences. If income falls or expenses rise, there will be a change in net operating income that will translate into a decrease in the value of the property. Care should be taken to determine if these are short-term alterations or if they are expected to continue in perpetuity. The relevant use issue is whether the detrimental condition impacts income, vacancy, expenses, or some combination of these. For example, rental rates may decline or vacancy might rise, either of which would cause the effective gross income to fall. It is also possible that operating expenses might be higher if the detrimental condition resulted in a period of higher utility charges, increased security requirements, or perhaps rental of auxiliary parking spaces on an adjacent or nearby property.

With non-income-producing or residential property, the use and utility issue is more straightforward. Quite apart from the issue of cost of repair and who is responsible for it, the question is whether the detrimental condition has had a sufficient impact on the use or utility of the property that the market would reflect a measurable discount in the value. This is clearly an empirical question that can only be answered by market data. In general, however, the more the "livability" of a home or neighborhood is affected by the detrimental condition, the more likely it is that use and utility will be affected with corresponding effects on market value.

Risk

There may be risks, as perceived by the market, associated with each applicable stage. These would generally fall into three categories for each of the three stages:

1. Risks associated with a property prior to the situation being assessed, termed an *uncertainty factor*
2. Risks and uncertainties associated with the cost to repair, termed a *project incentive*
3. Risks and uncertainties associated with an ongoing reluctance by the market to purchase a property with a history of a detrimental condition, including any reduced marketability or concern of third-party liability, which is termed *market resistance*

An *uncertainty factor* relates to a property that has been impacted by a detrimental condition that requires an assessment that has not yet been completed. Clearly, the risk is likely to be the highest and the value lowest at this point because, with value not yet being assessed, market participants may be extremely hesitant to purchase the property without the problem being characterized. This would be something like buying a car without being allowed to turn the key or open the hood.

Project incentive is the risk and uncertainties associated with the repair process. It may be that the detrimental condition being studied is common and that the procedures required to assess and repair it are well understood. Further, appropriate contingencies may be built into the cost estimates. As a result, it may be a reasonable assumption that there is no risk or uncertainty associated with the issue of repair costs; however, a financial incentive is generally required to assume the trouble of being responsible to make significant repairs. Additionally, there are many situations where reasonable repair cost estimates have been made but where there is a significant risk or uncertainty that the estimates could be exceeded, perhaps by a substantial amount. These considerations would likely weigh heavily in the mind of a prospective buyer and would therefore be reflected in either a cost contingency or the project incentive.

Ultimately, the project incentive reflects the certainty of the repairs being completed on time and on budget, the time to manage or oversee the repair process, and the general incentive necessary to accept responsibility for the repair process. This could be similar to purchasing a car where it is known that it needs a new transmission. While the situation is fully assessed and characterized, there may be a financial incentive to buy the car knowing that it will require this repair and all the associated problems and risks of getting those repairs completed.

Market resistance refers to the risks and uncertainties, if any, associated with the negative reactions by the market towards a property that has a history of being damaged. For example, deep groundwater contamination will usually not interfere with the use of improved commercial or industrial properties. Hence, the market may reflect that net operating income (NOI) is unaffected by the detrimental condition and that there is no risk or uncertainty that NOI will be affected in the future. In this situation, if the lenders do not require any premium on the loan terms and the equity market likewise does not require any premium, then there may be no market resistance.

Alternatively, a ground subsidence issue may have been adequately addressed at an improved industrial property with NOI being unaffected by the historical problem. There may be a significant risk, however, that the problem could reoccur, and if it did reoccur, use of the property would be significantly affected. In this case, the value of the property would likely reflect this risk or uncertainty.

Related to market resistance are any risks and uncertainties associated with third-party liability. This consideration relates primarily to litigation risk that is somehow associated with the detrimental condition. For example, a construction defect could have resulted in an accident where tenants were injured. As a result, the property owner may have the risk of potential legal exposure in personal injury suits brought by the tenants. Another situation where this kind of risk can occur is in environmental cases where the contamination has migrated from the source site to neighboring properties. Here the source site property owner may face considerable liability with respect to suits brought by neighboring property owners.

In other situations, there may have been no assessment stage or repair stage, but only a pure market resistance that is attributable to a negative event that occurred on the property, such as a crime scene. In all these situations, market resistance reflects any risks associated with the historical problems of the property. In the example of a car, this would be like any resistance by buyers toward a car that was damaged in an accident and later repaired. Depending upon the situation, the market may require a discount as an incentive to purchase the car, given its history.

The Detrimental Condition Model

Each detrimental condition is analyzed on a case-by-case basis because each can have any of a variety of impacts on value. The Detrimental Condition Model illustrates the fundamental issues graphically, from which a wide variety of additional illustrations may be derived. While the Detrimental Condition Model includes all possible stages, many detrimental conditions do not include all of the stages. The first step with any detrimental condition analysis is to consider the value of the property as if there is no detrimental condition, i.e., the *unimpaired value*. This is reflected as Point A in Exhibit 0.8. Upon the occurrence or discovery of the detrimental condition, the value may fall to Point B, if the facts and market data support such a decline. Some detrimental conditions require an assessment, such as conducting a soil, environmental, or engineering study. The value during this period is often the lowest, or the property is even unmarketable, as a potential buyer would likely require a significant discount as an enticement to purchase a property where the extent of damage is uncharacterized. However, in a retrospective

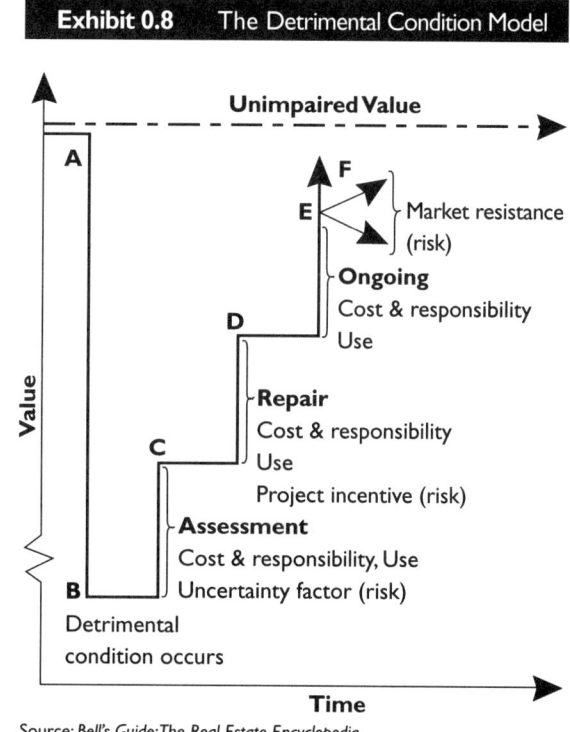

Exhibit 0.8 The Detrimental Condition Model

Source: Bell's Guide: The Real Estate Encyclopedia

appraisal assignment where all assessment, repair, and ongoing issues are studied, a determination of the value at Point B can be made.

While there are a variety of patterns that could accompany the assessment stage, the model reflects a simple increase to Point C. If repairs are required, the value will generally increase upon their completion, as reflected at Point D. Point E reflects the value of the property after considering the cost, responsibility for costs, and use issues in the ongoing stage.

Like any value issues, the risk that is associated within the ongoing stage could have a variety of impacts. To illustrate this concept, market resistance (risk) is reflected with multiple arrows, at Point F. While there are a variety of definitions of stigma, this is synonymous with many of these definitions. Of course, any issue within any stage could have a similar negative, positive, or neutral impact on value, which can only be determined on a case-specific basis.

The Bell Chart

Through the use of the Detrimental Condition Model framework showing the relationship of time and value, a variety of graphs emerge depending on the relevance and impact of each value issue during each stage. Out of the hundreds of detrimental conditions, certain common attributes arise that suggest distinct groupings. The Bell Chart organizes all detrimental conditions into 10 standard categories, as shown in Exhibit 0.9.

In determining the impact on value, it is critical that a distinction be made between the detrimental condition and unrelated issues. For example, market conditions may be responsible for a change in value that is unrelated to the condition being studied. In addition to the detrimental condition categories, the chart illustrates some of the various value patterns resulting from detrimental conditions.

The Three Detrimental Condition Approaches to Value

The impact of detrimental conditions on property values is ultimately an empirical question that requires the application of one or more of the three traditional approaches to value. While the fundamental detrimental condition issues seem straightforward, the real challenge of such an assignment lies in the skill of the appraiser or analyst to collect and properly analyze market data. As might be expected, each of the three approaches to value has potential applicability, depending upon the specific situation.

The Detrimental Condition Cost Approach

The cost approach employs data with and without the costs and losses associated with a detrimental condition. This approach deducts the costs or losses associated with each stage from the unimpaired value. Generally, only those costs and losses that are the responsibility of the property owner would be included, as only these would impact the market value. (As a practical matter, if market resistance were applicable, it would likely be determined from the sales comparison or income capitalization approaches.) The fundamental calculations for the detrimental condition cost approach are shown in Exhibit 0.10.

As corresponding to the Detrimental Condition Model:

- Point A relates to the estimate of market value as if unaffected by the detrimental condition.

Exhibit 0.9 The Bell Chart

Class		Detrimental Conditions	Analysis	Result
I	No Detrimental Condition (DC) or Benign Condition	Any DC if No Impact Sales Arrangement at Market (If Over Market: II or If Under: IV) Build-to-Suit/Tenant Purchase Threat of Condemnation/Auction First Right of Refusal/Double Escrow	There are hundreds of Detrimental Conditions (DCs) that may impact property values. The analysis of property damages starts with the DC Model, which illustrates the array of related issues. All six elements of the DC Model should be considered in every analysis. This can yield a variety of valuation patterns based upon the exclusion, inclusion, and timing of each element.	DCs have a variety of impacts upon analysis, vary on a case-by-case basis. No DC or Benign Premium One-Time Premium Increasing Market
II	Nonmarket Premium	Special Buyer Motivation Assemblage/Expansion Redevelopment Project Feng Shui Short-Term Windfall		

III	Market Condition	Economy/Supply & Demand
		Recession/Depression
		Lease Option/Rolling Option
		Exercise of Option/Takedown
			Detrimental Condition Model
			
			Value vs. Time graph showing Unimpaired value and Value With DC
			
			Key to Graphs
			- - - Unimpaired value —— Value With DC
			A: Unimpaired value
			B: DC occurs or discovered
			C: Assessment stage
			  Cost & responsibility
			  Use
			  Uncertainty factor (risk)
			D: Repair stage
			  Cost & responsibility
			  Use
			  Project incentive (risk)
			E: Ongoing stage
			  Cost & responsibility
			  Use
			F: Market resistance (risk)
				Market Cycles
				
				Decreasing Market
				
				Recovering
				
				Temporary Issue

IV	Temporary Condition	Distress Sale*/Tragedy** Bulk Portfolio Sale/Business Inc. High Vacancy/Temp. Easement Deferred Maintenance/Legal * Bankruptcy/Probate-Estate-Short Sale US Marshall/REO/Private REO/FDIC/RTC ** Crime Scene/Accident/Disease/Riot/Fire		
V	Imposed Condition	Neighboring Issue* Eminent Domain/Bond/Tax Deed Reconstruction/Ground Lease Leasehold/Leasehold Fee Physical Depreciation/Historical *Sewage-Power-Nuclear Plant/Blight Illegal Use/Jail/EMF/Traffic-Airport Noise		Permanent Declining Value One-Stage Repaired
VI	Building Construction Condition	Construction Defect Building Code Violations Poor Workmanship/Leaks ADA Noncompliance Functional Depreciation	Damages are benchmarked against the Unimpaired Value. In determining the impact on value, it is critical that a distinction be made between the DC and unrelated issues. For example, market conditions may be responsible for a change in value that is unrelated to the condition being studied. The impact of DCs on property values is ultimately an empirical question that requires the application of one or more of the three traditional approaches to value: 1. The sales comparision approach utilizing market data with and without the DC. 2. The income capitalization approach utilizing income and risk factors with and without the DC. 3. The cost approach utilizing data with and without the costs and losses associated with a DC. The DC Model, coupled with the three approaches to value, provides the fundamental framework for the analysis of DCs.	One-Stage Residual Two-Stage Repaired Two-Stage Residual Three-Stage Repaired
VII	Soil or Geotechnical Constuction Condition	Soil Construction Drainage/Tunneling Foundation/Cut & Fill Retaining Wall or Slope Grading/Soil Compaction		Three-Stage Residual
VIII	Environmental Condition	Soil Contamination Building Contamination Hydrocarbons/Metals/Solvents Asbestos/Radiation Groundwater/Landfill/LUST		Full DC Model
IX	Natural Condition	Natural Disasters Natural Habitat Flood/Earthquake/Volcano Tornado/Landslide/Soil Types Infestation/Sulfates/Wetlands		No Value Liability
X	Incurable Condition	Applicable to many DCs in severe situations where a complete loss or net liability exists		

Source: *Bell's Guide: The Real Estate Encyclopedia*

Detrimental Conditions and Property Values

Exhibit 0.10 Detrimental Condition Cost Approach

Unimpaired value	(Point A)
− Assessment stage value effects	(Point B to Point C)
Cost and responsibility	
Use	
Risk (uncertainty factor)	
− Repair stage value effects	(Point C to Point D)
Cost and responsibility	
Use	
Risk (project incentive)	
− Ongoing stage value effects	(Point D to Point F)
Cost and responsibility	
Use	
Risk (market resistance)	
= Impaired value	

- Point B relates to the estimate of value upon the realization that a detrimental condition has occurred.
- Point C relates to the estimate of value upon the assessment of the situation.
- Point D relates to the estimate of value upon the condition being repaired or otherwise resolved.
- Point E relates to the estimate of value upon considering any ongoing costs.
- Point F relates to the estimate of impact of any residual market resistance.

Proper evaluation of these costs requires consideration of each of the value issues, specifically repair costs and responsibility for those costs, effects on use, and risk.

There are numerous costs to consider in the detrimental condition cost approach. In the assessment stage, this could include all engineering studies, laboratory analysis, legal oversight, governmental oversight and fees, contractor estimates, and so on. In the repair stage, this includes not only the direct repair or remediation costs themselves but all the related costs, such as increased expenses, additional security, moving tenants, carrying costs, contingencies, rebuilding structures or tenant improvements destroyed in the process, moving costs, and so forth. During the ongoing stage, this could include monitoring wells, additional security, operations and maintenance (O&M) programs, and so forth.

Effects on use, as related to the detrimental condition cost approach, relate to a number of factors. During all the stages, consideration should be given to the utility of the property as compared to the unimpaired stage. For example, during the assessment stage or the repair stage, the detrimental condition may be disruptive or the situation may be dangerous, thereby preventing the property from being occupied. During the ongoing stage, the detrimental condition may result in a permanent and altered use of the property.

In general, with income-producing property, these use issues would take the form of either a decrease in income, an increase in vacancy rates, an increase in operating expenses, or a combination of these. For example, with a natural disaster such as a mudslide, there might be a complete loss of use from the time of the slide until the repair phase is completed. The loss of use for this period may be measured as the rental value, which would be added to the other costs associated with the mudslide. It is also possible that there may be a change in operating expenses associated with the mudslide, such as increased maintenance or preventative measures. If so, these changes will have to be estimated and incorporated into the analysis.

Risk must also be considered in the detrimental condition cost approach. Once all of the issues associated with repair costs, responsibility for repair costs, and effects on use have been addressed, a question remains as to whether there are remaining risks as a result of the detrimental condition. For an income-producing property, during any of the three detrimental condition stages, any risks are ultimately borne by the equity investor (the owner), and by the lender if the property is mortgaged. Thus, one way to characterize this risk issue is investigate whether, once allowance has been made for the costs already discussed, an additional discount is required to compensate for increased risk due to the detrimental condition. This could result from the equity investor requiring additional incentive because of risks associated with remediation cost overruns, subsequent effects on use or third-party lawsuits, or the costs of financing being increased due to lower loan-to-value ratios, higher borrowing costs, or higher interest rates.

As an illustration of a detrimental condition cost approach application, consider a property in an undamaged condition with a market value of $475,000. The assessment costs are $5,000, the repair stage costs $75,000, the ongoing costs are $4,000, and the market resistance (part of the ongoing stage) is $15,000. In addition, suppose the property owner is not responsible for $50,000 of the costs, which will be borne by others. The detrimental condition cost approach calculations would be as follows:

Unimpaired value	$475,000
Less:	
Assessment stage	(5,000)
Repair stage	(75,000)
Ongoing stage	(4,000)
Market resistance (risk)	(15,000)
Plus: Costs owner not responsible for	+ 50,000
Impaired value	$426,000

It must be noted that risk factors such as market resistance can only be estimated using the sales comparison approach or the income capitalization approach. While the detrimental condition cost approach is a useful way to organize the process and effects that detrimental conditions have on value, market evidence will ultimately have to be analyzed in the context of either the sales comparison approach or the income capitalization approach with regards to some of the value issues.

The Detrimental Condition Sales Comparison Approach

The sales comparison approach utilizes market data with and without the detrimental condition. This approach may not always be easy to apply because of the difficulty of finding relevant market data, but it still is a very strong approach in quantifying the value issues in a detrimental conditions assignment. As related to the Detrimental Condition Model, the detrimental condition sales comparison approach is summarized as shown in Exhibit 0.11.

Paired Sales Analysis. One of the most useful applications of this approach is paired sales analysis. This could be between the subject property, or similarly impacted properties, termed *test areas* (at Points B, C, D, E, or F), and unimpaired properties, which are termed *control areas* (Point A). Or an analysis could be made between the unimpaired value of the subject property before and after the detrimental condition. For example, the value diminution of a property that has been assessed but not repaired would be Point A to Point C. If a legitimate detrimental condition exists, there will likely be a measurable

Exhibit 0.11 Detrimental Condition Sales Comparison Approach

Control area market data
(No detrimental condition, Point A)
− Test area market data
(With detrimental condition, Points B, C, D, E, or F)
= Diminution in value

and consistent difference between the two sets of market data; if not, there will likely be no significant difference between the two sets of data. This process involves the study of a group of sales with a detrimental condition, which are then compared with a group of otherwise similar market data without the detrimental condition. For example, a group of properties near a sewage treatment plant can be compared with similar properties that are not located near a sewage treatment plant, an airport, traffic noise, or other neighborhood issue. Exhibit 0.12 is an example of a comparison between the test area and a control area. Five sales were located within the test area. Several control area sales were located that are similar to those in the test area, except for the detrimental condition does not impact the control area data.

The study indicates that properties that are impacted by a detrimental condition within the test area sell for an average of approximately 11% to 18% less than otherwise similar properties in the control area.

Impaired Sales Comparables. In the sales comparison approach, impaired sales data can be analyzed to determine if a diminution exists. For example, suppose a one-acre commercial land parcel was being valued that had previously been the location of a service station. Also, assume that the station had leaking underground storage tanks but also that the contamination had been cleaned up to the satisfaction of the relevant regulatory authorities and a "no further action" letter was in place on the property.

Since this set of facts is quite common in many large cities, it may be quite possible to find comparable sales that match the subject both in terms of their economic and location characteristics and in terms of their environmental characteristics. If four sales were found that were similar in size and location, each with a "no further action" letter

Exhibit 0.12 Paired Sales

	Test Area with Detrimental Condition	Control Area Comparables with no Detrimental Condition			Indication from Control Area Comparables	% Loss
		Sale 1	Sale 2	Sale 3		
Property 1	$495,000	$600,000	$585,000	$580,000	$588,000	15.8%
Property 2	$525,000	$590,000	$605,000	$575,000	$590,000	11.0%
Property 3	$490,000	$570,000		$600,000	$585,000	16.2%
Property 4	$505,000	$580,000		$605,000	$592,500	14.8%
Property 5	$485,000			$590,000	$590,000	17.8%

covering historical petroleum contamination, they might indicate the following for the subject after appropriate adjustments were made:

Impaired Comparable Sale 1, adjusted $7.40 per sq. ft.
Impaired Comparable Sale 2, adjusted $6.80 per sq. ft.
Impaired Comparable Sale 3, adjusted $8.20 per sq. ft.
Impaired Comparable Sale 4, adjusted $7.80 per sq. ft.

Given this market data, it is concluded that the impaired value of the subject was $7.60 per square foot, based on an evaluation of the adjusted four comparables.

To estimate the subject property's unimpaired value, the same procedure would be followed except the comparable sales would all be unimpaired with respect to any detrimental environmental condition. If the resulting estimate of unimpaired value were $7.60 per square foot, the conclusion would be that the environmental condition seems not to have had any ongoing or lasting impact on value. However, if the resulting unimpaired estimate were $8.40 per square foot, it would indicate that the market resistance associated with the environmental history of the property is approximately 10%.

Market Resistance Derivation. As a variable of the sales comparison approach, market resistance can be derived from sales comparables. For example, suppose an industrial property is being evaluated just after an earthquake. Further, suppose that several sales are located where the property sold in a damaged condition (impaired value) similar to the subject property. The unimpaired value can be determined from market data immediately prior to the earhquake. From verifying the market data, the total assessments costs, repair costs inclusive of project incentives, and ongoing costs for each property can be determined as well as whether these costs would be the responsibility of the owner. As might be expected in an earthquake, loss of use was a significant issue for several of the sales, and rental income loss estimates were made for the period of interrupted occupancy. Using the relationship between the unimpaired value and impaired value, the data can now be used to estimate market resistance as shown in the following table.

	Sale 1	Sale 2	Sale 3	Sale 4	Sale 5
Unimpaired value	$1,000,000	$2,500,000	$1,500,000	$3,000,000	$4,750,000
− (Assessment, repair, ongoing costs)	75,000	440,000	115,000	1,750,000	2,000,000
+ (Costs owner not responsible for)	None	None	None	None	None
− (Loss of use)	25,000	160,000	65,000	50,000	150,000
− Impaired value	800,000	1,600,000	1,200,000	800,000	2,000,000
= Market resistance	$100,000	$300,000	$120,000	$400,000	$600,000
As % of unimpaired value	10%	12%	8%	13%	13%

Assuming that the subject property and the comparable sales are similar in character, one could estimate from the market data that the market resistance is between 8% and 13% of the unimpaired value.

Sale/Resale Analysis. Another type of paired sales analysis involves the study of the sale and subsequent resale of the same property. This method is used to determine the influence of time on market values, or to determine the impact of a detrimental condition by comparing values before and after the detrimental condition is discovered.

The following table illustrates a neighborhood study that determines the net effects of market influences on properties between 1994 and 1999. Properties that had major renovations or remodeling during this time period may need to be eliminated, and adjustments for physical depreciation may also be necessary. The study illustrates five properties that sold in 1994 and then resold in 1999.

	1994	1999	Percent Change
Property A	$78,000	$85,500	9.6%
Property B	$75,000	$80,000	6.7%
Property C	$77,000	$86,000	11.7%
Property D	$77,500	$85,000	9.7%
Property E	$76,000	$83,500	9.9%

The illustration shows that property values have experienced a net increase ranging from 6.7% to 11.7% within the five-year period. Of course, the net impact could also be negative.

The same type of sale and resale analysis could be used for estimating the impact of a detrimental condition on property values. The following study illustrates a situation where five properties were sold prior to the discovery of a detrimental condition and then resold after the detrimental condition occurred or became apparent.

	Sale Before Detrimental Condition 1998	Sale After Detrimental Condition 1999	Percent Change	Percent Attributable to Market	Percent Attributable to Detr. Cond.
Property A	$482,000	$385,500	-20.0%	-5%	-15.0%
Property B	$476,500	$370,000	-22.4%	-5%	-17.4%
Property C	$478,000	$376,500	-21.2%	-5%	-16.2%
Property D	$477,000	$386,000	-19.1%	-5%	-14.1%
Property E	$480,000	$383,500	-20.1%	-5%	-15.1%

This illustrates that property values dropped from 14.1% to 17.4% as a result of the detrimental condition. Like any detrimental condition study, care should be taken to adjust for any market factors that are not associated with the issue being studied.

The Detrimental Condition Income Capitalization Approach

The income capitalization approach utilizes income and risk factors with and without the detrimental condition. This approach to value focuses on the impact that a detrimental condition has on 1) the income (both short term and in perpetuity) and 2) risk (the capitalization rate, discount rate, or both). The risk rate itself is a combination of both the mortgage and equity risks. Although the analysis of market data can get quite complicated, the basic principles are straightforward as they relate to the Detrimental Condition Model, as shown in Exhibit 0.13.

Direct Capitalization Approach.
As cited earlier, the income capitalization approach recognizes that value (V) reflects an anticipated stream of future benefits (income, or I) capitalized at a return (rate, or R) necessary to attract capital to the opportunity. The detrimental condition has the potential to decrease the stream of future benefits or to increase the return necessary to attract capital, either or both of which will decrease value. The valuation issue then becomes how to quantify the decrease in future benefits, the increased return, or both.

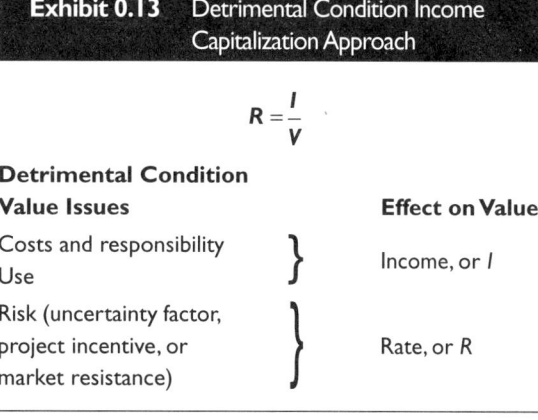

Exhibit 0.13 Detrimental Condition Income Capitalization Approach

$$R = \frac{I}{V}$$

Detrimental Condition Value Issues	Effect on Value
Costs and responsibility Use	Income, or I
Risk (uncertainty factor, project incentive, or market resistance)	Rate, or R

As an illustration, following are two sets of capitalization rates, one of which is impacted by a detrimental condition and one of which is not.

	Capitalization Rates Without Detrimental Condition	Capitalization Rates With Detrimental Condition
	10.0%	12.1%
	9.6%	11.8%
	10.5%	12.6%
	9.7%	11.9%
	10.2%	11.6%
Average	10.0%	12.0%

Detrimental Conditions and Property Values

In this example, unimpaired properties have a capitalization rate of approximately 10%, while impaired properties have a capitalization rate of approximately 12%. The capitalization rates must be derived from market data that are comparable to the subject property in both its impaired and unimpaired condition. Assuming that the net income of $100,000 is not impacted by the detrimental condition, value would be calculated as follows:

	Net Operating Income	Capitalization Rate	Indicated Value
Without detrimental condition	$100,000	10%	$1,000,000
With detrimental condition	$100,000	12%	$835,000 (rounded)

The overall capitalization rate can be estimated in one of two basic ways. It can be extracted from market data transactions or derived from the mortgage-equity technique.

With market data where both the sale price (V) and net operating income (I) are known, the capitalization formula can be used to extract the capitalization rate (R).

$$R = \frac{I}{V}$$

Suppose, for example, that an apartment is being valued after all repairs are completed following an earthquake and that it has no ongoing repair costs or any loss of use. Assume further that the subject property has NOI of $400,000 per year. After researching the market, suppose two transactions are found that involve very similar apartment complexes that had suffered earthquake damage but are now fully repaired. The basic data on the two transactions follows:

	Sale 1	Sale 2
NOI	$600,000	$525,000
Sale price	$7,250,000	$6,100,000
Extracted R_O	8.28%	8.61%

The appraiser or analyst might conclude from these sales an impaired rate for the subject of 8.5% and a value of $4,705,000 (rounded) based on NOI of $400,000.

The second approach to estimating the impaired capitalization rate uses the band of investment approach to build up a capitalization rate as a weighted average of a debt rate (R_M) and an equity rate (R_E) where the weight reflects the loan-to-value mortgage ratio (M):

$$R_O = (M) R_M + (1 - M) R_E$$

The overall capitalization rate has to reflect its two components, the debt rate and the equity rate, weighted by their relative magnitude in the capital base of the investment.

For example, suppose the facts applicable to an unimpaired industrial building are 70% loan-to-value (M) with a 9% mortgage constant and a 10.5% equity dividend rate (R_E).

$$\text{Unimpaired } R_O = (.70)\,.09 + (.30)\,.105 = .0945$$

Now, suppose a similar building has been subject to environmental contamination. Assume that the contamination has been remediated and that there is no effect on the use or utility of the property. There are, however, some significant risk issues because the contamination has migrated off-site and has affected several neighboring properties. By discussing these facts with brokers, lenders, and investors, useful insight can be gained on how they see the financing of the project being affected by the environmental issues.

Suppose systematic interviews are carried out with lenders and investors and the results indicate that the loan-to-value ratio would drop to 50%, the mortgage constant would be unchanged, and the equity dividend rate would have to be increased to 11.5% to attract equity capital. Every attempt would then have to be made to verify these opinions based on actual market transactions. The mortgage financing terms on similar properties with similar environmental issues are relatively easy to verify, and once these are known the equity dividend rate can be extracted.

Assuming that market data supports the interview results reported above, the impaired capitalization rate can be calculated as follows:

$$\text{Impaired } R_O = (.50)\,.09 + (.50)\,.115 = .1025$$

Thus, the impact of the detrimental condition is to raise R_O from 9.45% to 10.25%. If the NOI of the property (both unimpaired and impaired were $200,000), this would cause value to fall by approximately $165,000.

$$\text{Unimpaired value} = \$200{,}000\,/\,.0945 = \$2{,}115{,}000 \text{ (rounded)}$$
$$\text{Impaired value} = \$200{,}000\,/\,.1025 = \$1{,}950{,}000 \text{ (rounded)}$$

This analysis suggests that potential buyers would require a 5% to 10% discount to purchase the impaired property. The market resistance is due to the fact that the greater risk associated with the property requires a higher rate of return to attract capital to the project. This is because of the requirement by lenders that there be a larger equity investment relative to debt and the requirement by equity investors that their equity return be higher. Higher risk requires a higher return that lowers value.

A detrimental condition can also affect NOI because of repair costs or use issues. Since these repair costs and effects on income or expenses tend to be variable from year to year, they are best analyzed in a discounted cash flow framework. The point is that if the detrimental condition causes NOI to be permanently reduced by $15,000 in the example above (perhaps because of some ongoing cost or due to rental concessions), impaired value would fall by a total of $310,000.

$$\text{Unimpaired value} = \$200{,}000\,/\,.0945 = \$2{,}115{,}000 \text{ (rounded)}$$
$$\text{Impaired value} = \$185{,}000\,/\,.1025 = \$1{,}805{,}000 \text{ (rounded)}$$

Discounted Cash Flow Analysis. This valuation method involves the calculation of the present value of a stream of income that reflects the various costs and revenues as impacted by a detrimental condition over a period of time. For example, if a property is undergoing asbestos abatement or soils remediation, the cash flow study would incorporate all the costs related to the assessment stage, repair stage, and ongoing stage, including any change in effective income or operating expenses. (Exhibits 0.14 and 0.15 illustrate the application of those costs in an example of discounted cash flow calculations.[1]) Specifically, it could include air or groundwater monitoring costs and, if some contaminants remain, any future demolition, disposal, or cleanup costs. If rental rates or vacancy levels are impacted, the

Exhibit 0.14 Discounted Cash Flow (in thousands) – Unimpaired

Year	1	2	3	4	5	6	7	8	9	10	11
Potential gross income	$300	300	300	300	300	300	300	300	300	300	300
Vacancy (10%)	30	30	30	30	30	30	30	30	30	30	30
Effective gross income	270	270	270	270	270	270	270	270	270	270	270
Operating expenses	90	90	90	90	90	90	90	90	90	90	90
NOI	180	180	180	180	180	180	180	180	180	180	180
Reversion @ $R_o = 10\%$	–	–	–	–	–	–	–	–	–	1,800	–
Cash flow	180	180	180	180	180	180	180	180	180	1,980	–

Value unimpaired at beginning of year 3: present value @ 12% = $1,596,000.

Exhibit 0.15 Discounted Cash Flow (in thousands) – Impaired

	Unimpaired Stage		Discovery → Assessment Stage		Approved Repair Plan → Repair Stage			Repair Complete → Ongoing Stage			
Year	1	2	3	4	5	6	7	8	9	10	11
Potential gross income	$300	300	300	300	300	300	300	300	300	300	300
Vacancy	30	30	150	150	150	150	150	45	45	45	45
Effective gross income	270	270	150	150	150	150	150	255	255	255	255
Operating expenses	90	90	90	90	90	90	90	90	90	90	90
Repair costs:											
Assessment costs	–	–	20	20	–	–	–	–	–	–	–
Repair costs	–	–	–	–	60	40	20	–	–	–	–
Ongoing costs	–	–	–	–	–	–	–	15	15	15	15
NOI	180	180	40	40	0	20	40	150	150	150	150
Reversion @ $R_o = 10\%$	–	–	–	–	–	–	–	–	–	1,500	–
Cash flow	180	180	40	40	0	20	40	150	150	1,650	–

Value impaired at beginning of year 3: present value @ 13% = $972,000.

---

1. These examples do not include inflation factors in order to better isolate and illustrate the detrimental condition stages and issues. In an actual cash-flow study, inflation or growth factors are an essential component.

effective gross income would reflect that. Also, any changes in operating expenses due to the detrimental condition would have to be accounted for. Any market resistance or other risks could be incorporated in the reversionary capitalization rate or the discount rate. This type of analysis is particularly useful in situations where the income, vacancy, or expense impact of a detrimental condition are highly variable or occur over a long period of time.

As the discounted cash flow analysis illustrates, value drops by more than $600,000 due to the detrimental condition. The impact occurs in three areas—cost to repair, loss of use, and market resistance (risk). As shown, there are significant assessment costs in years 3 and 4, repair costs in years 5, 6, and 7, and ongoing costs from year 8 forward. In addition, the detrimental condition severely affected occupancy, with 50% of the property remaining vacant through the assessment and repair stages. Further, even after repair is completed, vacancy at 15% is higher than it was prior to discovery of the detrimental condition at the beginning of year 3. Finally, because of the changed risk profile of the property, the example assumes that the market will require a higher yield (discount rate) than is the case with the property in the unimpaired stage. This yield rate can be quantified using the same techniques as the capitalization rate—extraction from comparable sales, lender or investor surveys, and the band-of-investment approach.

Market Surveys

Generally, one or more of the above appraisal-based methods may be used in determining the impact, if any, of a detrimental condition. In some unusual circumstances, the detrimental condition may be so unique that finding situations where it has affected other properties is very difficult or even impossible. For example, if a single-family residence has a sewer manhole cover in the backyard and such a feature is not found anywhere else in the region, it may not be possible to find comparable market data from which to make a detrimental condition analysis. In these types of unusual situations, a market survey may be made of property owners and brokers to determine what their perspectives and perceptions are related to the effect on value, if any. Additionally, a market survey may be used as secondary or supporting documentation for market data. This is the case, for example, with lender and investor surveys where financing questions are asked about a specific set of property and detrimental condition facts.

The pitfalls with such surveys is that without proper discipline, planning, and thought, the "survey" can become little more than casual conversations where preconceived ideas and notions become superficially validated. To be truly valid, a survey must follow some fundamental guidelines. First, the survey should be carefully scripted to ensure that each participant is pre-qualified and that uniform questions are asked throughout the examination. The questions should be carefully and objectively worded. The survey should be designed in such a manner that no bias or preconceived notions are projected in the questions being asked, and the questions must be truly relevant to the issues at hand. Careful documentation must be made as to the complete conversations with each survey participant. Also, it is important that enough participants are surveyed that there is a meaningful analysis.

Two examples are set forth on the following pages. The first is a simple broker survey designed to assess the effect of earthquake damage on residential property value. The second is a survey to be administered to lenders and investors with respect to a contaminated property. Note the careful presentation of the case facts so that the respondents have a well-defined context in which to answer the questions.

Broker Survey

Hello. My name is Steve Preston and I'm calling from the consulting firm of XYZ Consulting. We're conducting a brief opinion survey of real estate agents and brokers in your area. Your answers will remain confidential and I will not need to contact you again. This survey has six questions and will take no more than two to three minutes. Would you be willing to help?

Question 1
This survey is among real estate brokers or agents who are licensed in the State of Ohio. Are you currently a licensed broker or agent?
- ❏ Yes   How long? _____
- ❏ No   Thank you for your time.

Question 2
In your experience, if a home is worth approximately $300,000 in good condition, yet it requires $20,000 to fix up to be inhabitable, what would you expect the house to sell for?
$_____

Question 3
In your experience, which statement is true? If a $300,000 home has $20,000 in flood damage:
- ❏ a) The buyer would pay full price.
- ❏ b) A buyer would take a $20,000 deduction off the normal price.
- ❏ c) A buyer would take a $20,000 deduction, plus an additional discount, off the price.
- ❏ d) Nobody would buy it.

  If the answer is "c," what is your opinion as to the percentage discount? _____%

Question 4
If a property has been damaged by a flood and has been fully repaired, do you feel that there is any residual "stigma" or market resistance towards the house after the repairs are completed?
- ❏ No
- ❏ Yes   If yes, how much? _____

Question 5
Have you had experience with transactions of this type?
- ❏ No
- ❏ Yes   If yes, could you give me one or two examples? _____
_____
_____

Question 6
Do you have any additional comments about the incentive to purchase damaged or repaired properties or the market's resistance towards such properties? _____
_____
_____

That completes the survey. Thanks for your help, and I hope you have a pleasant day/evening.

Lender or Investor Survey

The Subject Property is a 296-unit apartment complex comprising 13 three-story buildings and one single-story building located on a 6.1-acre site in west central Houston, Texas. The average apartment size is 836 square feet. The property provides 12 laundry rooms and two domestic hot water boiler rooms. Four elevators serve the three-story buildings. The pitched-roof, wood-frame structures have brick veneer, wood siding, and asphalt shingle (mansard roof) siding.

Site improvements include two swimming pools, landscaping, concrete-paved walkways, asphalt-paved parking/driveways, and secure entry systems for driving onto the property and for access to the buildings. There are 308 covered parking spaces.

The improvements were built in 1970 and remodeled in 1988 and 1995. The 1995 renovations included roof replacement, rehabilitation of the HVAC system, exterior painting and surface repair, required window and screen replacement, exterior stair repairs, and repairs to the parking lot and driveways.

Overall, occupancy, rents, and lease structures reflect general market conditions.

Environmental History and Condition

In July 1992, routine testing revealed that a gasoline delivery line connecting underground storage tanks to the gasoline pumps on the convenience store/gas station site (Source Site) adjacent to the Subject Property had failed. The Texas Water Commission (TWC) was immediately notified of the leak and that the delivery line was repaired in July 1992. Environmental consultants conducted a Phase II initial site assessment in October 1992 and concluded that soil and groundwater samples taken from borings and monitor wells on the Source Site were contaminated with petroleum hydrocarbons. As required by TWC, a program of free product removal and ongoing monitoring of soil and groundwater conditions was initiated at the Source Site in September 1992.

Between 1993 and 1997, monitoring wells installed on the Subject Property revealed petroleum hydrocarbon contamination of the soil and groundwater. Since 1993, monitoring of the soil and groundwater conditions at the Subject Property has been ongoing in accordance with the requirements of the Texas Natural Resource Conservation Commission (TNRCC replaced TWC as the regulatory agency). This is the only remediation activity that TNRCC has required at the Subject Property.

The location of the plume has been defined on the Subject Property.

Assumptions

- Regulatory compliance has been maintained with respect to all TWC/TNRCC-required assessment, remediation, and monitoring AT ALL TIMES since July 1992.
- All remedial activities have been approved and executed under the supervision of, and in accordance with, the requirements of TWC/TNRCC, at the expense of the Responsible Party.
- The Responsible Party will indemnify current and future lenders and owners of the Subject Property against liability for costs of any TNRCC-required remedial actions associated with the contamination emanating from the Source Site. The Responsible Party has the financial capacity to pay on all justified claims.
- All contaminant levels are below TNRCC risk-based standards accepted and approved for the Subject Property.
- Currently, the only TNRCC-required remedial activity is ongoing monitoring. If the current monitoring reveals no change in contaminant levels through September 1998, it is unlikely that there will be any additional remediation required.

Lender Questionnaire

Assume that you are contemplating providing an acquisition or refinance loan with the Subject Property as collateral, and assume that the applicant is creditworthy.

I. Lending Opportunity

1) In general, assuming no history or existence of contamination:
    (i) What interest rate or range would you charge for financing the purchase of the apartment property described in the case study?
    (ii) Would you require the buyer to pay any points?
    (iii) What would be the required loan-to-value ratio?
    (iv) What would be your minimum required debt coverage ratio?
    (v) Over what period would the loan be amortized?
    (vi) What would be the term of the loan?
2) What type of due diligence would you require on the subject property?
3) Considering the environmental history:
    (i) Would the environmental history and condition of this property prevent you from committing to acquisition financing?
    (ii) If yes, why?
    (iii) If no, would the environmental history and condition of this property impact the terms of the mortgage? Why?
    (iv) If yes, which of the following would change?
        Interest rate _____   Discount points _____
        Amortization period_____   Term _____
        Debt coverage ratio _____   LTV ratio _____

II. Company Policy

1) (i) Does your bank have a policy with regard to contaminated properties? If so, briefly, what is it and how long has it been in place?
    (ii) If not, what guidelines do you use to evaluate contaminated real estate?
2) (i) Are you familiar with any loans that your bank has considered for acquisition financing of environmentally contaminated property? If so, when were they considered?
    (ii) Did you extend or deny the loans? Why?
3) What are your title and general responsibilities?

III. Lending Characteristics

1) During the past 12 months, approximately how many loans has your bank made on improved income-producing properties for acquisition financing?
2) What percentage of your real estate loans is made on property in, or competitive with, the Houston area?

IV. Additional Comments

_____
_____
_____
_____
_____
_____

Investor Questionnaire

Assume that you are contemplating acquisition of the Subject Property and that lenders are willing to finance the acquisition at market rates and terms.

I. Acquisition Opportunity

In general, assuming no history or existence of contamination, what rate of return would you seek for acquisition of the apartment property described in the case study?
   (i) Would the environmental history and condition of this property deter you from proceeding with the acquisition? If yes, why?
   (ii) If no, would you require a risk premium (specify in what form) for your acquisition of the Subject Property?
   (iii) Apart from a possible risk premium, how else might your evaluation of the Subject Property be influenced by its environmental history and condition?

II. Company Policy

1) Does your company have a policy with regard to contaminated properties?
   (i) If so, briefly, what is it and how long has it been in place?
   (ii) If not, what guidelines do you use to evaluate contaminated real estate?
2) What is your title?
3) What are your general responsibilities?

III. Acquisition Characteristics

1) During the past 36 months, approximately how many investments in improved income-producing properties has your company made?
2) During the past 36 months, what percentage of your total real estate investments has your company made in apartment properties?
3) What percentage of your real estate portfolio is property in, or competitive with, the Houston area?

IV. Additional Comments

Further Applications to Residential and Income Properties

Detrimental conditions valuation methodologies are an important aspect of real estate and are universally applicable. Although the most appropriate methodology may vary by property type, detrimental conditions impact all types of properties. Therefore, the study of detrimental conditions is equally relevant to both residential and commercial appraisers and analysts. The task facing the appraiser or analyst given allegations of property value diminution is quite different for residential property than for income-producing property, though. In the residential context, the appraiser could determine what evidence exists from actual residential transactions that properties influenced by the detrimental condition are selling at a discount relative to properties uninfluenced by the detrimental condition. Interestingly, the detrimental condition-related issues in this context are determined by the various perceptions of market participants (buyers, sellers, brokers, etc.) and may take on a life of their own somewhat independent of the technical dimensions of the incident or events from which they originate. In the income-producing property context, an appraiser or analyst is more likely to look at the specific circumstances of the subject property and ask whether its anticipated future income flows are affected by the detrimental condition or whether the rate at which this income would be capitalized into value by the market would be affected by the detrimental condition. Conclusions on each of these issues would be supported by a combination of an examination of the facts of the subject property, discussions with knowledgeable market participants (particularly lenders and investors), and evidence derived from actual transactions.

Ultimately, the successful analysis of detrimental conditions depends on selecting the appropriate methodology and on the skill and perseverance shown in locating, collecting, and verifying the market data necessary to implement the methodology. As many detrimental conditions involve litigation or insurance claims, an additional concern is organizing and presenting the analysis in such a way that it is understandable to the client, as well as possibly to judges, juries, and others.

Some appraisers or analysts may be of the opinion that a certain detrimental condition always or never causes a loss of property value. This is simply not true. Each situation must be individually considered based upon relevant market data, within a specific market, and at a specific date of value. Clearly the conclusions of one detrimental condition study cannot be applied universally. While case studies are valuable in illustrating the methodologies used to gather and analyze market data, the conclusions may or may not be relevant to another situation, in another market, or at a different time. Related to this is the common misconception that there are "off-the-shelf" solutions for analysis of detrimental conditions, with no need to conduct an analysis of the local market data. This is not a realistic expectation. It is ultimately up to the appraiser or analyst to collect relevant market data, analyze it, and apply the results to their situation. In fact, it is entirely possible for the same detrimental condition to result in different value impacts in different markets or at different times. For example, studies show that electromagnetic fields (EMFs) have caused a diminution in value in some areas of the country, have no impact in others, and yet increase property values in some areas where the open corridors are used for snowmobiles or are otherwise considered an amenity. While there are hundreds of scientific studies on this and other topics, the relevant issue is how the specific market perceives the situation as of a specific date of value, not what is said by certain members of the scientific community.

The analysis of detrimental conditions has to be grounded in the fundamental principles of the appraisal profession. These are

1. Defining the appraisal problem
2. Using the appropriate definition of value
3. Setting forth the scope and conditions of the appraisal
4. Applying the principles of supply and demand, balance, substitution, change, conformity, and externalities
5. Adhering to concepts of highest and best use
6. Always looking to the market for support for analyses and opinions, even when the market is narrow

Market data for detrimental conditions are not necessarily as easy to obtain as conventional appraisal market data, but that process is an essential aspect of the analysis. Leads for data can be obtained from government lists of similar detrimental conditions, such as environmental action lists, flood zone maps, earthquake maps, endangered species zones, and so forth. Brokers are often an excellent source for market data. Utility companies often have maps of tunnels, power lines, easements, water, and gas and sewer lines. From these maps, the market can be searched for sales transactions. Many detrimental conditions receive media attention, making historical newspaper articles an invaluable tool in locating market data leads. COMPS Infosystems, Inc., based in San Diego, California, now publishes market data classified according to the Bell Chart. Another excellent source of market data comes from the engineers involved in the assignment, and chances are they have files of many other similar situations. The Internet has also become an invaluable tool for searching for information on certain detrimental conditions. Retirement homes are often filled with people who have intimate knowledge of a neighborhood and know of the reactions to certain detrimental conditions. The multiple listing services (MLS) often have clues about properties that are impacted by a detrimental condition. For example, comments such as "needs tender loving care," "bring your hammer," "fixer-upper," "handyman's dream," or "jewel in the rough" can be a tip-off that a detrimental condition may be involved. All considered, there are numerous sources of information that can lead to the market data required for an analysis.

Residential Property

Causality. Claims of residential property value diminution frequently have to be evaluated in the framework of a broadly stated question, such as if the detrimental condition-related issues have caused residential property values to be lower than they otherwise would have been, other things being equal. Issues critical to the question of legal liability (e.g., the actual nature, extent, and location of the detrimental condition, whether particular properties have been physically impacted or are just proximate to the detrimental condition, and the timing associated with the detrimental condition) are difficult to disentangle in the actual marketplace. Market participants (buyers, sellers, brokers, lenders, builders, etc.) have their own understanding of these issues, which in turn may or may not influence their behavior.

The core of the task of asserting causality, therefore, lies in imposing some kind of control that allows isolation of the consequences of the detrimental condition-related issues. Some of the challenges in this regard relate to the following:

- Distinguishing the effects of a detrimental condition, which have often occurred over a substantial period of time, from the effects of the real estate cycle
- Distinguishing the effects of a detrimental condition from simple proximity to noncomforming facilities
- Distinguishing the effects of a detrimental condition from the more traditional sources of neighborhood change such as changing public education opportunities, transportation patterns, location of employment centers, location of shopping centers, and so forth

Interpreting the Market Evidence

Retrospective appraisals of allegedly affected properties that have sold. Sometimes the relationship of the allegedly affected properties to the detrimental condition may be defined with some precision—e.g., in the case of contamination transported by floodwater, the subject properties, as the allegedly affected properties are often referred to, may include all riparian properties from the source to some downstream dam. In other cases the relationship of properties to the contamination may be highly variable—e.g., all properties within a one-mile radius of the groundwater contamination source site. Whatever the specifics, the probability of being able to definitively evaluate the allegation is a direct function of the number of actual transactions of subject properties during the time period in which they are thought to have been affected.

For example, suppose that in the 10 years after a spill there have been 15 residential property transactions. Because actual sale prices exist for these transactions, assuming they are all arm's-length transactions, the appraiser or analyst must determine whether the properties would have sold for a higher price if not for the contamination issues. To answer this question, each of the sale properties is appraised effective the date of the sale (hence "retrospective appraisal") using comparable sales that, to the extent possible, mirror the subject property in every respect except for the influence of the contamination. This controls for the influence of the real estate cycle, for all the characteristics of the property itself (size, age, condition, garage, pool, etc.), and for characteristics of the neighborhood that may affect value (school district boundaries, proximity to industrial areas, proximity to public transportation routes, etc.).

Comparing the actual sale price to the retrospectively appraised value then gives an indication of whether the sale price was affected by the detrimental condition-related issues. Such a comparison for any single transaction would be a slender thread on which to form a broader conclusion, but after examining 10, 15, or 20 such comparisons, a clearer picture may emerge as to whether there seems to be any systematic diminution in value associated with the detrimental condition-related issues.

In addition, the retrospective appraisal process always involves trying to contact the parties to the transaction and discussing with them their motivation and the particular role played by the detrimental condition-related issues. After the appraiser locates the parties, if they have no strategic objection to talking about the transaction, their insights can be a valuable complement to the information contained in the market data.

Appraisals of subject properties as influenced and as uninfluenced by the detrimental condition. Often a particular assignment focuses on a small number of subject properties. The transactions will most often not have taken place after the date of the alleged effect. If they have, then the retrospective appraisal procedures described above would be implemented. In the more common circumstance where no such sale has occurred, it will generally be useful to appraise the property twice, once using comparable sales that are influenced by the detrimental condition and once using sales that are not.

This serves two useful functions. First, it forces the appraiser or analyst to draw whatever implications are possible for the subject property from the influenced and uninfluenced sales that exist. Second, it ensures that the specific characteristics of the subject property are thoroughly understood, particularly as they might relate to either vulnerability to or insulation from the particular effects of the detrimental condition.

Comparing the appraisals as influenced and uninfluenced by the detrimental condition-related issues would obviously suggest a conclusion with respect to diminution in the value of the subject properties due to the detrimental condition.

Neighborhood Comparison Approach. As opposed to the previous two approaches, which try to reach a conclusion about the effects of a detrimental condition on a particular property, the neighborhood comparison approach and the proximity approach look at a large number of transactions to see whether generalizations can be made for the area. An appraiser or analyst must recognize that if some systematic effect of the detrimental condition does reveal itself in the analysis of a neighborhood in the aggregate, he or she must still quantify the effect on individual properties. This would require application of one or both of the appraisal techniques discussed earlier.

The neighborhood comparison approach requires the definition of a test area that contains the allegedly affected properties and one or more control areas that are generally agreed to have been unaffected by the detrimental condition. The more similar the control areas are to the test area, except for the influence of the detrimental condition, the better. A variety of secondary data sources can be used to try to match land use, property, and demographic characteristics. Realistically, however, all areas have their own unique features, and it is a mistake to think of the comparison areas as "comparables" in the sense that appraisers use the term in the sales comparison approach. Rather the comparison (control) areas may be a little "better" or a little "worse" than the test area.

The critical consideration in neighborhood comparison is whether there appears to be any change in the relationship between the test area and the control (unimparied) area after the market became aware of the detrimental condition-related issues. This issue is usually resolved by observing trends in price or price per square foot of living area. If the trends start to diverge in favor of the control areas after the market becomes aware of the detrimental conditions, there is a suggestion that the divergence (i.e., diminution in the test area) is due to the detrimental condition. To reach this conclusion, however, other plausible explanations of the divergence must be investigated.

If the test and control areas have had active markets, the simplest approach to calculating the trend for each area is to calculate the mean and/or median sale price for each time period. The control area trends can then be compared to the test area trend. In many cases the timing associated with discovering and publicizing the detrimental condition may be well-defined—e.g., a high-profile accident or spill—and the relationship of the trends in price between the two areas can be compared before and after the detrimental condition with some precision. The resulting analysis can be summarized simply in a chart of the types shown in Exhibit 0.16. In this example, Control Area A appears to be inferior (on average) to the subject neighborhood, while Control Area B is a little stronger than the test area. Further, in the first graph there is no evidence of any change in the

Exhibit 0.16 Neighborhood Comparison Approach

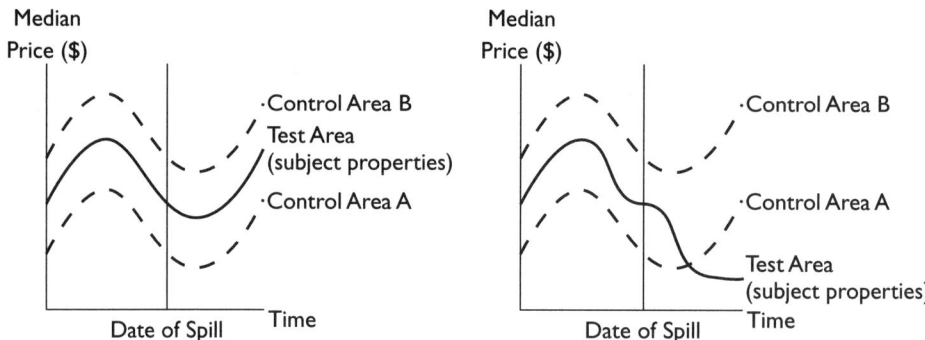

value relationship subsequent to the date of the incident, hence no empirical support for a claim of value diminution. However, if the spill did cause a diminution in value, it might have a pattern similar to the second graph in Exhibit 0.16.

Three issues commonly arise with this kind of analysis:

1. Ambiguity in the date of impact
2. Appropriate controls for other factors influencing sale prices in the neighborhoods
3. Correct interpretation and application of the results

*1. **Ambiguity in the date of impact.*** In Exhibit 0.16, a well-defined point in time when the market became aware of a highly publicized spill is assumed; however, the market may have come to understand the detrimental condition over a considerable period of time. Local press coverage may be a good proxy for market knowledge, so it is often useful to plot the number of articles dealing with the detrimental condition-related issues over time.

Exhibit 0.17 shows a hypothetical history of coverage. The trend line shows that there were occasional articles in the 1980s, but then intense coverage occurred from 1990 to 1994. This would suggest that the appraiser or analyst look carefully for changes in the trend relationship between the test and the controls beginning in 1990.

*2. **Controls for other factors.*** The previous discussion was based on a simple comparison of mean (or median) values of price (or price per square foot) between a test area and one or more control areas. If the mix of sales between large custom homes and tract homes was changing over time between the areas, though, then a change in the relationship of the trends between the different areas could mistakenly be attributed to the detrimental condition. The appraiser or analyst will often try, therefore, to control for other factors that could impact value. These would include property-specific variables (size of house, age, condition, garage, size of lot, number or rooms, number of bathrooms, etc.) and location-specific variables (school district, adjacency of a high-traffic road, proximity of shopping, etc.).

If a very small number of sales were being analyzed, the appraiser or analyst could make adjustments for these factors using the traditional methodology of the residential appraiser. More frequently, however, the assignment deals with relatively large areas over significant periods of time. This situation generates a sufficiently large number of observations so that statistical methods can be used to isolate the time trend, holding other factors constant. Multiple regression is commonly used for this kind of analysis

3. **Correct interpretation of the results.** Particular care has to be exercised in the interpretation of the results of the neighborhood comparison analysis. First, a divergence in the value trends of the test and control areas does not necessarily prove causality due to the detrimental condition; it simply indicates that there is *some* cause of divergence beyond the variables that are controlled in the study. Other possible causes of the divergence must be carefully analyzed and eliminated before attribution to the detrimental condiiton is concluded. Second, the conclusion that results from this analysis is a conclusion about the neighborhood in the aggregate, not about individual properties. Additional, property-specific research would be required to understand how the aggregate results would apply to individual properties.

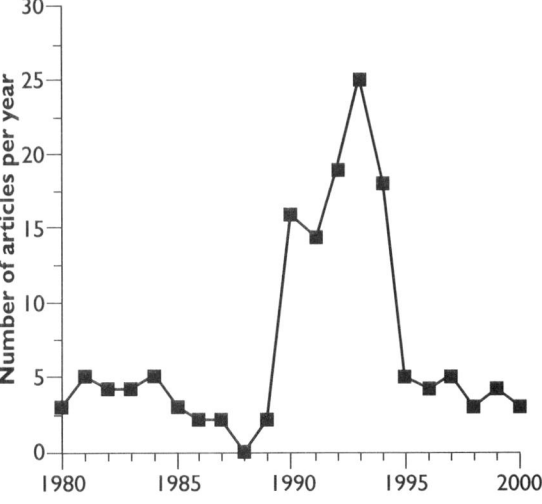

Exhibit 0.17   Local Press Coverage of the Contamination Issues

Proximity Approach. The proximity approach has several elements in common with the neighborhood comparison approach, but the former focuses exclusively on the test area, asking the question whether there is any evidence of a systematic effect on value associated with proximity to the detrimental condition.

Proximity can be defined in several different ways, as long as any plausible hypothesis of effect can be tested. It might be distance to the property boundary of the source site, the distance to the nearest contaminated water well, a binary variable reflecting whether the property is over the plume, distance from airport noise, or other variables.

The basic test is estimating the trend of values over time associated with the various proximity variables. Suppose, for example, the appraiser or analyst was testing for differences in value trends within the test area based on three different distance zones from an environmental source site—less than 1,000 feet, from 1,000 to 2,000 feet, or more than 2,000 feet. Suppose further that, other things equal, the value trends were higher as distance from the source site increased, as shown in Exhibit 0.18. Does this result suggest that contamination has affected home values? Suppose the contamination-related event occurred in 1990 and was well publicized in the market at that time. Under this assumption, the detrimental condition does not seem to have affected value if the pattern resembles the first graph. The same value relationships that existed before the detrimental condition-related event also exist after. There does not appear to have been any change in proximity-related value trends due to the detrimental condition. However,

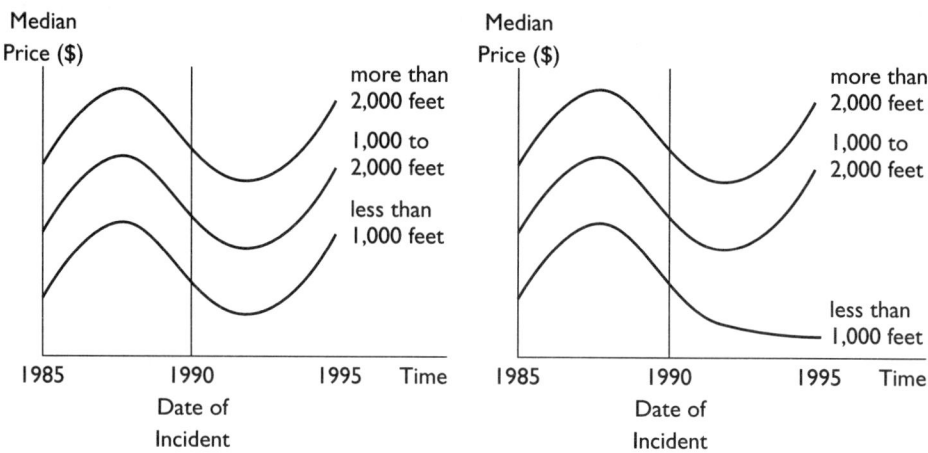

Exhibit 0.18 Value Trends Associated with Proximity to the Test Site

in the second graph the pattern suggests that the contamination does impact properties less than 1,000 feet from the spill.

Like neighborhood comparison analysis, proximity analysis can be carried out based on simple mean or median sale price data or on multiple regression analysis used to control for property- and neighborhood-specific variables that may affect value. Similarly the admonitions that apply to the interpretation of results in neighborhood comparison analysis are relevant here as well.

Issues in Residential Property Analysis. The most significant issue in assessing the consequences of a detrimental condition on residential property values is the general predisposition of people to believe that detrimental conditions affect residential property values. When a home owner is posed the question, "Other things equal, how would you like to live next to a _____?" answers are uniformly in the negative. No one views landfills, sewage treatment, plants, jails, airport noise, and soil or groundwater contamination as a positive attribute of a residential property. But that is only part of the story. If market value is going to be affected, then this particular attribute has to be given enough weight in the decision process of buyers and sellers to have a material effect on price. In other words, the detrimental condition issue has to be important relative to all the other variables that influence the home purchase decision (public safety, quality of schools, access to employment, church or synagogue, or friends and relatives, special features of the home, affordability, etc.). Like any detrimental conditon, an analysis of market data is necessary to determine if the issue causes a diminution in value or if it is a Class I benign condition.

Income-Producing Property

Conceptual Framework. The fundamentals of real property valuation recognize that value reflects an anticipated stream of future benefits capitalized at a return necessary to attract capital to the opportunity. Detrimental conditions have the potential to decrease the stream of future benefits and to raise the return necessary to attract capital, both of which will decrease value. The valuation issues then become quantifying the decrease in future benefits (i.e., the effects on net operating income) and the increase in yields (i.e., the risk premiums due to the detrimental conditon). Exhibit 0.19 illustrates the basic steps in the process.

Initially there is an investigative phase in which the nature and extent of the detrimental condition must be assessed and fully characterized. In addition, an evaluation of the detrimental condition from the public and regulatory perspectives is necessary as well as a full understanding of the consequences of the problem (i.e., remediation costs and alternatives, liability, use restrictions). The results of the investigative phase become a critical component throughout the remainder of the valuation process and allow for the preliminary assessment of whether the value of the property may have been diminished.

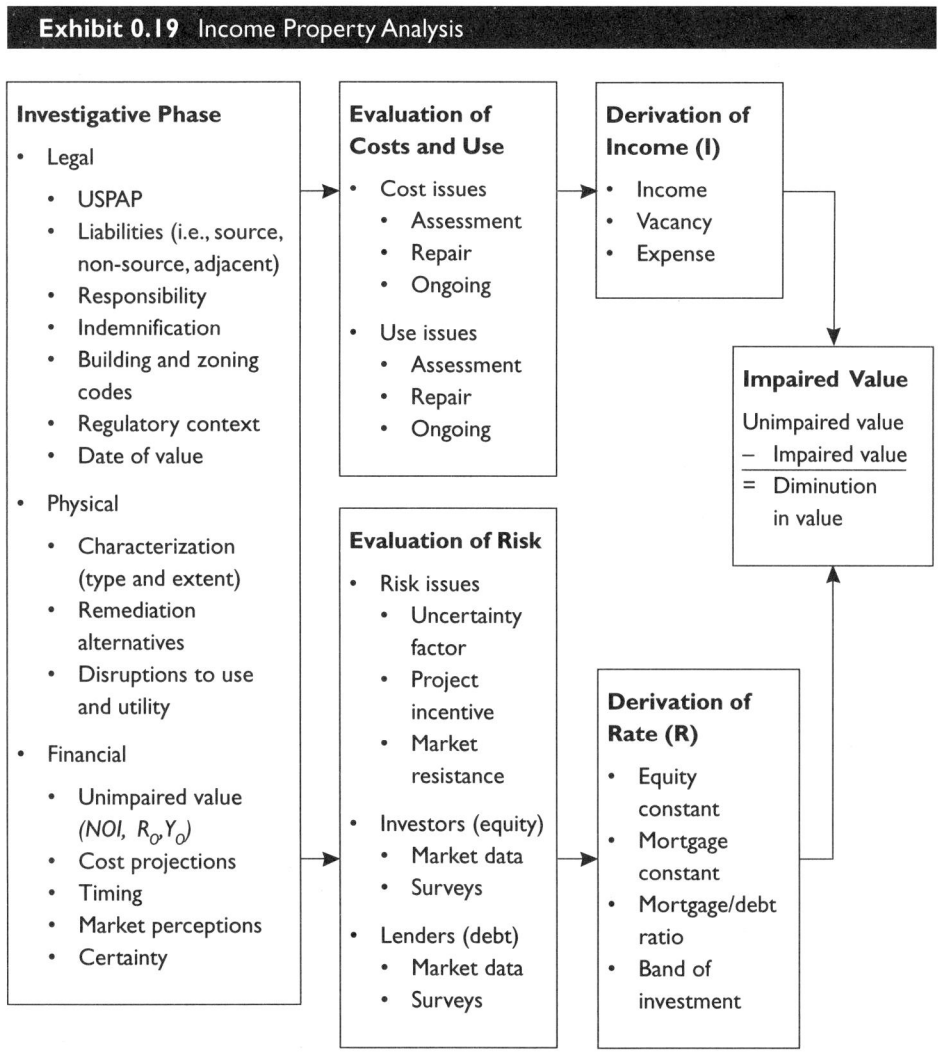

Exhibit 0.19 Income Property Analysis

The findings from the investigative phase provide the basis for determining the direct costs associated with the property as well as for developing the fact pattern from which to evaluate the risk perceptions of market participants relative to the affected property. The fact pattern becomes the foundation for assessing whether the market perceives additional risk associated with the property (i.e., project incentive or market resistance). If the property and its history are well described, it is usually possible to obtain definitive opinions with a high degree of consensus from users, lenders, and investors regarding the impact of the detrimental condition on their business decisions. The direct costs and the risk-adjusted capitalization or yield rates are then used in conjunction with the anticipated future cash flows of the property to determine the property's value in an impaired state.

Risk Quantification by Market Participants. As is illustrated in Exhibit 0.19, the valuation of a property impacted by a detrimental condition depends on estimates of net operating income effects combined with adjustments for the risks perceived by market participants. Quantification of appropriate risk adjustments in light of particular, site-specific fact patterns is typically the most challenging part of the valuation problem.

Under the detrimental condition income approach, risk analysis and quantification may begin with the perceptions of lenders and equity investors. Research on the perceptions and reactions of these participants can provide great understanding of the range and type of market responses to the changes caused by the detrimental condition in the risk characteristics of real property. For mortgage investors, market response to detrimental condition takes the form of adjustments in the underwriting standards for loan decisions or in the availability or terms at which credit is offered. For equity investors, market response includes adjustments to the yield, or return, requirements necessary to compensate for the increased risk associated with the detrimental condition or hazard. The approach to quantifying these effects has two components—structured interviews and comparable sales.

Structured interviews. Appraisers and analysts have always depended heavily on firsthand discussions with market participants (buyers, sellers, brokers, lenders, investors, users, etc.) to understand and evaluate the market. With detrimental conditions, this is no less the case. In fact, due to the large number of important, property-specific issues associated with a detrimental condition, structured interviews are both important and highly instructive. As discussed, the person being interviewed is given a short but detailed description of the economic characteristics of the property and whatever is known about the nature and extent of the detrimental condition, the regulatory status, likely repairs or remediation, liability, indemnification, off-site issues, and so forth. The interview is then guided by an outline of questions that, in the case of a lender, begins with the terms that credit would be available under, if at all, in the absence of detrimental condition issues. This is then followed up by a series of questions dealing explicitly with the detrimental condition and its effect on the credit terms already described for the property.

Through careful selection of market participants (specifically those the subject property presents a relevant loan or investment opportunity for) and with careful delineation of the facts that such decisions are based on, a clear consensus usually emerges after relatively few interviews (three to ten), which gives the appraiser or analyst a reliable basis on which to form an opinion.

Comparable sales. Analysis of actual transactions is involved here in the context of the income capitalization approach, not the sales comparison approach. Specifically, the object is to find actual transactions with characteristics similar enough to the subject that the self-reported behavior of lenders and investors can be checked. For example, the terms under which a large regional bank has extended credit on a property with considerable contamination but with very strong indemnity from an economically strong responsible party may shed considerable light on a subject property with similar contamination facts, even if it has somewhat different economic characteristics.

Guidelines to Detrimental Condition Analysis

In summary, several questions should be asked, and some key points and rules should be applied for a credible and professional study of detrimental conditions, as follows.

1. Real Estate Type

Is the subject property a commercial property or a residential property? If it is residential, is it a tract home for which sales comparable will be plentiful, or is it a unique custom home for which comparable transactions will be more difficult to find? If it is an income-producing property, is it a generic product that will be relatively easy to value using sales comparison and income capitalization approach methods, or is it a property with special use characteristics that will require significant reliance on the cost approach?

In general, it is important to understand the subject property's market segment, as well as the basic characteristics of the subject property in an unimpaired condition. A crack running through a warehouse floor may be perceived quite differently than the same crack running through a living room. The demand for an upscale luxury apartment may be very sensitive to amenities, as opposed to a mid-level complex catering to singles and students that is price-sensitive. Property owners in an urban area may have an entirely different perception about a large water tunnel underneath their property than those in a rural area. Older neighborhoods may have different dynamics than a younger neighborhood. An inner-city area may react differently towards the development of a jail nearby than a suburban area. Reactions towards a detrimental condition may differ in an increasing market, as opposed to a period when the market is declining. All of these dynamics can influence market perceptions.

2. Detrimental Condition Fundamentals

What is the nature of the problem? What is the extent of the problem? Are regulatory authorities involved with the problem? If so, what is their perspective on the problem? Is the problem well-defined? What is the public profile of the problem? Has a qualified professional provided a clear characterization of the problem? Is the engineering report reasonable?

Understanding the basics of detrimental conditions is central to preliminary investigation of the areas of impact on which a detrimental analysis depends. It is essential to understand the full implications of the detrimental condition in terms of the assessment, repair, and ongoing stages, as well as the full implications of cost and responsibility, use, and risk issues as they relate within each stage. The Detrimental Condition Matrix,

Detrimental Condition Model, and Bell Chart, coupled with the three detrimental condition approaches to value, provide a fundamental framework for these questions and the analysis of detrimental conditions.

3. Costs

What kinds of assessment activities will be required? How long will they take? What will they cost? What kinds of repair or remediation costs are anticipated? Is there a reliable basis for anticipating their costs and timing? Are the costs guaranteed? What are the contingencies? Is "cost cap" insurance available, where the costs are guaranteed? Are there other costs, such as tenant improvements, moving costs, carrying costs, and so forth? Once the repairs are complete, is there a reason to expect that ongoing costs will be required to monitor or maintain the repairs?

A full and complete accounting must be made of all costs. This could include absorption, administrative, assessment, agency oversight, backfill, carrying costs, contingencies, disposal, engineering, excavation, fixed costs, insurance, laboratory analysis, landscaping, leasing commissions, legal oversight, monitoring, moving, operations and maintenance programs, paving, permits, repairs, remediation, sampling, structural, tenant relocation, transport and hauling, treatment, trenching, utility disconnect or moving, well site removal, and so on.

4. Responsibility for Costs and Repairs

Who will pay the costs? Is the property owner responsible for the repairs, or are previous owners, neighbors, or other parties responsible? Are they financially capable? Is responsibility for the detrimental condition in dispute? Is there an indemnification? How solid is it?

It is imperative that there be a clear understanding about the party responsible for repairs. Those costs paid by another party do not cause a diminution to the property value, in terms of repair costs, provided that the responsible party has the financial capacity and willingness to fund the necessary costs.

5. Effects on Use

Is the property safe to occupy? In the case of an income-producing property, are there any effects on rents or occupancy? Are there any effects on operating expenses? Do expenses increase, perhaps due to increased security requirements, or could they decrease if the facility were partly or totally closed for some period of time? Is there a tangible nuisance in the form of noise or odor, or is something going on in a deep acquifer under the property that has little or nothing to do with surface activity? Is the bottom line impacted?

With income-producing properties, the detrimental condition must impact the income or risk to have an effect on value. With residential property, understanding the effect on use requires a more general inquiry into the way in which the detrimental condition would affect the livability of the property.

6. Risks

Are there perceived risks? Are they justified? Can they be validated from the market data?

Depending on when the property is being valued, there may be significant uncertainty associated with estimated costs to repair. A first important step, therefore, is to work systematically through the various stages of risk and to determine whether each is an issue and, if so, the magnitude of the issue.

7. Selection of Appropriate Detrimental Condition Approaches to Value

Is primary reliance on the income capitalization approach, or is primary reliance on the cost approach with the estimate of market resistance extracted from the sales comparison approach? Is the discounted cash flow approach appropriate? How will the discount rate be estimated? Is the income capitalization approach appropriate? Is the cost approach appropriate? Is the sales comparison approach appropriate?

It is imperative to properly select and apply the appropriate valuation methodology. With the preceding points addressed, the strategic decision can be made as to which of the three detrimental condition approaches to value will be relied upon.

8. Market Data

Has a thorough investigation for market data been conducted? What market data are available? Are they verified? Are they reliable? Are they truly relevant to the detrimental condition being studied?

It should be recognized that there are specialized techniques for collecting market data and that conclusions should be drawn that are properly supported by relevant market data. Whatever approach or approaches are chosen, it is important that the quality of the market data ultimately drives the quality of the analysis. Quantifying damages based *solely* upon "experience and professional judgment" is reckless at best and probably unethical, particularly when market data exist to measure the impact of most detrimental conditions. Failing to research and apply relevant market data is the single most common flaw in detrimental condition analysis. While preconceptions to the analysis of detrimental conditions do exist, the issue is ultimately an empirical question that can only be resolved with relevant market data. A detrimental condition cannot be universally generalized, and it is unique to a particular market and the facts of a particular property as of a specific date of value.

9. Competence and Ethics

Is the appraiser or analyst experienced in this type of situation? What specialized detrimental condition training has the appraiser received? Are the methodologies consistently and competently applied?

An appraiser must not go beyond his or her area of expertise. A detrimental conditions assignment will frequently require an understanding of engineering and legal issues. Assessing soil conditions, identifying contaminants, designing remediation systems, or estimating the duration of various repair activities are all technical issues that require appropriate engineering or scientific knowledge. Similarly, there are issues of regulatory compliance, contract interpretation, or statutory liability that are equally critical to the analysis but which require legal expertise. The appraiser or analyst must advise the client that the assignment requires this foundational information from qualified sources and that without it he or she is unable to proceed. It is always imperative to incorporate and apply the Ethics and Standards of Professional Practice of the Appraisal Institute when estimating the effects of detrimental conditions on real estate values.

As a practical matter, some may feel that a proper market-driven analysis is simply too time-consuming. However, providing clients with conclusions that are not based upon a proper analysis is a violation of the standards of the Appraisal Institute and of the Uniform Standards of Professional Appraisal Practice (USPAP) of The Appraisal Foundation. Regardless, once an assignment is accepted, the appraiser or analyst has an ethical duty to carry out a full and proper study, regardless of the financial consequences. Of course, the ethics and standards of the Appraisal Institute and USPAP are an integral part of any proper detrimental conditions analysis.

10. Reliance on the Reports of Others

Did an engineer, scientist, or other qualified professional issue a report? Was the appraiser or analyst able to have any questions about the report answered satisfactorily? Does the appraisal report clearly state what reports were relied upon and what assumptions were made?

While most real estate appraisers and analysts are not engineers, it is not only possible but also appropriate that these costs be reviewed for basic reasonableness. In addition to repair or remediation costs, contingencies should also be considered. These costs may be reviewed by general comparison to other assignments or in discussions with other engineers.

Further Reading[2]

Bell, Randall. "The Impact of Detrimental Conditions on Property Values." *The Appraisal Journal* (October 1998).

___. "Detrimental Conditions: A Profile of Valuation Methodologies with Environmental Contamination, Crime Scene Stigma, and Natural Disaster Case Studies." Paper presented at the National Symposium of the Appraisal Institute, Washington, D.C., June 1997.

Chalmers, James A., and Thomas O. Jackson. "Risk Factors in the Appraisal of Contaminated Property." *The Appraisal Journal* (January 1996).

Harris, Timothy J. "The Requirement of Expert Testimony in Appraisal Litigation." *The Appraisal Journal* (January 1992).

Love, Terrence L. "Guidelines for the Witness: Pointers for Giving Effective Testimony." *The Appraisal Journal* (October 1995).

Mundy, Bill. "The Impact of Hazardous and Toxic Material on Property Value." *The Appraisal Journal* (April 1992), and "The Impact of Hazardous and Toxic Material on Property Value: Revisited." *The Appraisal Journal* (October 1992).

---

2. While some of these articles are written on environmental topics, they provide some of the framework used to value detrimental conditions.

___. "Stigma and Value." *The Appraisal Journal* (January 1992).

Neustein, Richard A. "Estimating Value Diminution by the Income Approach." *The Appraisal Journal* (April 1992).

Patchin, Peter. "Contaminated Properties and the Sales Comparison Approach." *The Appraisal Journal* (July 1994).

___. "Contaminated Properties—Stigma Revisited." *The Appraisal Journal* (April 1991).

___. "Valuation of Contaminated Property." *The Appraisal Journal* (January 1988).

Rabianski, Joseph, and Neil G. Carn. "Cross-Examination: How to Protect Yourself and the Appraisal Report." *The Appraisal Journal* (October 1992).

CHAPTER 1

Class I—No Detrimental Conditions or Benign Condition

Class I is the most straightforward classification because it involves the absence of material detrimental conditions. As many detrimental condition assignments include the initial step of determining the *unimpaired value*, many studies begin with the basic valuation as a benchmark for later comparisons. The Detrimental Condition Model generates an illustration of Class I detrimental conditions as seen in Exhibit 1.1.

Benign Conditions

Class I detrimental conditions also involve acts or events wherein the issue has no effect on value. This can involve any one of the detrimental conditions in Classes II through IX. While this concept is straightforward, it can be the grounds for litigation. For example, a plaintiff may contend that some condition affected his or her property value, while the defendant claims that the event had no impact on value.

Virtually any detrimental condition can be benign and not have any impact at all, or it can be so severe that all value is lost. For example, if a shopping center is the scene of a shoplifting crime, this one occurrence is not likely to have an impact on the property value. However, if the same shopping center is the scene of a particularly violent and well-publicized crime, it may have a significant impact. If a home owner accidentally kicks over a can of paint in the garage, it is not likely to have any impact on the value of the property. However, if a large manufacturing firm spills thousands of gallons of contaminants into the soil, it would likely have a profound impact. The impact of a detrimental condition, and therefore its ultimate classification, can only be determined by a comprehensive analysis based on relevant market data.

Exhibit 1.1 Class I—No Detrimental Conditions or Benign Condition

The primary graph for DC Class I has been highlighted here; however, DCs have a variety of impacts, which, upon analysis, vary on a case-by-case basis. Ultimately any graph may be applicable based upon the case-specific facts.

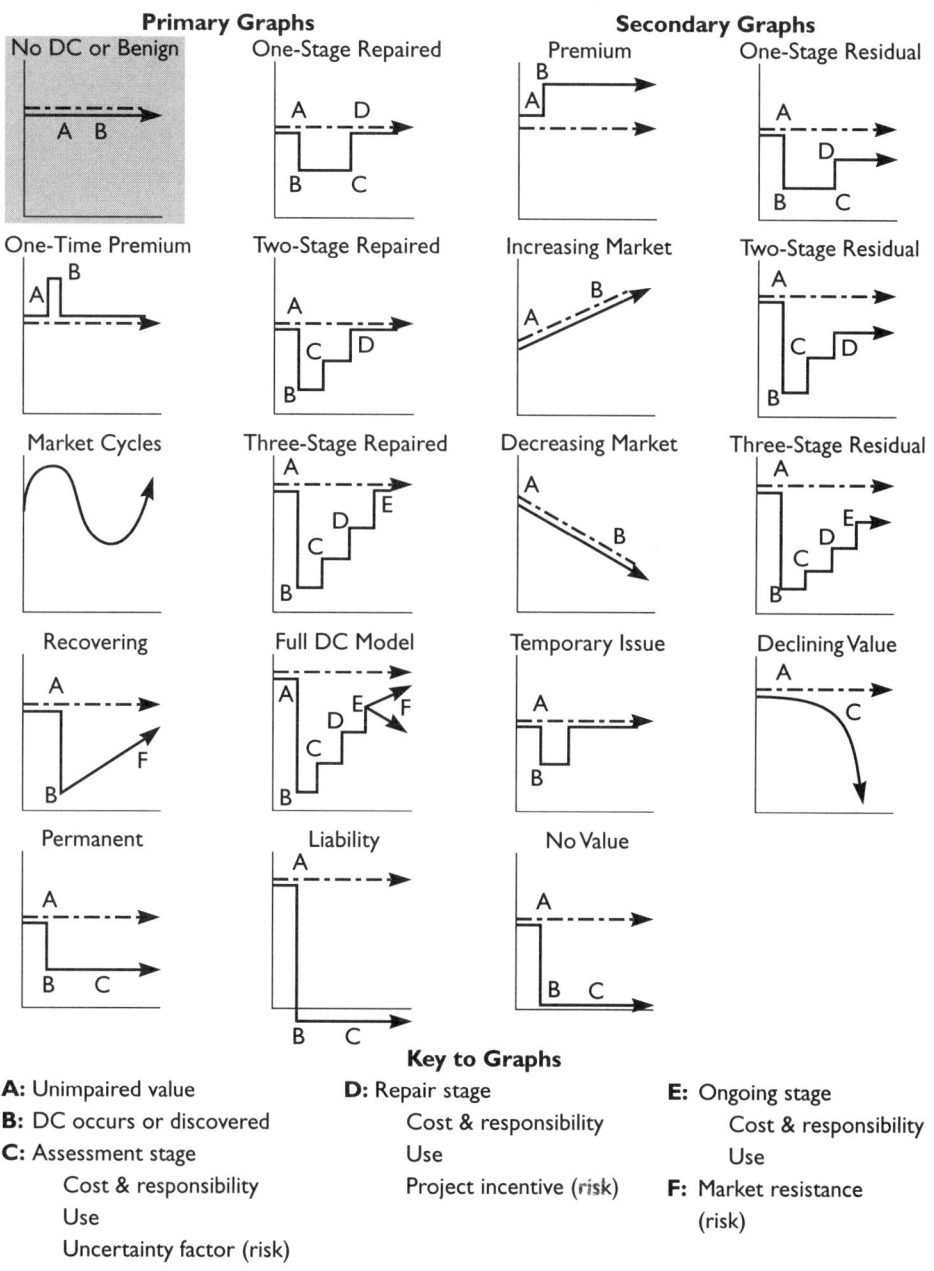

Key to Graphs

- **A:** Unimpaired value
- **B:** DC occurs or discovered
- **C:** Assessment stage
  - Cost & responsibility
  - Use
  - Uncertainty factor (risk)
- **D:** Repair stage
  - Cost & responsibility
  - Use
  - Project incentive (risk)
- **E:** Ongoing stage
  - Cost & responsibility
  - Use
- **F:** Market resistance (risk)

Source: *Bell's Guide: The Real Estate Encyclopedia*

Chapter 1 Case Study

By Randall Bell, MAI

Bruce McNall House—White-Collar Crime
Class I Detrimental Condition—Benign Condition

The former owner of the Los Angeles Kings, Bruce McNall, was convicted of various white-collar crimes and sentenced to prison. The bank foreclosed on McNall's 12,214-sq.-ft. home, which sold promptly for full value when put on the market. This was a high-profile case but only regionally reported by the local media. This indicated that the market did not require a discount for white-collar crimes in this instance. If a violent crime had been committed, it would likely be a Class IV detrimental condition.

This West Los Angeles home was previously owned by Bruce McNall, who formerly owned the Los Angeles Kings hockey team. After being convicted of white-collar crimes, the home was sold for its full market value and had a normal marketing period. As opposed to violent crimes, white-collar crimes tend to not impact property values.

CHAPTER 2

Class II—Nonmarket Motivations

Most commonly, real estate transactions involve "arm's-length" situations, where the parties are each acting in their own best interests. One of the definitions of *market value* states that

> "Market value" means the most probable price which a property should bring in a competitive and open market under all conditions requisite to a fair sale, the buyer and seller each acting prudently and knowledgeably, and assuming the price is not affected by undue stimulus. Implicit in this definition is the consummation as of a sale of a specified date and the passing of title from seller to buyer under conditions whereby:
>
> (1) buyer and seller are typically motivated;
> (2) both parties are well informed or well advised, and acting in what they consider their best interests;
> (3) a reasonable time is allowed for exposure in the open market;
> (4) payment is made in terms of cash in U.S. dollars or in terms of financial arrangements comparable thereto; and
> (5) the price represents the normal consideration for the property sold unaffected by special or creative financing or sales concessions granted by anyone associated with the sale.[1]

While the definition of market value is clear, the reality of the real estate market is that not all buyers and sellers are knowledgeable and well informed. Additionally, the transaction may have involved considerations other than cash, special financing may have been a factor, and one of the parties may have been knowledgeable but not typically motivated. In fact, by no means does the term *market value* define all the situations that actually take place in the real estate market, and many real estate transactions fall into categories other than market value. Class II nonmarket motivations are those situations where a premium was paid for the property above its market value.

---

1. *Office of the Comptroller of the Currency* under 12 CFR, Part 34, Subpart C-Appraisals, 34.42 Definitions (f).

The classification of certain price premiums as detrimental conditions becomes apparent when a transaction is viewed from the perspective of a buyer who pays more than necessary to acquire a property. The classification includes assemblages, over-heated markets, expansions, and nonknowledgeable buyers who overpaid. Generally, the premium is expressed as a percentage of the Class I value.

An illustration of a common Class II detrimental condition would be the assemblage of two parcels. If a group of developers or property owners strongly desire to combine the adjoining parcel with their property, they may be willing to pay a premium to acquire it. In fact, the two properties combined as one may be of more use, and have a higher value, than two separate properties. If land is worth $10 per square foot and a specially motivated property owner is willing to pay $12 per square foot for the adjoining parcel, then the premium would be a factor or 1.20, or 20%. In Exhibit 2.1, Class II detrimental conditions reflect a normal property value and an increase over the normal property value.

This concept can be illustrated by the following example. Terrence Donnelley, a major local developer owns a 3,500-sq.-ft. fast-food restaurant on the main traffic thoroughfare in Phoenix, Arizona. Recently, the franchisee, Sandy Hampton, wanted to install a drive-through window that she expected would increase her business by 20% to 40%. The increase in business would require a 1,000-sq.-ft. addition to the restaurant, and in turn another 15 parking spaces would be needed to meet the city's parking code. Donnelley would be able to increase the rent significantly if he could assemble some land next to his site to accommodate the additional required parking. He spoke to the owner of the land adjacent to the restaurant site, who was reluctant to sell. Donnelley eventually enticed the owner to sell the land; however, the owner required a price that reflected a 20% premium over the market value.

Donnelley performed some calculations showing that if the rents could be increased from the current rate of $1.50 net per square foot to $1.85, then he would recover the premium paid for the land in two years. From that point on, Donnelley would make a profit from the lease. He presented a proposal to the franchisee that he would purchase the adjoining land if the franchisee would construct the additional improvements and sign a five-year lease at $1.85 net per square foot. The franchisee agreed, so Donnelley went ahead and purchased the land knowing that he was paying 20% over the market value.

Further Reading

Easements

Graham, Lannie M. "Prescriptive Easements and a Highest and Best Use Decision." *The Appraisal Journal* (October 1991).

Knipe, William B. (Trey) III. "Valuing the Probability of Rezoning." *The Appraisal Journal* (April 1988).

West, Robert J. "Statistical Inference: An Aviation Easement Analysis." *Real Estate Issues,* vol. 13, no. 1 (Spring/Summer 1988).

Exhibit 2.1 Class II—Nonmarket Motivations

The graphs for DC Class II have been highlighted here; however, DCs have a variety of impacts, which, upon analysis, vary on a case-by-case basis. Ultimately any graph may be applicable based upon the case-specific facts.

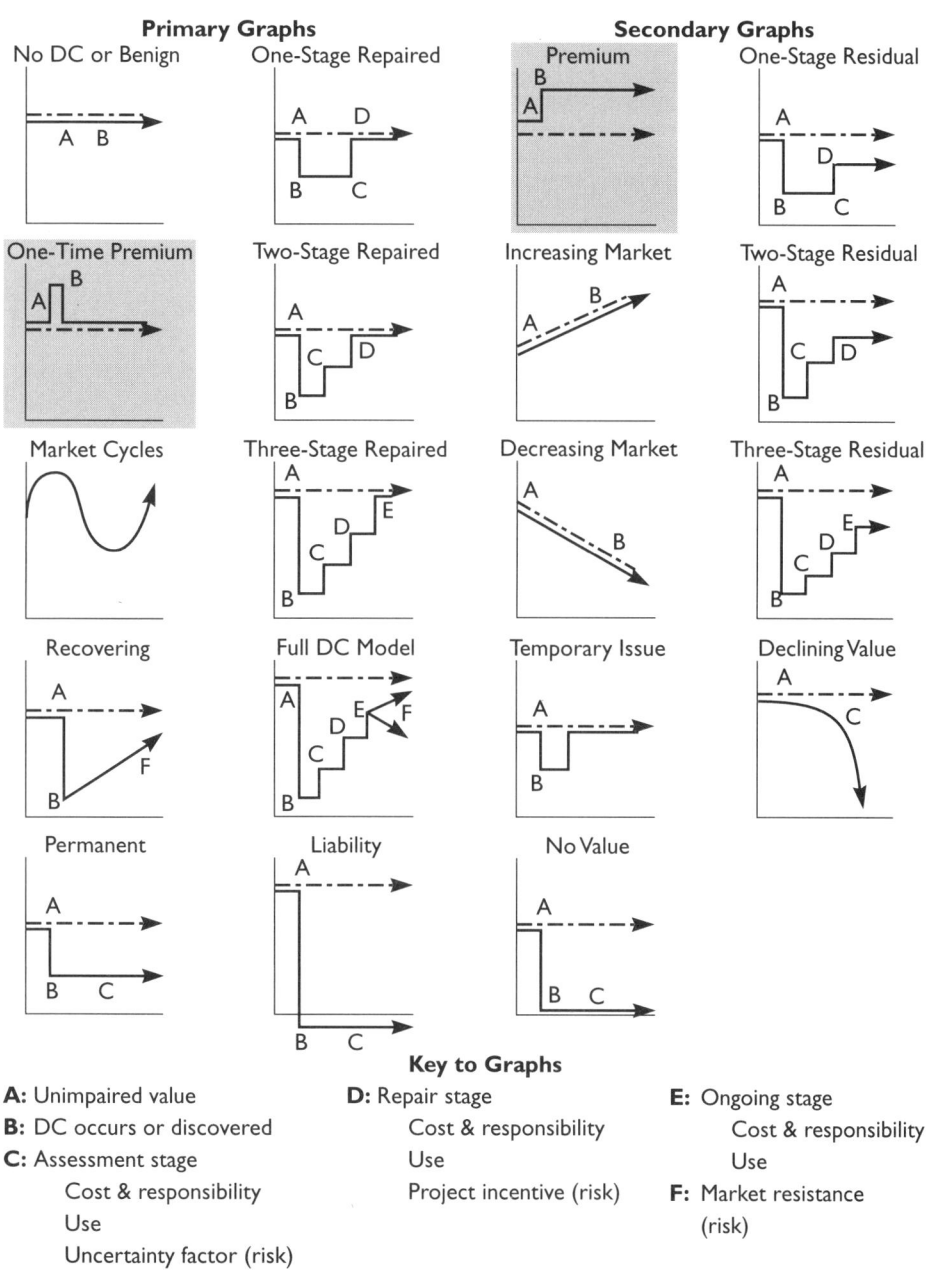

Key to Graphs

A: Unimpaired value
B: DC occurs or discovered
C: Assessment stage
    Cost & responsibility
    Use
    Uncertainty factor (risk)
D: Repair stage
    Cost & responsibility
    Use
    Project incentive (risk)
E: Ongoing stage
    Cost & responsibility
    Use
F: Market resistance
    (risk)

Source: *Bell's Guide: The Real Estate Encyclopedia*

Chapter 2 Case Study

By Orell C. Anderson, MAI

Feng Shui
Class II Detrimental Condition—Nonmarket Motivation

Feng shui (literally meaning "wind and water") is an ancient Chinese system of beliefs governing the arrangement of physical living and working environments using the concept of harmony. These beliefs can impact the price paid for either residential or commercial land or for improvements in the areas of the world where a buyer's choices are motivated by these issues. Premiums may be paid for properties that have good feng shui, or, on the other hand, properties with bad *feng shui* may be burdened by extended marketing periods, may receive a lower price, or may not be considered altogether as a purchase option.

According to Sheida Hodge in her book *Feng Shui - A Guide for Increased Real Estate Sales to Asians*, the application of feng shui is proper, harmonious placement—the proper siting of a building, its architectural configuration, and its interior layout.

A survey was conducted with real estate agents, brokers, and other active market participants in the Southern California area working with clients who hold these beliefs. The following questions were asked:

- What percentage of the Asian population is motivated by *feng shui*?
- What significant items are typically considered by potential buyers as very negative or positive features?
- If a property is suffering from bad *feng shui*, what can be done to mitigate the issues?

The study indicated that approximately 70% of purchasers consider it in their buying decisions. If the property has bad *feng shui*, these buyers generally will not consider purchasing it. Of this 70%, 25% to 30% retain the services of a *feng shui* master *(geomaster)* to inspect the property or give input before buying.

Items that are considered undesirable include homes that have garages or front doors facing the street. The survey also indicated that most prospects did not want a home with this type of street orientation. The number "4" in an address was also considered detrimental, as this unlucky number means death to those who subscribe to *feng shui* beliefs. Developers marketing directly to the Asian community also will go to great lengths to avoid including the number in an address. Finally, lots with a **T** orientation (a street pointing at it) or buildings at a **Y** junction are undesirable.

The ideal property has hills or mountains to the north and water to the south of a gently sloping lot with a southerly orientation. It is desirable to have trees located on the northwest lot line. Commercial property with good *feng shui* is located on a corner or convergence of two-way streets. In certain Chinese cities, apartment complexes with a southerly orientation receive higher lease rates. Building size and style should conform to other buildings in the neighborhood. In Hong Kong, where the Bank of China constructed a blade-like high-rise office building that jutted out of the center of the city, neighboring businesses and residents complained that it destroyed the good feng shui of surrounding buildings. The high-rise has reportedly suffered from high vacancy rates and a stigma of bad luck resulting in lower rental rates as an incentive to lease.

If a property suffers from bad *feng shui*, several things can be done to mitigate its state. The survey, as well as Hodge's book, indicated that landscaping or remodeling are typical remedies. This may take the form of relocating the front door to face a different direction, installing a curved staircase that does not face the front door, installing party walls and/or a fountain, changing the address, planting trees, or placing wind chimes in key areas. However, the greatest incentive was the perception of a good value on the part of the buyer. This is not limited to just discounting the price, but may include the perception of increasing market values or nonquantifiable items known only to a particular buyer.

Based upon the above discussion two case studies were conducted to investigate this Class II detrimental condition and specific nonmarket motivation.

The first case study is a vacant, rectangular industrial site located in Anaheim, California. The subject property contains 122,425 square feet with frontage on three streets in an industrial/business park. The parcel was purchased in fall 1995 for $10.68 per square foot. It has good freeway access. The intended use was to construct a user-owned, 70,000-sq.-ft. industrial/office building (i.e., flex space). In terms of good *feng shui*, hills were located to the north, the lot sloped slightly to the south where there was vacant land and a lake, and the site was situated on a corner.

In analyzing this transaction, it became apparent that it had sold for a slight premium over other properties in the area. This was verified by one of several brokers involved with the transaction. One broker noted that the buyer had special *feng shui* motivations, which amounted to a premium of approximately 5% being paid. As a check of reasonableness, five comparable land sales were analyzed. The following chart sets forth the most pertinent comparable sales:

Land Sales Summary

No.	Location	Size	Sale Date	Price per Square Foot
Subject	Anaheim	122,425	Fall 1995	$10.68
1	Huntington Beach	26,160	Winter 1995	$12.96 −
2	Santa Ana	54,711	Spring 1995	$10.00 +
3	Anaheim	142,267	Spring 1995	$10.02
4	Huntington Beach	21,830	Winter 1994	$12.00 −
5	Santa Ana	33,780	Spring 1994	$9.92 +

The unadjusted price per square foot ranged from $9.92 to $12.96 per square foot. No adjustment for market conditions was necessary. Sales 1 and 4 were considered superior as compared with the subject property in terms of their location in a beach city and their smaller size. Sales 2 and 5 were considered inferior in terms of location. Sale 3 was considered the most similar to the subject property in terms of location and size, and sold for approximately 6.18% less than the subject property. The market data supported the comments of the broker who believed that the market value of the subject property was approximately $10.00 per square foot. Because of his special motivations, the buyer had purchased the property for a premium of 5%. This was supported by both the market data and broker opinion.

The second study involves a residential subdivision in Southern California that was built near two other competing developments. Some buyers in the area held *feng shui* beliefs. The subject development included 96 homes ranging in size from 1,300 to 1,700 square feet with two or three bedrooms. The two-story homes are located on small lots of approximately 3,500 square feet. Amenities included private parks, swimming pools, tennis courts, and a central recreation center/clubhouse. Prices in 1996 ranged from $218,000 to $235,000 with incentives of $10,000 to $12,000.

Knowing that some buyers who held beliefs in *feng shui* would pay premiums, one developer consulted with a *feng shui* expert who gave planning input that included site orientation, landscaping, space planning, and structural design. The sales strategy included the elimination of the address numbers 4, 14, 24, and 34 for the first two phases. Additionally, the developer went to great lengths to restrict lots facing a **T** intersection. According to on-site agents, the residential market was "soft" at the time. Absorption rates for the subject property, for the first year, averaged one unit per week with gradual elimination of incentives. The competing developments that had not gone to any efforts to address *feng shui* issues had considerably lower absorption rates of one unit per month. In June 1997, the market became "hot," absorption increased to approximately 3.75 homes per week, while the competing developments had absorption of 2.5 homes per week.

As many buyers were enticed to buy in the subdivision with *feng shui* incentives, the competing developments incurred some losses for lots and homes with bad *feng shui*. Although many lots with "unlucky" addresses and locations were discounted to offset the unlucky numbers, they remained on the market for six to eight months longer as compared to other similar undeveloped lots. They did not sell until they were developed with homes and landscaping, at additional costs and risk to the developer, and after the market had significantly improved. Lots that faced **T** intersections did not sell until they were discounted $5,000. A young Asian couple not aware of the bad *feng shui* perceived this discount as a great value and made an offer to purchase the lot. However, when informed by their agent as to the meaning, they pulled their offer and refused to look at any homes that were not three lots away from **T** intersections.

As the surveys and market data indicated, certain buyers may pay a premium if a property is perceived to have good *feng shui*, as compared to a residence that is functionally similar.

CHAPTER 3

Class III—Market Conditions

As is commonly known, real estate values fluctuate over time. In a strong market—commonly referred to as a *seller's market*—prices are increasing, listing periods tend to be short, fewer properties are on the market, and construction is active. Conversely, in a weak market, prices are falling, listing periods are long, an overabundance of properties are available for sale, and construction activity is limited. This is commonly referred to as a *buyer's market* because buyers can be selective and demand lower prices.

Class III includes these normal cycles of the real estate market, when values increase, decrease, or remain level over a specific period of time. The detrimental effect of this condition may be viewed from the perspective of the buyer in an increasing market, or a property owner in a decreasing market. These patterns of value are simply the effects of the general economy, which are driven by the issues of supply and demand.

Market Trends

The forces of real estate economics cause fluctuations in the real estate market. While predicting future trends is speculative, quantifying historical trends is relatively simple, as it involves only the accumulation of historical market data, as shown in Exhibit 3.1.

In Exhibit 3.2, Class III market conditions simply reflect the increase, decrease, or level market condition over time. One way of measuring Class III conditions involves the study of several comparable sales that resold at a later date (i.e., sale/resale analysis). By comparing the initial and subsequent sale dates and values, a determination can be made as to the market condition trends. For example, if market conditions have declined 5% per year and the situation involves an 18-month time period, then the adjustment would be a factor of -0.075.

Exhibit 3.1 Market Trends Graph

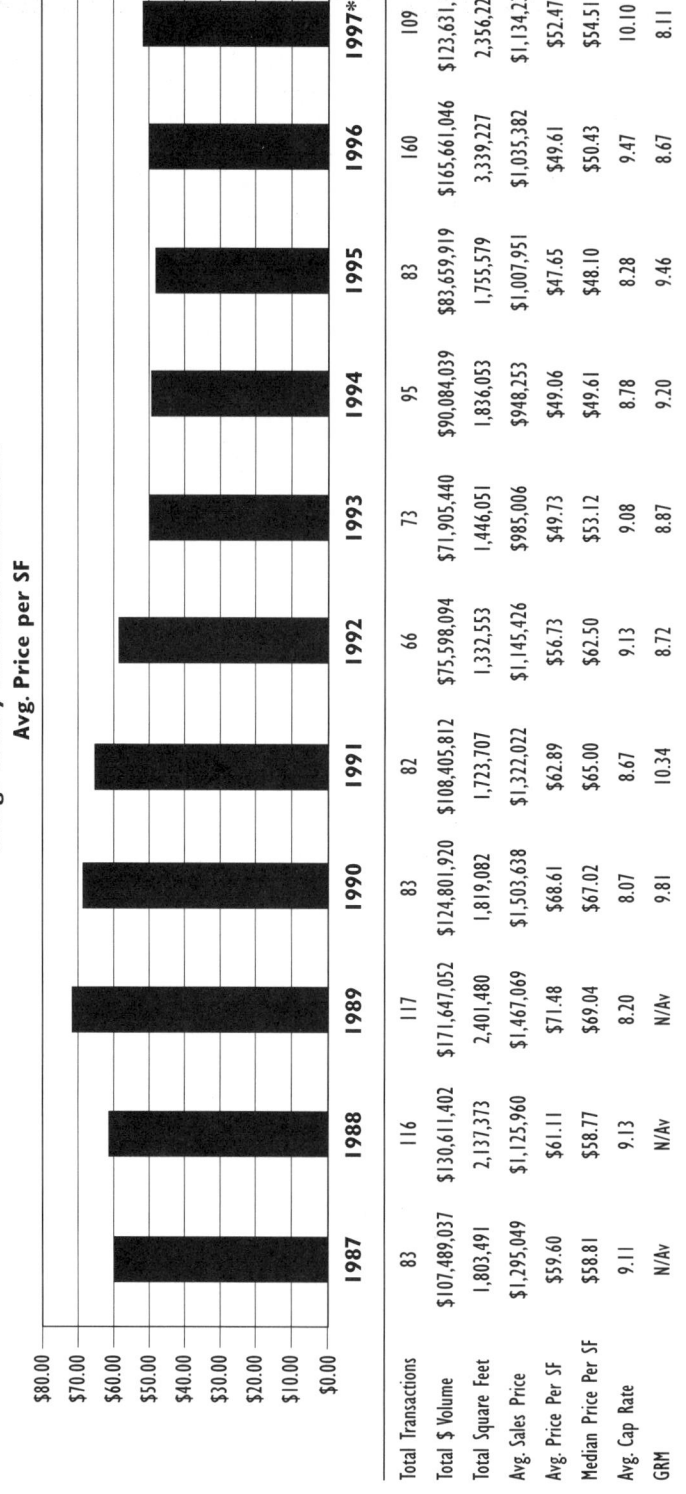

Orange County Industrial Transactions
Avg. Price per SF

	1987	1988	1989	1990	1991	1992	1993	1994	1995	1996	1997*
Total Transactions	83	116	117	83	82	66	73	95	83	160	109
Total $ Volume	$107,489,037	$130,611,402	$171,647,052	$124,801,920	$108,405,812	$75,598,094	$71,905,440	$90,084,039	$83,659,919	$165,661,046	$123,631,195
Total Square Feet	1,803,491	2,137,373	2,401,480	1,819,082	1,723,707	1,332,553	1,446,051	1,836,053	1,755,579	3,339,227	2,356,227
Avg. Sales Price	$1,295,049	$1,125,960	$1,467,069	$1,503,638	$1,322,022	$1,145,426	$985,006	$948,253	$1,007,951	$1,035,382	$1,134,231
Avg. Price Per SF	$59.60	$61.11	$71.48	$68.61	$62.89	$56.73	$49.73	$49.06	$47.65	$49.61	$52.47
Median Price Per SF	$58.81	$58.77	$69.04	$67.02	$65.00	$62.50	$53.12	$49.61	$48.10	$50.43	$54.51
Avg. Cap Rate	9.11	9.13	8.20	8.07	8.67	9.13	9.08	8.78	8.28	9.47	10.10
GRM	N/Av	N/Av	N/Av	9.81	10.34	8.72	8.87	9.20	9.46	8.67	8.11

© 1997 COMPS InfoSystems, Inc. All rights reserved. COMPS has obtained the information contained herein from sources which it believes to be reliable. COMPS makes no representation, warranty or guarantee, express or implied, as to the accuracy or reliability of the information contained herein.

* **Special Notes:**

Property Type is Industrial. Market: Orange County. Submarket Areas: 01, 02, 03, 04, 05, 06, 07, 08, 10. SF: 10,000 to 50,000
1997 data is through 9/30/97, however, due to an extensive confirmation process, additional transactions will continue to be added.

Exhibit 3.2   Class III—Market Conditions

The primary and secondary graphs for DC Class III have been highlighted here; however, DCs have a variety of impacts, which, upon analysis, vary on a case-by-case basis. Ultimately any graph may be applicable based upon the case-specific facts.

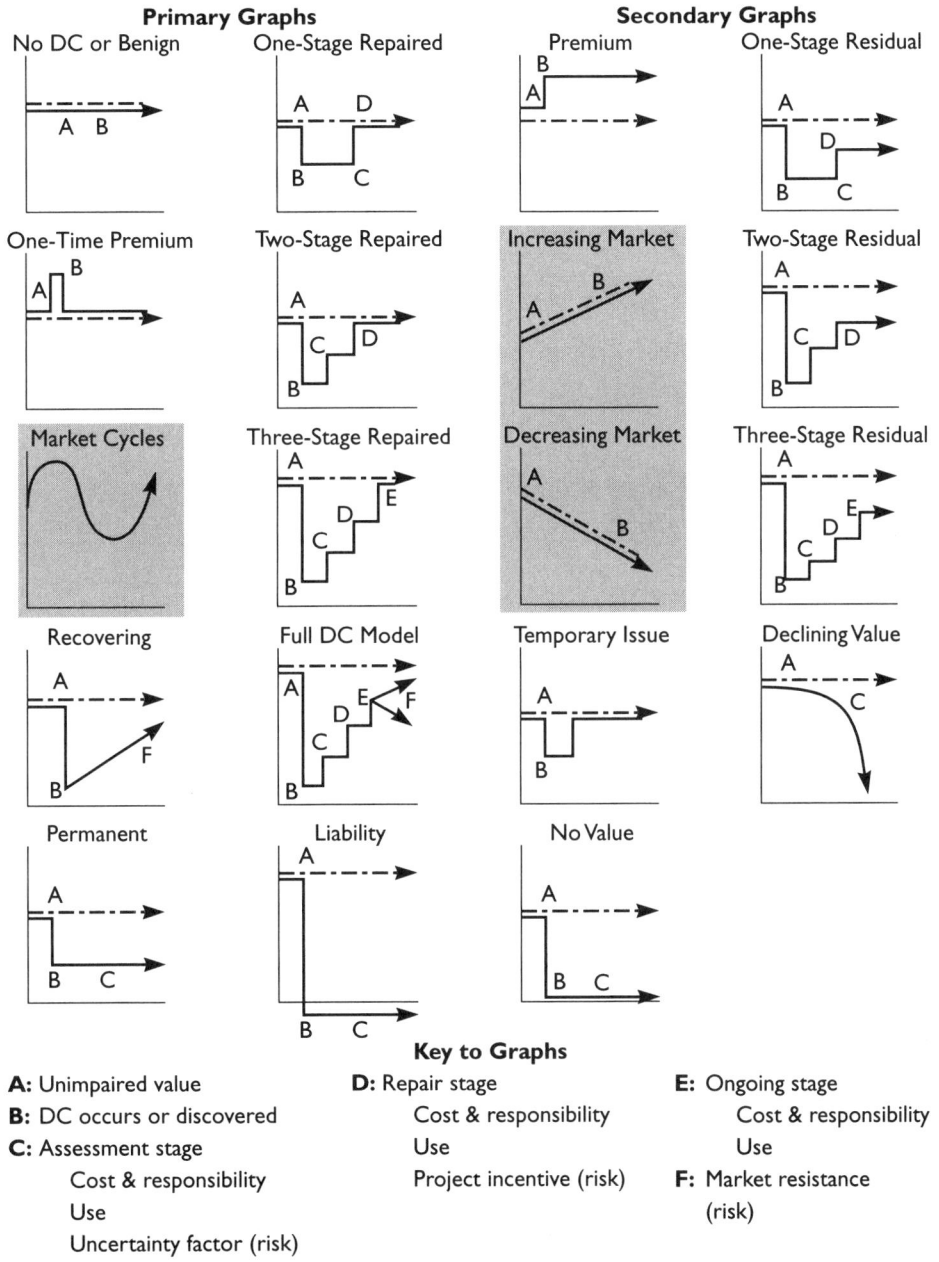

Key to Graphs

A: Unimpaired value
B: DC occurs or discovered
C: Assessment stage
  Cost & responsibility
  Use
  Uncertainty factor (risk)
D: Repair stage
  Cost & responsibility
  Use
  Project incentive (risk)
E: Ongoing stage
  Cost & responsibility
  Use
F: Market resistance
  (risk)

Source: *Bell's Guide: The Real Estate Encyclopedia*

Despite the simplicity of the concept of market conditions, this is a significant classification. For example, a contention may exist that a certain condition had an effect on value, whereas that condition was actually benign while market conditions caused the observed loss or gain in value.

A typical application of this situation can be illustrated through the following example. A property owner named Chris Anderson built a large lakeside house outside Appleton, Wisconsin. He put the property on the market for $350,000, and it promptly went into escrow for $340,000 to Lane King, a local mortgage banker. King asked for, and received, several extensions of the escrow. After six months, King broke the contract and pulled out of the sale, although Anderson had met every requirement of the escrow. The market conditions had been declining, and at the time King pulled out of the escrow, the house had a market value of $300,000. Anderson filed suit against King for the $40,000 lost due to market conditions and delays caused by King.

The appraisal assignment under this situation requires a simple appraisal at the time of the opening of the escrow and at the time that the contract was broken. Additionally, secondary data, such as market trend reports, could be collected to show that the decline was typical for the area. A study of local market conditions could be collected by looking at sales and subsequent resales of local properties during this time period.

The appraisal process verified a market value of $340,000 and $300,000 as of their respective dates of value, so the market conditions over time amounted to -11.76%.

Real Estate Economics

The factors that determine the value of a real property are complex and interconnected. Each property has unique characteristics, such as location, size, and topography. Just like people, no two properties are alike, so in some cases estimates based upon market data become as important to real estate valuation as laboratory study is to a doctor in assessing a patient's condition. There are four interdependent factors critical to the creation of value—utility, scarcity, desire, and effective purchasing power—which are in concert with the economic principles of supply and demand.

The theory of supply and demand is the basic concept by which value is determined in economics. Typically, supply and demand curves are represented on a two-dimensional graph with price measured on the y, or vertical, axis and quantity represented on the x, or horizontal, axis. Demand curves are typically downward-sloping. In other words, higher prices mean less quantity of the item will be demanded. Similarly, a relationship exists between the price of a good and the quantity of that good supplied by the market. A normal supply curve is represented on the aforementioned graphical plane as upward-sloping. This means that higher prices result in more quantity available for sale.

The point at which the supply and demand curves intersect represents the equilibrium combination of price and quantity from which the market has no intrinsic pressures to move away, as shown in Exhibit 3.3. To illustrate the equilibrium concept, at all points to the right of the equilibrium the supply will exceed demand. Thus the prices will fall to accommodate a buyer's market. At all points to the left of the equilibrium demand will outpace supply. So prices will rise as buyers compete with each other for the goods. Therefore, at any point away from the equilibrium, market pressures tend to bring the price and quantity of the good in that market back to equilibrium. It is important to note that the supply of land is virtually a fixed stock (i.e., one cannot create more land in the way that one could manufacture more VCRs). However, through efficiencies the supply of land can be effectively increased somewhat. The supply of improvements, such as housing or office space, can be increased through development. Therefore, movements in the demand for land mainly drive land values.

Supply and demand analysis provides a model for understanding general market forces and cycles and how they affect real property values. For example, a recession or depression leads to a contraction of general market wealth. Having less income and less wealth for investment leads to a fall in demand for real property acquisitions at every price level. Accordingly, there is a downward shift in the demand curve where for every given price level there is less quantity of property demanded. The downward or left shift of the demand curve causes the equilibrium point to move down the supply curve—i.e. the equilibrium price for the property at every quantity level is now lower, as shown in Exhibit 3.4. The converse is true for prices in an economic boom. This explains the fall in real property prices associated with recessions and the rise in real property prices during periods of economic expansion.

Other market forces also affect real property values. For example, general economic uncertainty brought about by factors such as high inflation, high relative unemployment rates, and political uncertainty can also affect real property values. Periods of uncertainty increase the perceived risk in all investments.

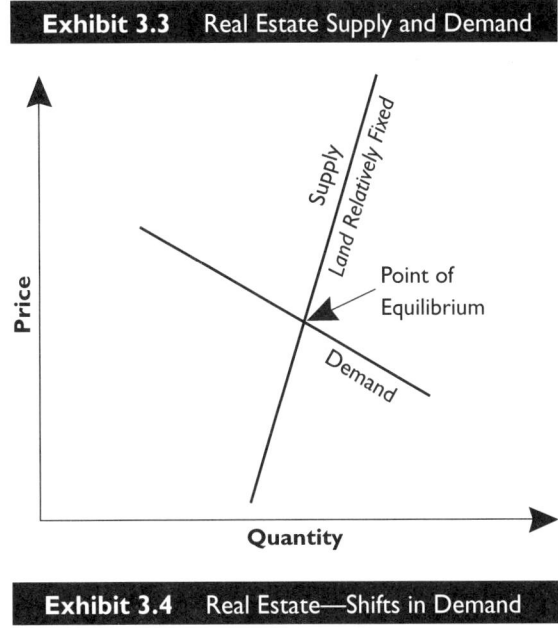

Exhibit 3.3 Real Estate Supply and Demand

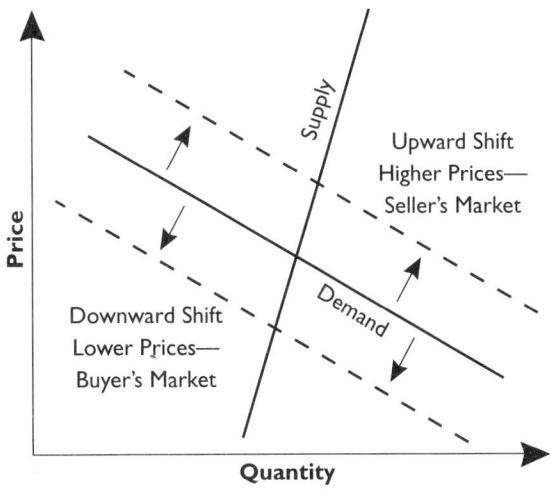

Exhibit 3.4 Real Estate—Shifts in Demand

Class III—Market Conditions

Further Reading

Market Conditions

Bottum, MacKenzie S., and Scott D. Evans. "Supply-Saturation-Induced External Obsolescence: Two Techniques for Quantifying Value Loss." *The Appraisal Journal* (October 1993).

Ling, David C. "The Valuation of Income Property in Overbuilt Markets." *The Appraisal Journal* (July 1993).

Chapter 3 Case Study

By Orell C. Anderson, MAI

Weatherby Pointe—Fox River, California
Class III Detrimental Condition—Market Conditions

Weatherby Pointe is a residential subdivision located in the community of Fox River, California. The subject property is located within the subdivision and is a two-story tract home with four bedrooms and three bathrooms. This development was built in 1972 and contains 632 homes with four models. Because of the rolling topography, many of the homes, including the subject property, enjoy a view amenity.

In 1991, the Schultz family purchased the subject property on Summit Avenue, which had a sweeping, panoramic view. At the time they inspected the home, there was a large shopping center (Center A) located approximately 150 yards directly behind the house, and a large vacant tract of land located about 1.5 miles away to the far right peripheral view, as shown in Exhibit 3.5. Most of the surrounding areas were developed with residential housing, schools, and churches.

Soon after they purchased the home, construction began on a shopping center (Center B) on the large vacant site. The Schultz family filed a lawsuit against the broker for not disclosing that a 24-hour shopping center would be built on the vacant site. Their contention was that the shopping center was an eyesore and had caused their property value to drop.

Exhibit 3.5 Map of View

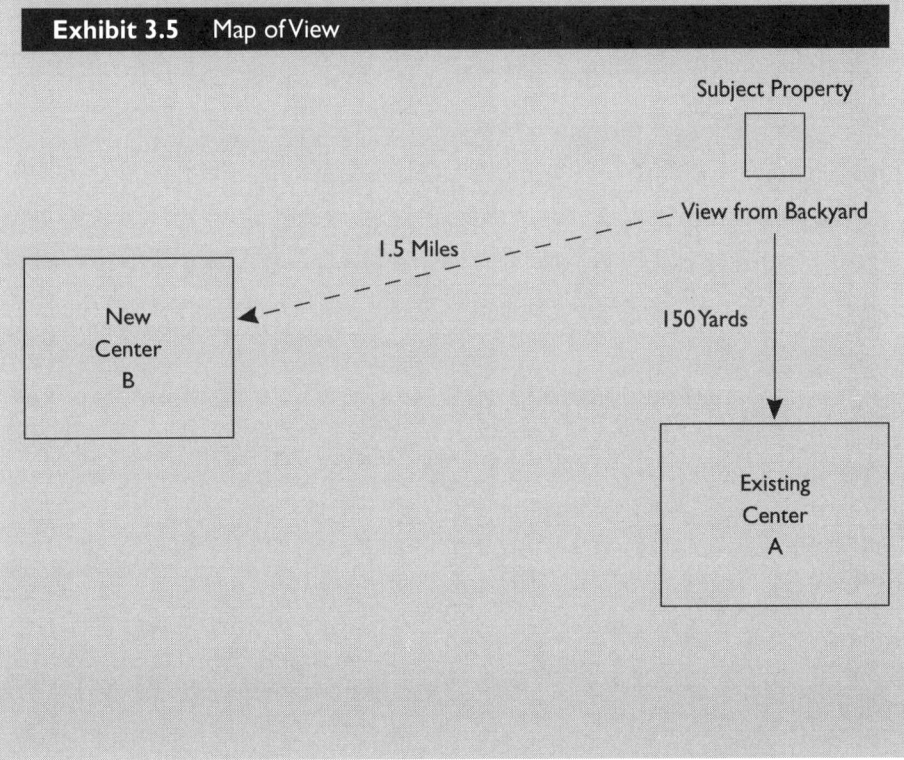

Exhibit 3.6 Land Use Ranking

Police Department	Long Beach	Torrance	Redondo Beach	Carson	La Habra	Mission Viejo	Santa Ana	Huntington Beach	Tustin	Mean
Land use										
Public park	6	2	5	7.5	8	8	8.5	N/Av	4.5	6.2
24-hour quick mart	2	5	5	6	4	3	3.5	N/Av	1.5	3.8
Industrial	2	7	8	8	5	5.5	3.5	N/Av	7.8	5.9
Shopping center	8	7	5	8	5	5.5	8.5	N/Av	5.6	6.6
24-hour center	2	7	5	8	6	4.5	8.5	N/Av	5.6	5.8
Apartments	2	6	4	6	4	N/Av	8.5	N/Av	5	5.1
Office	5	8	8	9	5	5.5	8.5	N/Av	7.5	7.1
Chamber of Commerce										
Land use										
Public park	7	8	N/Av	N/Av	8	10	N/Av	8.5	8	8.3
24-hour quick mart	7	3.5	N/Av	N/Av	9	2	N/Av	1	2.5	4.2
Industrial	7	N/Av	N/Av	N/Av	5	2	N/Av	2.5	6	4.5
Shopping center	9	3.5	N/Av	N/Av	8	9.5	N/Av	5	5	6.7
24-hour center	9	3.5	N/Av	N/Av	9.5	9.5	N/Av	3.5	3	6.3
Apartments	8	N/Av	N/Av	N/Av	7	5	N/Av	2.5	4	5.3
Office	9	8.5	N/Av	N/Av	7	2.5	N/Av	8.5	5	6.8
Cities										
Land use										
Public park	N/Av	N/Av	N/Av	N/Av	3.5	8	8.5	8	8	7.2
24-hour quick mart	1.5	N/Av	N/Av	N/Av	5	4	4	4	3	3.6
Industrial	5	N/Av	N/Av	N/Av	7	7	4.5	6	5	5.8
Shopping center	4	N/Av	N/Av	N/Av	7	7	9.5	5	8	6.8
24-hour center	4	N/Av	N/Av	N/Av	8	7	7	4	8	6.3
Apartments	6	N/Av	N/Av	N/Av	7.5	4	3.5	6	9	6.0
Office	8	N/Av	N/Av	N/Av	8.5	9	7.5	7	9	8.2

Key: Ranking of land use 1 = bad, 5 = neutral, 10 = good

Real Estate Damages: An Analysis of Detrimental Conditions

The analytical assignment was to determine if it was reasonable to conclude that a shopping center 150 yards away did not cause a diminution in value but one 1.5 miles away did. Indeed, the value of the subject property had dropped 10% over the past two years.

An examination of the subject property was conducted to evaluate the impact of a 24-hour shopping center on the adjacent residential neighborhood. Extensive interviews and surveys were performed, and a quantitative analysis of the possible impact of 24-hour operated shopping centers on residential home values was derived through a paired sales analysis. The analysis provided a quantitative technique to compare homes near 24-hour retail operations with similar properties that are not near those types of operations, in an effort to determine if there is any impact on home values.

Exhibit 3.6 is a summary of responses from police departments, chambers of commerce, and municipal leaders such as city managers, community development directors, and senior planners. The participants were asked to rate specific land uses on a scale of 1 (bad) to 5 (neutral) to 10 (good) on its potential impact on homes at night.

The survey indicated that a 24-hour retail center basically had a neutral rating of 5.8 to 6.3. The major concern derived from the survey was that of late night noise and parking lights disturbing adjoining homes. This could be mitigated with proper planning and restrictions regarding truck delivery and garbage pickup times, such as structure and landscaping buffering. The John's Grocery Store chain has successfully accomplished this with approximately 150 stores, 75 of which are operated on a 24-hour basis, with the remaining stores open from 6 a.m. until 2 a.m.

Sixteen retail centers in the region were investigated. Of these, five 24-hour retail facilities in five cities were located that abut residential properties. These were studied to determine if they had any impact on value. Areas included Long Beach (John's), Torrance (First-Save Drug), Carson (First-Save Drug), La Habra (Mega-Mart), Mission Viejo (John's), and Huntington Beach (John's). Paired sales analyses were conducted comparing the sale price of homes adjacent to these retail facilities to the sale price of homes not impacted by the retail operations. Exhibit 3.7 sets forth the net overall effect of this study as a percentage.

Exhibit 3.7 Paired Sales Analysis Summary

Net Overall Effect

	Test No. 1	Test No. 2	Test No. 3	Test No. 4
Long Beach	6.30%	-10.90%	3.30%	5.00%
Torrance	10.50%			
Carson	-1.50%	-2.40%	1.00%	
La Habra	3.30%			
Mission Viejo	-4.00%	7.20%	-5.50%	
Huntington Beach	-7.90%	-7.60%		

Positive numbers indicate that homes away from the shopping center sell for more as compared with homes directly adjacent to the facility.

Negative numbers indicate that the homes further from the retail area sell for less as compared with the home adjoining the 24-hour retail operation.

Based upon the paired sales analysis, no correlation exists between home values and adjacent 24-hour shopping centers.

Three sale/resale analyses (sale and resale of the same properties in the area) revealed that the majority of homes in the subject property neighborhood with or without similar view amenities had decreased in value. They are set forth in Exhibits 3.8, 3.9, and 3.10.

Exhibit 3.8 Sales Trend Study No. 1—Weatherby Pointe (Exclusive of Summit Ave.)

No.	Original Price	Date	Sale Price	Date	% Change	Annual Change	Total Gain/Loss
1	$400,000	19-Apr-89	$395,000	15-Jan-93	-1.3%	-0.3%	($5,000)
2	$502,200	6-Feb-81	$319,000	21-Jan-93	-36.5%	-3.1%	($183,200)
3	$695,000	31-Aug-90	$395,000	15-Apr-93	-43.2%	-16.4%	($300,000)
4	$705,000	28-Aug-90	$388,000	13-Aug-93	-45.0%	-15.2%	($317,000)
5	$557,200	22-Oct-92	$445,000	26-Feb-93	-20.1%	-57.6%	($112,200)
6	$1,220,600	17-Jun-87	$927,000	23-Jul-93	-24.1%	-3.9%	($293,600)
7	$575,000	6-Feb-89	$668,500	22-Apr-93	16.3%	3.9%	$93,500
8	$555,000	12-Jul-89	$425,000	3-Sep-93	-23.4%	-5.7%	($130,000)
9	$795,000	9-Nov-90	$725,000	10-Jun-93	-8.8%	-3.4%	($70,000)
10	$773,000	25-May-90	$649,000	19-Mar-93	-16.0%	-5.7%	($124,000)
11	$420,000	28-Feb-89	$377,000	1-Sep-93	-10.2%	-2.3%	($43,000)
12	$628,000	28-Nov-90	$450,000	11-Aug-93	-28.3%	-10.5%	($178,000)
13	$390,000	8-May-90	$437,000	29-Jun-93	12.1%	3.8%	$47,000
14	$352,000	6-Apr-90	$480,000	13-May-93	36.4%	11.7%	$128,000
15	$365,000	31-Aug-89	$304,000	13-Sep-93	-16.7%	-4.1%	($61,000)
16	$416,000	21-Apr-89	$387,500	7-May-93	-6.9%	-1.7%	($28,500)
17	$448,500	29-Jun-89	$400,000	27-Jan-93	-18.1%	-5.1%	($88,500)
18	$460,000	16-Feb-89	$520,000	28-May-93	13.0%	3.0%	$60,000
19	$612,000	16-Aug-91	$550,000	6-Aug-93	-10.1%	-5.1%	($62,000)
20	$567,000	6-Mar-89	$475,000	22-Jun-93	-16.2%	-3.8%	($92,000)
21	$469,000	27-Feb-89	$405,000	23-Mar-93	-13.6%	-3.4%	($64,000)
22	$460,000	10-May-90	$341,000	2-Sep-93	-25.9%	-7.8%	($119,000)
23	$389,000	16-Nov-89	$320,000	21-May-93	-17.7%	-5.0%	($69,000)
24	$345,000	7-Aug-90	$303,000	26-Jul-93	-12.2%	-4.1%	($42,000)
25	$690,000	21-Jun-91	$745,000	23-Jul-93	8.0%	3.8%	$55,000
26	$679,500	16-Aug-90	$545,000	7-Jan-93	-19.8%	-8.3%	($134,500)
Mean	$558,038	—	$476,000	—	-12.6%	-5.6%	(82,038)

Exhibit 3.9 Sales Trend Study No. 2—Fox River

No.	Original Price	Date	Sale Price	Date	% Change	Annual Change	Total Gain/Loss
1	$328,000	02-Nov-90	$326,000	02-Feb-93	-0.6%	-0.3%	($2,000)
2	$390,000	23-Aug-91	$365,000	11-Jun-93	-6.4%	-3.6%	($25,000)
3	$355,000	13-Jan-89	$320,000	9-Sep-93	-9.9%	-2.1%	($35,000)
4	$343,000	07-Nov-92	$337,500	24-Mar-93	-1.6%	-3.5%	($5,500)
5	$435,000	03-Apr-90	$338,500	23-Jul-93	-22.2%	-6.7%	($96,500)
6	$343,000	29-Sep-89	$305,000	27-Apr-93	-11.1%	-3.1%	($38,000)
7	$401,500	22-Mar-89	$300,000	16-Apr-93	-25.3%	-6.2%	($101,500)
8	$350,000	29-Aug-90	$375,000	08-Jul-93	7.1%	2.5%	$25,000
9	$519,000	09-Apr-91	$430,000	02-Jul-93	-17.1%	-7.7%	($89,000)
10	$332,000	09-Dec-91	$300,000	30-Jun-93	-9.6%	-6.2%	($32,000)
11	$475,000	28-Mar-91	$335,000	21-Jul-93	-29.5%	-12.7%	($140,000)
12	$399,000	30-Aug-91	$345,000	24-Aug-93	-13.5%	-6.8%	($54,000)
13	$476,500	09-Jul-89	$430,000	01-Sep-93	-9.8%	-2.4%	($46,500)
14	$431,000	12-Sep-89	$458,000	03-May-93	6.3%	1.7%	$27,000
15	$453,000	06-Dec-91	$451,000	26-Jan-93	-0.4%	-0.4%	($2,000)
16	$404,000	12-Oct-90	$390,000	17-Jun-93	-3.5%	-1.3%	($14,000)
17	$433,000	24-May-90	$405,500	30-Jul-93	-6.4%	-2.0%	($27,500)
18	$446,000	10-Jun-91	$366,000	30-Jun-93	-17.9%	-8.7%	($80,000)
19	$425,000	04-Mar-92	$385,000	27-Jul-93	-9.4%	-6.3%	($40,000)
20	$485,000	04-Oct-89	$352,000	30-Jun-93	-27.4%	-7.3%	($133,000)
21	$393,000	16-Nov-90	$370,000	31-Aug-93	-5.9%	-2.1%	($23,000)
22	$490,000	15-May-92	$435,000	04-Jun-93	-11.2%	-10.7%	($55,000)
23	$450,000	09-Nov-90	$400,000	26-Feb-93	-11.1%	-4.8%	($50,000)
24	$370,000	22-Feb-92	$370,000	31-Mar-93	0.0%	0.0%	$0
25	$440,000	01-Feb-91	$438,000	09-Jul-93	-0.5%	-0.2%	($2,000)
26	$547,000	20-Dec-89	$430,000	16-Jul-93	-21.4%	-6.0%	($117,000)
27	$558,500	01-Mar-89	$480,000	07-May-93	-14.1%	-3.4%	($78,500)
28	$565,000	22-Sep-89	$380,000	18-Aug-93	-32.7%	-8.4%	($185,000)
29	$680,000	04-Jan-89	$539,000	01-Dec-93	-20.7%	-4.2%	($141,000)
30	$712,000	10-Apr-89	$625,000	28-May-93	-12.2%	-3.0%	($87,000)
Mean	$447,650	—	$392,717	—	-11.3%	-4.2%	($54,933)

Exhibit 3.10 Sales Trend Study No. 3—Pleasant Grove

No.	Original Price	Date	Sale Price	Date	% Change	Annual Change	Total Gain/Loss
1	$420,000	27-Aug-91	$380,000	24-Aug-93	-9.5%	-4.8%	($40,000)
2	$485,000	31-May-91	$395,000	22-Jun-93	-18.6%	-9.0%	($90,000)
3	$390,000	30-May-90	$327,000	05-Feb-93	-16.2%	-6.0%	($63,000)
4	$381,000	15-Mar-90	$330,000	01-Jun-93	-13.4%	-4.2%	($51,000)
5	$314,500	25-May-90	$338,000	15-Sep-93	7.5%	2.3%	$23,500
6	$332,500	28-Mar-91	$354,000	16-Apr-93	6.5%	3.2%	$21,500
7	$365,000	23-Apr-91	$330,000	21-Jan-93	-9.6%	-5.5%	($35,000)
8	$314,500	15-Mar-91	$332,500	23-Jun-93	5.7%	2.5%	$18,000
9	$438,000	30-Jul-92	$400,000	04-Jun-93	-8.7%	-10.3%	($38,000)
10	$327,000	08-Mar-91	$315,500	10-Feb-93	-3.5%	-1.8%	($11,500)
11	$360,000	25-Apr-90	$305,000	14-May-93	-15.3%	-5.0%	($55,000)
12	$387,500	20-Oct-90	$340,000	27-Jan-93	-12.3%	-5.4%	($47,500)
13	$425,000	06-Sep-91	$457,500	21-Jul-93	7.6%	4.1%	$32,500
14	$362,500	05-Apr-91	$379,000	02-Sep-93	4.6%	1.9%	$16,500
15	$442,500	18-Jul-89	$300,000	14-Jul-93	-32.2%	-8.1%	($142,500)
16	$422,500	01-Jun-90	$349,000	02-Aug-93	-17.4%	-5.5%	($73,500)
17	$390,000	12-Mar-92	$357,000	23-Mar-93	-8.5%	-8.2%	($33,000)
18	$345,000	19-Mar-91	$315,000	14-Jan-93	-8.7%	-4.8%	($30,000)
19	$398,000	19-Aug-91	$365,000	26-Feb-93	-8.3%	-5.4%	($33,000)
20	$422,000	05-Jul-91	$370,000	01-Mar-93	-12.3%	-7.4%	($52,000)
21	$400,000	13-Sep-91	$370,000	06-Aug-93	-7.5%	-4.0%	($30,000)
22	$517,000	17-Apr-89	$390,000	21-May-93	-24.6%	-6.0%	($127,000)
23	$445,000	04-Feb-92	$385,000	27-Aug-93	-13.5%	-8.6%	($60,000)
24	$555,000	26-Jun-90	$450,000	30-Aug-93	-18.9%	-5.9%	($105,000)
25	$510,000	26-Apr-91	$475,000	02-Apr-93	-6.9%	-3.5%	($35,000)
26	$795,000	09-Feb-90	$700,000	03-May-93	-11.9%	-3.7%	($95,000)
27	$365,000	27-Dec-90	$425,000	22-Apr-93	16.4%	7.1%	$60,000
28	$508,500	26-Sep-89	$479,000	14-Jul-93	-5.8%	-1.5%	($29,500)
29	$429,000	30-Mar-93	$385,000	06-May-93	-10.3%	-102.8%	($44,000)
30	$420,000	19-Apr-91	$368,500	28-Apr-93	-12.3%	-6.1%	($51,500)
31	$457,500	07-Apr-89	$410,000	06-Aug-93	-10.4%	-2.4%	($47,500)
32	$505,000	12-Jul-89	$507,000	20-Aug-93	0.4%	0.1%	$2,000
33	$544,500	05-Jan-90	$420,000	08-Sep-93	-22.9%	-6.2%	($124,500)
34	$375,000	10-Mar-92	$310,000	28-Apr-93	-17.3%	-15.3%	($65,000)
35	$462,500	28-Jul-89	$435,000	26-May-93	-5.9%	-1.6%	($27,500)
36	$550,000	18-Nov-80	$450,000	12-Jul-93	-18.2%	-1.4%	($100,000)
37	$488,000	30-Oct-89	$415,000	09-Aug-93	-15.0%	-4.0%	($73,000)
38	$460,000	18-Dec-89	$390,000	25-Aug-93	-15.2%	-4.1%	($70,000)
Mean	$434,461	—	$389,579	—	-9.5%	-6.5%	($44,882)

Sales Trend Study 1, Weatherby Point subdivision (excluding the street where the subject property is located), indicated that only 5 of 26 resales had increased in value, while the remainder all decreased in value. The overall mean indicated a -12.6% change with an average of -5.6% change annually. Sales Trend Study 2, the community of Fox River (excluding Weatherby Point), indicated that only 2 of 30 resales had increased in value, while the remainder all decreased in value by 11.3% on average. The mean annual change was -4.2%. Sales Trend Study 3, the community of Pleasant Grove (an adjacent city considered similar to the subject property area), indicated that 7 of 38 resales had increased in value, while the majority on average decreased in value by 9.5%. The mean annual change was -6.5%.

In conclusion, the Schultz family's contention that the decline of their home value was a result of the construction of Center B was, in fact, a benign condition. The home did indeed incur a 10% drop in value. However, this decrease was due to general market conditions that had impacted nearly all homes in the region. Furthermore, the interviews and paired sales analysis indicated no correlation existed between the presence or absence of a shopping center on nearby residential property values.

CHAPTER 4

Class IV—Temporary Conditions

Class IV includes detrimental conditions that are only temporary in nature. Therefore, the loss in value is limited to the disruption caused by the temporary condition. This classification includes distress sales due to bankruptcy, probate, REOs, short sales, and other conditions where the real estate is "dumped" by non-typically motivated sellers. Another common Class IV situation involves temporary construction easements, wherein a portion of a property is utilized by another party while adjoining construction is underway. Upon completing the construction, the full use of the property is returned to its original state. As depicted in Exhibit 4.1, these types of conditions may either have a brief effect with no long-term impact or be serious enough to have a long-lasting effect that often diminishes in time. Because of their temporary nature, there are three important components of the property loss:

1. The amount of the loss
2. The timing of such loss
3. The net effect of both increases and decreases over time

This temporary disruption can have an impact on value. For example, if temporary construction disrupts the traffic patterns of a shopping center, the diminution in value may be extracted from the lost revenues, higher vacancy rates, and other related losses. This would be in addition to the "rental rate" of the land being used during the temporary construction. Additionally, while the effects of bankruptcy are often a benign Class I detrimental condition, this situation may be a Class IV detrimental condition, particularly if there is substantial deferred maintenance or if there are other temporary conditions that affect the value.

Another type of Class IV detrimental condition would include absorption losses. For example, if a particular situation causes a large tenant to abruptly vacate the building, the

Exhibit 4.1   Class IV—Temporary Conditions

The primary and secondary graphs for DC Class IV have been highlighted here; however, DCs have a variety of impacts, which, upon analysis, vary on a case-by-case basis. Ultimately any graph may be applicable based on the case-specific facts.

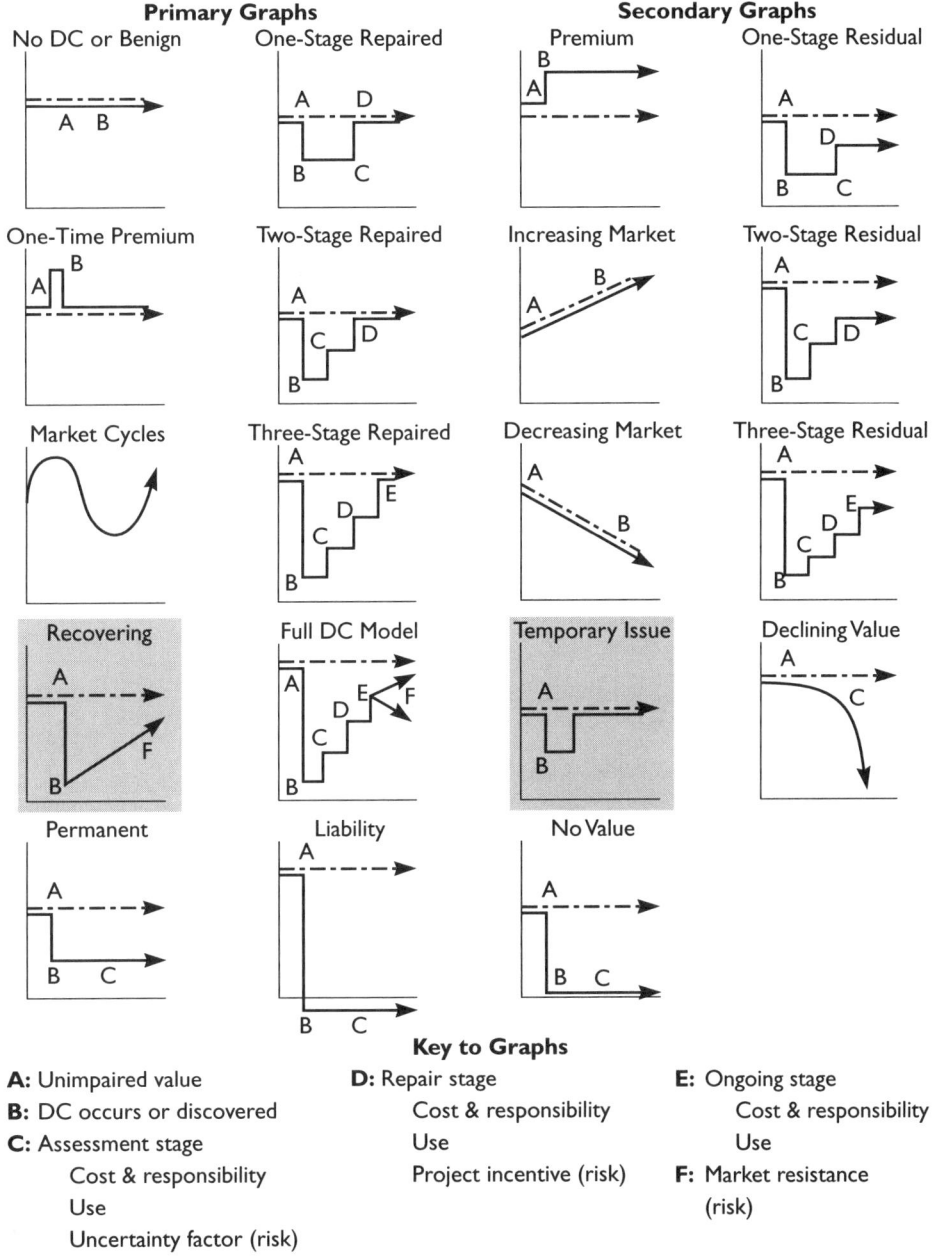

Key to Graphs

A: Unimpaired value
B: DC occurs or discovered
C: Assessment stage
  Cost & responsibility
  Use
  Uncertainty factor (risk)

D: Repair stage
  Cost & responsibility
  Use
  Project incentive (risk)

E: Ongoing stage
  Cost & responsibility
  Use
F: Market resistance
  (risk)

Source: Bell's Guide: The Real Estate Encyclopedia

value of the property would drop upon their leaving and then increase over time as the vacant space is absorbed. Specific absorption losses include lost rents, leasing commissions, and tenant improvements.

Class IV conditions may also involve a crime scene or other similar tragic event. In these cases, because of the incident and the subsequent media coverage, the general public may be aware of the events that took place, and the market's perception of the property may be negatively impacted. Interviews with brokers and agents indicate, almost without fail, that a violent crime committed within a residence has an adverse effect on value when disclosed.

The following example illustrates such a situation. In a middle-class upstate New York suburb, a violent crime was committed in a two-story, 2,223-sq.-ft. house containing 3 bedrooms and 2½ bathrooms. The situation shocked the community, which prided itself as a safe and quiet place to live. The incident was reported in the local papers and was a local topic of conversation for months. Because of the tragedy, the occupants moved out of the area and put the house on the market. The house was well kept and no physical traces of the incident remained. However, every local real estate broker and agent knew of the situation and tended to steer their clients away from the house.

While most detrimental conditions involve some physical issues and some detrimental conditions involve both physical and stigma issues, crime scenes involve only market resistance, or stigma, yet its effects can be profound. Because crime scenes involve only market resistance, these situations provide some valuable insight into the study of pure stigma. The market resistance may actually cause two losses, the carrying costs associated with the extended marketing time (if the property is not occupied) and a discount to entice a buyer to purchase the property.

For example, on March 26, 1997, police discovered 39 bodies of former Heaven's Gate members within a mansion in Rancho Santa Fe, California, an exclusive suburb of San Diego. The first police to arrive at the scene were overcome by the odor created by decaying bodies and bodily fluids. The cult members believed that they were discarding their "vehicles" to return to a spaceship that followed the Hale-Bopp Comet. The house is the site of the largest mass suicide in the history of the United States. The property is a two-story, single-family residence that contains 9,011 square feet of livable area, seven bedrooms, seven bathrooms, a two-car garage, a limousine garage, sauna, pool, spa, tennis court, and a view amenity on 3.11 acres. The house is very private and is not visible from the public streets or from the entry gate. The Heaven's Gate members rented the house, and the lease specifically limited occupancy to seven people.

Prior to March 1997, this large home in Rancho Santa Fe, California, was just one of hundreds of estates located throughout the prestigious community. When police discovered the bodies of 39 followers of the Heaven's Gate cult inside, it shocked the world and had a significant impact on the perceptions toward this property.

The property was purchased by the owner on June 24, 1994, for $1,375,000. As of the date of the event, the property was listed for sale for $1,595,000. The house was cleared of the bodies and all belongings by county authorities, but significant physical damage remained. The physical damage amounted to well over $100,000. This created significant carrying costs for the property. A false rumor was generated that local home owners would pay full value for the house and bulldoze it. The property was marketed, but all offers were less than $800,000, approximately 50% of its undamaged value, which attests to the profound impact of stigma. In October 1998, the owner gave the deed back to the bank.

Another lesson from these situations is that it may be easier to rent or lease the property as opposed to selling it. Generally, time does tend to help in these situations, as depicted in Exhibit 4.2 and in the following examples.

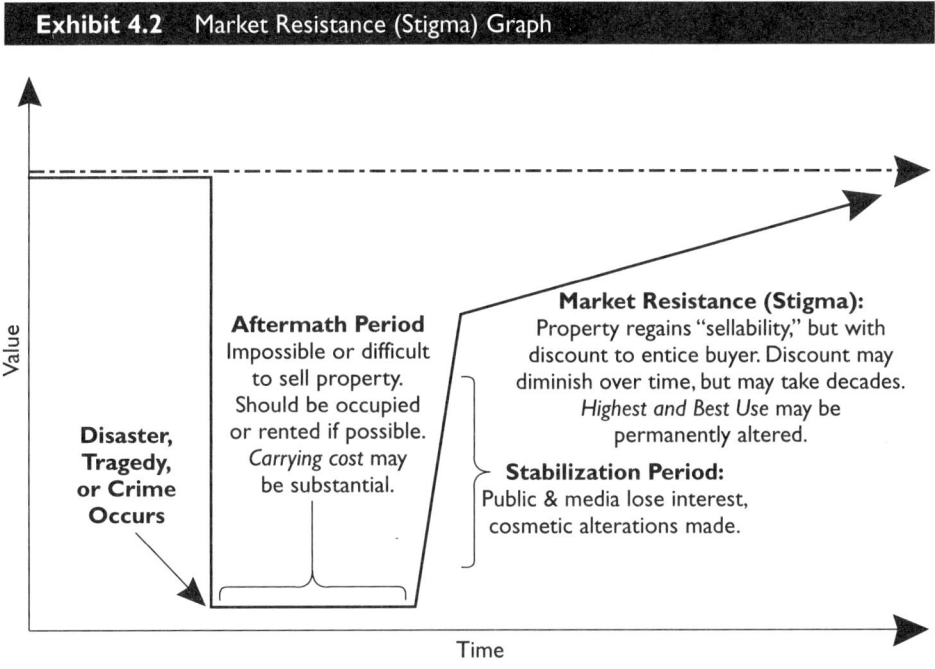

Exhibit 4.2 Market Resistance (Stigma) Graph

On August 9, 1969, the followers of Charles Manson committed the murders of actress Sharon Tate and others in a small farmhouse-style home off Benedict Canyon Road in an area north of Beverly Hills, California. Throngs of curiosity seekers found the home and visited the property for years after the crime. The house was built in 1941 on a site that has an outstanding view of the Los Angeles basin. It contained 2,324 square feet, three bedrooms, four bathrooms, a guest house, and a pool. In 1991, the original house was demolished, the site was re-graded, and a new, large Mediterranean home was built. The grading has dramatically altered the appearance of the site. Research indicates that today, more than 30 years after the crimes, there is little or no residual stigma associated with the property. Aided by the remote location of the site and the extensive grading, curiosity seekers have long forgotten about the property. The current property owner states that he did not receive any discount due to stigma when he purchased the property, and local residents state that the issue rarely arises. Apparently time has cured the stigma associated with this property.

The studies of properties that have been impacted by crime scene stigma yield some other interesting lessons. First, market resistance or stigma cannot be easily eliminated by simply demolishing the structure. In these instances, the stigma goes to the site, not the improvements, so bulldozing them solves little or nothing. For example, in October 1984, a man walked into a McDonald's Restaurant in San Ysidro, California, and shot and killed 21 people before he was shot and killed. McDonald's donated the restaurant to the city within 90 days of the incident. A long debate ensued amongst local leaders as to what to do with the property. The community expressed a strong desire to demolish the improvements and erect a memorial. Due to lack of action by the city, one night, beginning at 10 p.m., McDonald's bulldozed the improvements, and by the next morning nothing was left but dirt and two palm trees. McDonald's then acquired another site one-quarter mile away and constructed a new restaurant, which still exists today.

This site was once improved with the house where the followers of Charles Manson murdered Sharon Tate and her friends. Today the site has been re-graded and improved with a large Mediterranean villa and looks nothing like it did in 1969, when the crimes occurred. Although one of the most infamous crimes in history, the real estate market has long forgotten about the stigma that was once associated with this site.

This memorial, in San Ysidro, California, marks the spot where the largest mass murder, up to that time, had occurred in the United States. McDonald's bulldozed its restaurant, and eventually the land was donated for use as an educational center.

Various ideas were presented for possible uses, such as a park. This use was thought of as nonconforming within the business-area location. Therefore, the best location for the memorial was thought to be in another part of the city, with proceeds from the subject site sale financing it. The subject site stood vacant for approximately six months. The city listed the property for sale at $425,000, and then for $300,000, but there were no legitimate inquiries. Finally, a local community college offered to build an education annex if the site was donated. The school had a competition for an on-site memorial and design, and 2½ years after the tragedy, an educational annex was constructed, with a small memorial on-site.

In addition to the long-lasting effects of stigma on the site of a crime scene, market resistance tends to be more pronounced in bad economic times than in good, as the market tends to "forgive" more problems when demand is high. High-end properties tend to be impacted more than basic properties. For example, a buyer in the market for an expensive home tends to be more in a comfortable stage of life and less willing to accept the inconvenience associated with market resistance. In contrast, a person seeking low-income housing has more basic needs to fill and may have fewer options.

As an example, on March 20, 1996, a jury convicted Lyle and Erik Menendez of first-degree murder for the August 1989 slayings of their parents in their Beverly Hills mansion. The property contains 9,063 square feet, six bedrooms, and eight bathrooms for a total of 23 rooms. Amenities include a pool, tennis court, and guest house. Tourist buses still stop at the house today, over 10 years after the incident.

The murders occurred approximately one year after the parents purchased the home for $4 million. The living room where the murders occurred was completely renovated, and no physical trace of the crime remains. The house was placed on the market in April 1991 and was listed for sale for approximately 1½ years before a buyer came forward in October 1992. The property sold for $3 million. By 1992 the property was worth approximately $4.2 million with no stigma. The $3 million sales price indicated that there was an approximate 35% discount attributed primarily to stigma. In addition, the property suffered from an extended marketing period of approximately 1½ years, which is significantly longer than a typical six-month time frame in the neighborhood.

The issues of rural or urban settings should also be considered when evaluating market resistance. It is possible that market resistance may be more pronounced in rural settings, while it may be diluted by the hustle and bustle of urban life. A good example of this phenomenon is the World Trade Center in New York City.

In February 1993, a bomb-loaded vehicle was detonated on the second level within the underground parking structure beneath the World Trade Center. The blast was so powerful that a crater was formed that penetrated six levels downward. Five people died in the tragedy. Although the

From the air, the Menendez home can be seen to be a large estate with a tennis court, swimming pool, guest house, and other amenities associated with the grand Beverly Hills lifestyle.

Class IV—Temporary Conditions

blast occurred underground approximately between the two towers, there was no permanent damage to the towers themselves.

The 1993 bombing of the World Trade Center occurred in a parking structure between the two towers.

Before the World Trade Center bombing, the building tenants and their visitors simply took an elevator to the various offices above. Today, any tenant or visitor wishing to enter an office suite must first be registered at a visitor's desk in the lobby.

Despite the tragedy, leasing activity largely went unchanged. For example, Bank of America, which had commenced lease negotiations for six floors before the explosion, continued with talks and consummated a lease after the bombing. Some tenants did not renew their leases, but it is unknown if this was related to the bombing. The property manager instituted new and advanced security measures and provided seminars to building tenants regarding these changes. The most noteworthy effect was that currently all visitors must show photo ID at a "visitor's reception" counter and verify that they have legitimate business within the building. They are then issued a card that is scanned by a guard at the elevator.

Measuring Class IV detrimental conditions often involves the comparison of the subject property to other properties that incurred similar Class IV situations and subsequently were sold to buyers who were informed of the detrimental condition. Often, a lower sales price is required to entice buyers to purchase properties under these conditions, and this type of market data is essential in quantifying Class IV detrimental conditions. In addition, the extended marketing times should be considered, as this can effectively increase the loss.

Further Reading

Legal Issues

Bridging the Gap Using Findings in Local Land Use Decisions. 2d ed. Sacramento, Calif.: Governor's Office of Planning and Research, 1988.

Clark, Robert Emmet. *Water and Water Rights, Eastern, Western, Federal.* Indianapolis: Allen Smith Co., 1976, vols. 1, 2, and 4-7; Charlottesville, Va.: The Michie Co., 1988, vol. 3.

Chapter 4 Case Study

By Mark W. Smith, MAI

Davis Building
Class IV—Absorption Loss and Profit Potential Study

The subject property is an average quality, four-story, steel frame and glass curtain wall office building. The building is 13 years old and contains about 77,000 rentable square feet. It has generally been kept in good condition.

Shortly after the building was completed, the owner leased the entire building to two tenants. Each tenant leased two full floors. The tenant on the lower two floors signed a 12-year lease, and the tenant on the upper two floors signed a 14-year lease. Both tenants had somewhat atypical tenant improvement (TI) requirements. The tenant on the lower floors, a major aerospace contractor, had highly specialized testing facilities installed in its space. The tenant on the upper two floors, a major insurance company, had a need for large open spaces for back-office employees.

The local economy entered a period of decline just prior to the expiration of the lower tenant's lease. The tenant of the lower two floors decided not to exercise its renewal options and vacated the two lower floors at the end of its lease. Given the highly specialized nature of the TIs, the lower two floors were gutted and brought down to a shell condition.

The tenant of the two upper floors was purchased by a competing firm. The new parent company gave notice it would not renew the lease of the upper two floors. The tenant vacated the premises and offered the upper two floors for sublease for the 18 months remaining on the existing lease. The consensus among local brokers was that the insurance company would be unable to find a sublessee for such a short remaining lease term. Given the minimal TIs, consisting primarily of ceiling panels, lighting, electrical outlets, and carpeting (no interior walls), the upper two floors would likely need to be substantially reworked prior to re-leasing the space.

The building is part of a fairly large portfolio. The portfolio manager is contemplating the sale of the building prior to re-tenanting the property. The purpose of the assignment was to estimate the potential profit associated with re-leasing the building to stabilized occupancy prior to sale.

The assignment began by using the income capitalization approach to estimate the value of the building assuming stabilized multitenant occupancy. A rent survey was conducted as a portion of the income approach. The rent survey served not only to estimate the potential income from the building once it is re-leased but also to give an indication of the anticipated absorption period, or the likely amount of time necessary to achieve stabilized occupancy. Based upon the rent survey and an expense analysis, the net operating income of the subject was estimated as shown in Exhibit 4.3. Based upon observed conditions in the subject's local market, the anticipated time necessary to attain stabilized occupancy was two years as of the date of this analysis.

Exhibit 4.3   Net Operating Income Calculations

Monthly potential gross income	
77,000 sq. ft. @ $1.30:	$100,100
Vacancy and collection loss:	− $7,510
Collected rents:	$92,590
	× 12 Mos.
Effective annual gross income:	$1,111,080
Total expenses:	− $529,889
Net operating income:	$581,191

A search was then conducted to locate and verify transfers of office buildings that were operating at stabilized occupancy at the time of sale. Of the sales found generally meeting the search criteria, the four shown in Exhibit 4.4 were thought to be the most similar to the subject property.

Exhibit 4.4   Stabilized Office Building Sales

	Subject	Sale A	Sale B	Sale C	Sale D
Square footage:	77,000	107,252	161,778	91,437	56,192
Year built:	1984	1981	1987	1987	1980
Quality:	Average	Average	Good	Average	Average
Condition:	Average	Average	Good	Good	Average
Scheduled gross income:		$1,801,834	$3,203,204	$1,536,142	$876,336
Less: vacancy:		$230,634	$160,160	$153,614	$43,817
Effective gross income:		$1,571,200	$3,043,044	$1,382,528	$832,519
Less: expenses:		$643,512	$1,213,335	$594,341	$359,559
Net operating income:		$927,668	$1,829,709	$778,187	$472,960
Cash equivalent price:		$9,400,000	$20,500,000	$8,600,000	$5,000,000
Date of sale:		5/28/97	12/20/96	12/4/96	10/1/96
Overall rate:		9.87%	8.93%	9.16%	9.46%

A 9.4% overall rate was considered appropriate for the subject property. With a 9.4% overall rate and net operating income as shown above, the value of the subject property, assuming stabilized multitenant occupancy on the date of value, was estimated to be $6,180,000.

As mentioned earlier, local market conditions had declined prior to the expiration of the lower tenant's lease. Market conditions had declined to a point where there were numerous sales of office buildings operating well below stabilized occupancy. Five sales of under-occupied buildings (four of which were entirely vacant), including the relatively recent sale of the building adjacent to the subject property (Sale I) were verified and documented as shown in Exhibit 4.5.

Exhibit 4.5 High-Vacancy Office Building Sales

	Subject	Sale E	Sale F	Sale G	Sale H	Sale I
Square footage:	77,000	35,051	91,404	59,725	84,500	76,800
Year built:	1984	1981	1981	1980	1979	1984
Quality:	Average	Average	Average	Average	Average	Average
Condition:	Average	Fair	Average	Average	Average	Average
Cash equivalent price:		$950,000	$3,750,000	$3,500,000	$3,800,000	$4,050,000
Date of sale:		6/2/97	4/29/97	3/31/97	11/21/96	8/31/95
Vacancy at sale:		100%	100%	90%	100%	100%
Anticipated mo. lease rate:	$1.30	$1.40	N/A	$1.30	$1.50	N/A
Price per square foot:		$27.10	$41.03	$56.09	$40.00	$52.73
Anticipated absorption costs:		$28.50	$21.88	$4.05	$15.00	$7.60
Adjusted price/sq. ft.:		$55.60	$62.91	$60.14	$55.00	$60.33

The unadjusted price per square foot of the five comparables ranges from $27.10 to $56.09. This is a wide range, suggesting there is no rhyme nor reason to the market's reaction to under-occupied office buildings.

During the verification process it was discovered most buyers of under-occupied office buildings in the area use a simplified price per square foot analysis when making their purchase decisions. Many of those interviewed stated they simply deduct the cost of rehabilitating and re-leasing the building from their estimate of the value of the property once it is leased, then deduct their desired profit to arrive at the maximum price per square foot they can afford to pay.

After adding the buyer's anticipated rehabilitation and re-leasing costs to the price per square foot paid, it appears the market does act rationally. After adjusting each comparable for these anticipated costs, the range of adjusted square foot prices for the five comparables narrows considerably to $55.00 to $62.91 per square foot, suggesting that a rehabilitated office building, inclusive of all absorption costs, has a value of approximately $60 per square foot. Anticipated absorption costs for the subject (including tenant improvement costs and leasing commissions) were estimated at about $18 per square foot, indicating a value as is of $42 per square foot, or $3,235,000 (rounded).

Profit, or the benefit from re-leasing the building prior to sale, was then calculated as follows:

Value assuming stabilized occupancy	$6,180,000
Value inclusive of acquisition and absorption costs (at $60/sq. ft.)	– $4,620,000
Profit	$1,560,000

The cost of earning this profit is $18 per square foot. With both the cost and profits of re-leasing known, the investor is now able to make an informed investment decision after assessing the risk involved with re-leasing the building.

CHAPTER 5

Class V—Imposed Conditions

Class V detrimental conditions involve adverse external factors, undesirable acts, or forced events by another person or entity that affect the value of a property. Class V conditions can include imposed governmental conditions such as downzoning, special bond assessments, or the designation of a property as a historical site. Examples of adverse external factors are dumps, landfills, factories that produce noise and bad odors, neighbors who allow their property to deteriorate, and transmission lines. They may also include the discovery that improvements were illegally constructed or the development of surrounding issues (or perceived nuisances) such as a sewage treatment plant, airport, or prison. Additionally, Class V detrimental conditions apply to eminent domain situations.

These situations often involve a *conditions adjustment,* which may be determined from the marketplace. For example, if comparing homes under an airport flight corridor with similar homes that are not indicates a 10% loss attributable to being under the flight corridor, then the conditions adjustment is -0.10.

In some situations, the effects of an imposed condition may be relatively easy to assess, and no special studies are necessary to clarify the situation. In other cases, the imposed condition may be unclear, and special studies are required to decipher how these events will alter the status quo. Upon full investigation and assessment, the uncertainties are eliminated and the actual situation is revealed. With uncertainties eliminated, the value of the property generally will increase.

As seen in the primary graph of Exhibit 5.1, Class V imposed conditions reflect a sudden drop in value upon the occurrence of the detrimental condition and a permanent loss in value as a result of the imposed condition. This would include eminent domain or an imposed neighborhood nuisance, such as a jail, airport, or power plant. In a situation involving diminishing effects, such as a ground lease, the leasehold value gradually decreases over time.

Exhibit 5.1 Class V—Imposed Conditions

The primary and secondary graphs for DC Class V have been highlighted here; however, DCs have a variety of impacts, which, upon analysis, vary on a case-by-case basis. Ultimately any graph may be applicable based on the case-specific facts.

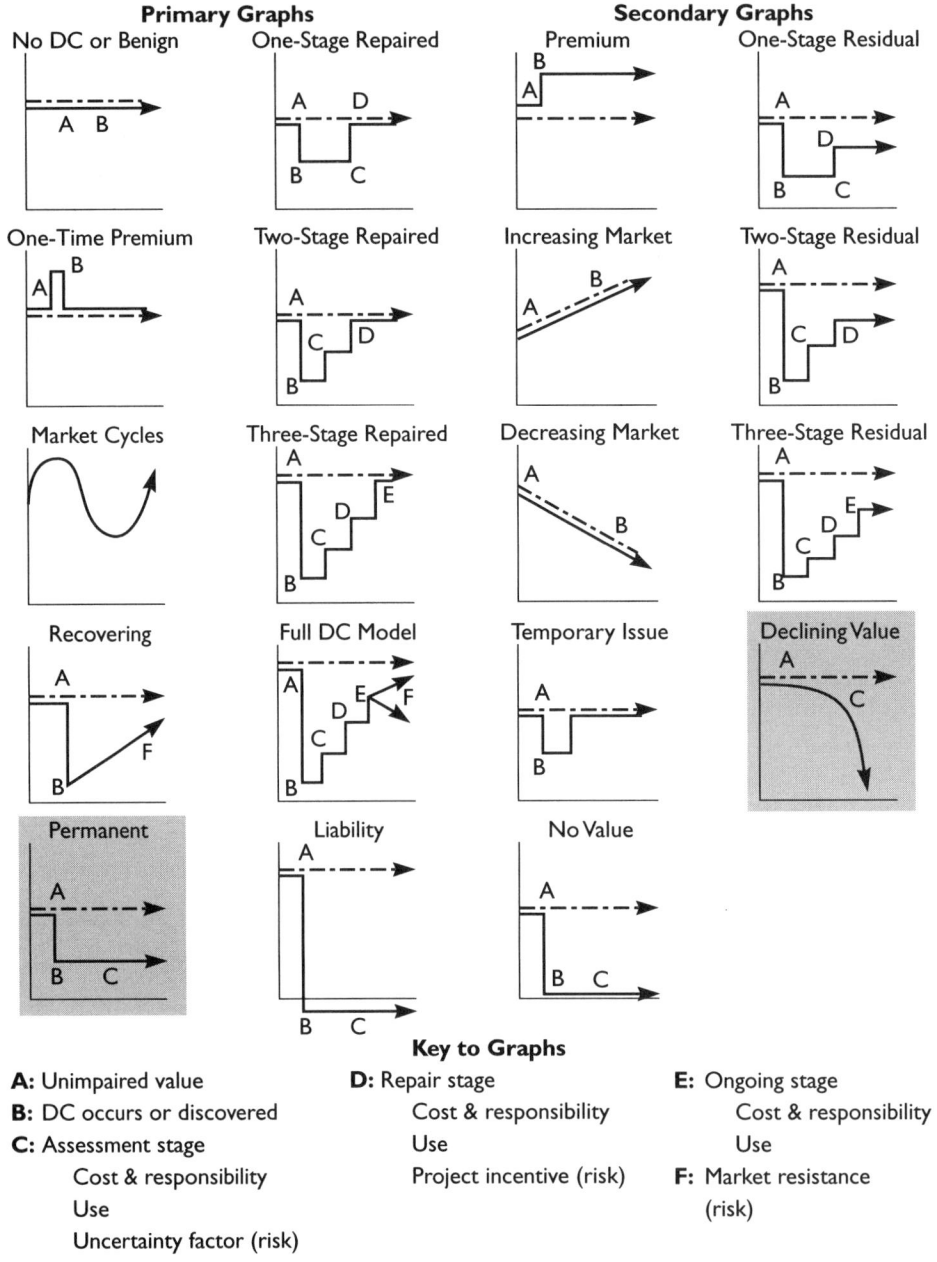

Key to Graphs

A: Unimpaired value
B: DC occurs or discovered
C: Assessment stage
   Cost & responsibility
   Use
   Uncertainty factor (risk)
D: Repair stage
   Cost & responsibility
   Use
   Project incentive (risk)
E: Ongoing stage
   Cost & responsibility
   Use
F: Market resistance
   (risk)

Source: *Bell's Guide: The Real Estate Encyclopedia*

Real Estate Damages: An Analysis of Detrimental Conditions

The secondary graph is also identical for the simple effects of physical depreciation, or a leasehold position.

This chapter discusses three of the broad categories of imposed conditions:

1. The effects of time
2. Eminent domain
3. Neighborhood issues

The Imposed Effects of Time

Improvements depreciate over time, so their value drops to the point where they no longer contribute to the land value. While Class V detrimental conditions are often imposed by time or other unpreventable factors, they can also include willful acts of the property owner, such as entering into a ground lease. For example, from the perspective of the ground lessee (tenant), a 99-year lease is worth virtually the same as the fee simple estate assuming the same discount rate applies. However, the value of the ground lease diminishes over time, and at the point of about 30 years remaining, the value of the ground lease as a percentage of the fee estate starts to drop significantly. Mathematically, the value of the leasehold (tenant) estate as compared to the fee simple estate is equivalent to a present value annuity multiplied by the reciprocal of the discount rate.[1] By computing a 99-year lease, the imposed effects of time can be seen graphically to be nearly unaffected for periods of over 30 years, and then start to drop until the leasehold estate has no value at the termination of the lease, at year 0, as shown in Exhibits 5.2 and 5.3 on the following pages.

Eminent Domain

From 1997 to 2030 the United Nations expects population growth of 25% in the United States. To facilitate the increase in population there will be a great need for the expansion of roads, increase in utility lines, and growth of other vital public services. However, this expansion will inherently affect the resident population and existing private property owners.

Eminent domain is the power of the government to take private property for public use without the owner's consent, and it is only restricted by the constitutional provision for "just compensation." The first instance of eminent domain is not exactly known. However, the federal government clearly established the power in 1875. The Fifth Amendment to the U.S. Constitution protects private property owners and promises that they be paid just compensation for property that is taken. As long as state and local governments do not contradict the U.S. Constitution, they have power in non-federal court proceedings. Eminent domain proceedings are determined either by a jury in a court of law or by an arbitrator.

Just Compensation

According to the U.S. Constitution, a private property owner who has to give up land as a result of eminent domain is due compensation for the loss of the property. The compen-

---

1. Robert N. Jones and Steven D. Roach, "Valuation of Long-Term Leases," *The Appraisal Journal* (October 1989): 451.

Exhibit 5.2 Leasehold versus Fee Simple Value

Discount Rate = 12.50%

Years Remaining	Annuity Factor	Reciprocal of Discount Rate	Leasehold As % of Fee Estate	Years Remaining	Annuity Factor	Reciprocal of Discount Rate	Leasehold As % of Fee Estate
99	7.999931	8.00	0.999991	60	7.993178	8.00	0.999147
98	7.999922	8.00	0.999990	59	7.992325	8.00	0.999041
97	7.999913	8.00	0.999989	58	7.991365	8.00	0.998921
96	7.999902	8.00	0.999988	57	7.990286	8.00	0.998786
95	7.999889	8.00	0.999986	56	7.989072	8.00	0.998634
94	7.999876	8.00	0.999984	55	7.987706	8.00	0.998463
93	7.999860	8.00	0.999983	54	7.986169	8.00	0.998271
92	7.999843	8.00	0.999980	53	7.984440	8.00	0.998055
91	7.999823	8.00	0.999978	52	7.982495	8.00	0.997812
90	7.999801	8.00	0.999975	51	7.980307	8.00	0.997538
89	7.999776	8.00	0.999972	50	7.977845	8.00	0.997231
88	7.999748	8.00	0.999968	49	7.975076	8.00	0.996885
87	7.999716	8.00	0.999965	48	7.971961	8.00	0.996495
86	7.999681	8.00	0.999960	47	7.968456	8.00	0.996057
85	7.999641	8.00	0.999955	46	7.964513	8.00	0.995564
84	7.999596	8.00	0.999950	45	7.960077	8.00	0.995010
83	7.999546	8.00	0.999943	44	7.955086	8.00	0.994386
82	7.999489	8.00	0.999936	43	7.949472	8.00	0.993684
81	7.999425	8.00	0.999928	42	7.943156	8.00	0.992895
80	7.999353	8.00	0.999919	41	7.936051	8.00	0.992006
79	7.999272	8.00	0.999909	40	7.928057	8.00	0.991007
78	7.999181	8.00	0.999898	39	7.919064	8.00	0.989883
77	7.999079	8.00	0.999885	38	7.908947	8.00	0.988618
76	7.998964	8.00	0.999870	37	7.897565	8.00	0.987196
75	7.998834	8.00	0.999854	36	7.884761	8.00	0.985595
74	7.998688	8.00	0.999836	35	7.870356	8.00	0.983795
73	7.998524	8.00	0.999816	34	7.854151	8.00	0.981769
72	7.998340	8.00	0.999792	33	7.835920	8.00	0.979490
71	7.998132	8.00	0.999767	32	7.815410	8.00	0.976926
70	7.997899	8.00	0.999737	31	7.792336	8.00	0.974042
69	7.997636	8.00	0.999705	30	7.766378	8.00	0.970797
68	7.997341	8.00	0.999668	29	7.737175	8.00	0.967147
67	7.997009	8.00	0.999626	28	7.704322	8.00	0.963040
66	7.996635	8.00	0.999579	27	7.667362	8.00	0.958420
65	7.996214	8.00	0.999527	26	7.625782	8.00	0.953223
64	7.995741	8.00	0.999468	25	7.579005	8.00	0.947376
63	7.995208	8.00	0.999401	24	7.526381	8.00	0.940798
62	7.994609	8.00	0.999326	23	7.467178	8.00	0.933397
61	7.993936	8.00	0.999242	22	7.400575	8.00	0.925072

Real Estate Damages: An Analysis of Detrimental Conditions

Exhibit 5.2 Leasehold versus Fee Simple Value *(continued)*

Years Remaining	Annuity Factor	Reciprocal of Discount Rate	Leasehold As % of Fee Estate	Years Remaining	Annuity Factor	Reciprocal of Discount Rate	Leasehold As % of Fee Estate
21	7.325647	8.00	0.915706	10	5.536431	8.00	0.692054
20	7.241353	8.00	0.905169	9	5.228485	8.00	0.653561
19	7.146523	8.00	0.893315	8	4.882045	8.00	0.610256
18	7.039838	8.00	0.879980	7	4.492301	8.00	0.561538
17	6.919818	8.00	0.864977	6	4.053839	8.00	0.506730
16	6.784795	8.00	0.848099	5	3.560568	8.00	0.445071
15	6.632894	8.00	0.829112	4	3.005639	8.00	0.375705
14	6.462006	8.00	0.807751	3	2.381344	8.00	0.297668
13	6.269757	8.00	0.783720	2	1.679012	8.00	0.209877
12	6.053476	8.00	0.756685	1	0.888889	8.00	0.111111
11	5.810161	8.00	0.726270	0	—	8.00	0.000000

Exhibit 5.3 Leasehold versus Fee Simple Value

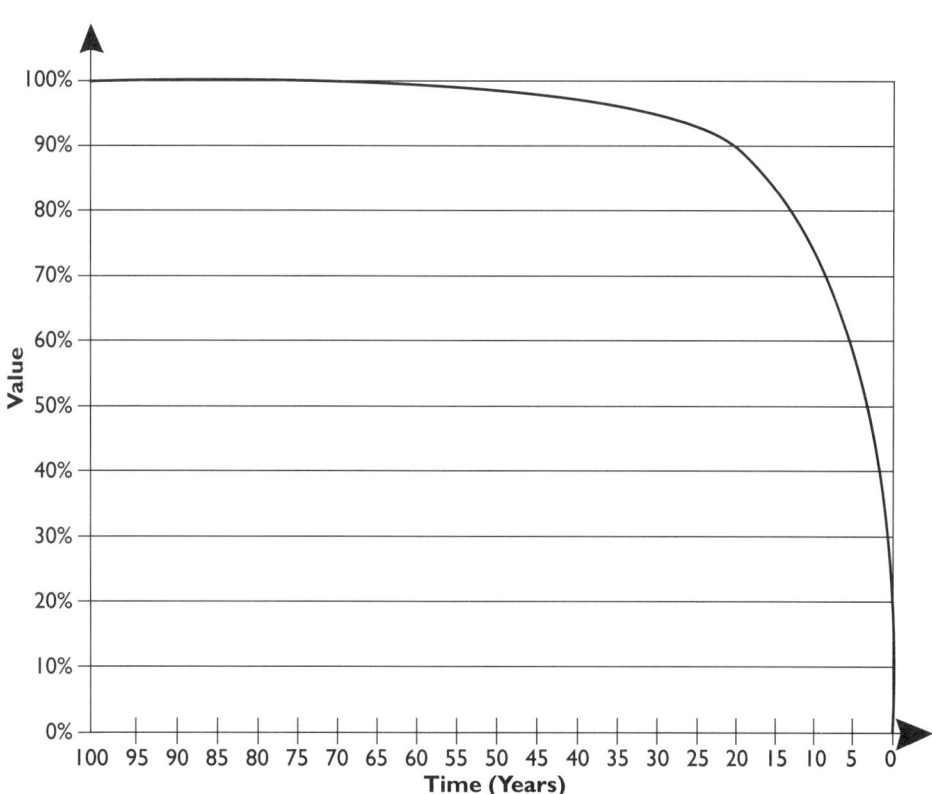

Infrastructure, such as these major freeways in Southern California, is a necessity for any community. When a freeway is widened, it may require the taking or partial taking of properties along its path.

Exhibit 5.4   Eminent Domain Diagram

Eminent domain is the right of government to take, or condemn, a property from the property owner for the good of the general public (i.e., roadways, fire stations, road widening). When taking a property, the government is obliged to pay *just compensation*.

Value of Partial Acquisitions

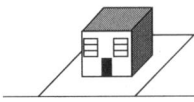 Value of the whole before acquisition

 Value of the part acquired as part of the whole

 Value of the remainder as part of the whole

 Value of the remainder after the acquisition and before consideration of special benefits

 Value of the remainder after the acquisition and after consideration of special benefits

sation for property loss in many jurisdictions is referred to as *just compensation*. The challenge to real estate appraisers is to estimate what the just compensation ought to be, which has many permutations, as shown in Exhibit 5.4. The answer to this question depends on which state the eminent domain proceeding takes place in. There are two rules of measurements of just compensation, the "before and after" (federal) rule and the "value plus damage" (state) rule.

The before and after (federal) rule is a valuation method used in federal cases, as well as in many specific states. (Only the Fifth Circuit Court of Appeals of the United States has ruled that the before and after rule is the only acceptable valuation method; other Circuit Courts will accept other variations of the rule.) Generally, the rule states that the value of the property taken is calculated by using the value of the property before the property is taken minus the value after the property is taken. The difference in values equals just compensation. Exhibit 5.5 outlines the states that use the before and after rule.

There are some recognized problems with the before and after rule. One problem is that it does not provide a component to exclude benefits from the after value. Also, the before and after rule does not provide a way to exclude noncompensable damages from the after value. Because of these problems, there are some jurisdictions that instituted variations of the rule.

Exhibit 5.5: Before and After (Federal) Rule

Alabama	Maryland	New Jersey	Tennessee
Arkansas	Michigan	New Mexico	Virginia
Connecticut	Minnesota	Ohio	Washington
Delaware	Mississippi	Oklahoma	Wisconsin
Hawaii	Missouri	Pennsylvania	Wyoming
Iowa	North Carolina	Rhode Island	
Maine	New Hampshire	South Dakota	

Source: J.D. Eaton, MAI, SRA, *Real Estate Valuation in Litigation,* 2d. ed. (Chicago: Appraisal Institute, 1995).

One variation of the before and after rule is used in cases where a small portion of a much larger piece of land is taken. Then, the calculation of just compensation is as follows:

> Value of the part taken PLUS Damages to the remainder LESS Special benefits

Special benefits are benefits that the remainder obtains as a result of the public improvement.

With the value plus damage (state) rule, the property owner is given just compensation through payment of a *fair market value* for the piece of property taken plus severance damages for the remaining piece of land. This rule is best applied when a small piece of land is taken and a larger piece of land remains. Also, this rule takes a more detailed and in-depth analysis than the before and after rule. Exhibit 5.6 demonstrates the procedures of the value plus damage rule, and Exhibit 5.7 sets forth the states that use the value plus damage rule. Exhibit 5.8 sets forth the federal and state eminent domain setoff rules and policies.

Exhibit 5.6 Value Plus Damage Rule Calculations

Value before taking		$1,500,000
Value of part taken	−	$50,000
Remainder value before taking		$1,450,000
Remainder value after taking	−	$1,250,000
Damages to remainder		$200,000
Special benefits to remainder	−	$50,000
Net damage to remainder		$150,000
Value of part taken	+	$50,000
Just compensation		$200,000

Class V—Imposed Conditions

Exhibit 5.7 Value Plus Damage (State) Rule

Arizona	Illinois	Montana	South Carolina
California	Indiana	Nebraska	Texas
Colorado	Kansas	Nevada	Utah
Florida	Kentucky	New York	Virginia
Georgia	Louisiana	North Dakota	Vermont
Idaho	Massachusetts	Oregon	West Virginia

Source: J.D. Eaton, MAI, SRA, *Real Estate Valuation in Litigation*, 2d. ed. (Chicago: Appraisal Institute, 1995).

Exhibit 5.8 Federal and State Eminent Domain Setoff Rules and Policies

Of Jurisdictions that Set Off Compensation with both General and Special Benefits

Jurisdiction	Benefits Applied to Compensation	Benefits are Applied Against		Percent of Total Cases	Future Damages and Benefits		
		Damages to Remainder	Value of Part Taken		Future Years to Count	Discount Future Values	Typical Rates
Federal*	Special	Yes	No*	10%-15%	3–5 Years	Yes	8%-12%
Illinois	General and Special	Yes	No	1%±	1 Year	No	—
New Mexico†	General and Special	Yes	No	2%±	1 Year	Yes†	—
New York	General and Special	Yes	No	5%±	3–5 Years	No	—
West Virginia	General and Special	Yes	No	1%±	2–7 Years	Yes	9%-11%
California**	General and Special	Yes	No	1%–2%**	3–5 Years	Yes	8%-12%

* The Federal Government applied both general and special benefits to both damages and the value of the part taken as recently as 1992.

† New Mexico ordinarily only counts benefits realized with the first year. These needn't be discounted. In some cases, incremental income ascribable to benefits may be discounted for many years into the future.

** An August 25, 1997, decision by the California Supreme Court merged general and special benefits into "benefits." Historically special benefits were 1% to 2% of cases.

Source: Richard A. Neustein, MAI and Orell C. Anderson, MAI, "Condemnation in California: Redefining Damages for Partial Takings," *Right of Way* (Spring 1998): 34-36.

Neighborhood Nuisances

There are many neighborhood nuisances, such as prisons, tunneling projects under properties, power plants, sewage treatment plants, and landfills. However, few have received the attention of one of the biggest nuisances for property owners, airport noise. This issue demonstrates many of the concepts that are central to neighborhood nuisances. For decades, the use of commercial jet aircraft has increased. Consequently, airport noise has become a growing concern for a number of communities located near airports. In the 1970s, the FAA developed policies that required airlines to phase in quieter aircraft. However, the number of flights nationally is expected to increase 37% by the year 2007. This increased volume can be expected to have growing adverse effects. Some studies have linked airport noise to a variety of health problems. In addition to the annoyance and disruption caused by airport noise, home owners in particular may feel its impact in terms of reduced property values.

Measuring Airport Noise

There exist numerous measurements of noise. Some measurements gauge only single noise events, while others take average exposure levels over a 24-hour period, weighting more heavily for noises that occur in the evening and overnight. Simply measuring airport noise does not necessarily predict the human reaction to it, though. As the FAA states in its Noise Abatement Policy, it is "uncertain whether people, in reacting to aircraft noise, are more annoyed by the number of aircraft noise events or the noise levels of individual events."

The most widely known measurement of noise to the lay person and the most commonly used is the decibel. The decibel scale starts at 0, where only the faintest sounds are heard, and increases in a logarithmic pattern for which every increase of 10 dB, the sound pressure doubles. The dB scale is somewhat ineffective in measuring the true loudness or the "judged intensity" of noises due to the human ear's selective response to various frequencies. True loudness is also a function of frequency levels of the sound wave length—i.e., a low frequency sound is perceived as louder than a higher frequency sound of equal intensity on the dB scale. Another scale that accounts for sound intensity and frequency was developed: the dBA scale, which is illustrated in Exhibit 5.9. For every 3 dBA increase, sound doubles.

Exhibit 5.9   Common Sounds and their dBA Rating

Sound Element	dBA
Rustling leaves	20
Room in a quiet dwelling at midnight	32
Soft whispers at 5 feet	34
Window air conditioner	55
Conversational speech	60
Busy restaurant	65
Vacuum cleaner in private residence (at 10 feet)	69
Ringing alarm clock (at 2 feet)	80
Beginning of hearing damage if prolonged exposure over 85 dBA	
Printing press plant	86
Heavy diesel-propelled vehicle (about 25 feet away)	92
Home lawn mower	98
Air hammer	107
Jet airliner (500 feet overhead)	115

Source: *FAA Report on Airport Noise* (March 1988)

Assessing the Effects of Airport Noise on People

There is currently no agreement on the exact physiological and psychological effects of airport noise on human beings. A housing survey conducted by the Bureau of the Census for the Department of Housing and Urban Development indicated that of those households experiencing airport noise, 34.2% considered the noise to be "disturbing, harmful, or dangerous," and 6.3% would like to move from the neighborhood because of the noise. Airport noise is not thought to cause any direct health problems (such as hearing loss), but nonetheless its indirect effects may still be harmful.

Reducing the Effects of Airport Noise

The FAA has developed policies that require airlines to phase quieter aircraft into their fleets. However, simply lowering the level of noise may not be a complete solution. In its Noise Abatement Policy, the FAA states that "Airport Proprietors are primarily responsible for planning and implementing action designed to reduce the effect of noise on residents of the surrounding area. Such actions include *optimal site location,* improvements in airport design, noise abatement ground procedures, land acquisition . . ." In essence, the FAA is stating that airports should be constructed in areas that will least affect people—i.e., away from highly populated areas where people live and work, for example, the location of the new Denver International Airport.

While some efforts have been made to mitigate the effects of airport noise, many properties are nevertheless located in proximity to major airports. Several studies have been conducted that have measured the diminution in value from airport noise. Usually these studies are based upon paired sales analyses whereby homes that are located under or near a flight corridor are compared to otherwise similar homes that are not located near any airport flight corridor.

Power Lines and Electromagnetic Fields

Electromagnetic fields (EMFs) are produced by power lines, electrical wiring, and electrical equipment. EMFs are invisible lines of force that surround any electrical device. By definition, an *electromagnetic field* is a property of space caused by the motion of an electric charge. A stationary charge will produce only an electric field in the surrounding space. If the charge is moving, a magnetic field is also produced. An electric field can be produced also by a changing magnetic field. The mutual interaction of electric and magnetic fields produces an electromagnetic field.

Electromagnetic fields are created by electric charges. Electric fields represent the forces that charges exert on other charges, while magnetic fields result from the additional forces that moving charges exert on other moving charges. Electric fields are produced by voltage, and they increase in strength as the voltage increases. The electric field strength is measured in units of volts per meter (V/m). Magnetic fields increase in strength as the current increases. They are measured in units of gauss (G) or tesla (T). A major difference between electric and magnetic fields is that as long as electrical equipment remains connected to the source of electrical power, electrical fields are still present, even when the equipment is switched off. Magnetic fields, on the other hand, are produced when electrical equipment is turned on—i.e., current must be flowing.

Electric power lines and appliances produce low frequency fields, which typically operate at a frequency of 60 Hz. Much research is now underway concerning the health effects of 60 Hz fields. These are the kind of EMFs found in virtually every home and workplace. Both electric and magnetic fields are present around electrical equipment and power lines, but the concern about potential health effects are focused on magnetic fields. Electric fields are shielded or weakened by materials that conduct electricity, such as trees, buildings, and human skin. Magnetic fields, on the other hand, pass through most materials.

Some scientific studies have shown that electromagnetic fields are not linked to childhood leukemia. Regardless of these conclusions, the impact on real estate values is determined by the market and not by scientific analysis.

Most high-voltage transmission lines in the United States are rated at 115, 230, 345, 500, and 765 kV. Those with voltages of less than 345 kV are ordinary high-voltage lines, and those with voltages over 345 kV are *extra high-voltage* lines. For some 500 kV lines, the maximum magnetic field of about 140 mG directly under the line will drop to about 3.0 mG at approximately 300 feet, depending on the amount of current within the line.

Before extra high-voltage lines were introduced, the concern about transmission lines was their impact on the landscape's aesthetic appearance. Their 60 Hz fields were considered weak, so very few people were concerned about potential health hazards from direct exposure. Not until extra high-voltage transmission lines were used did the public show concern over the stronger electric fields.

Despite the various concerns raised about EMFs, the role of the appraiser or analyst is to examine real estate market data to determine whether there is any evidence of effects on property values.

Further Reading

Eminent Domain

Patel, Purushottam H. "Eminent Domain." *The Appraisal Journal* (January 1995).

Bolton, David R. *Properties Near Power Lines and Valuation Issues: Condemnation or Inverse Condemnation?* Paper presented at Annual Conference of the Institute on Planning, Zoning and Eminent Domain, Dallas, Texas, November 17-19, 1993.

Buesing, Robert H. "Condemnation for Electric Transmission Lines: Meeting the Challenge of Adequate Proof." *Probate & Property* (May/June 1994).

Airport Proximity

Bornis, Sanford F. "Mieszkowski and Saper's Estimate of the Effects of Airport Noise on Property Values: A Comment." *Journal of Urban Economics,* vol. 9, no. 1 (January 1981).

Crowley, Ronald W. "A Case Study of the Effects of an Airport on Land Value." *Journal of Transport Economics and Policy,* vol. VII, no. 2 (May 1973).

Frankel, Marvin. "Aircraft Noise and Residential Property Values: Results of a Survey Study." *The Appraisal Journal* (January 1991).

Gautrin, Jean-Francois. "An Evaluation of the Impact of Aircraft Noise on Property Values with a Simple Model of Urban Land Rent." *Land Economics* (February 1975).

Mieszkowski, Peter, and Arthur M. Saper. "An Estimate of the Effects of Airport Noise on Property Values." *Journal of Urban Economics,* vol. 5, no. 4 (October 1978).

Nelson, Jon P. "Airports and Property Values: A Survey of Recent Evidence." *Journal of Transport Economics and Policy,* vol. XIV, no. 1 (January 1980).

___. "Airport Noise, Location Rent, and the Market for Residential Amenities." *Journal of Environmental Economics and Management* (December 1979).

___. *Aircraft Noise and the Market for Residential Housing: Empirical Results for Seven Selected Airports.* Washington, D.C.: Department of Transportation, Research and Special Programs Administration, September 1978.

O'Byrne, Patricia Habuda, Jon P. Nelson, and Joseph J. Seneca. "Housing Values, Census Estimates, Disequilibrium, and the Environmental Cost of Airport Noise: A Case Study of Atlanta." *Journal of Environmental Economics and Management,* vol. 12, no. 2 (June 1985).

Pennington, G., N. Topham, and R. Ward. "Aircraft Noise and Residential Values Adjacent to Manchester International Airport." *Journal of Transport Economics and Policy,* vol. XXIV, no. 1 (January 1990).

Walters, A.A. "Airports—An Economic Survey." *Journal of Transport Economics and Policy,* vol. XII, no. 2 (May 1978).

High-Pressure Natural Gas Pipeline Proximity

Kinnard, William N., Jr. *The Impact of Proximity to High-Pressure Natural Gas Pipelines on Single-Family Residential Property Values.* Paper presented at the 1993 Annual Meeting of the American Real Estate Society, Key West, Fla., April 1993.

Kinnard, William N., Jr., Sue Ann Dickey, and Mary Beth Geckler. *Fear (As a Measure of Damages) Strikes Out: Two Case Studies, Comparisons of Actual Market Behavior with Opinion Survey Research.* Paper presented at 1994 Annual Conference of American Real Estate Society, Santa Barbara, Calif., April 1994.

___. "Natural Gas Pipeline Impact on Residential Property Values: An Empirical Study of Two Market Areas." *Right of Way* (June/July 1994).

High-Voltage Transmission Line Proximity

Ball, Thomas A. *A Study of the Economic Effects of High Voltage Electrical Transmission Lines on the Market Value of Real Property.* Tempe, Ariz.: Salt River Project, 1989.

Beasley, Ben. "High Voltage Power Lines: Impact on Nearby Property Values." *Right of Way* (February 1991).

Beauregard Conseil Eur. *Final Report: Assessment of the Impacts of the Hydro Line River Crossing on the Residents of the Immediate Region.* Hydro Quebec, Environmental Vice Presidency, 1990.

Blomquist, Glenn. "The Effects of Electrical Utility Power Plant Location on Area Property Value." *Land Economics,* vol. 50 (February 1974).

Callanan, Judith, and R. V. Hargreaves. "The Effect of Transmission Lines on Property Values: A Statistical Analysis." New Zealand, 1995.

Case, Bradford, and Charles M. Quigley. *Statistical Analysis of Sales Data to Verify Appraisal Information.* Working Paper no. 88-150. Berkeley, Calif.: Center for Real Estate and Urban Economics, October 1988.

Colwell, Peter F. "Power Lines and Land Values." *The Journal of Real Estate Research,* vol. 5, no. 1 (Spring 1990).

Cost Effectiveness Analysis: Mitigation of Electromagnetic Fields Compared to a Study of the Potential Health Effects of EMF Emissions from High-Voltage Transmission Lines. Providence, R.I.: Public Utilities Commission, 1993.

Cowger, John R., Steven C. Bottemiller, and James M. Cahill. "Transmission Line Impact on Residential Property Values." *Right of Way* (September/October 1996).

Delaney, Charles J. *Valuation Implications for Residential Property Proximate to High Voltage Power Lines: A New Environmental Concern?* Baylor University, Department of Real Estate, Spring 1991. Unpublished Manuscript.

Delaney, Charles J., and Douglas Timmons. "High Voltage Power Lines: Do They Affect Residential Property Value?" *The Journal of Real Estate Research,* vol. 7, no. 3 (Summer 1992).

Economics Consultants Northwest. *Garrison-West High Voltage Transmission Line Social Monitoring Study.* Montana Department of Natural Resources and Conservation, and Bonneville Power Administration, 1990.

Florig, H. Keith, and M. Granger Morgan. "Measurements of Housing Density Along Transmission Lines." *Bioelectromagnetics,* vol. 9 (1988).

Furby, Lita, Robin Gregory, Paul Slovic, and Baruch Fischhoff. "Electric Power Transmission Lines, Property Values, and Compensation." *Journal of Environmental Management,* 27 (1988).

Hamilton, Stanley W., and Gregory M. Schwann. "Do High Voltage Electric Transmission Lines Affect Property Value?" *Land Economics* (November 1995).

Ignelzi, Patrice C. "Successfully Conducting Transmission Line Impact Assessments of Property Values." *Transmission Lines in Residential Neighborhoods: Issues in Siting and Environmental Planning.* Portland, Oreg.: Edison Electric Institute, October 12-13, 1989.

Ignelzi, Patrice C., and Thomas Priestley. *A Statistical Analysis of Transmission Line Impacts in Six Neighborhoods.* Albany, Calif.: Pacific Consulting Services, February 1991. Two Volumes.

———. *A Methodology for Assessing Transmission Line Impacts in Residential Communities.* Washington, D.C.: Edison Electric Institute, June 1989.

Jack Faucett Associates, Inc. *Evaluation of Power Plant Externalities, A Land Value Approach—Final Report.* Prepared for Maryland Department of Natural Resources, PB01-203747, January 1976.

Kinnard, William N., Jr. "The Effect of High-Voltage Overhead Transmission Lines on Sales Prices and Market Values of Nearby Real Estate: An Annotated Bibliography and Evaluative Analysis." *Transmission Lines in Residential Neighborhoods: Issues in Siting and Environmental Planning.* Portland, Oreg.: Edison Electric Institute, October 12-13, 1989.

___. "The Impact of High Voltage Transmission Lines on Real Estate Values." *Journal of Property Tax Management,* vol. I, no. 4 (1990).

___. "Patterns of Property Value Impacts from Proximity to High-Voltage Transmission Lines: Analytical Update." Paper presented at Edison Electric Institute Conference, Duluth, Minn., August 1992.

Kinnard, William N., Jr., Sandy Bond, Paul M. Syms, and Jake W. DeLottie, "Effects of Proximity to High-Voltage Transmission Lines on Nearby Residential Property Values: An International Perspective on Recent Research." Paper presented at the 1997 International Conference of the American Real Estate and Urban Economics Association, Berkeley, Calif., May 1997.

Kinnard, William N., Jr., and Sue Ann Dickey. "A Primer on Proximity Impact Research: Residential Property Values Near High-Voltage Transmission Lines." *Real Estate Issues* (Spring 1995).

Kinnard, William N., Jr., Mary Beth Geckler, and Jake W. DeLottie. "Effects of Proximity to High-Voltage Transmission Lines on Nearby Residential Property Values: An International Perspective." Paper prepared for Chartered Surveyors' Education Channel Television Education Network, Ltd., Royal Institution of Chartered Surveyors, London, England, August 1996.

Kinnard, William N., Jr., Phillip S. Mitchell, and James R. Webb. "The Impact of High-Voltage Overhead Transmission Lines on the Value of Real Property." Paper presented at the American Real Estate Society Annual Conference, Arlington, Va., April 1989.

Kroll, Cynthia A. "Property Valuation: A Primer on Proximity Impact Research." Paper presented at the Conference on Electric and Magnetic Fields, San Francisco, Calif., February 8, 1994.

Kroll, Cynthia A., and Thomas Priestley. *The Effects of Overhead Transmission Lines on Property Values: A Review and Analysis of the Literature.* A report prepared for the Siting and Environmental Planning Task Force, Edison Electric Institute, Piedmont, Calif., December 1991.

Kung, Hsiang-te, and Charles F. Seagle. "Impact of Power Transmission Lines on Property Values: A Case Study." *The Appraisal Journal* (July 1992).

Mitchell, Phillip S., and William N. Kinnard, Jr. "Statistical Analysis of High-Voltage Overhead Transmission Line Construction on the Value of Vacant Land." *Valuation,* vol. 40, no. 1 (June 1996).

Porter, Jeffrey R., and Carolyn S. Langer. "Electromagnetic Fields: Courts Deal with EMFs Effect on Property Values." *Massachusetts Lawyer's Weekly* (February 27, 1995).

Priestley, Thomas. "Perceptions of Transmission Lines in Residential Neighborhoods: Results of a California Case Study." *Transmission Lines in Residential Neighborhoods: Issues in Siting and Environmental Planning.* Portland, Oreg.: Edison Electric Institute Workshop, October 12-13, 1989.

Priestley, Thomas, and Gary Evans. *Perceptions of Transmission Lines in Residential Neighborhoods: A Case Study in Vallejo, California.* Southern California Edison Company, 1990.

Reed, Richard A. "Fear and Lowering Property Values in New York: Proof of Consequential Damages from 'Cancerphobia' in the Wake of *Criscuola v. Power Authority of the State of New York.*" *New York State Bar Journal* (March/April 1994).

Rhodeside & Harwell, Inc. (Andrew A. White, PhD, statistical consultant). *Transmission Line Impact on Property Values.* Richmond, Va.: Virginia Power Company, June 1992.

___. *Perceptions of Power Lines: Residents' Attitudes.* Richmond, Va.: Virginia Power Company, 1988.

Rigdon, Glenn J. "138 kV Transmission Lines and the Value of Recreational Land." *Right of Way* (December 1991).

Rikon, Michael. "Electromagnetic Radiation Field Property Devaluation." *The Appraisal Journal* (January 1996).

Sewell, E. Larry. *230 kV Transmission Lines: Impact Study on Real Estate Marketability.* Sarasota, Fla.: Sewell, Valentich, Tillis & Thatcher, 1989.

Taubes, Gary. "Fields of Fear." *The Atlantic Monthly* (November 1994).

University of California at Berkeley. "Electrophobia: Overcoming Fear of EMFs." *Wellness Letter* (November 1994).

Wellman, Juliana B. "The Threat of EMF Litigation and the Case for Sound Science." *The Litigation Journal* (Fall 1993).

Transportation Corridor Proximity

Allen, Gary R. "Highway Noise, Noise Mitigation, and Residential Property Values." *Transportation Research Record,* no. 812 (1981).

Allen, W. Bruce, and David E. Boyce. "Impact of High Speed Rapid Transit Facility on Residential Property Values." *High Speed Ground Transportation Journal,* vol. 8, no. 2 (Summer 1974).

Gamble, Hays B., Owen H. Sauerlender, and C. John Langley. "Adverse and Beneficial Effects of Highways on Residential Property Values." *Transportation Research Record,* no. 508 (1974).

Hall, Fred L., Barbara E. Breston, and S. Martin Taylor. "Effects Of Highway Noise on Residential Property Values." *Transportation Research Record,* no. 686 (1978).

Hall, Fred L., and J. Douglas Welland. "The Effect of Noise Barriers on the Market Value of Adjacent Residential Properties." *Transportation Research Record,* no. 1143 (1987).

Hirschman, Ira, and Michael Henderson. "Methodology for Assessing Local Land Use Impacts of Highways." *Transportation Research Record,* no. 1274 (1990).

Hughes, William T., and C.F. Sirmans. "Traffic Externalities and Single-Family House Prices." Unpublished Paper, College of Business Administration, Louisiana State University, March 1992.

Hyde, James V., Jr. "The Appraiser's Approach to Noise Damage." *The Real Estate Appraiser* (November-December 1976).

Kamerud, Dana B., and Calvin R. von Buseck. "The Effects of Traffic Sound and its Reduction on Houses Prices." *Transportation Research Record,* no. 1033 (1985).

Langdon, F. J. "Noise Nuisance Caused by Road Traffic in Residential Areas: Part III." *Journal of Sound and Vibration,* vol. 49, no. 2 (1976).

Langley, C. John, Jr. "Adverse Impacts of the Washington Beltway on Residential Property Values." *Land Economics,* vol. 52, no. 1 (February 1976).

___. "Highways and Property Values: The Washington Beltway Revisited." *Transportation Research Record,* no. 812 (1981).

___. "Time-Series Effects of a Limited-Access Highway on Residential Property Values." *Transportation Research Record,* no. 583 (1976).

Lewis, Harold J. "The Appraisal of Highway Noise Damages." *The Appraisal Journal* (October 1977).

McGough, B. C. "Methodology for Highway Impact Studies." *The Appraisal Journal* (January 1968).

Nelson, Jon P. "Highway Noise and Property Values. A Survey of Recent Evidence." *Journal of Transport Economics and Policy,* vol. 16, no. 2 (May 1982).

Nelson, Roland D., and Laurence G. Allen. "Expressway Proximity Damages to Residential Property." *Right of Way,* vol. 30, no. 1 (February 1983).

Palmquist, Raymond B. "Impact of Highway Improvements on Property Values in Washington State." *Transportation Research Record,* no. 887 (1982).

Taylor, S. M., B. E. Breston, and F. L. Hall. "The Effect of Road Traffic Noise on House Prices." *Journal of Sound and Vibration,* vol. 80, no. 4 (February 1982).

Wigle, W. G. "The Effect of Urban Expressways on Adjacent Land Values." *Right of Way* (February 1975).

Historical Site Designation

Benson, Virginia O., and Richard Klein. "The Impact of Historic Districting on Property Values." *The Appraisal Journal* (April 1988).

Neighboring Landfills and Hazardous Waste Facilities

Bachrach, Kenneth M., and Alex J. Zautra. "Assessing the Impact of Hazardous Waste Facilities: Psychology, Politics, and Environmental Impact Statements" in *Advances in Environmental Psychology, Volume 6 Exposure to Hazardous Substances: Psychological Parameters.* Edited by Lebovits, et al. Hillsdale, N.J.: Lawrence Erlbaum Associates, 1984.

Baker, Brian. *Land Value Surrounding Waste Disposal Facilities.* Ithaca, N.Y.: Department of Agricultural Economics, New York State College of Agricultural and Life Sciences, Cornell University, October 1982.

Baker, Mary Dunn. *Property Values and Potentially Hazardous Production Facilities: A Case Study of the Kanawha Valley, West Virginia.* Florida State University, PhD Dissertation, 1986.

Bleich, Donald H., M. Chapman Findlay, and G. Michael Phillips. "An Evaluation of the Impact of a Good Landfill on Surrounding Property Values." *The Appraisal Journal* (July 1990).

Carother, Andre. "Living Next to the Landfill: The Coming Age of Sumter County." *Greenpeace* (July-September 1987).

Cartee, Charles P. "A Review of Sanitary Landfill Impacts on Property Values." *The Real Estate Appraiser and Analyst* (Spring 1989).

Centaur Associates and U.S. Environmental Protection Agency, Office of Waste and Waste Management. *Siting of Hazardous Waste Management Facilities and Public Opposition.* Document SW-809, 1979.

Coughlin, R., H. Newburger, and C. Seigner. *Perceptions of Landfill Operations Held by Nearby Residents.* Philadelphia, Pa.: Regional Science Research Institute, Discussion Paper Series, no. 65, 1973.

Elliot-Jones, Michael. "Real Estate Value and Toxic Sites." *The Digest of Environmental Law,* vol. 5, no. 7 (1992).

———. "Rents and Proximity to Toxic Sites." *Spectrum Economics.* San Francisco, Calif.: 1991.

Gamble, Hays B., and Roger H. Downing. "Effects of Sanitary Landfills on Property Values and Residential Development." Chapter 28 of *Solid and Liquid Wastes: Management, Methods and Socioeconomic Consideration.* Edited by S. K. Majumdar and E. Willard Miller. Philadelphia, Pa.: Pennsylvania Academy of Sciences, 1986.

Gamble, Hays B., Roger H. Downing, J. S. Shortle, and D. J. Epp. *Effects of Solid Waste Disposal Sites on Community Development and Residential Property Values.* Institute for Research on Land and Water Resources, Pennsylvania State University, Final Report for Bureau of Solid Waste Management Department of Environmental Resources Commonwealth of Pennsylvania, November 1982.

Garippa, John E., and Kenneth R. Kosco. "The Developing Law of Landfill Valuation." *Journal of Property Tax Management,* vol. 6, no. 4 (Spring 1995): 1-15.

Goldberg, L., et al. *The Effects of Solid Waste Disposal Sites on Property Values.* Washington, D.C.: U.S. Environmental Protection Agency, 1972.

Greenberg, Michael R., and Richard F. Anderson. *Hazardous Waste Sites: The Credibility Gap.* New Brunswick, N.J.: Center for Urban Policy Research, 1984.

Greenberg, Michael R., and James Hughes. "Impact of Hazardous Waste Sites on Property Value and Land Use: Tax Assessors' Appraisal." *The Appraisal Journal* (January 1993).

Harrison, David, Jr., and James H. Stock. *Hedonic Housing Values, Local Public Goods, and the Benefits of Hazardous Waste Cleanup.* Cambridge, Mass.: Harvard University Energy and Environmental Policy Center, Discussion Paper E-84-09, November 1984.

Havlicek, Joseph, Jr., Robert Richardson, and Lloyd Davies. *Measuring the Impacts of Solid Waste Disposal Site Location on Property Values.* Chicago: University of Chicago Urban Economics Report no. 65, November 1972.

Institute for Environmental Studies, University of North Carolina. *Costs and Benefits to Local Governments Due to the Presence of a Hazardous Waste Management Facility and Related Compensation Issues.* March 1985.

Ketkar, Kusum. "Hazardous Waste Sites and Property Values in the State of New Jersey." *Applied Economics* 24: 647-659.

Kiel, Katherine A. "Measuring the Impact of the Discovery and Cleaning of Identified Hazardous Waste Sites on House Values." *Land Economics* (November 1995).

Kinnard, William N., Jr. "Measuring Locational Obsolescence from Nearby Hazardous Facilities." Seminar on Appraising Contaminated Properties. Boston, Mass.: Appraisal Institute National Conference, July 29, 1992.

———. "Measuring Locational Obsolescence: Proximity to Hazardous Materials Sites." *Silver Anniversary Professional Seminar on Appraisal of Distressed Properties.* Montreal, Quebec, Canada: International Association of Assessing Officers, October 13, 1990.

Kleindorfer, P. R. "Compensation and Negotiation in the Siting of Hazardous Waste Sites." *Sci. Total Environ.* (The Netherlands), vol. 51 (1986).

Kolhase, Janet E. "The Impact of Toxic Waste Sites on Housing Values." *Journal of Urban Economics* (1990).

Lautenberg, Sandra. *The Effects of Abandoned Hazardous Waste Dump Sites on Land Use and Values in Edison, New Jersey.* New Brunswick, N.J.: Department of Urban Planning and Policy Development, Unpublished Paper, 1982.

Lawson, Jeffrey T., and Barbara H. Cane. *Hazardous Waste and the Real Estate Transaction: A Practical and Theoretical Guide (for the Technical Consultant, Real Estate Attorney, Business Person, Investor, or Anyone Involved in Buying and Selling Land).* Washington, D.C.: National Symposium, Management of Uncontrolled Hazardous Waste Sites, November 29-December 1, 1982.

Long, F. A., and Glenn E. Schwietzer (editors). *Risk Assessment at Hazardous Waste Sites.* Washington, D.C.: American Chemical Society, ACS Symposium Series 204, 1982.

Massey, D. *Attitudes of Nearby Residents Toward Establishing Sanitary Landfills.* Washington, D.C.: U.S. Environmental Protection Agency, 1978.

McClelland, Gary H., William D. Schulze, and Brian Hurd. "The Effect of Risk Beliefs on Property Values: A Case Study of a Hazardous Waste Site." *Risk Analysis* (December 1990).

Mitchell, Robert, and W. H. Desvousges. "The Value of Avoiding a LULU: Hazardous Waste Disposal Sites." *Review of Economics and Statistics* 68: 293-299.

Mundy, Bill. *The Impact of Waste Disposal Sites on Nearby Property Values: A Bibliography of Related Literature.* Seattle, Wash.: Mundy and Associates, January 1991.

___. "The Impact of Waste Disposal Sites on Nearby Property Values: Summary of Literature." *Environmental Analysis and Valuation Seminar.* Seattle, Wash.: Mundy and Associates, March 1992.

Nelson, Arthur C. *Anticipated Market Impacts on Sales Prices of Residential Properties Near Proposed Laidlaw Waste Systems Landfill.* Northeast Kansas City, Mo.: Unpublished Report, March 1991.

Nelson, Arthur C., John Genereux, and Michell Genereux. "Price Effects of Landfills on House Values." *Land Economics,* vol. 68, no. 4 (November 1992).

Pettit, C. L., and Dr. Charles Johnson. "The Impact on Property Values of Solid Waste Facilities." *Waste Age* (April 1987).

Price, Joe R. *The Impact of Solid Waste Management Facilities on Surrounding Real Estate Values.* West Palm Beach, Fla.: Callaway & Price, Inc., 1989.

Reichert, Alan K. *The Impact of a Toxic Waste Superfund Site Upon Residential Property Values.* Hilton Head, S.C.: Paper presented at the Annual Meeting of the American Real Estate Society, April 1995.

Reichert, Alan K., Michael Small, and Sonil Mohanty. "The Impact of Landfills on Residential Property Values." *The Journal of Real Estate Research,* vol. 7, no. 3 (Summer 1992).

Rudzitis, G., and E. G. Hwang. "The External Costs of Sanitary Landfills." *Journal of Environmental Systems,* vol. 7, no. 4 (1977-78).

Smith, Martin A., F. M. Lynn, and R. N. Andrews. "Economic Impacts of Hazardous Waste Facilities." *Hazardous Waste and Hazardous Materials* (1986).

Smith, V. Kerry, and William H. Desvousges. "The Values of Avoiding a LULU: Hazardous Waste Disposal Sites." *The Review of Economics and Statistics* (May 1986).

___. "Asymmetries to the Valuation of Risk and the Siting of Hazardous Waste Disposal Facilities." *American Economic Review* (May 1986).

Smolen, G. E., G. Moore, and L. V. Conway. "Hazardous Waste Landfill Impacts on Local Property Values." *Real Estate Appraiser* (April 1992).

Wise, Kenneth T. *Analysis of Property Value Impacts in the Uniontown Class Area.* Cambridge, Mass.: The Brattle Group, February 1993.

Zeiss and Atwater. "Waste Facility Impacts on Residential Property Values." *Journal of Urban Planning and Development* (1989).

Solid Waste Disposal Proximity

Jessup, Deborah H. "Laws, Issues, and Solutions." *Waste Management Guide.* Washington, D.C.: The Bureau of National Affairs, Inc., 1998.

U.S. Congress, Office of Technology Assessment. "What Next for Municipal Solid Waste?" *Facing America's Trash,* OTA-0-124. Washington D.C.: U.S. Government Printing Office, October 1989.

U.S. Environmental Protection Agency. "Solid Waste Disposal in the United States." *Report to Congress,* vol. 11, EPA530-SW-99-011B. Washington, D.C.: U.S. Government Printing Office, 1988

Chapter 5 Case Study

Sea-Tac International Airport
Class V—Imposed Condition Study

Initial Assessment and Recommendations
February 1997
Prepared Under a Grant from
The State of Washington for the:
    City of Burien, Washington
    City of Des Moines, Washington
    City of Federal Way, Washington
    City of Normandy Park, Washington
    City of Tukwila, Washington
    Highline School District
    Highline Community Hospital

Prepared by:
    Hellmuth, Obata + Kassabaum, Inc., Dallas, Texas
    Raytheon Infrastructure Services, Inc., Denver and Philadelphia

In Association with:
    Thomas Lane & Associates, Inc., Seattle, Washington
    Michael J. McCormick, AICPA, Olympia, Washington

Airport Noise Study
Potential Socioeconomic Impacts and Mitigation

Expected changes in land values, land uses, home ownership tenure, local government revenue, and social service needs resulting from construction of the third runway and related facilities

Aircraft operations at Sea-Tac International Airport impact the value of nearby properties in two ways.

First, the airport's operations depress property values below the level that real estate markets would produce if the airport did not exist. If a single-family residential house located in, for example, Burien could be physically transported to an identical location on an identical lot in another part of King County, its value would be increased, and the amount of its increase is the depression in value caused by proximity to the airport. The next section of this study estimates the average loss in value of real estate located in close proximity to Sea-Tac International Airport by comparing a large sample of comparable single-family housing units in northwest and southwest King County holding constant the non-airport factors that also influence real estate values.

A second way in which Sea-Tac International Airport operations impact the value of real estate is in the variation in value among properties caused by their proximity to the flight paths of arriving and departing aircraft. Such changes are the "shadow" effects (noise pollution, visual pollution, possible air quality pollution, and a generally degraded environment for human habitat) caused by living under low-flying aircraft. The third section of this study uses a statistical technique known as regression analysis to estimate Sea-Tac International Airport's shadow effects by measuring the difference in value of a property, holding other factors constant, when it is located at different distances from directly under one of Sea-Tac International Airport's arrival/departure flight paths.

The remaining subsections provide information on the changes in land use produced by airport-induced depressions in adjacent land values and on the alteration in the demographic profile of persons living in jurisdictions where depressed land values result in altered land uses.

It is important to remember that the following analysis addresses the issue of depressed but not declining land values. All parts of the Puget Sound Region have experienced population growth in the recent past, and the entire area is expected to experience rates of population growth above the national average in the foreseeable future. This means that the Puget Sound Region is expected to have significant net in-migration. As a result, average real estate values will undoubtedly rise. Real estate located in close proximity to the airport will participate in these growth trends and will also experience rising land values.

Because of the airport, however, the rate of appreciation in the value of nearby real estate is expected to be less than it otherwise would have been. The correct measure of the airport-induced depression in land values, consequently, is the price difference between comparable properties located close to and distant from the airport. Neither a simple calculation of whether or not property values have increased nor a comparison of properties inside or outside any specific L_{DN} (level day night) contour line provide an appropriate basis for comparison.

Airport impacts on average property values

The impact of proximity to the airport was evaluated using average property values for comparable housing units in 10 census tracts in southwest King County immediately around Sea-Tac International Airport and 10 census tracts in northwest King County—the area that generally conforms to the city of Shoreline.

Northwest King County was chosen for comparison based on the following criteria:

- The census tracts are all located in King County and are equally affected by county and state land use and development policies. The census tracts are all bordered by Puget Sound to the west and Lake Washington to the east.
- Both clusters of census tracts contain commercial areas bordering Highway 99, and both have a mix of residential areas ranging from low/moderate income to high/upper income.
- Both clusters of census tracts contain racially and ethnically diverse populations.

The cluster of 10 census tracts around the airport contained 17,046 housing units in 1990, of which 11,526 (67.6%) were single-family. The cluster of 10 census tracts in northwest King County contained 19,523 housing units in 1990, of which 12,683 (65.0%) were single-family.

The following parameters were used to screen housing units in the two clusters of census tracts for comparability:

- Only units rated as being in "very good" condition by the King County Assessors Office were included.
- All units with a "view" were excluded.
- All units were in "single-family" zoned areas and were classified as single-family land uses.
- All units had an above-ground structure of 1,000 square feet or more.
- All units were located on lots of between 10,000 and 14,999 square feet.
- All units had three or more bedrooms.
- All units had two or more bathrooms.

These screening criteria excluded the top and the bottom of the distribution of housing units in both areas and resulted in a total of 739 of the 11,526 single-family properties (6.4%) in the 10 census tracts around the airport (southwest King County) and 760 of the 12,683 single-family properties (6.0%) in 10 census tracts in northwest King County being used for comparison of real estate values. Summary statistics from the King County Assessors Office for these units are contained in Exhibit 5.10.

The two groups of properties compared closely in terms of their physical attributes. The difference in average lot size between the southwest and northwest King County properties was 3.3%. The difference in size of structure was 2.0%, in number of bedrooms 1.4%, and in number of baths 0.6%. In terms of property values, however, the differences were more pronounced. The average assessed value of land was 14.1% higher in northwest King County than it was in areas immediately surrounding the airport, and the assessed value of structures was 7.7% higher. The assessed value of land and structures combined was 10.1% higher.

Standardized for view, condition of structure, size of structure, lot size, number of bedrooms, number of baths, zoning, land use, county/state development policies, and similarity of neighborhoods, a housing unit selling for $141,400 in the immediate vicinity of the airport would sell for $155,700, or $14,300 (10.1%) more, if it were located elsewhere.

The average difference of 10.1% in the assessed value of real estate (property plus structure) when all other factors are adjusted for is attributable to the impact of low-flying

Exhibit 5.10 Comparison of Housing Units in Northwest and Sorthwest King County—1993

	Southwest Mean Value	Northwest Mean Value	Difference (SW–NW)	Percent Difference
Size				
Lot size	11,914 sq. ft.	11,522 sq. ft.	+392 sq. ft.	3.3%
Above ground structure size	1,538 sq. ft.	1,507 sq. ft.	-31 sq. ft.	-2.0%
Rooms				
Number of bedrooms	3.6	3.6	0	-1.4%*
Number of bathrooms	2.0	2.0	0	0.6%*
Value				
Assessed value of land	$52,734	$60,181	-$7,447	-14.1%
Assessed value of structure	$88,703	$95,550	-$6,847	-7.7%
Total assessed value	$141,437	$155,731	-$14,294	-10.1%

* Differences due to rounding.
Source: King County Assessors Office

aircraft in the immediate vicinity of Sea-Tac International Airport. The resulting depression of property values as of 1993, taking community differences into account, is shown in Exhibit 5.11.

Exhibit 5.11 Estimated Average Depression in Single-Family Residential Property Values by Community—1993

Community	Actual Average Assessed Value of Housing Unit	Estimated Assessed Value Without Airport	Difference
Burien	$129,900	$143,000	-$13,100
Des Moines	$136,100	$149,800	-$13,700
Federal Way	$142,900	$157,300	-$14,400
Normandy Park	$173,600	$191,100	-$17,500
Tukwila	$122,400	$134,800	-$12,400

Between 1993 and 2000, operations (i.e., landings and takeoffs) at Sea-Tac International Airport are forecast to increase by 39,700, or 11.7%. Between 2000 and 2020, operations are forecast to increase by an additional 62,400, or 16.5%. Applying these same rates of change to the estimated 1993 difference in single-family residential property values caused by aircraft operation at Sea-Tac International Airport produces the depressed values shown

Class V—Imposed Conditions

in Exhibit 5.12. The next to the last column of the table contains the expected reduction of value for the average single-family residential housing unit between 2000 and 2020. The last column shows the average difference in value experienced over the entire 20-year period 2000 through 2020.

There will be no reduction in property value attributable to the Sea-Tac International Airport expansion until 2000. The decline will be small the first year because there will be few operations over the airport's annual service volume (ASV). As operations over the ASV threshold increase, the relative decline in property value will increase, reaching, in the case of Burien, $36,356 in 2020. Averaged over the entire 20-year period, the decline is $13,179, as shown in the last column of Exhibit 5.12.

This loss of value occurs after Sea-Tac International Airport would have reached its ASV capacity limit had the third runway and related facility improvements not been built.

Exhibit 5.12 Forecast of Average Depression in Single-Family Residential Property Values Caused by Aircraft Operations at Sea-Tac

Community	1993	2000	2020	Change 2000-2020	Average Difference 2000-2020
Burien	-$13,100	-$29,831	-$56,187	-$26,356	-$13,179
Des Moines	-$13,700	-$31,227	-$58,835	-$27,608	-$13,804
Federal Way	-$14,400	-$32,804	-$61,795	-$28,991	-$14,496
Normandy Park	-$17,500	-$39,859	-$75,079	-$35,220	-$17,610
Tukwila	-$12,400	-$28,172	-$53,016	-$24,844	-$12,422

Flight track impacts on average property values

The impact on a parcel's value of its location under, or in close proximity to, the approach/departure flight track of aircraft operating at Sea-Tac International Airport was estimated using the following linear regression model:

$$y = a + \hat{a}_1 X_1 + \hat{a}_2 X_2 + \hat{a}_3 X_3 + \hat{a}_4 X_4 + \hat{a}_5 X_5 + \hat{a}_6 X_6 + \hat{a}_7 X_7 + \hat{a}_8 X_8 + \hat{a}_9 X_9 + \hat{a}_{10} X_{10}$$

where:

y = Assessed value of land and structures
X_1 = Lot size (square feet)
X_2 = Structure size (square feet)
X_3 = Number of bedrooms
X_4 = Number of bathrooms
X_5 = Distance from center of jet flight track (east of runway 16/34R or west of runway 16/34L), measured in tenths of a mile
X_6 = A binary variable representing the city of Des Moines
X_7 = A binary variable representing the city of Normandy Park
X_8 = A binary variable representing the city of Sea-Tac
X_9 = A binary variable representing Unincorporated King County
X_{10} = A binary variable representing the city of Tukwila

The model's parameters were estimated from assessors data on 3,026 properties in 10 census tracts in the immediate vicinity of the airport. The regression coefficient (adjusted R^2) was 0.65.

The model initially contained variables for the cities of Federal Way and Kent, but these places had too few cases to be meaningful and were dropped from the final model. The distance from each parcel to the center of the airport was also initially used as a variable, but its coefficient was not statistically significant and it was also dropped from the final model. The following housing units were excluded in estimating the regression model:

- Units with fewer than three bedrooms
- Units whose condition was less than "good" or "very good"
- Units with a view
- Units not in single-family residential zoned areas

The ratio of the regression's standard error to the standard deviation of the dependent variable was 0.59. The log likelihood ratio was -35379, and the F-statistic was 566. The Durbin-Watson statistic was 1.44.

All of the independent variables in the model were statistically significant at the 90% level, and seven were statistically significant at the 99% level. The variable measuring a property distance from a flight track was significant at the 99% level.

The coefficient on the variable for distance from a jet aircraft flight track was 17,784, meaning that all other things remaining equal, the value of a house and lot increases by about 3.4% ($4,450 on the average valued house of $129,900) for every one-quarter mile the house is farther away from being directly underneath the flight track of departing/approaching jet aircraft. This relationship is shown in Exhibit 5.13 and illustrated in Exhibit 5.14.

Exhibit 5.13 Model Estimated Impact of Jet Flight Track on Average Property Values

Miles from Flight Track	Burien	Des Moines	Federal Way	Normandy Park	Tukwila
0.00	$104,151	$109,122	$114,574	$139,189	$98,138
0.25	$107,843	$112,990	$118,636	$144,123	$101,617
0.50	$111 666	$116,996	$122,241	$149,232	$105,210
0.75	$115,625	$121,143	$127,196	$154,522	$108,949
1.00	$119,724	$125,438	$131,705	$160,000	$112,811
1.25	$123,822	$129,732	$136,214	$165,478	$116,673
1.50	$128,062	$134,174	$140,878	$171,143	$120,668
1.75	$132,446	$138,767	$145,701	$177,002	$124,799
2.00	$136,980	$143,518	$150,689	$183,062	$129,072

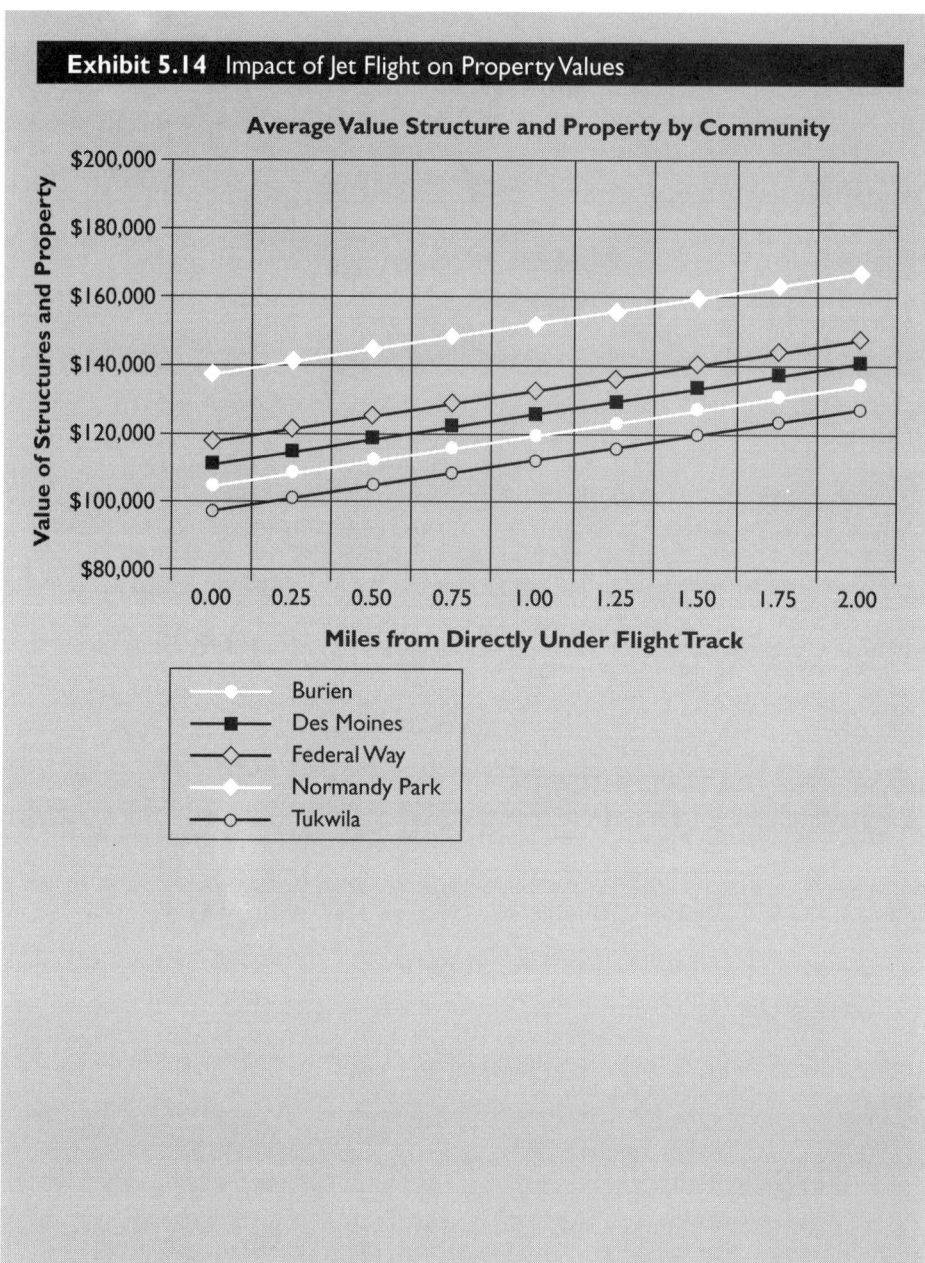

Exhibit 5.14 Impact of Jet Flight on Property Values

Real Estate Damages: An Analysis of Detrimental Conditions

CHAPTER 6

Class VI—Building Construction Conditions

Class VI includes all detrimental conditions associated with the construction of the improvements, such as construction defects, improvements not built to code, ADA noncompliance, and functional obsolescence. It also includes issues of poor workmanship that may result in leaks, plumbing or electrical problems, and other issues.

A basic premise of Class VI detrimental conditions is that they are *man-made* construction defects, which generally means that they can be physically repaired. However, they may or may not be able to be repaired economically. (See Exhibit 6.1 for common construction terms.) Within the analysis of detrimental conditions, a distinction is made between above- and below-grade construction defects to reflect the fact that those above grade are generally much easier to access, assess, and repair. Class VI detrimental conditions involve construction issues above grade. As such, they often result in the full value of the property being restored upon the completion of the repairs. Sometimes the problems are self-evident, and no special studies are required to determine the scope of the problem; however, all detrimental condition stages and issues should be addressed.

Quantifying these types of detrimental conditions involves studying the cost of repairs, engineering, and related costs such as relocating the tenant, free rent for the tenant while repairs are being made, post-repair cleanup, etc. Some tenant relocation costs can be at least partially, if not entirely, mitigated simply by waiting until the property is vacant to make the repairs.

In the primary graph of Exhibit 6.2., Class VII super-surface construction issues reflect a drop in value upon the discovery of the condition and a return to full value upon the repair of the condition. In some circumstances, as shown in the secondary graph, there may be an ongoing condition that remains because it is not physically or economically possible to cure, thereby resulting in a permanent loss in the value of the improvements.

To illustrate the latter situation, consider the Ashby Building, a three-story, 45,600-sq.-ft. mixed-use complex in Eugene, Oregon. The ground level has retail uses, while the upper levels have mixed office and apartment uses. The building was constructed in 1991 with a frame and stucco design. The builder failed to install the insulation required by the architectural plans, and as a result the property is very "energy inefficient." In addition, the building is "noisy," with sound traveling between rooms because of the lack of insulation. Most of the tenants have lodged complaints with the owner over these issues.

Class VI detrimental conditions are above-grade construction issues and may be relatively easy to access. Because Class VI situations are man-made problems, they can generally be repaired, and, once fully repaired, the property will typically return to full value.

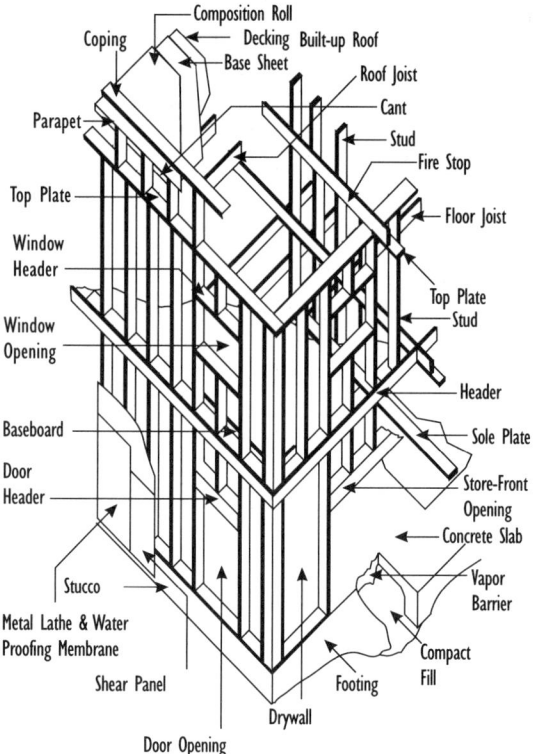

Exhibit 6.1 Building Diagram

The issues of economics of the situation must be examined carefully. If the damages cannot be fully repaired for economic reasons, there may be an ongoing condition that results in a diminution in value. For the Ashby Building, the income levels would need to justify the intrusive repairs to install insulation in all the walls (curable functional obsolescence versus incurable functional obsolescence). Under this condition, there is a permanent loss of value because the condition remains, or is perceived to remain, unchanged over time.

There is no general rule for comparing or correlating the costs of the repairs with loss of value. As an extreme example, if a 747 jet airliner has a $5 fuse go out, the delay may cause the flight to be canceled at a loss of revenue of $50,000. Likewise, a relatively small matter may cause very significant loss of value in a building. Of course, common sense must play a role in diminution in value studies. Unless a liability is caused by the detrimental condition, the loss cannot exceed the value of the property. For example, if a property has a value of $250,000 and is impacted by the discovery of major construction defects within the improvements, the maximum loss would be the undamaged value less the contributing value of the improvements and demolition costs. In other words, the value could not fall below the land value less demolition costs.

Exhibit 6.2 Class VI—Building Construction Conditions

The primary and secondary graphs for DC Class VI have been highlighted here; however, DCs have a variety of impacts, which, upon analysis, vary on a case-by-case basis. Ultimately any graph may be applicable based on the case-specific facts.

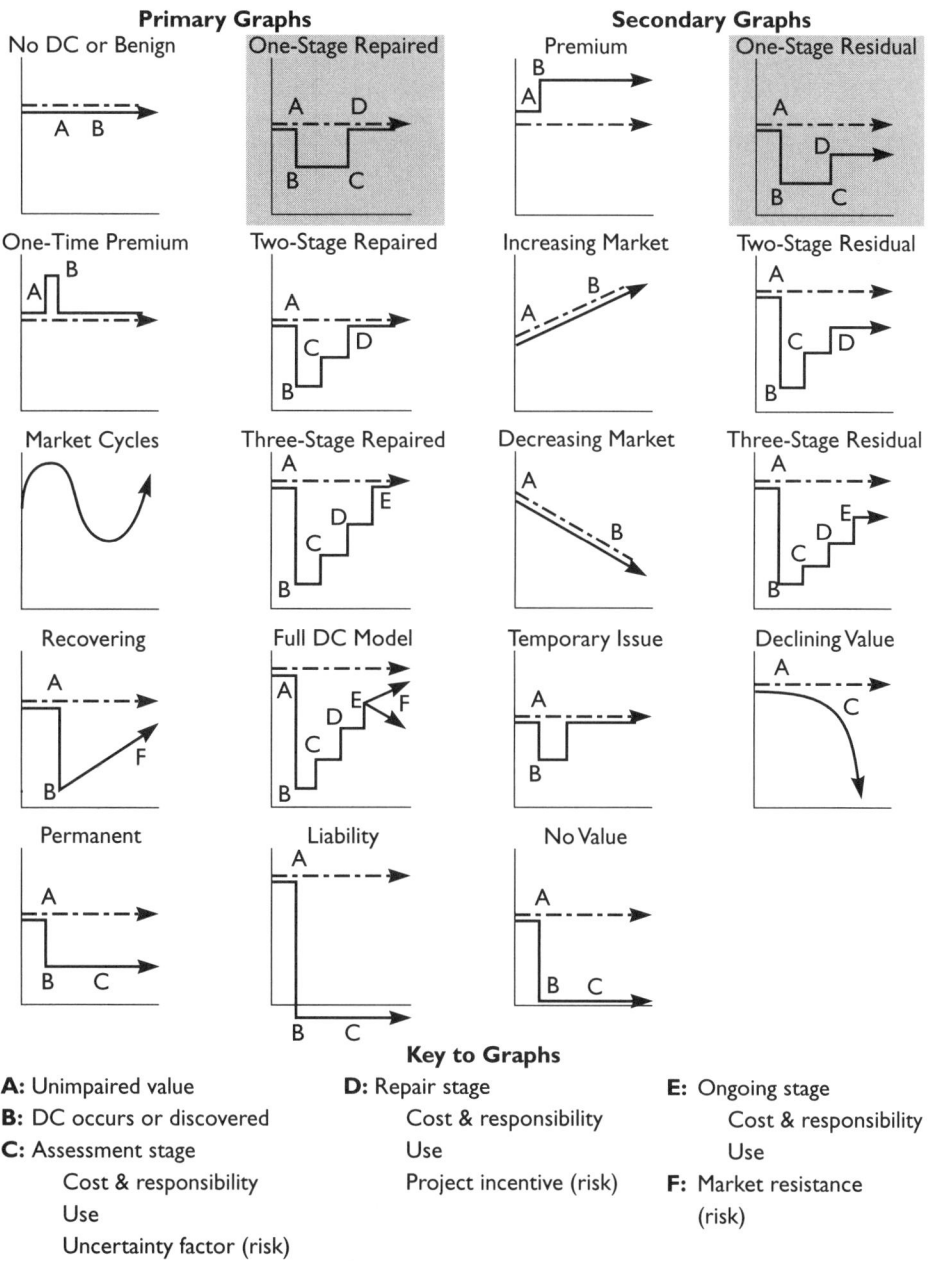

Key to Graphs

- **A:** Unimpaired value
- **B:** DC occurs or discovered
- **C:** Assessment stage
  - Cost & responsibility
  - Use
  - Uncertainty factor (risk)
- **D:** Repair stage
  - Cost & responsibility
  - Use
  - Project incentive (risk)
- **E:** Ongoing stage
  - Cost & responsibility
  - Use
- **F:** Market resistance
  - (risk)

Source: Bell's Guide: The Real Estate Encyclopedia

Chapter 6 Case Study

By Richard A. Neustein, MAI, SRA

Fine Mountain Condominiums
Class VI Detrimental Condition—Construction Defect

This situation involves a construction defects matter for a 543-unit condominium project, which was built in phases from 1982 to 1988. Owners of individual units encountered various problems (plumbing, roof leaks, etc.), but it took a few years for the home owners to become aware that these were project-wide problems. In 1991, the board of directors of the home owners association sent a letter to each home owner giving notice of the systemic nature of the problems, the likelihood that a lawsuit might ensue, and the home owner's obligation to disclose this information to a prospective purchaser.

The engineering estimates of repair cost amounted to approximately half of the value in the undamaged condition. The appraisal analyses for this matter were done in mid-1995. The market had risen in the late 1980s, peaked in the early 1990s, and then turned down as a protracted recession brought about a general lowering of market values, which was still in effect in 1995.

In order to investigate this market, approximately 1,500 sales of condominiums within the city were downloaded from a phone-linked computer database that was based on public records. The transactions included both one- and two-bedroom units, reflecting the mix in the subject property, and included sales from the beginning of 1988 through mid-1995. Approximately 10% of these sales were tested and verified by MLS files and/or private broker records. The unit value investigated was price per square foot of living area.

The pattern of values depicted in Exhibit 6.3 conforms to general knowledge about market trends but reveals little about whether values of the subject property moved with the market. In order to make this distinction, the data points for sales at the subject property were kept dark, while those for sales at all other projects were made white so that they would fade into the background. This feature is available in most spreadsheet programs. The result is the following foreground/background graph (Exhibit 6.4).

In Exhibit 6.4 it is easy to see that during the late 1980s the price per square foot paid at the subject property was near the upper end of the range for the market. Values at the subject property then declined with respect to the market until they reached the lower end of the range from 1994 to 1995. This suggests that while the entire market had gone up and then down, the subject property had started higher and fallen farther than the market in general.

Trend lines were added to the graph in order to aid the visualization of the pattern. It is noteworthy that as the trend line for the subject property declined, it crossed the trend line for the general market at approximately the time when home owners at the subject property were first required to disclose defects to prospective purchasers.

In this case, foreground/background analysis was an aid to visualizing and evaluating subtle value changes that were not easily discernible by such techniques as paired sales analysis.

Exhibit 6.3 and 6.4 Price per Square Foot Paid for Condominium Units

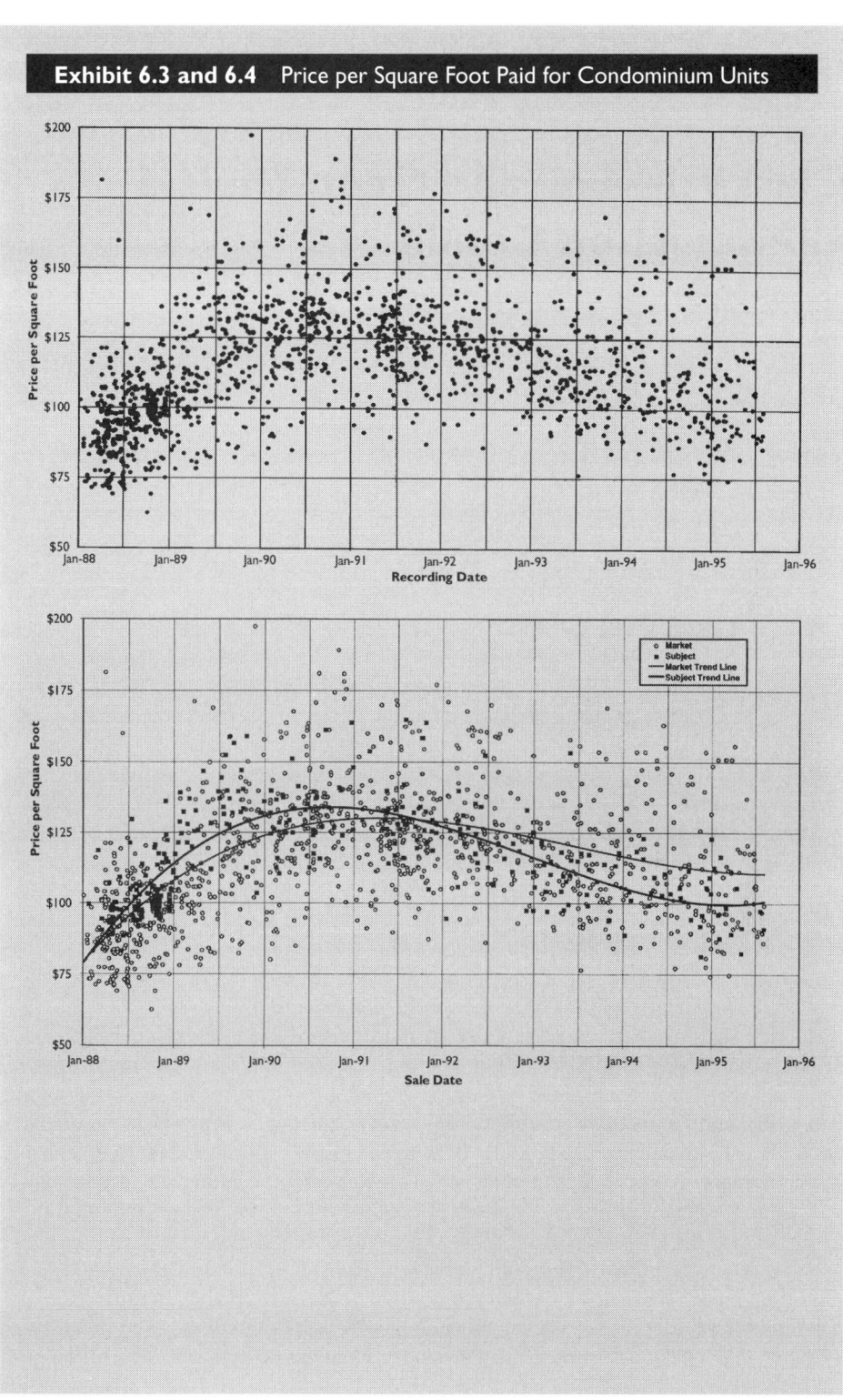

Class VI—Building Construction Conditions

CHAPTER 7

Class VII—Soil and Geotechnical Construction Conditions

Class VII detrimental conditions involve soils and geotechnical construction issues below grade. Generally, these problems are more difficult to repair than Class VI conditions because of the challenges of assessing conditions below grade and the associated drilling, coring, and earth moving. This category of detrimental conditions could include site grading, soil cut, soil fill, soil compacting, slopes, drainage, tunneling, and retaining walls.

There are two basic categories of geotechnical problems. First are those that occur naturally, such as expansive soils, subsidence of unstable soils, slope creep, slope instability, etc. Second are those that are construction defects, or "man-made" problems, such as improperly compacted soils, improper construction, leaking pipes under the foundation, inadequate drainage, retaining walls, or slopes, etc. Both situations may result in the foundation cracking, cracks in walls, doors and windows going out-of-joint, and other problems. This chapter addresses the man-made problems.

Tell-tale signs of geotechnical problems include cracks in the foundation, walls, driveway, porch, or garage. Also, a sinking foundation is a symptom of soil problems. Some problems may be prevented by sloping the yard away from the house and installing rain gutters and spouts to divert water away from the foundation. Any cracks should be promptly patched and any leaks should be quickly repaired. It is important to note that when dealing with geotechnical problems, the problem must be addressed, not just the symptoms. If only the symptom is addressed (i.e., the cracked foundation and not the underlying cause), the problem may reoccur or even worsen.

As shown in the primary graph of Exhibit 7.1, Class VII subsurface construction conditions reflect a loss in value when the condition is discovered and a return to the nonimpacted value upon the assessment and repair of the condition. In some situations, as shown in the secondary graph, there may be residual market resistance remaining even after repairs are made.

Exhibit 7.1 Class VII—Soil and Geotechnical Construction Conditions

The primary and secondary graphs for DC Class VII have been highlighted here; however, DCs have a variety of impacts, which, upon analysis, vary on a case-by-case basis. Ultimately, any graph may be applicable based upon the case-specific facts.

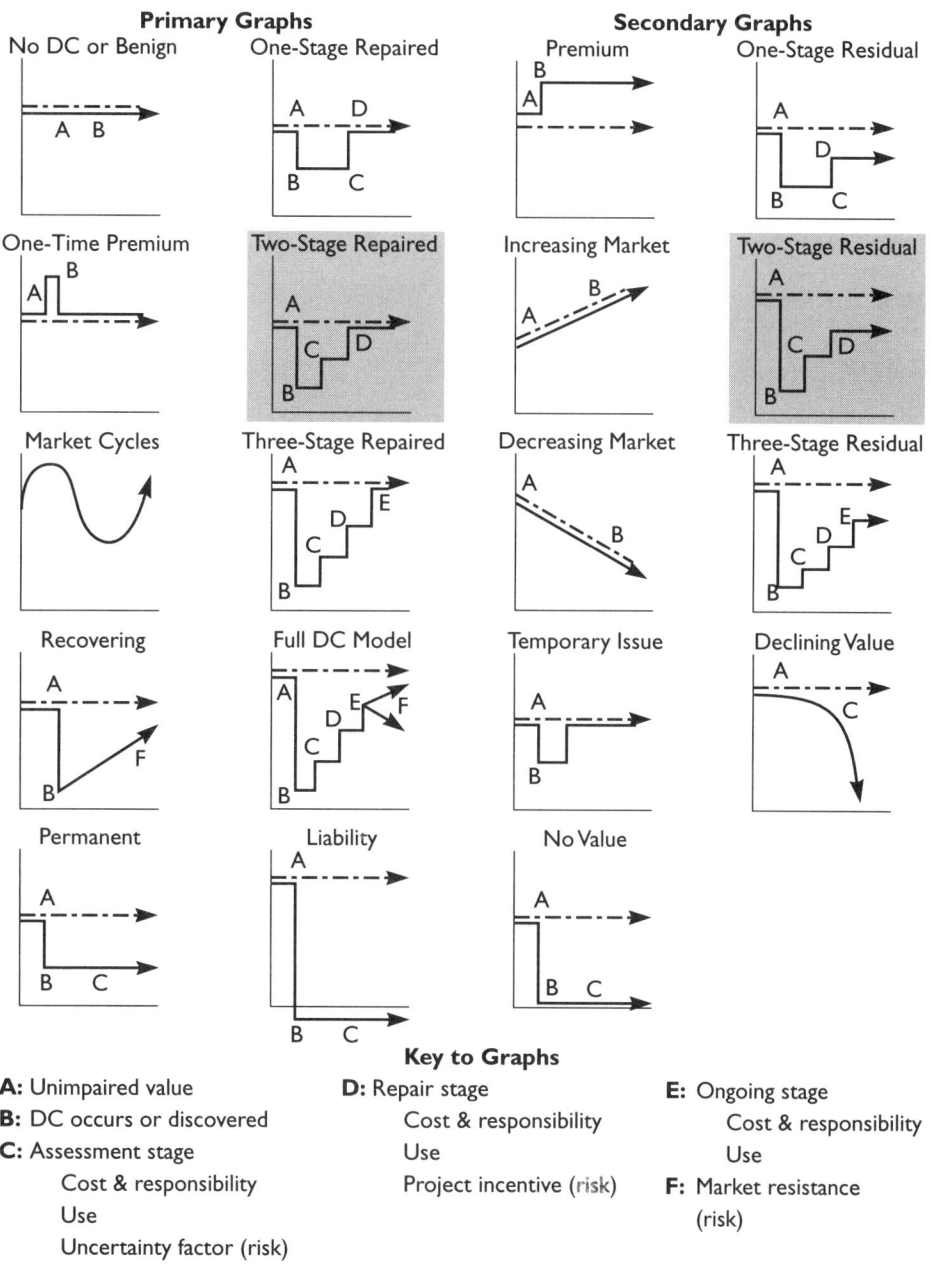

Key to Graphs

A: Unimpaired value
B: DC occurs or discovered
C: Assessment stage
    Cost & responsibility
    Use
    Uncertainty factor (risk)

D: Repair stage
    Cost & responsibility
    Use
    Project incentive (risk)

E: Ongoing stage
    Cost & responsibility
    Use
F: Market resistance
    (risk)

Source: *Bell's Guide: The Real Estate Encyclopedia*

These issues can be illustrated through the example of Preston Manor, a low-income housing development outside of Cleveland, Ohio. The area has slightly rolling topography, and a number of small hills were graded to fill in the "valleys." The contractors did not properly compact the soils, so after the homes were built, several experienced differential settlement. A number of foundations cracked, and the community pool leaned to one side, causing the water level to be three inches higher on one side. The soils engineers agreed that the soils had then fully settled.

With Class VII detrimental conditions, subterranean problems often require drilling and soils samples in order to determine the problems. Appraisers and analysts have an ethical obligation to consider the reasonableness of the soils reports and any report they rely on. Appraisers and analysts should also be aware that various remediation efforts are more effective than others, and the economics of the repair costs as compared to the benefits should be considered. Also, the likelihood and perception of the problems recurring should be considered. With any detrimental condition, scientific opinions are important, but the perceptions of the market drive property values.

Geotechnical Issues

Geotechnics involves the use of engineering principles to understand the behavior and interaction of earth materials, including solid materials (rock and soil) and fluid materials (water and gases). Geotechnical expertise is often critical in design and construction, and the failure of buildings or other structures due to geotechnical problems often requires the services of an appraiser or analyst to measure loss in value. Such problems include casualty losses caused by natural forces such as earthquakes, sinkholes, and landslides, as well as man-made problems resulting from accidental damage or construction defects.

Although detailed knowledge of geotechnics is well beyond the expertise of most appraisers, an elementary understanding of some of the types of situations likely to be encountered is helpful. While geotechnical problems often involve the physical movement and associated damage of structural improvements, damage can sometimes result from other factors. Where movement of structures results in damage, such damage can be sudden, as in an earthquake, or much more gradual, as in subsidence or settlement. Because the sources of geotechnical problems are often located beneath the surface, determining the appropriate repairs and associated costs often requires estimates, which may leave residual uncertainty as to the effectiveness of repairs and probability of recurrence.

Some knowledge of geotechnical issues is therefore essential for appraisers and analysts involved in this type of work, allowing communication with engineers, geologists, and other professionals, as well as proper evaluation of significant detrimental condition factors, including cost of repair, loss of use, ongoing costs, incentives, and market resistance.

Settlement

While buildings may be founded on bedrock or have loads that are transferable to bedrock via caissons or piles, many structures are built on unconsolidated material (i.e., soil) where bedrock is too far below the surface to feasibly provide support. Imposition of vertical loads to the ground results in consolidation of the soil, causing all buildings to settle. Modern construction invariably makes an allowance for normal settlement, which is considered acceptable if not excessive or differential.

Uniform settlement is considered excessive only if it is at a magnitude that threatens underground infrastructure (utilities, pipelines, etc.) or disrupts surface drainage. Differential settlement is generally much more problematic and tends to produce the greatest damage to structural improvements, as shown in Exhibit 7.2. The Leaning Tower of Pisa, Italy, is perhaps the best-known example of this phenomenon.

Differential settlement can occur on both natural and filled soils, but it is generally more prevalent on filled ground, particularly with deep fills and differing fill thicknesses, and common with cut and fill grading on hilly topography. Settlement may also occur where there is a buried stratum of weak soil beneath a site, particularly organic soils that can hold many times their weight of groundwater, commonly known by topographic names such as *bogs*, *marsh*, *peat*, and *swamps;* these are often not detected at the time of original construction and are particularly prone to settlement and associated structural failure.

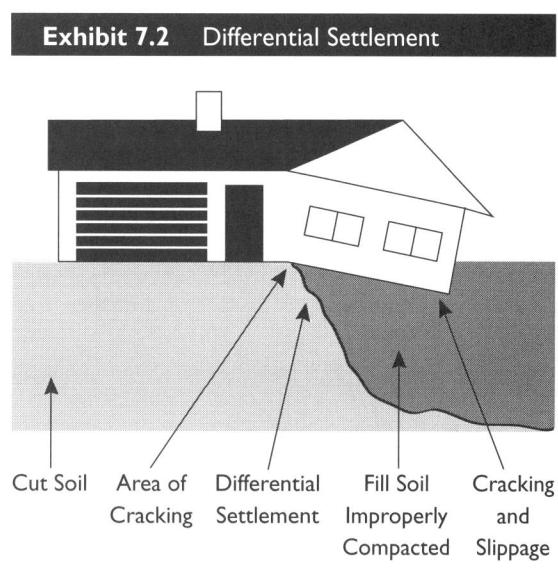

Exhibit 7.2 Differential Settlement

Cut Soil | Area of Cracking | Differential Settlement | Fill Soil Improperly Compacted | Cracking and Slippage

Geotechnical problems are as old as civilization itself. The ancient city of Machu Picchu in Peru has suffered from ground settlement problems. The stones that normally fit so well that a knife blade would not fit in between are now separating in some areas because of differential settlement.

Subsidence

Subsidence is related to settlement, often caused by the extraction of underlying minerals, water, oil, or natural gas. Where settlement is usually a localized condition, subsidence is normally spread over a wide area, which may have less impact on individual properties. Even so, subsidence over a wide, low-lying area might lead to increased risk of flooding. Extraction of minerals or other materials is often accompanied by injection of water to replace the material removed, which is designed to minimize subsidence. Sinkholes are a related but much more localized phenomenon.

Expansive Soils

Expansive soils are generally those with a high clay content, which experience volume changes in response to moisture changes. Such soils tend to expand when wet and shrink when dry, and they are capable of generating forces that can easily lift buildings. It is estimated that expansive soils cause more damage annually than the combined impact of floods, hurricanes, tornadoes, and earthquakes. Differential movement is the main problem of expansive soils, especially when allowed to become saturated or dry at varying locations. Heavy vegetation, especially large trees, planted in expansive soils close to buildings are particularly troublesome, drawing large quantities of water, which can dry the soil and undermine support for adjacent structures.

Slope Movement

Slope movement is an all-inclusive term encompassing both sudden movements, popularly known as *landslides,* and more gradual movements such as subsidence. Slope movements are often classified by type of failure, including falls, topples, slides, spreads, and flows. Slope movement is a natural occurrence due to the force of gravity but can be exacerbated by increased loading from buildings or accumulation of moisture.

Slope instability often develops slowly over time, with sudden landslides usually the result of a critical event such as an earthquake. Changes in groundwater conditions from overwatering, water retention from devegetation, and/or heavy rainfall are frequently to blame for landslides, causing an increase in the effective weight of the soil and weakening unconsolidated materials.

Slope movement involving deep failures frequently occurs on the site of ancient slides, which are inherently unstable, and can be reactivated by head loading (grading on top of the hill) or toe removal (excavating the "toe" of a hill). Unstable natural slope conditions often involve sedimentary bedrock and layers of clay. These conditions can usually be mapped based upon topographic interpretation of aerial photographs but are sometimes missed during preliminary site investigations, leading to subsequent structural failures, often many years after original construction.

Slopes composed of clay soils are most susceptible to shallow failures, due to both a decrease in the frictional resistance of saturated soils with a high content of clay minerals and a decrease in permeability when compared to sandy soils. The expansive qualities of clay soil are also instrumental in generating a phenomenon known as *slope creep*, in which soil moves outward and downward during successive cycles of wetting and drying.

Erosion

While clay soils are often a contributing factor to slope instability, erosion can be a problem in areas of sandy soil. Erosion is most prevalent along coastal beaches, lakeshores, and coastal bluffs. Erosion can be generated by a number of factors, primarily water and wind, and can act on both rock and soil.

Volcanoes and Earthquakes

Volcanoes and earthquakes are natural disasters, among the most powerful geologic forces known to man. Major earthquakes and volcanic eruptions are not frequent, but as the most devastating of natural phenomena, they often result in severe property damage, injury, or death, as discussed more fully in Chapter 9. Earthquakes are particularly affected by local geologic conditions, which can significantly impact the intensity and duration of tremors.

Liquefaction

Liquefaction is strongly associated with seismicity, involving the temporary loss of shear resistance in the soil, which is transformed into a fluid mass (similar to quicksand) during an earthquake. Liquefaction occurs almost exclusively in water-saturated sandy soils that are exposed to strong tremors, causing the soil to lose strength as water pressure increases and absorbs more load, predictably impacting the structural integrity of buildings.

Sulfates/Corrosives

Building foundations are typically constructed of concrete, a material whose service life and durability can be impacted by many factors, including environmental exposure to deleterious compounds of sulfates or chlorides, frost, fire, etc. Sulfates are naturally occurring mineral salts in sedimentary rock and some soils, and they are widely acknowledged as corrosive due to chemical reactions between the cement and sulfate salts, resulting in deterioration of concrete when sulfates are present in sufficient concentration.

The effects of sulfates on concrete have been known for many years and can usually be prevented by use of the proper cement type, water-cement ratio, and/or admixtures that make the concrete less permeable and more resistant to sulfate attack. Moisture barriers are also helpful in protecting concrete from sulfate damage, although common plastic moisture barriers often lack integrity, particularly where penetrations are necessary for plumbing or mechanical systems.

Other natural compounds may also attack concrete, which has been noted particularly in areas previously used for dairy operations. Slabs and other large expanses of relatively thin concrete are most vulnerable, although footings have also been known to sustain damage due to the action of sulfates and other corrosive materials.

The consideration of soil mechanics is much more prevalent now than in the past, although there is still a vast array of inherent problems associated with construction and soils. An additional problem is lack of funds for adequate site investigation in many cases, which sometimes leads to discovery of serious geotechnical difficulties long after completion of construction.

Core samples are taken to determine the thickness and quality of the concrete and foundation construction. Here two workers are drilling samples for analysis.

Remediation of geotechnical problems may be accomplished by a variety of methods, including excavation and removal of defective soils, de-watering, foundation replacement or underpinning, soil grouting, construction of retaining structures, and so forth. Such remedies will invariably involve engineering professionals, although it is important for the appraiser or analyst to get an adequate layman's understanding of the proposed fix and its estimated effectiveness.

There are three primary repairs made to cracked foundations or other structural damages caused by geotechnical or natural forces. These are

1. reinforced repair
2. underpinning
3. caissons or piles

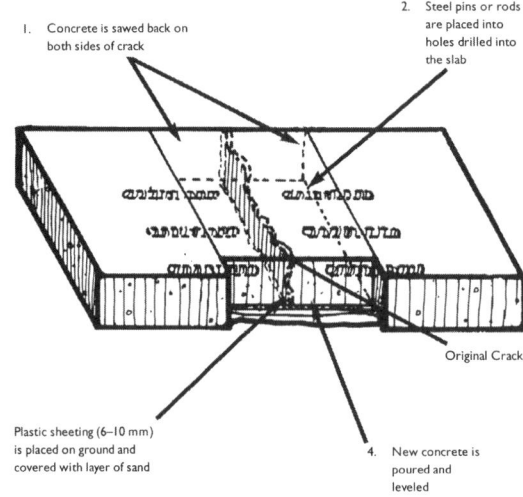

Exhibit 7.3   Reinforced Repair for Cracked Foundation

Small cracks may be filled by injecting epoxy. Larger cracks require this four-step process.

1. Concrete is sawed back on both sides of crack
2. Steel pins or rods are placed into holes drilled into the slab
3. Plastic sheeting (6–10 mm) is placed on ground and covered with layer of sand
4. New concrete is poured and leveled

Original Crack

The reinforced repair for cracked foundations involves small cracks that may be filled by injecting epoxy. Larger cracks require a multiple-step process whereby the crack is saw cut on both sides, the slab is drilled for steel dowels, and the area is refilled with concrete, as shown in Exhibit 7.3. Underpinning may be used in a situation where the foundation has settled and can be lifted back into place, as shown in Exhibit 7.4. This repair is used where the soils have subsided because of hillside construction, drainage problems, expansive soils, and improper soil compaction. With the most serious geotechnical problems, caissons (columns with a widened base) or piles (columns only) may be utilized to set the structure upon firm bedrock or to prevent soil movement in a hillside area. These structures may be over 50 feet in depth and several feet in circumference. Both caissons and piles are constructed of steel-reinforced concrete, as shown in Exhibit 7.5.

Valuation Analysis

Class VII detrimental conditions can often be assessed and repaired, even if doing so requires reinforced foundations or underpinning the improvements. As with Class VI detrimental conditions, calculating the diminution in value involves the review of the functional utility of the property, repairs that are necessary to prevent a loss to life or property, repair costs, engineering costs, disruption to the property, and so on. Additionally, like Class VI detrimental conditions, these conditions are man-made and can generally be physically corrected. In some extreme conditions, however, if the condition cannot be fully assessed or repaired, there may be an ongoing condition that impacts the value if the remaining issue diminishes the functional utility of the property or creates an ongoing issue that is perceived to impact the value. Like Class VI detrimental conditions, the functional use of the property must be carefully reviewed, as well as necessary repairs.

For example, if a site has fill soil that is up to 100 feet deep and differential settlement occurs, it may not be economically or physically possible to install the

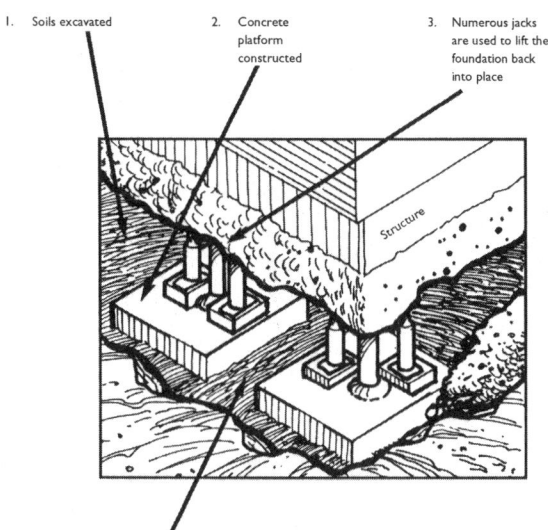

Exhibit 7.4 Underpinning

1. Soils excavated
2. Concrete platform constructed
3. Numerous jacks are used to lift the foundation back into place
4. The excavated area is filled with concrete. The jacks may be removed or left in place. This process often causes significant cracking in both exterior and interior walls, which are then repaired

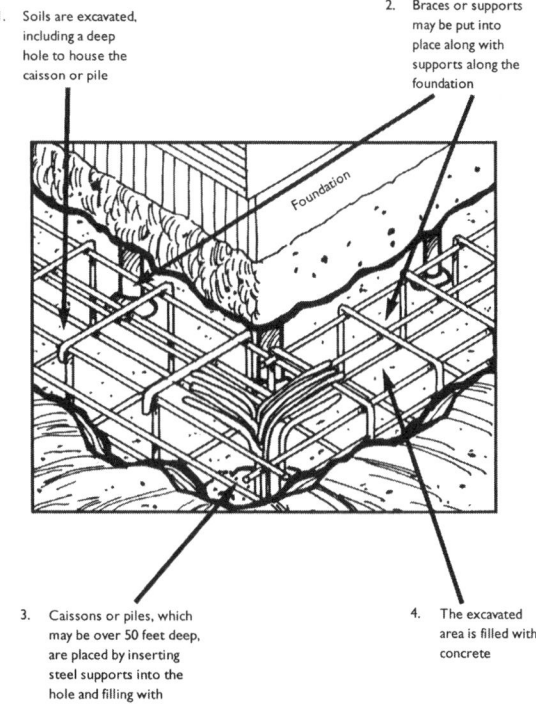

Exhibit 7.5 Caissons or Piles

1. Soils are excavated, including a deep hole to house the caisson or pile
2. Braces or supports may be put into place along with supports along the foundation
3. Caissons or piles, which may be over 50 feet deep, are placed by inserting steel supports into the hole and filling with concrete
4. The excavated area is filled with concrete

piles and extra building foundations to the bedrock that would support the improvements and fully mitigate the situation. As a result, it may be reasonable to expect that the property will be more prone to earthquake damage or continued settlement damage. A naturally occurring sinkhole may be a sign of significant further risk of future subsidence. In this type of condition, the value of the property may be permanently impaired, as opposed to other Class VI and VII detrimental conditions where the problem can be economically and physically cured.

On the other hand, some construction defects may be so minor that they do not have any effect on the rental rates paid by tenants, on liability, or on the utility of the property, and therefore those conditions may not be Class VI or VII detrimental conditions at all. For example, if improperly compacted shallow soils cause some minor settlement cracks in the floor area of a warehouse building and similar settlement cracks are commonly found in comparable properties with no known soils problems, the issue may not have any impact on value. This is particularly true if the tenants' use of the property is unaffected by the condition and if the marketability of the space is comparable with other similar properties.

Further Reading

Tunneling

Lea, Robert M. "Subway Tunnel Easement in Metropolitan Areas." *The Appraisal Journal* (April 1994).

Toma, Darrell M. "The Effects of Pipelines on Agricultural Land Values." *Right of Way* (October 1983).

Geotechnical Issues

Sanders, Michael V. "Post-Repair Diminution on Value from Geotechnical Problems." *The Appraisal Journal* (January 1996).

Chapter 7 Case Study

By Michael V. Sanders, MAI, SRA

California Condominiums
Class VII Detrimental Conditions—Construction Defects versus Market Conditions

Construction defect litigation has become increasingly common over the past decade, particularly in situations where prices have declined significantly due to market conditions. Declining values are sometimes blamed on defects related to construction, causing home owners, often through their associations, to sue for these losses. In some parts of the country, this has effectively curtailed the construction of condominiums and other attached for-sale housing. The challenge for the analyst is to determine whether losses in value are due to defects in construction, the litigation, market conditions, or some combination of these.

This study relates to a 300-unit condominium project in Southern California that was constructed in the mid-1980s, consisting of both one-bedroom and two-bedroom floor plans. Residents subsequently filed suit against the developer and subcontractors alleging serious defects in construction. The suit was ultimately settled, with payment to the plaintiff of several million dollars.

Direct sales comparison is often of little help in analyzing this type of situation. Only comparison with sales outside the subject project will allow the appraiser to isolate the effects of the construction defects that are unique to the subject, and the availability of suitably similar comparables is often limited. An alternative is the comparison of prices over time, to ascertain whether or not the subject has experienced price trends different from the market as a whole.

The case study involved the compilation of a 10-year sales history for the subject project dating back to the time of construction, encompassing the litigation and including the period immediately following the settlement. For comparison purposes, similar data were compiled for three other condominium projects in the same market area, verifying that none were impacted by defects or associated litigation over the time period under study. One was a project of similar vintage and roughly comparable prices, and the other two were older projects of inferior appeal with lower prices, though all would be expected to respond similarly to changes in general market conditions.

Exhibit 7.6 is a graphic comparison of price per square foot over the relevant time period for the subject project (Case Study) and the three control properties (designated Projects 1 through 3). If construction defects impacted prices in the subject project, it would be expected that the trendline would have a significantly different shape, sloping downward more sharply than for the other three projects. Instead, however, the trendlines show much the same pattern, suggesting that value declines in the subject project are similar to those experienced by other projects, which would be attributed to a softening of the general market for condominiums, rather than to the impact of alleged defects in construction.

Because the subject and all three control projects have a significant number of two-bedroom units, a comparison of prices for two-bedroom units was also undertaken, reflecting slightly higher correlation with similar results, as shown in Exhibit 7.7.

The same analysis of one-bedroom units in the subject and one other project (not shown) produced similar results.

This type of analysis using a single independent variable (time) is relatively simple and is particularly useful for conforming projects that are large enough to have a substantial

Exhibit 7.6 Price per Square Foot—All Sales

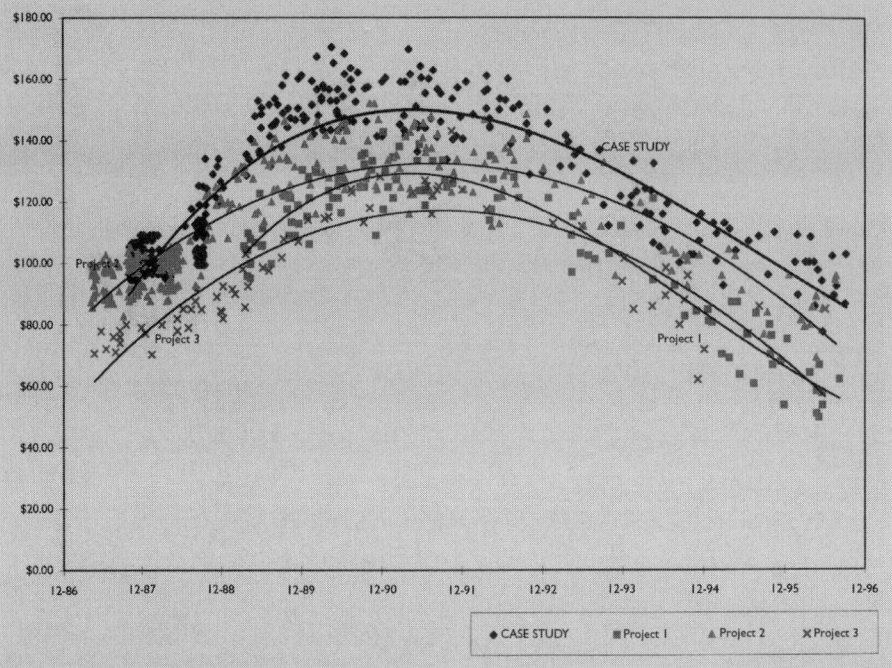

amount of relevant sales data. Similar analyses of sales velocity, time on market, etc. could also be undertaken. Based on price comparison, the case study suggests that value diminution in the subject project could reasonably be attributed to market conditions, rather than to the impact of defective construction.

Exhibit 7.7 Price for Two-Bedroom Units

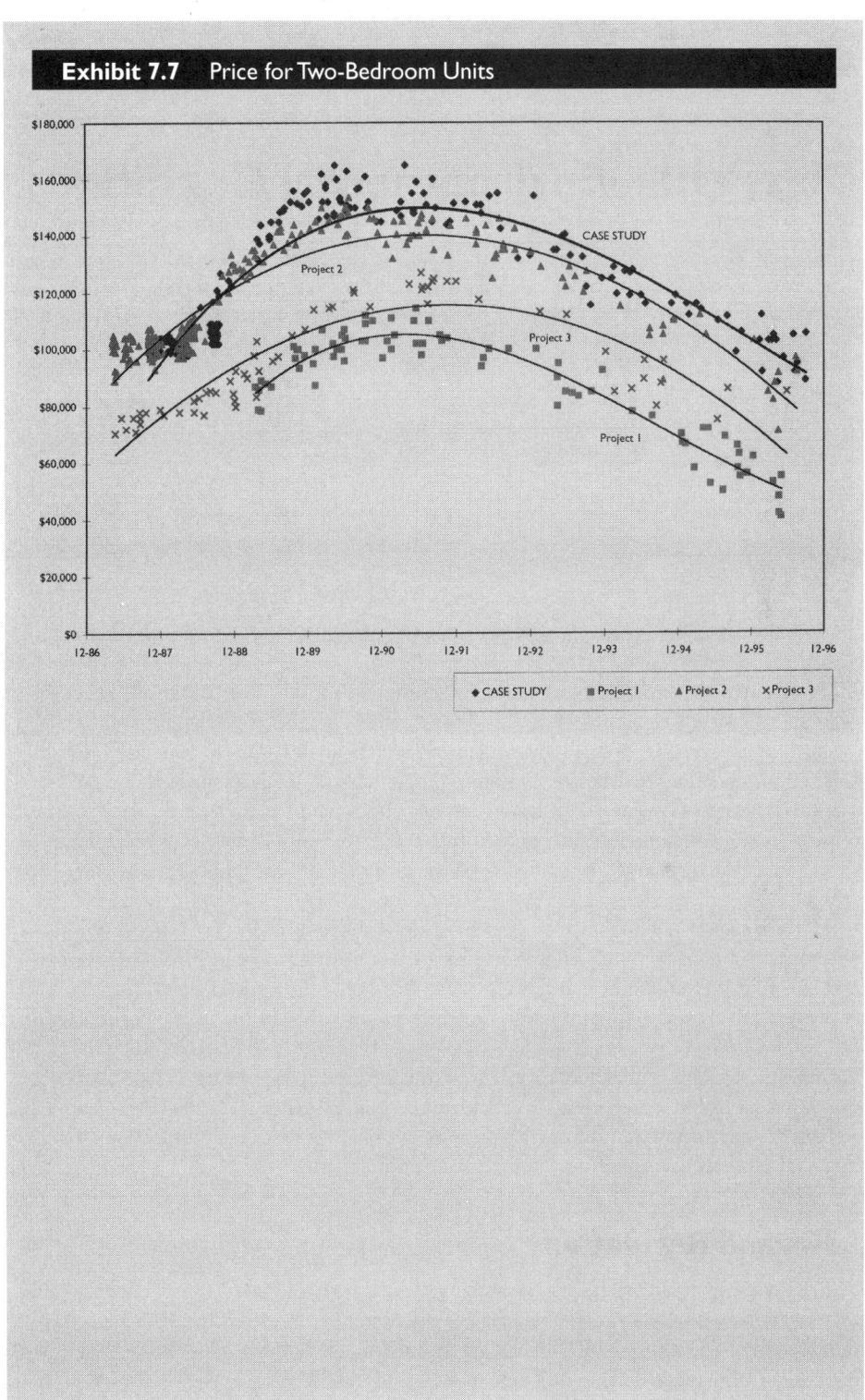

Class VII—Soil and Geotechnical Construction Conditions

CHAPTER 8

Class VIII—Environmental Conditions

Class VIII involves curable, man-made environmental conditions that may be economically and physically repaired. These conditions may affect the improvements, site, subsurface, or even air space. They range from archaeological sites to contamination in soil and groundwater to asbestos containing materials (ACMs), radon, or lead-based paints. Contamination can result from a variety of pollutants being emitted in a number of ways. Some contaminants are released into the air through factory or vehicle emissions. Other are discharged or spilled onto the ground or directly into oceans, lakes, or rivers.

Modern society depends upon many hazardous substances. Fuels are needed for automobiles and to heat buildings. Solvents are necessary for manufacturing processes and also to dry-clean clothes. Other chemicals are needed to control agricultural pests and weeds, to ensure that paint goes onto surfaces smoothly, or to make a plastic bag that keeps food fresh. In years past, society was largely ignorant of the health effects of hazardous materials, but as more was learned, it became apparent that contaminants are directly responsible for a variety of serious diseases and health problems. These and other revelations have prompted new laws and regulations, many of which impose severe financial burdens on property owners, lenders, and tenants.

Laws and Regulations

While environmental laws have been established for many decades, the public was jolted into awareness of the detrimental effects of contamination in the early 1960s with the publication of *Silent Spring* by Rachel Carson, in which the author reported on how the insecticide DDT entered the food chain and caused the thinning of egg shells, which in

Exhibit 8.1 Class VIII—Environmental Conditions

The graphs for DC Class VIII have been highlighted here; however, DCs have a variety of impacts which, upon analysis, vary on a case-by-case basis. Ultimately any graph may be applicable based upon the case-specific facts.

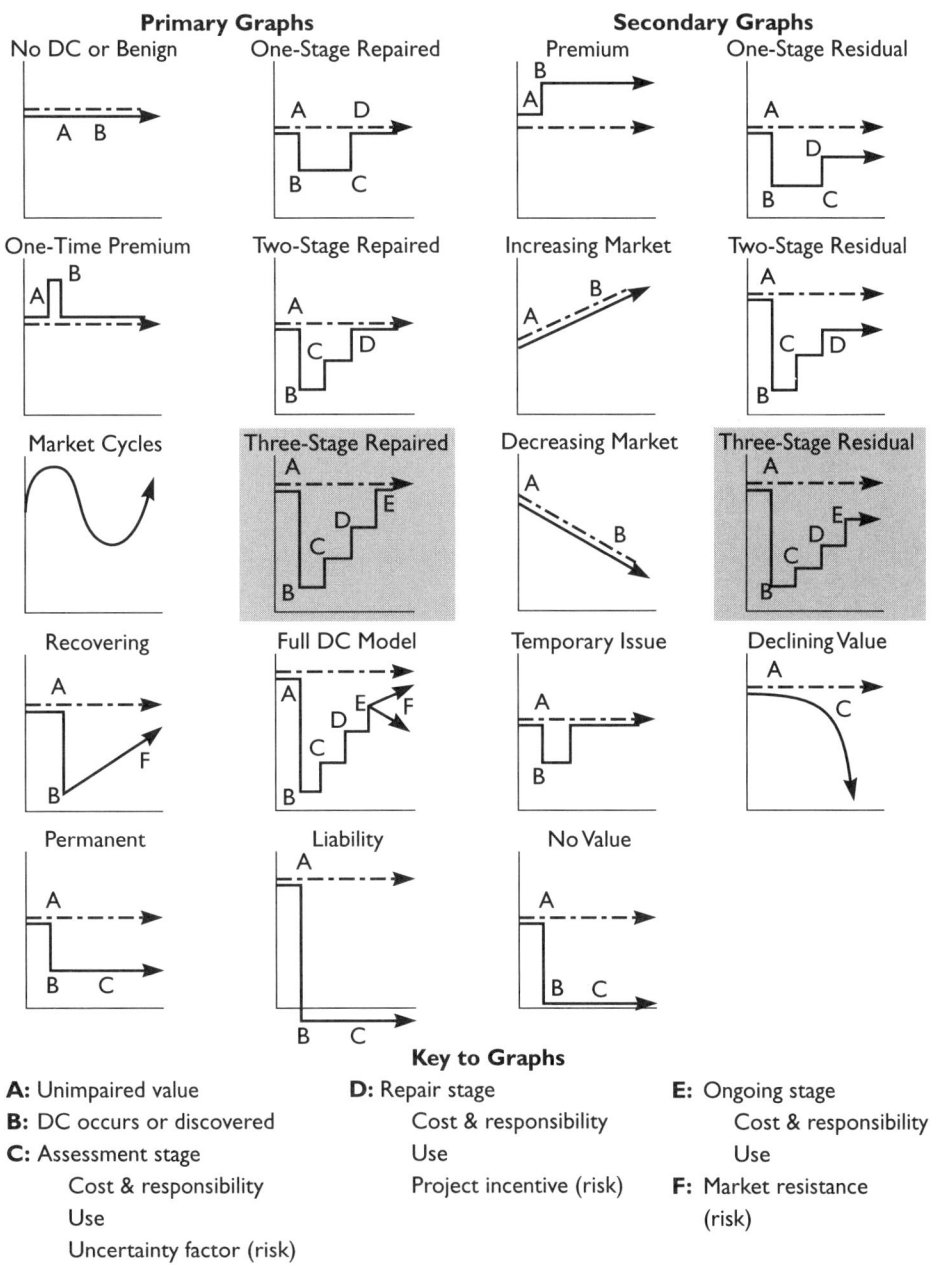

Key to Graphs

- **A:** Unimpaired value
- **B:** DC occurs or discovered
- **C:** Assessment stage
  - Cost & responsibility
  - Use
  - Uncertainty factor (risk)
- **D:** Repair stage
  - Cost & responsibility
  - Use
  - Project incentive (risk)
- **E:** Ongoing stage
  - Cost & responsibility
  - Use
- **F:** Market resistance (risk)

Source: Bell's Guide: The Real Estate Encyclopedia

turn would cause eggs to break before hatching. That book is generally acknowledged as a catalyst for the creation of the modern environmental movement, which spawned a network of new federal, state, and local laws and regulations, as shown in Exhibit 8.2. Two of the more recent acts deserve special attention because they and their derivative regulations established many of the terms and precedents that are almost universally used today. They are the Resource Conservation and Recovery Act (RCRA) of 1976 and the Comprehensive Environmental Response, Compensation, and Liability Act (CERCLA) of 1980, which is commonly referred to as the Superfund Act. The intent of all these laws is to protect human health and the environment from harm caused by hazardous materials.

Exhibit 8.2 Chronology of Selected Environmental Acts, Laws, Regulations, and Cases

Year	Act, Law, Regulation, Policy, or Case
1899	**Rivers and Harbors Act (The "Refuse Act")** Designed to protect navigable waters, especially the Mississippi River system, from floating debris that constituted hazards to navigation.
1947	**Federal Insecticide, Fungicide, and Rodenticide Act (FIFRA)**
1948	**Federal Water Pollution Control Act (Old Clean Water Act)**
1954	**Atomic Energy Act**
1956	**Clean Water Act**
1963	**Clean Air Act (CAA)**
1966	**National Historic Preservation Act**
1967	**Clean Air Act Revision**
1969	**National Environmental Policy Act**
1972	**Marine Protection, Research, and Sanctuaries Act**
1972	**Federal Coastal Zone Management Act**
1972	**Federal Water Pollution Control Act Amendments (Clean Water Act)**
1973	**Federal Endangered Species Act**
1974	**Safe Drinking Water Act**
1976	**Resource Conservation and Recovery Act (RCRA)** Defined what was hazardous and drew a distinction between hazardous material and hazardous waste.
1976	**Toxic Substances Control Act (TSCA)**
1977	**Clean Water Act Amendments**
1978	**Uranium Mill Tailings Radiation Control Act**
1979	**Hazardous Liquid Pipeline Safety Act**
1980	**Comprehensive Environmental Response, Compensation, and Liability Act (CERCLA) "Superfund"** Intended to take care of cleanups at sites that were no longer being operated.
1984	**Hazardous and Solid Waste Amendments**

Exhibit 8.2 Chronology of Selected Environmental Acts, Laws, Regulations, and Cases *(continued)*

Year	Act, Law, Regulation, Policy, or Case
1985	Supreme Court Support of Adjacent or Isolated Wetlands as "Waters of the U.S."
1986	Safe Drinking Water and Toxic Enforcement Act (California Proposition 65)
1986	Superfund Amendment and Reauthorization Act (SARA)
1986	Maryland Bank and Trust Superfund liability can attach to a lender that takes title to a property through foreclosure.
1987	Federal Water Quality Act
1987	Air Toxics "Hot Spots" Information and Assessment Act
1990	Oil Pollution Act
1990	Pollution Prevention Act
1990	Hazardous Waste Operations and Emergency Response Act
1990	Fleet Factors A lender doesn't even have to hold title to have liability under CERCLA. If the lender exerts control over a business, then it may become liable.
1992	OSHA Process Safety Management Standards
1992	Title X Housing and Community Development Act (lead-based paint)
1992	EPA Issues Lender Liability Rule Attempted to protect lenders, etc., and struck down by Appeal Court 2/4/94.
1994	ASTM Standard Practice for Site Assessment
1995	EPA Officially Begins Brownfields Programs Contaminated Aquifer Policy Prospective Purchaser Agreements Comfort Letters
1995	EPA Issues Lender Liability Policy Attempts to protect still unconvinced lenders.

Resource Conservation and Recovery Act (RCRA)

Under the RCRA of 1976, when a party generates hazardous waste, it must be labeled, manifested, placarded, and shipped by an approved transporter to a permitted storage or disposal facility. The waste remains the property of the generator, and the generator remains liable for it, even when it is stored elsewhere. This has been termed *cradle to grave* responsibility. RCRA also provides for sizable daily penalties for knowingly violating its strictures.

A material is defined as hazardous if it has at least one of the four characteristics of *ignitability*, *corrosivity*, *reactivity*, or *toxicity*, or if it appears on one of the lists maintained by the Environmental Protection Agency (EPA). Ignitability and toxicity are the characteristics that most often qualify a waste material as an RCRA hazardous waste. If a material spontaneously catches fire at a temperature below 140° F, then it is considered to be hazardous because of ignitability.

Exhibit 8.3 Lists of Hazardous Materials (or Wastes) Maintained by EPA

EPA List Code	Characteristic	Description
D001	Ignitability	Flashpoint <140°F (spontaneously catches fire)
D002	Corrosivity	pH is less than 2.0 (acid) or more than 12.5 (base)
D003	Reactivity	Reacts violently or generates pressure
D004-D017	Toxicity	Toxic at specified concentrations
F List	Listed wastes	Listed wastes from non-specific sources
K List	Listed wastes	Wastes from listed sources or processes
P List	Listed wastes	Specific substances
U List	Listed wastes	Off-spec or discarded products and/or residues

The hazard characteristics are so significant that they are the basis of a commonly seen, diamond-shaped sign on nearly every building that contains hazardous materials. The sign, as shown in Exhibit 8.4, was devised by the National Fire Protection Association (NFPA) as a way to quickly inform firefighters about the nature of the materials within a building and the appropriate firefighting techniques to use. Real estate professionals would also find the knowledge of the risks posed by a building's contents useful.

Superfund Act

Some of the most seriously contaminated sites in the U.S. are the result of what were accepted business practices in the distant past. Some of these sites have posed dangers to resident populations while the parties who contributed to the contamination are no longer around or not easily found. CERCLA, the Superfund law, was enacted in 1980 to marshal the forces needed to clean up the worst of these sites and to get those who are responsible to pay the bill. Originally, the worst 400 sites were going to be cleaned up. These were placed on a National Priority List (NPL), which at one time grew to over 1,100 sites.

CERCLA conferred extraordinary powers on regulators by providing for swift response to emergency situations and by defining liability broadly to fall on generators (those with whom the contaminants originated), transporters (those who carried the materials to the site), operators (those who accepted the materials at the site), and owners of the site.[1] Those who are considered likely to be responsible under CERCLA are termed *potentially responsible parties* (PRPs). Often, a group of PRPs will band together in order to handle a regional problem they all contributed to because costs can quickly run into the millions of dollars as they fund the steps in the Superfund process. The basic steps in the process are shown in Exhibit 8.5.

---

1. These terms have very specific definitions under the statutes and as they have been interpreted by the courts. There is no intent here to provide a formal or exhaustive definition.

Exhibit 8.4 NFPA Hazard Identification System

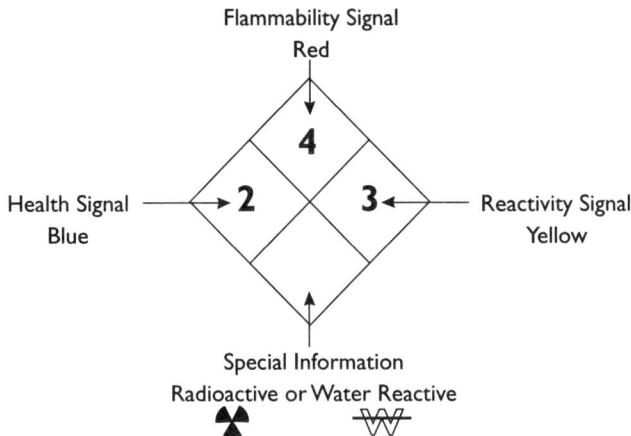

Identification of Health Hazard	Identification of Flammability	Identification of Reactivity
Color Code: Blue	**Color Code: Red**	**Color Code: Yellow**
Signal / Type of Possible Injury	**Signal / Susceptibility of Materials to Burning**	**Signal / Susceptibility to Release of Energy**
4 — Materials that on very short exposure could cause death or major residual injury even though prompt medical treatment were given	4 — Materials that will rapidly or completely vaporize at atmospheric pressure and normal ambient temperature or which are readily dispersed in air and which will burn readily	4 — Materials that in themselves are readily capable of detonation or of explosive decomposition or reaction at normal temperatures and pressures
3 — Materials that on short exposure could cause serious temporary or residual injury even though prompt medical treatment were given	3 — Liquids and solids that can be ignited under almost all ambient temperature conditions	3 — Materials that (1) in themselves are capable of detonation or explosive reaction but require a strong initiating source or (2) must be heated under confinement before initiation or (3) react explosively with water
2 — Materials that on intense or continued exposure could cause temporary incapacitation or possible residual injury unless prompt medical treatment is given	2 — Materials that must be moderately heated or exposed to relatively high ambient temperatures before ignition can occur	2 — Materials that (1) in themselves are normally unstable and readily undergo violent chemical change but do not detonate or (2) may react violently with water or (3) may form potentially explosive mixtures with water
1 — Materials that on exposure could cause irritation but only minor residual injury even if no treatment is given	1 — Materials that must be preheated before ignition can occur	1 — Materials that in themselves are normally stable but that can (1) become unstable at elevated temperatures or (2) react with water with some release of energy but not violently
0 — Materials that on exposure under rare conditions would offer no hazard beyond that of ordinary combustible material	0 — Materials that will not burn	0 — Materials that in themselves are normally stable, even when exposed to fire, and that do not react with water

Class VIII—Environmental Conditions

Exhibit 8.5   Steps in the Superfund Process

Name of Step	Comments
Preliminary assessment	Initial reconnaissance to ascertain whether there is a need for emergency action.
Emergency removal action	If needed, materials that pose an immediate threat to human health or the environment are removed.
Site inspection	This is a more thorough inspection in order to get a better idea of the problem and to better plan the investigations to come.
Hazard ranking	The hazard ranking score (HRS) is computed for the known conditions at the site in order to see whether the property should be added to the National Priority List. If the HRS is 28.5 or greater, then the property gets listed.
Remedial investigation (RI)	This involves both field and laboratory investigations and is usually done iteratively with the feasibility study until the site is sufficiently characterized.
Feasibility study (FS)	Based upon information from the remedial investigation, various technologies are studied in order to select those that will achieve the remediation goals most cost effectively.
Remedial action plan (RAP)	This is the plan to remediate the problem. It brings together scientific, engineering, regulatory, and community concerns into a unified program.
Record of decision (ROD)	This is the formal document that accepts and records the remedial action plan.
Remedial design	The systems and procedures to implement the plan are designed.
Remedial action	The contamination is remediated according to the RAP.

Source: Environmental Protection Agency

Source, Non-Source, and Adjacent Properties

One of the fundamental issues related to contamination and liability under the law is whether a property is the source of a release that poses a risk (the source site) or is a property onto or into which the contamination has migrated (a non-source site). This is a fundamental distinction for contaminated properties and one that is especially important to liability under CERCLA. Under the Superfund Law, a *source property* has strict joint and several liability for all costs to remediate the entire area affected by the problem. The affected area, called a *facility* for Superfund purposes, is defined to include all the air, soils, and waters contaminated by the risk source, and the facility may include any number of legal parcels.

A *non-source property* may contain a part of the facility created by the release of the risk source, but the owner of the non-source property does not generally have liability for the costs of remediation. An *adjacent property* is not a part of the facility, but adjoins either a source or non-source property. It is not directly affected by the release at the facility and has no liability for any part of the remedial process. Clearly it is imperative that this distinction be made in any valuation analysis, as the category could have a profound effect on value. Exhibit 8.6 illustrates these three various types of fundamental property classifications.

Geology and Hydrogeology

The sciences of geology and hydrogeology enable environmental engineers to understand the structure of the subsurface and how groundwater and contaminants move through that structure. The reason that these sciences are important is that one of the focal points of environmental engineering is protection of drinking water resources.

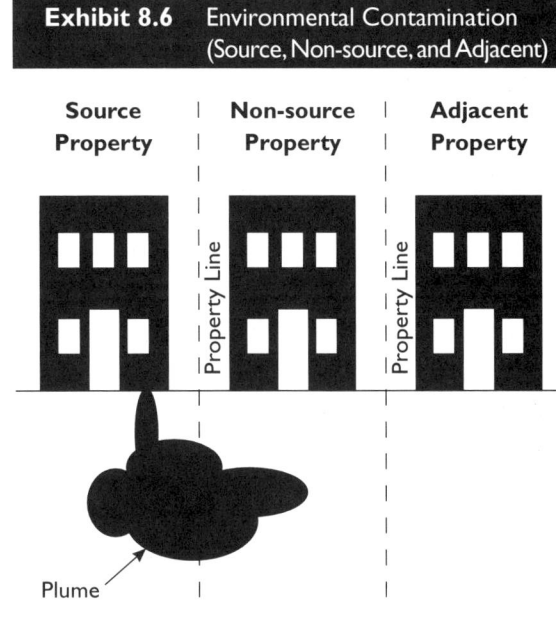

Exhibit 8.6 Environmental Contamination (Source, Non-source, and Adjacent)

Groundwater is a major source of the water used for drinking and irrigation, and it accounts for 40% of the water consumed in the United States.[2]

When contamination enters a site, it typically first sinks into the soil. There, gravity prompts the contaminant to continue its downward path. Most contaminants move more quickly through porous layers like sand and gravel and are slowed by clays, but they generally continue their descent under gravity's influence. When a descending plume of contaminant runs into an aquifer, its direction of travel may change significantly. Movement of water within the aquifer is generally to the side, not downward. Thus, when the plume reaches the aquifer, it makes a turn and starts to migrate to the side, towards the property of others. Once the moving plume crosses a property line, it has carried contamination into the property of others.

Floating and Sinking Contaminants

Water is known as the universal solvent because it dissolves most contaminants and many hydrocarbons. A dissolved contaminant is said to be in the *aqueous phase*. Once the water has dissolved all it can, the contaminant then begins to develop a separate layer of undissolved material, a non-aqueous phase liquid (NAPL). Materials that are less dense than water are called light non-aqueous phase liquids (LNAPLs) and float and accumulate near the upper water surface. This makes LNAPLs relatively easy to find. In contrast, some contaminants sink in water, as they are more dense than water. These dense non-aqueous phase liquids (DNAPLs) are usually harder to find and treat than LNAPLs.

---

2. United States Geological Survey, Water Supply Paper 2220.

Toxicology

Toxicology is often called the science of poisons, or the study of the harmful effects of chemicals on living things. Within the context of contamination, it is more rightly viewed as a way to define and quantify the adverse effects of chemicals in order to establish safe human exposure levels. This latter definition is more appropriate because our society has chosen to live with a broad spectrum of chemicals, some of which have the potential to cause harm or death. An important distinction exists between the terms *hazardous* and *toxic*. For example, table salt is generally not considered hazardous, but if ingested at high levels it becomes toxic. Likewise, gasoline is a hazardous substance but is considered toxic, again, only if ingested at certain levels. A hazardous material is considered toxic only if it becomes *bioavailable,* meaning that harmful levels come into contact with humans.

A particularly important set of safe exposure levels was put forward by the EPA in the Drinking Water Standards in publication EPA 822-B-96 002 (October 1996). The government document lists over 250 elements or compounds and has maximum contaminant levels (MCLs) for about 100 of them. The MCL is the maximum concentration of a substance allowed in drinking water, usually expressed as milligrams or micrograms per liter (mg/L or ug/L) or parts per million or per billion (ppm or ppb). Because one of the primary goals of environmental policy is to protect drinking water resources, MCLs often play important parts in establishing cleanup goals.

Types of Contaminants

Lead

Lead may be found in paints, car batteries, dust, pipes and solder, and drinking water. When exposure is excessive, lead can accumulate in the blood, tissues, and bones. As a result, there may be damage to the brain, kidneys, male reproductive organs, and nervous systems. Lead accumulation can cause learning disabilities, decreased IQ, and behavioral problems.

The two most common sources of lead are paint and water. The Environmental Protection Agency estimates that lead-based paints were used in about two-thirds of the homes built before 1940, one-third of the homes built between 1940 and 1960, and in some homes built after 1960. Beginning in 1978, the federal government required that paints for home use contain less than 0.06% lead. Paints for other uses, such as industrial, military, marine, and other situations, may have lead contents much higher than this. For this reason, a home owner should only use a paint intended for residential properties when painting a house.

Any home that was painted before 1978 has the potential to contain lead-based paint. If home paints contain lead, they may be covered by more recent layers of non-lead paint or by wallpaper or paneling. A test called x-ray fluorescence (XRF) can now distinguish if any of the paint layers contain lead and, if so, which layers. Removing the paint in some ways, such as sanding, may actually increase the risk of exposure to lead in the form of inhaled or ingested dust.

Lead may enter the drinking water via lead pipes or lead solder used on copper pipes. Lead pipes are usually found only in homes built before 1930, and lead soldering materials have been banned since 1988. Since October 1996, the EPA's MCL action level for lead in drinking water has been 0.015 mg/L, or 0.015 parts per million (ppm) or 15 parts per billion (ppb). If lead is found within drinking water, then the plumbing system may need to be renovated, filters may be employed, or only bottled water used. If any reason exists to suspect that lead is in paints or water, laboratory testing of samples should be conducted. If lead concentrations above MCL are detected in any samples, then corrective measures need to be taken.

Formaldehyde

Formaldehyde is a colorless gas emitted from a variety of products and categorized as a probable carcinogen (i.e., a cancer-causing substance) by the EPA. Household products that possibly contain formaldehyde include wood-pressed products such as particleboard, urea-formaldehyde foam, insulation, fabrics, paints, plastics, photographic materials, and resins. Two main areas of concern are materials used in mobile homes and wood-pressed products, though formaldehyde may also be produced by improperly vented gas or kerosene heaters. Newer products are more likely to emit formaldehyde gas than older ones.

Formaldehyde exists in the outside air at levels ranging from 0.0002 to 0.050 ppm. Many people experience throat or eye irritation at levels of 0.1 ppm or above. The only way to determine if formaldehyde levels are excessive (over the outdoor air levels) is through laboratory testing of air samples. Gas levels, if excessive, may be reduced by removing the materials that contain formaldehyde and generally increasing air circulation.

Radioactive Contamination

Radioactive materials emit high speed particles or energetic photons, collectively called *ionizing radiation*. Ionizing radiation includes alpha and beta particles, gamma rays, x-rays, neutrons, and heavy ions. Nearly all of human exposure to radiation comes from natural background radiation (81%) or medical tests (14%). Contrary to some perceptions within the real estate market, nuclear power plants actually emit only a small amount of radiation, which is sometimes even less than coal- or oil-powered plants. Neutrons, x-rays, and gamma rays can penetrate deeply into the human body. Alpha and beta particle sources cause damage mainly if they are inside the body from being inhaled, ingested, or directly applied to the skin. Radioactive particles move at velocities that approach the speed of light—186,000 miles per second. It is theorized that these fast moving particles can break up or alter molecules, thereby causing cancer.

Among the Japanese atom bomb survivors, a carefully monitored group of 8,500 people were exposed to doses of radiation measured at 100,000 to 600,000 millirem. To date, there have been 200 (2.4%) cases of excess cancers amongst this group (i.e., 2.4% more cases than the normal probability). Another study followed British medical patients exposed to unusually high levels of radiation. About 14,000 British patients received x-ray doses averaging 300,000 millirem, resulting in 100 excess cancers (0.7%).[3]

As related to real estate, by far the most problematic source of radioactive exposure is from radon, as can be seen in exhibit 8.7. Radon is a colorless and odorless naturally

---

3. American Council on Science and Health.

Exhibit 8.7 Sources of Radiation

Radiation Source	Dose (Millirem/Year)	Percent of Total
Natural indoor radon	200	54%
Natural cosmic radiation	100	27%
Medical procedures	53	14%
Nuclear bomb testing	6	2%
Other man-made (soot, dust)	10	3%
Nuclear power plant	0.1	0%
Totals	369	100%

Source: American Council on Science and Health

Exhibit 8.8 Radon

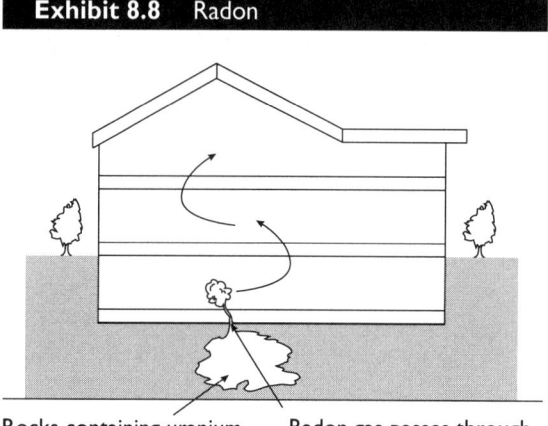

Rocks containing uranium, usually shales and granite, form a radioactive gas—radon

Radon gas passes through cracks in the basement or foundation and circulates within the structure

occurring radioactive gas that forms when radioactive uranium and radium decay within rocks, as shown in Exhibit 8.8. The gas has been determined by the EPA to be a carcinogen. It accumulates in areas closest to the source, usually the ground or basement levels. Smokers are impacted more by radon, although the effects may take over 20 years to become apparent. The EPA recommends that action be taken if radon levels are over 4 pico-curies per liter of air (pCi/L). In addition to gases, radon may also enter the water system, particularly when water comes from wells. Water treatment for radon includes a granular-activated carbon unit (GAC) or an aeration unit.

Radon gas is unpredictable and may affect one property and not the one next door. If any reason exists to suspect radon gases may be present, only a special laboratory test will provide conclusive answers. Often, a modestly priced system of fans and ducts provides sufficient ventilation to disperse radon and reduce its concentration to acceptable levels.

Hydrocarbons

Hydrocarbons is a general term for all carbon-based chemicals. These include methane gas, gasoline, oils and greases, asphalt, solvents, pesticides, plastics, and even DNA. Most contamination matters have been concerned with only the categories of fuels and solvents, many of which are considered hazardous because of their flammability or toxicity characteristics.

The fuel hydrocarbons of most concern have been the four ubiquitous components of gasoline: benzene, toluene, ethylbenzene, and xylene, known collectively as BTEX. One of the most hazardous of these is benzene, a known carcinogen. Many sites that have had a gasoline tank have some BTEX in the soil and perhaps even in the groundwater. Once viewed with great alarm, BTEX contamination in soil is now treated as a fairly routine matter, although it is still considered very dangerous if a drinking water supply is threatened.

Asbestos

Although asbestos and asbestos containing materials (ACMs) have been used in building construction since they were introduced by the Romans and Greeks in the first century A.D., their days of being considered staple building materials are clearly over. Asbestos is a naturally formed fibrous material with properties that suit it well to building uses. It is non-combustible, has high tensile strength, and has outstanding thermal, electrical, and acoustical insulating properties. According to some studies, it also has been shown to pose health risks. Accordingly, its use has been mostly discontinued and it has been removed from some buildings.

In the past, the use of asbestos in the building industry was tremendous. The EPA estimates that of the 30 million tons of asbestos used from 1900 to 1980, 60% to 70% was in the construction industry. (The United States produced 25% of the asbestos it consumed and imported 97% of the remainder from Canada.) Two terms frequently used when referring to ACMs are *friable* and *non-friable*. Friable simply means that the ACMs can be pulverized or crushed with hand pressure. Non-friable ACMs are formed into solid building materials and cannot be crushed with hand pressure. Examples of friable uses are sprayed acoustical ceilings and sprayed fireproofing on structural steel. Non-friable materials include vinyl flooring, insulating bricks, and roofing materials. Typical locations of ACMs in buildings include sprayed surfaces such as thermal insulation on structural steel, sprayed acoustical ceilings or walls, pre-formed block insulation surrounding furnaces, insulation on boilers and hot water tanks, drywall, pipe wrap, patching compounds, texture paints, vinyl floor tiles, and floor sheeting.

While asbestos was widely used for centuries, in the early 1970s it was declared a health

The office building above was photographed just a few weeks before an asbestos abatement program was initiated. Asbestos abatement, like many remediation processes, can be highly intrusive and result in the demolition of the tenant improvements.

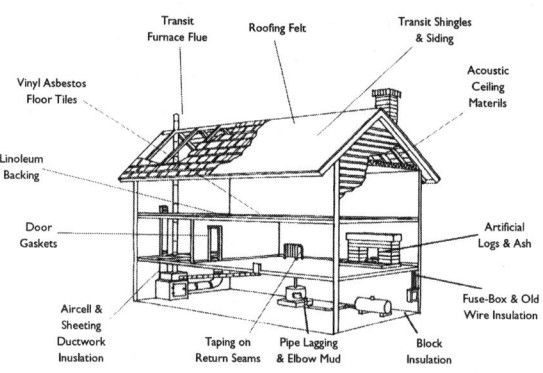

Exhibit 8.9 Asbestos in the Home

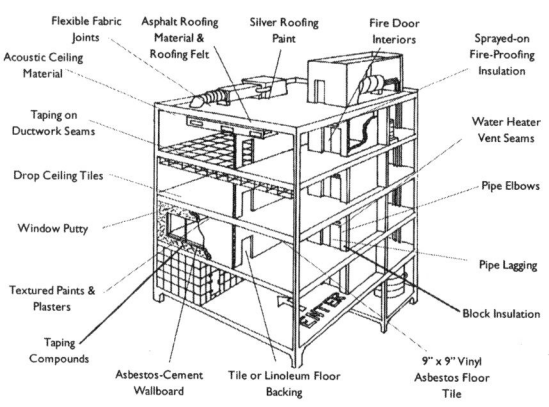

Exhibit 8.10 Asbestos in the Office

risk. No safe threshold has ever been established for exposure to asbestos. ACMs in and of themselves do not pose a health hazard, but asbestos fibers released by disturbance, destruction, or decay can cause serious health problems. There are about six diseases attributed to asbestos, the two most common being mesothelioma, a lung cancer, and asbestosis, a chronic lung disease. Because of these health risks, the federal government has intervened and restricted asbestos use. As would be expected, the demand for ACMs has fallen dramatically, with the 1989 use level approximately 15% of what it was in 1979. The EPA estimates that as many as 31,000 schools and 733,000 public and commercial buildings contain friable ACMs. ACMs can be found in approximately 20% of the 3.6 million commercial properties in the United States.

Following is a summary of the legal limitations placed on ACMs used in new construction or products:

1973	All sprayed ACMs that contain an amount of 1% asbestos by weight or volume.
1978	All friable ACMs.
1989	A phased-in ban of virtually all ACMs.
1990	Phase I includes roofing and flooring felt, sheeting, tile, and clothing.
1993	Phase II includes brake linings, transmission components, clutches, and other friction products.
1996	Phase III includes floor coatings, paper, brake blocks, pipes, and shingles.

With the exception of school buildings, ACMs in existing buildings were not affected by the EPA bans and regulations.

In ascertaining whether or not a building contains ACMs, the first consideration is the construction date. Properties constructed prior to 1979 are more likely to have ACMs. Friable or sprayed construction materials are also a warning sign that there may be ACMs within a building. It is important to review building records of any building in question, but the only way to be certain of the presence of ACMs is to test air and building material samples.

Air sampling, as the name implies, means taking samples of the air for laboratory testing. The air is tested in the laboratory for fiber counts using one of three microscopy methods. The Occupational Safety and Health Administration (OSHA) has established an action level of 0.1 fibers per cubic centimeter of air. Samples of building materials are often taken in conjunction with air sampling. For the study, small amounts of various building materials are collected for laboratory testing. Building materials are considered an ACM if the lab analysis indicates that the materials contain 1% or greater of asbestos (by either volume or weight). Asbestos sampling is usually unobtrusive and can be done without causing any risk of exposure to the building occupants.

Attitudes towards asbestos have changed dramatically since the 1970s and 1980s. The high profits that attracted many contractors to the asbestos abatement business in the 1980s have fallen, and contractors now number approximately 1,600, which is down 27% from 1989.[4] Abatement revenues fell from $3.9 billion to $3.2 billion in 1989 and 1990 respectively, yet asbestos will continue to be an important issue in the real estate industry with an estimated $75 billion in asbestos-related cleanup costs remaining over the next 25 years.

In 1990, the EPA issued the *Green Book,* which recommends various means of treating or managing ACMs. As a result of this and other studies, most banks do not require ACM removal as a condition of financing.

Solvents

A variety of solvents used for cleaning and manufacturing purposes are usually carcinogenic materials that do not biodegrade easily. They often are compact, dense molecules that may move fairly quickly through soil and sink through groundwater to the bottom of an aquifer, where they may be difficult to remediate.

Contamination and its Impact on Real Estate

When dealing with contamination that impacts a specific property, two broad categories must be considered, building contaminants and soil contaminants. Building contaminants include those hazards that are part of or contained within the improvements, such as asbestos, radon, lead paint, and formaldehyde. Soil contaminants include hydrocarbons, solvents, chemicals such as pesticides and herbicides, and other toxins that threaten the environment. It is entirely possible for the same contaminant to be found in both buildings and soils. For example, lead-based paints can be found in many buildings, and lead in the drinking water is a soils condition. Also, although asbestos is most commonly associated with asbestos containing building material, it is also possible for asbestos to contaminate soil.

Contaminants in Building Improvements

Several contaminants are most commonly found within the improvements on a property, as seen in Exhibit 8.11. These include asbestos, radon, lead paint, formaldehyde, and

---

4. United Press International, "New Attitudes and Litigation over Asbestos," *Los Angeles Times* (September 22, 1993): Business section, 7.

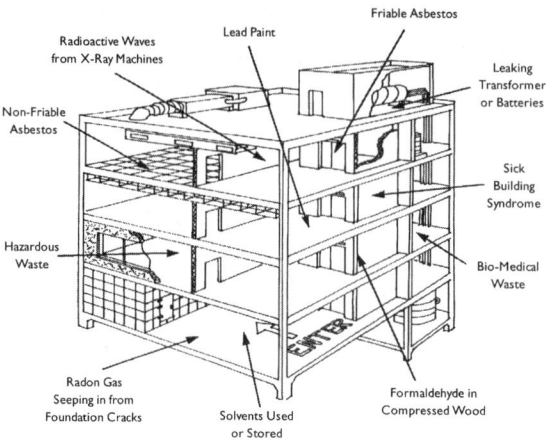

Exhibit 8.11 Environmental Conditions Within Building Improvements

others. The risk associated with these hazardous materials as part of, or within, the improvements is that there may be direct human contact. A child may eat lead paint chips, asbestos fibers may be inhaled by the occupants of an office building, or radon gas or formaldehyde fumes may by inhaled by a family in their home.

A laboratory analysis is virtually always required to determine the presence and concentrations of these contaminants. An assessment is easier for improvements than it is for soils contamination because the materials are easily accessed, as opposed to having to drill in the soil. All the work is above-grade, so remediation is easier.

When dealing with a property that has contaminants within the improvements, there are various alternatives, including encapsulation, enclosure, immediate removal, staged removal, or an operations and management program with removal at demolition.

Encapsulation

Encapsulation is a term used when sealants are sprayed onto the contaminant. The sealants surround, coat, and bond the contaminant and prevent any particles from being released into the air. A simple analogy would be the hard coating surrounding the soft chocolate in M&M candies. Encapsulation may be less expensive than removal or, in many cases, enclosure, but it has disadvantages as well. The added weight of the encapsulating materials may hasten the decay of the contaminant, and encapsulated contaminants are more difficult to remove than if they had not been treated at all. Encapsulation is usually considered a temporary solution. It is currently not recommended as being a viable abatement choice, except in special circumstances.

Enclosure

Enclosure involves the construction of air-tight walls that surround the building contamination materials (BCMs). Often this means that the BCMs are surrounded with drywall. This is an effective technique and is less expensive than removal, although it has important engineering considerations because of the added weight of the enclosures. Additionally, access is not always available to all the areas within buildings that contain BCMs. Like encapsulation, enclosure is also considered only a temporary solution, as all BCMs must be removed from a building prior to demolition.

Removal

As the name indicates, this method involves removing the BCMs from the building. It has permanent results, but the process is usually expensive, with asbestos removal costs often ranging from $10 to $70 per square foot. (In actual abatement projects, costs are not calculated on gross building area but rather on *reflective* area, which refers only to the areas within the building that have BCMs.) With removal, the building owner retains legal ownership, and thus liability, for up to 40 years for any disposed materials, even when taken to a landfill or storage site. Another negative aspect of removal is that, according to a study by the Energy and Environmental Policy Center at Harvard University, removal may actually increase asbestos exposure for building occupants because of the disruption of the asbestos.

There are three alternatives for removing BCMs:

1. Immediate or initial removal
2. Staged removal over a period of time
3. Removal at the end of the economic life (demolition) of the building

Operations and Management

Another option for dealing with BCMs is an *operations and management* (O&M) program. This means that the BCMs in good condition are simply left alone while the situation is monitored to ensure that there are no health hazards to the occupants of the building. According to the EPA, a good O&M program is 95% as effective as a non-asbestos building. The EPA recommends an O&M program over removal when the BCMs are in good condition.

When implementing an O&M program, the building owner or manager hires a qualified O&M consultant, who in turn trains the building management, engineers, custodians, and occupants concerning the handling of BCMs. The consultant may also conduct routine air sampling and building inspections to ensure that no fibers are released into the air through disturbance. The O&M program is generally continued until the BCMs are removed or the building is eventually demolished. Even with an O&M program, BCMs must be eventually removed, whether initially, staged removal over a number of years, or at the end of the building's economic life. In the event that the BCMs are removed at demolition, special BCM handling and disposal can double the demolition costs.

Soil and Groundwater Contamination

Soil contamination is a general term that sometimes includes the contamination of both soil and groundwater. The contamination may consist of materials in a variety of locations, such as on or near the surface, as is often the case with heavy metals or asbestos. Gases or vapors can form from volatile materials in the subsurface. They can also be found within the subsurface soils, which is usual for leaking underground storage tanks (LUSTs). In these cases, they may impact the groundwater, either dissolved, as a separate phase, or both. Various forms of soil contamination are illustrated in Exhibit 8.12

The danger with some contaminants, such as lead or asbestos, is that they are on the surface and can be ingested by humans or animals. If a contaminant is capable of being absorbed downward into the soils, the concern is the risk to the groundwater, aquifers, or

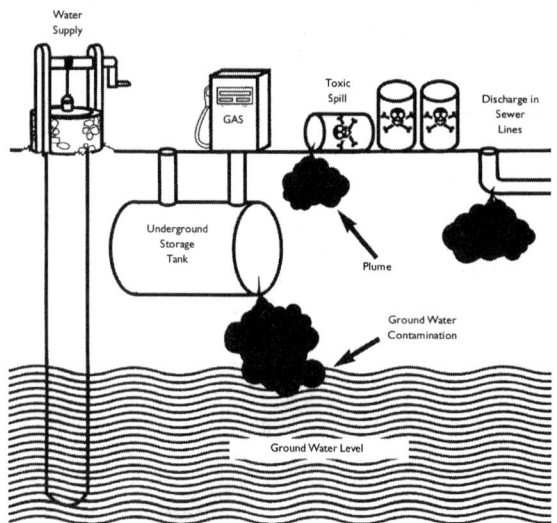

Exhibit 8.12 Contamination in the Soil

the water supply. If the groundwater is contaminated, then the contaminants may be ingested by humans, animals, or plants and cause a variety of health-related problems. When mixed with groundwater, some contaminants dissolve, some float on the surface, and some sink to the bottom, much in the same way that salad dressing separates. These attributes create additional problems in terms of assessing and remediating the contamination.

Site Assessment

Properties that have been impacted by soils contamination undergo a four-phased process of a preliminary site assessment (Phase I), an intrusive site investigation involving subsurface exploration to ascertain whether contamination in fact exists (Phase II), systematic testing to fully describe (or "characterize") the nature and extent of the contamination (Phase III), and the remediation of the contaminants (Phase IV).[5]

Phase I: Surface and Records Review. A Phase I study is an initial review of a site to determine if there is any reason to suspect that there is contamination. It may also address compliance with environmental or OSHA laws and regulations. This study is done by a trained environmental engineer or assessor who inspects the site and reviews aerial photographs to determine if there were any historical uses that might be linked with contamination, such as a manufacturing facility or agricultural uses with pesticides. Records of such agencies as the Fire, Health, Planning, Building and Safety, and Public Works Departments may be reviewed to see if any historical uses, permits, or records exist of underground tanks, special manufacturing permits, or other issues that may warrant further investigation. Agencies such as the EPA and Air and Water Quality Control Boards are also contacted, and their lists are reviewed to determine if there are any records reflecting historical or current contamination issues related to the property. Current and former tenants may be interviewed to learn of any actions taking place on the property associated with contamination.

Nearly all regulatory agencies maintain databases of properties that are somehow connected with contamination. There are lists of properties with suspected contamination, contamination that is still to be cleaned up, sites that have been remediated and approved, sites that are partly remediated and contain residuals, and so forth. Usually when a property is put on a list, it remains on that list permanently. Some recent pro-

---

5. It is important to note that many professionals combine Phases II and III, effectively creating a three-phased process where the final phase is remediation.

grams provide for listings to be removed as certain goals are met. With databases being maintained by federal, state, and local agencies, a single agency will likely have two or more overlapping databases, particularly if it enforces regulations for two or more programs. Nearly every database or list is available to the public, and the EPA and many state agencies have Internet sites that can be a helpful research source. There are even environmental research services that charge a very modest fee to tap into all applicable lists, produce a summary report and map for any address, and fax and mail the report to a caller.

If the Phase I study indicates that no reason exists to suspect contamination, then no other studies may be necessary. However, if evidence indicates that the site may be contaminated, then a Phase II study may be required.

Phase II: Subsurface Study. The goal of the Phase II study is to establish whether contamination exists at a site. A Phase II assessment may include collecting samples of soil, groundwater, surface water, sediment, soil vapor, and even building materials. Samples are usually taken near likely sources (tanks and plumbing) and from suspicious areas such as discolored soil and standing puddles of unidentified fluids.

The EPA and other agencies have prescribed sampling techniques and laboratory analyses to be done for a broad spectrum of contaminants. Often samples must be kept cool or frozen and must be delivered to a certified lab in a timely manner. Chain of custody is documented, and the labs have quality control and assurance programs that must be strictly followed. These assure that the samples have not been altered by activities in the field or in the lab.

The Phase II study may find no contamination or concentrations that are below regulatory action limits. These are usually seen as positive findings because the property is then deemed to be unimpaired by contamination. If contamination is found and is present at levels that require remediation, then a Phase III investigation will be necessary.

Phase III: Characterization. Before a cleanup plan can be designed, it is necessary to define the nature and extent of the contamination. For a groundwater plume, for example, this involves knowing the three-dimensional shape of the plume—its length, width, and depth as well as the direction and speed at which it is moving. These studies are more often referred to as *remedial investigations* (RI) than Phase III studies and are necessary before the effectiveness and cost of various remedial alternatives can be examined in feasibility studies (FS).

The culmination of the site assessment process is the development of the remedial action plan (RAP). This plan is subject to careful review by the regulatory agencies involved and must be approved by them. It is the blueprint for the schedule and the methods to be applied, and the results to be achieved in the cleanup process. An approved RAP sets the stage for the start of the actual remediation process.

Phase IV: Remediation. The remediation process is the actual cleanup of the released material. Its goal is not necessarily to return the property to an uncontaminated state but to remedy the problem to the satisfaction of the regulatory authorities. Parts of the property may be excavated and refilled, piping may be extended into the soil, and wells may be used to reach and treat groundwater. Numerous remediation technologies are available, depending upon the specific mix of contaminants and where they are found. The choices of remedial technologies for various categories of contaminants are summarized in Exhibit 8.13. In many cases, a succession of technologies is used as concentrations change in order to get the most remedial efficiency.

Exhibit 8.13 Remedial Technology Choices for Various Contaminants

Remediation Method or Process	Aqueous Solutions		Organic Liquids	Sludges and Slurries	Solids
	Inorganic	Organic			
Adsorption		√	√		
Bioremediation		√	√	√	
Dewatering	√		√	√	
Distillation			√		
Drying			√		
Emulsion Breaking		√	√		
Extraction		√	√	√	
Incineration		√	√	√	√
Landfarming		√	√	√	
Landfill/Landspreading				√	√
Neutralization	√	√		√	
Oxidation	√	√	√	√	√
Precipitation	√				
Solidification	√				
Stabilization	√			√	√
Steam Stripping		√	√		
Surface Impoundments	√	√		√	
Wastewater Treatment	√	√		√	

All remedial options fall under one of two categories, *in situ* and *ex situ*. In situ remediation means that the treatment of the soils or groundwater are completed with them in place. In other words, they are not excavated as they are with ex situ remediation measures. In situ processes are less disruptive and less expensive than ex situ methods. However, they may take longer and are often not as thorough as when soil is excavated for treatment.

In Situ Remediation Methods. There is a variety of in situ procedures:
- Bioremediation and bioventing involve the injection of oxygen or oxygen-releasing compounds through pipes into the soils or groundwater. The oxygen injected in this process stimulates aerobic biodegradation of the carbon-based contaminants.
- Biodegradation is a process where the microorganisms that are mixed and added to soils break down contaminants within the soils or groundwater.

- Soil vapor extraction (SVE) is a process whereby fresh air is drawn into the ground with a vacuum pump. The air mixes with the contaminant's vapors and is then vacuumed back to the surface. The mix of air and contaminants is filtered, incinerated, or otherwise treated.
- Passive biodegradation involves the concept of natural attenuation, allowing the natural biodegradation of contaminants by the microbes that are already in the soil.
- Groundwater treatment involves boring wells or driving pipes down to the contaminated groundwater tables and pumping the subsurface contaminated groundwater to the surface, much like a regular water well. The contaminated water is filtered or otherwise treated and then, according to permit, is either discharged as waste or pumped back down into the ground through an injection well. An alternative treatment, called air sparging, involves injecting air into the groundwater to stimulate aerobic degradation and microbial activity and to promote migration of contaminants to the remedial process.

Ex Situ Remediation Processes. There is also a variety of ex situ remediation methods:

Most people traveling on and around this service station may never notice the small enclosed area near the corner. However, a closer investigation reveals a vapor extraction unit that has been installed to remediate the contaminants located in the soils.

- Excavation and off-site disposal, sometimes called *scoop and haul,* is the simplest concept. Contaminated soil is merely excavated, exported, and disposed of in an approved off-site landfill. Then the soil is replaced with imported clean soils. While conceptually straightforward, this process is relatively costly, and there may be a lingering liability associated with the contaminated soils that were shipped off-site.
- A variation of this idea is to excavate the soils, treat them on- or off-site, and then put them back into the excavation. One way of treating excavated soils, either on- or off-site, is by incineration where the contaminants are simply burned. In a process known as *on-site low temperature thermal desorption,* the soils

Class VIII—Environmental Conditions

are heated to vaporize and release the contaminants, which are then collected and treated.
- Bioremediation, biomounding, and land farming all involve excavating contaminated soils, adding nutrients or bacteria to stimulate microbes already in the soil, and perhaps adding microbes as well, all in order to facilitate biodegradation. The soils are spread by a bulldozer over a lined treatment area or kept in mounds. The soils are tilled from time to time to stimulate the process.
- Fixation or encapsulation involves the excavation of contaminated soils and the addition of fixation materials that stabilize, enclose, and/or encapsulate contaminants.
- Capping is used when it is considered best not to disturb the subsurface material but there is still a chance that rain or other water moving through the soil could promote contaminant migration. Some contaminants may be removed and an impermeable cap is placed over the contamination and prevents water from moving down into the site, thereby halting any movement of the contaminants.

Site Closure

When all the remedial goals are met, the responsible government agency generally confirms that fact in writing. The written document is often called a *closure letter* or a *no further action letter* (NFA letter), which states that the case is closed or that no further action is required. An NFA letter is a positive step, as it is evidence that regulators are satisfied for the time being. It may also signal that a listing of the property has been moved from one publicly available database to another one with less onerous connotations. This may reduce the potential risks of property ownership and is often viewed favorably by potential lenders. Nevertheless, an NFA letter does not mean that a property is free of contamination, that it poses no further risks, that all of the contamination has even been found, or that there will not be additional, future investigations interfering with property use. The letter simply means that no further action is required on the project for which the letter was issued. No governmental agency will irrevocably certify a site as clean, even if the site has undergone remediation and has *site closure* status; however, while a technical risk may exist, the market perceptions may be such that no material risk exists at that point. Of course market data must be used to make such a determination.

Further Reading

Air Contamination

Freeman, A. Myrick, III. "On Estimating Air Pollution Control Benefits from Land Value Studies." *Journal of Environmental Economics and Management* (May 1974).

Smith, V. Kerry, and Timothy A. Deyak. "Measuring the Impact of Air Pollution on Property Values." *Journal of Regional Science* (July 1986).

Smith, V. Kerry, and Ju-Chin Huang. "Can Markets Value Air Quality? A Meta-Analysis of Hedonic Property Value Models." *Journal of Political Economy,* vol. 103, no. 1 (February 1995).

Vanderver, Timothy A., Jr. *Clean Air Law and Regulation.* Washington, D.C.: The Bureau of National Affairs, Inc., 1992.

Asbestos

Bell, Randall. "The Impact of Asbestos on Real Estate Values." *Right of Way,* vol. 41, no. 5 (October/November 1994).

Fisher, Jeffrey D., George H. Lentz, and K.S. Maurice Tse. *Effects of Asbestos on Commercial Real Estate: A Survey of MAI Appraisers.* Bloomington, Ind.: Center for Real Estate Studies, Indiana University, February 1991.

___. "Valuation of Effects of Asbestos on Commercial Real Estate." *The Journal of Real Estate Research,* vol. 7, no. 3 (Summer 1992).

Ramsland, Maxwell O., Jr. "Asbestos: Risk and the Remediation Process." *Technical Report.* Chicago, Ill.: Appraisal Institute, 1992.

Tenenbaum, Wayne A. "The Effect of Asbestos on Market Value: A Suggested Methodology." *14th Annual IPT Conference* (June 1990).

Wilson, Albert R. "Probable Financial Effect of Asbestos Removal on Real Estate." *The Appraisal Journal* (July 1989): 378–391.

Class VIII—Environmental Conditions

Access EPA. Washington, D.C.: Information Access Branch, Information Management and Services Division, USEPA (updated annually).

Chalmers, James A., and Thomas O. Jackson. "Risk Factor in the Appraisal of Contaminated Property." *The Appraisal Journal* (January 1996).

Gale, Charles M., Esq. "Common Environmental Myths, When Selling, Buying, or Leasing Real Property." *Los Angeles Business Journal* (October 5, 1992).

Jessup, Deborah Hitchcock. *Guide to State Environmental Programs.* 3d ed. Washington, D.C.: The Bureau of National Affairs, Inc., 1994.

Mays, Richard H. "Environmental Laws; Impact on Business Transactions." *A Practical Guide with Forms.* Washington, D.C.: The Bureau of National Affairs, Inc., 1992.

McLain, Wallis E., Jr. *U.S. Environmental Laws.* Washington, D.C..: The Bureau of National Affairs, Inc., 1991.

Rabe, Barry G. *Fragmentation and Integration in State Environmental Management.* Washington, D.C.: The Conservation Foundation, 1986.

Simons, Robert. "How Clean is Clean?" *The Appraisal Journal* (July 1994).

Stimson, James A., Jeffrey J. Kimmel, and Sara Thurin Rollin. *Guide to Environmental Laws from Premanufacture to Disposal.* Washington, D.C.: The Bureau of National Affairs, Inc., 1993.

Sullivan, Thomas F. P. *Environmental Information Sources.* 5th ed. Rockville, Md.: Government Institutes, Inc., 1995.

Sullivan, Thomas F. P., and Richard F. Hill. *Environmental Information Sources.* Rockville, Md.: Government Institutes, Inc., September 1986.

Who's Who in Environmental Engineering. Annapolis, Md.: American Academy of Environmental Engineering, 1988.

Environmental Contamination

Bell, Randall. "Quantifying Diminution in Value Due to Detrimental Conditions: An Application to Environmentally Contaminated Properties." *Environmental Claims Journal* (Autumn 1996).

Ciambrone, David F. *Environmental Life Cycle Analysis*. Boca Raton, Fla.: Lewis Publishers, 1997.

___. *Waste Minimization as a Strategic Weapon*. Boca Raton, Fla.: Lewis Publishers, 1996.

Directory of Environmental Attorneys. Englewood Cliffs, N.J.: Prentice-Hall Law and Business (updated annually).

Worobec, Mary Devine, and Girard Ordway. "Federal Regulation of Chemicals in the Environment." *Toxic Substances Controls Guide*. Washington, D.C.: The Bureau of National Affairs, Inc. 1992.

General Overviews of On-Site Contamination Impacts on Property Value

Arnold, Alvin L. "Protecting Lenders from Hazardous Waste Liability." *The Mortgage and Real Estate Executives Report* (February 1, 1991).

Bell, Randall. "Quantifying Diminution in Value Due to Detrimental Conditions: An Application to Environmentally Contaminated Properties." *Environmental Claims Journal* (Autumn 1996).

Bingham, Gail. "Resolving Environmental Disputes: A Decade of Experience." *The Conservation Foundation*. Washington D.C.: 1988.

Campanella, Joseph A. "Valuing Partial Losses in Contamination Cases." *The Appraisal Journal* (April 1984).

Chalmers, James A., and Jeffre B. Beatty. "Environmental Hazards Devastate Property Values." *Real Estate Valuation*, no. 39 (Spring 1994). Reproduced in part from *Environmental Compliance and Litigation Strategy Newsletter*.

Chalmers, James A., and Scott Roehr. "Issues in the Valuation of Contaminated Property." *The Appraisal Journal* (January 1993).

Christensen, Barbara. "Can Pollution Contaminate Value?" *The Real Estate Appraiser and Analyst,* vol. 53, no. 3 (Fall/Winter 1987).

Dunmire, Thea D. "Environmental Redlining: Phase I Auditing Concerns in Real Estate Transactions." *10th Annual IAAO Legal Seminar*. Grenelefe, Fla.: November 15–16, 1990.

Elliot-Jones, Michael. "Real Estate Value and Toxic Sites." *Digest of Environmental Law*, vol. 5, no. 7 (1992).

Farrah, George R. "Strategies for Compliance." *Environmental Tax Handbook*. Washington, D.C.: The Bureau of National Affairs, Inc., 1989.

Ferruggia, Frank E. "Valuation of Contaminated Property: New Jersey's *Inmar* Decision." *Assessment Digest* (March/April 1991).

Garippa, John E., and Seth I. Davenport. "The Effects of Environmental Contamination on Property Values for Tax Assessment Purposes." *15th IPT Annual Conference*. Reno, Nev.: June 26, 1991.

Gladstone, Robert A. "Contaminated Property: A Valuation Perspective." *Toxics Law Reporter* (November 27, 1991).

Goodman, Gary A., and Dennis P. Harkawik. "Handling Transactions Involving Environmentally Contaminated Property." *Real Estate Review* (Spring 1991).

"Hazardous Waste Movement in the United States." *Environmental Information Limited.* Washington, D.C.: National Solid Wastes Management Association, 1991.

Healy, Patricia R., and John J. Healy, Jr. "Lenders' Perspectives on Environmental Issues." *Real Estate Issues,* vol. 16, no. 2 (Fall/Winter 1991). Reprinted in July 1992 issue of *The Appraisal Journal.*

Hunsperger, Wayne L. "Case Example: Impact of Hazardous Waste Material on Appraisal." *Focus: The Bulletin of Environmental Risk Evaluation and Management* (February 1, 1991).

International Association of Assessing Officers. *Standard on the Valuation of Property Affected by Environmental Contamination.* Chicago, Ill.: 1992.

Kinnard, William N., Jr. "Current Techniques and Procedures for Dealing with the Effects of Property Contamination." *1990 SREA Symposium.* San Antonio, Texas: September 13, 1990.

___. "Measuring the Effects of Contamination on Property Values." *Environmental Watch,* vol. IV, no. 4 (Winter 1992).

___. "Measuring the Effects of Contamination on Property Values: The Focus of the Symposium in the Context of Current Knowledge." *Technical Report.* Chicago, Ill.: Appraisal Institute, 1992.

___. "What Appraisers Can Do and Must Do to Estimate the Impact of Contamination on Property Value." Paper presented at American Bar Association Meeting, New York, N.Y., March 1993.

Kinnard, William N., Jr., Sue Ann Dickey, and Mary Beth Geckler. "Fear and Property Value: Opinion Survey Results vs. Market Sales Evidence." Paper presented at the IAAO 1994 Annual Conference, Seattle, Wash., October 1994.

Kinnard, William N., Jr., Mary Beth Geckler, and Jake W. DeLottie. "The Effect of Varying Levels of Negative Publicity on Single-Family Property Values: A Case Study of Soil Contamination." *Assessment Journal,* vol. 3, no. 5 (September/October 1996).

Kinnard, William N., Jr., Mary Beth Geckler, and John K. Geckler. "Are Residential Property Values Affected by Proximity to Alleged Hazards to Human Health and Safety?" *The Journal of Property Tax Management,* vol. 7, no. 2 (Fall 1995).

Kline, Stephen M. "Valuing Contaminated Property: New and Unfamiliar Territory." *Journal of Technical Valuation* (August 1991).

McGregor, Gregor I. "Land Owner Liability for Hazardous Waste." *The Journal of Real Estate Development* (Winter 1989).

Milligan, Peter A. "Contaminated Land or Toxic Real Estate: Lessons from Ontario." *Journal of Property Tax Management,* vol. 16, no. 3 (Winter 1995).

Mundy, Bill. "Analog Research: Market Evidence of Impaired Property Sales and Case Studies." *Environmental Analysis and Valuation Seminar.* Seattle, Wash.: March 1992.

___. "Effect of Contamination of Real Estate Values." *Insider* (February 28, 1990).

___. "The Impact of Hazardous and Toxic Material on Property Value: Revisited." *The Appraisal Journal* (October 1992).

___. "The Impact of Hazardous Materials on Property Value." *The Appraisal Journal* (April 1992).

___. "Survey Cites Impacts of Contaminants on Value and Marketability of Real Estate." *News Release.* Chicago, Ill.: American Society of Real Estate Counselors, November 1988.

Neustein, Richard A. "Estimating Value Diminution by the Income Approach." *The Appraisal Journal* (April 1992).

O'Brien, James P., and Frank William Harris. *Environment Due Diligence: The Complete Resource Guide for Real Estate Lenders, Buyers, Sellers, and Attorneys.* Washington, D.C.: The Bureau of National Affairs, Inc., 1989.

Patchin, Peter J. "Contaminated Properties and the Sales Comparison Approach." *The Appraisal Journal* (July 1994).

___. "Valuation of Contaminated Properties." *The Appraisal Journal* (January 1988): 7–16.

___. "The Valuation of Contaminated Properties." *Real Estate Issues,* vol. 16, no. 2 (Fall/Winter 1991). Special issue on environmental conditions in real estate.

___. "Valuing Contaminated Properties: Case Studies." *Measuring the Effects of Hazardous Materials Contamination on Real Estate Values: Techniques and Applications.* Chicago, Ill.: Appraisal Institute, 1992.

Peters, Bill Thomas. "How the Cost of Cleanup, Liability Factors, and Governmental Regulation of Hazardous Wastes Impacts Property Values for Purposes of Ad Valorem Taxation." *Ninth Annual IAAO Legal Seminar.* New Orleans, La.: November 9, 1989.

Rinaldi, Anthony J. "Contaminated Properties—Valuation Solutions." *The Appraisal Journal* (July 1991).

Silverman, Gerald B. (Bureau of National Affairs, Inc.). "Love Canal: A Retrospective." *Environmental Reporter,* vol. 20, no. 20, part II (September 15, 1989).

Smart, Miles M., and David L. Wynes. "The Impact of Environmental Conditions on Real Property." *Assessment Digest* (November/December 1990).

Svoboda, Robert S. "Valuation Case Studies Involving Environmental Issues." *15th Annual IPT Conference.* Reno, Nev.: June 23, 1991.

"Valuing Contaminated Land." *Environmental Law 14.* London, England: Denton Hall, 1994.

Vidich, Charles. "Calculating the Risk of Purchasing Toxic Real Estate." Paper presented at 1991 Annual Conference, American Real Estate Society, Sarasota, Fla., April 12, 1991.

White, Mark A. "The Environmental Impact on Valuation." Charlottesville, Va.: Virginia Association of Assessing Officers, 39th Annual Property Assessment Program, July 20-22, 1994.

Wilson, Albert R. "Appraisal Practice Considering Environmental Risks." *Focus,* vol. 2, no. 2 (November 1, 1989).

___. "Calculation of an Extraordinary Risk Premium." *Focus,* vol. 5, no. 2 (January 2, 1992).

___. "Emerging Approaches to Impaired Property Valuation." *Environmental Watch,* vol. VII, no. 2 (Summer 1994).

___. "The Environmental Opinion: Basis for an Impaired Value Opinion." *Focus,* vol. 5, no. 3 (September 1, 1992).

___. *Environmental Risk: Identification and Management.* Chelsea, Mich.: Lewis Publishers, 1991.

___. "Environmentally Impaired Valuation: A Team Approach to a Balance Sheet Presentation." *Technical Report.* Chicago, Ill.: Appraisal Institute, 1992.

Wilson, Albert R., Maxwell O. Ramsland, Jr., Thomas Wilhelmy, and Roger Groves. "Ad Valorem Taxation and Environmental Devaluation (Parts I and II)." *Journal of Property Tax Management* (Summer and Fall 1993).

General Overviews of Contamination Proximity Impacts (Stigma Effects) on Property Value

Abelson, Peter W. "Property Prices and the Value of Amenities." *Journal of Environmental Economics and Management,* vol. 6, no. 1 (March 1979).

Dear, Michael. "Understanding and Overcoming the NIMBY Syndrome." *Journal of The American Planning Association,* vol. 58, no. 3 (Summer 1992).

Elliot-Jones, Michael. *Rents and Proximity to Toxic Sites.* San Francisco: Foster Associates, Inc., 1991.

___. *'Stigma' in Light of Bixby Ranch, DeSario, and T&E Industries.* San Francisco: Foster Associates, Inc., 1995.

Guidotti, Tee L. "The Cancer Non-Epidemic of County 20: Case Study of an Epidemiological Mistake." *Public Health Review* 19 (1991/92): 179-190.

Guidotti, Tee L., and Sheila Abercrombie. "Voices of Leadership in a Community Under Stress: Personal Observations By Officials on an Epidemiologic Mistake." *Journal of Public Health Medicine* (Oxford University Press, 1994).

Guidotti, Tee L., and Philip Jacobs. "The Implications of an Epidemiological Mistake: A Community's Response to a Perceived Excess Cancer Risk." *American Journal of Public Health* 83 (1993): 233-239.

Healy, John J., and Patricia R. Healy. "Lenders' Perspectives on Environmental Issues." *Real Estate Issues,* vol. 16, no. 2 (Fall/Winter 1991). Reprinted in July 1992 issue of *The Appraisal Journal.*

Jaconetty, Thomas. "Stigma, Phobias, and Fear: Their Effect on Valuation." *Assessment Journal,* vol. 3., no. 1 (January/February 1996).

Kiel, Katherine A., and Katherine T. McClain. "House Prices During Siting Decision Stages: The Case of an Incinerator from Rumor Through Operation." *Journal of Environmental Economics and Management* 28 (March 1995): 241–55.

Kiel, Katherine A., and Katherine T. McClain. "The Effect of An Incinerator Siting on Housing Appreciation Rates." *Journal of Urban Economics* 37(3): 311–23.

Kinnard, William N., Jr. "Analyzing the Stigma Effect of Proximity to Hazardous Materials Sites." *Environmental Watch,* vol. II, no. 4 (December 1989).

___. "Fear (As A Measure of Damages) Strikes Out: Two Case Studies Comparisons of Actual Market Behavior with Opinion Survey Research." Paper presented at American Real Estate Society Annual Conference, Santa Barbara, Calif., April 1994.

___. "Property Valuation: A Primer on Proximity Impact Research." Paper presented at Executive Enterprises Conference on Electric and Magnetic Fields, Washington, D.C., December 1993.

___. "The Stigma Effects of Contamination on Real Property Values." Paper presented at the IAAO Legal Seminar, Scottsdale, Ariz., November 1995.

Kinnard, William N., Jr., Mary Beth Geckler, and Jake W. DeLottie. "Post-1992 Evidence of EMF Impacts on Nearby Residential Property Values." Paper presented at the 1997 Annual Conference of the American Real Estate Society, Sarasota, Fla., April 1997.

Kinnard, William N., Jr., Mary Beth Geckler, and John K. Geckler, "Are Residential Property Values Impacted By Proximity to Alleged or Perceived Hazards to Human Health and Safety?" *Journal of Property Tax Management* (Fall/Winter 1995).

McClelland, Gary H., William D. Schulze, and Brian Hurd. "The Effect of Risk Beliefs on Property Values." *Policy Analysis,* vol. 10, no. 4 (1990).

Mitchell, Robert C., and Richard T. Carson. *Using Surveys to Value Public Goods: The Contingent Valuation Method.* Washington, D.C.: Resources for the Future, 1989.

Mundy, Bill. "Contamination, Fear, and Industrial Property Transactions." *Professional Report.* Washington, D.C.: Society of Industrial and Office Realtors, May/June 1993.

___. *Hazardous & Toxic Materials, and Property Valuation: Bibliography.* Seattle, Wash.: Mundy and Associates, March 1992.

___. "The Impact of Hazardous and Toxic Material on Property Value: Revisited." *The Appraisal Journal* (October 1992).

___. "The Impact of Hazardous Materials on Property Value." *The Appraisal Journal* (April 1992).

___. "Stigma and Value." *The Appraisal Journal* (January 1992).

___. "Stigma Influences on Value." *Methodologies for Valuation of Real Property Impacted by Pollution from Hazardous and Toxic Materials.* Seminar presented and prepared by The Real Estate Counseling Group of America, Inc., Orlando, Fla., February 28, 1991.

___. "Summary of Methodologies for Measuring Impaired Property Value." *Environmental Analysis and Valuation Seminar.* Seattle, Wash.: Mundy and Associates, March 1992.

Patchin, Peter J. "Contaminated Properties—Stigma Revisited." *The Appraisal Journal* (January 1991).

"Property Devaluation from Off-Site Environmental Hazards." *Environmental Strategies for Real Estate,* vol. 2, no. 8. (Boston: Warren Gorham & Lamont, May 1995).

U.S. Department of Commerce, *Report of the NOAA Panel on Contingent Valuation.* Washington, D.C.: National Oceanographic and Atmospheric Administration, January 1993. Published in *Federal Register,* vol. 58, no. 10 (January 15, 1993).

Wise, Kenneth, and Johannes P. Pfeifenberger. "The Enigma of Stigma: The Case of the Industrial Excess Landfill." *Toxics Law Reporter* (May 1994).

Hazardous Waste

Ferguson, Jerry T., and Phyllis S. Myers. "Managing the Hazardous Waste Risk of Landlords and Lenders." Paper presented at the Annual Meeting of the American Real Estate Society, Hilton Head, S.C., April 1995.

Mundy, Bill. "Hazardous Waste: Contamination, Fear, and Industrial Property Transactions." *Professional Report.* Washington, D.C.: Society of Industrial and Office Realtors, May/June 1993.

Olsen, Ralph K. "Hazardous Waste Sites." *The Appraisal Journal* (April 1989).

Leaking Underground Storage Tanks (LUSTs)

Simons, Robert A., and Rudy R. Robinson, III. "Negative Proximity Influence of Leaking Underground Storage Tanks/Toxic Neighbors on Residential Property: Issues of Information and Measurement." Paper presented at Annual Meeting of the American Real Estate Society, Hilton Head, S.C., April 1995.

Radioactive Materials Proximity

Abkowitz, Mark D., Moses Karakouzian, and James A. Cardle. "Developing an Impact Analysis System for the Transport of High-Level Nuclear Waste." *Transportation Research Record,* no. 1264 (1990).

Bjornstad, David J., and David P. Vogt. "Some Comments Relating to Model Specification on 'Effects of Nuclear Power Plants on Residential Property Values.'" *Journal of Regional Science,* vol. 24, no. 1 (1984).

Capitol Region Planning and Development Agency. *Adverse Housing Related Impacts on Viability of Neighborhoods Due to the Three Mile Island Accident.* Report to Pennsylvania Department of Community Affairs, Bureau of Policy Planning, August 21, 1980.

Chalmers, J. D., K. Pijawka, K. Branch, P. Bergmann, and J. Flynn. *Socioeconomic Impacts of Nuclear Generating Stations: Summary Report.* Washington, D.C.: Nuclear Regulatory Commission (CR-2750), 1982.

Egar, Francis J. *Air Pollution and Property Values in the Hartford Metropolitan Region.* Unpublished PhD dissertation, Fordham University, 1973.

Galster, George. "Nuclear Power Plants and Residential Property Values: A Comment on Short-run vs. Long-run Considerations." *Journal of Regional Science* (1986).

Gamble, Hays B., and Roger H. Downing. "Effects of Nuclear Power Plants on Residential Property Values." *Journal of Regional Science* (1982).

———. *Effects of the Accident at Three Mile Island on Residential Property Values and Sales.* Institute for Research on Land and Water Resources, Pennsylvania State University. Prepared for U.S. Nuclear Regulatory Commission (NUREG/CR-2063), 1981.

Griffin, C. R. "Assessing the Impact on Housing Prices of the Environmental Hazard of Rocky Flats, Colorado: An Initial Examination." Paper presented at the Annual Meeting of the American Real Estate Society, Sarasota, Fla., April 11, 1991.

Griffin, C. R., and Daniel R. Vellenga. "Homeowner Attitudes Toward Purchasing and Living in the Near Proximity to a Nuclear Facility." Paper presented at annual conference of American Real Estate Society, Key West, Fla., April 17, 1993.

Hageman, Ronda K. "Nuclear Waste Disposal: Potential Property Value Impacts." *Natural Resources Journal* (October 1981).

Hoyt, Richard W., R. Keith Schwer, and William Thompson. "A Note on Homebuyer Attitudes Toward a Nuclear Repository." *The Journal of Real Estate Research,* vol. 7, no. 2 (Spring 1992).

Kinnard, William N., Jr. "Analyzing the Stigma Effect of Proximity to a Hazardous Materials Site." *Environmental Watch,* vol. 11, no. 4 (December 1989).

Kinnard, William N., Jr., and Mary Beth Geckler. "The Effects on Residential Real Estate Prices from Proximity to Properties Contaminated With Radioactive Materials." *Real Estate Issues,* vol. 16., no. 2 (Fall/Winter 1991).

Kinnard, William N., Jr., Phillip S. Mitchell, and Gail L. Beron. "The Market Impact of a Release of Radioactive Materials on Local Housing Values: An Econometric Study." *Journal of Property Tax Management* (Fall 1990).

Kinnard, William N., Jr., Phillip S. Mitchell, Gail L. Beron, and James R. Webb. "Market Reactions to an Announced Release of Radioactive Materials: The Impact on Assessable Value." *Property Tax Journal,* vol. 10, no. 3 (September 1991).

Miller, Norman G. "A Geographic Information System-Based Approach to the Effects of Nuclear Processing Plants on Surrounding Property Values: The Case of the Fernald Settlement Study." Paper presented at the American Real Estate Society Annual Meeting, San Diego, Calif., April 1992.

Nelson, Jon P. "Three Mile Island and Residential Property Values: Empirical Analysis and Policy Implications." *Land Economics* (August 1981).

Payne, B. A., S. J. Olshansky, and T. E. Segel. "The Effects on Residential Property Values of Proximity to a Site Contaminated with Radioactive Waste." *Waste Management Conference.* Tucson, Ariz.: March 24, 1985. Presented by Argonne National Laboratory, Ill.

Pijawka, D., and J. Chalmers. "Impact of Nuclear Generating Plants on Local Areas." *Economic Geography* (January 1983).

Shearer, Don Paul. *Three Mile Island Nuclear Accident Community Impact Study on Real Estate.* Greater Harrisburg Board of Realtors, Inc., TMI Impact Study Committee, 1978.

Silverman, Gerald B. (Bureau of National Affairs, Inc.). "Love Canal: A Retrospective." *Environmental Reporter,* vol. 20, no. 20, part II (September 1989).

Twark, Richard D., Raymond W. Eyerly, and Roger H. Downing. *The Effect of Nuclear Power Plants on Residential Property Values: A New Look at Three Mile Island.* University Park, Pa.: Environmental Resources Research Institute, Pennsylvania State University, September 1990.

Webb, James R. "Nuclear Power Plants: Effects on Property Values." *The Appraisal Journal* (April 1980).

Refinery Proximity

Flower, Patrick C., and Wade R. Ragas. "The Effects of Refineries on Neighborhood Property Values." *Journal of Real Estate Research,* vol. 9, no. 3 (Summer 1994).

Ragas, Wade R., and Patrick C. Flower. "Refineries and Neighborhood Property Values." *Technical Report 1018.* College Station, Texas: Texas A&M University, April 1994.

___. "Petroleum Refineries—Can Larger Site Buffers Limit Adjacent Property Value Impacts?" *Professional Report of the Society of Industrial and Office Realtors,* October 1994.

Soil Contamination

Hunsperger, Wayne L. "Heavy Metal Pollution and Residential Property Damages." *Environmental Watch,* vol. VI, no. 3 (Fall 1993).

Kinnard, William N., Jr., Jake W. DeLottie, Mary Beth Geckler, and Benjamin H. Noble. "The Impact of Widespread, Long-Term Soil Contamination on Residential Property Values: A Case Study." Paper presented at the Annual Meeting of the American Real Estate Society, Hilton Head, S.C., April 1995.

Phillips, Beverly S., Peter D. Bowes, and John Reisse, Jr. "Environmental Issues and Diminution of Value: A Case Study." *The Canadian Appraiser* (Summer 1994).

Spillage

Kimmel, Jeffrey J. *Spill Reporting Procedures Guide.* 1994 ed. Washington, D.C.: The Bureau of National Affairs, Inc., 1989.

Stigma From On-Site Contamination (Including Post-Remediation)

Elliot-Jones, Michael. *Bixby Ranch: Some Observations on Plaintiffs Expert's Appraisal of Post-Clean-Up 'Stigma'.* San Francisco, Calif.: Foster Associates, Inc., 1995.

___. *'Stigma' in Light of Bixby Ranch, DeSario, and T&E Industries.* San Francisco, Calif.: Foster Associates, Inc., 1995.

___. *Toxic Sites, Property Values & Liquidity.* San Francisco, Calif.: Foster Associates, Inc., 1991.

Hogin, Bradley R. "Post-Cleanup Stigma Claims: The Latest Front in the War Over Hazardous Waste Cost Recovery." *Analysis and Perspective.* Washington, D.C.: The Bureau of National Affairs, January 1995.

Mundy, Bill. "Stigma and Value: The Impact of Hazardous Materials." *Measuring the Effects of Hazardous Materials Contamination on Real Estate Values: Techniques and Applications.* Chicago: Appraisal Institute, 1992.

Water Contamination

Anderson, Terry L. "Water Rights." *Scarce Resource Allocation.* Cambridge, Mass.: Ballinger Publishing Co., 1983.

Houghton, Mary J. *The Clean Water Act Amendments of 1987: A BNA Special Report.* Washington D.C.: The Bureau of National Affairs, Inc., 1987.

Starr, Beth L. "Funding Wastewater Treatment Facilities." *The Complete Guide to the New State Revolving Fund Program: A BNA Special Report.* Washington, D.C.: The Bureau of National Affairs, Inc., 1988.

Chapter 8 Case Study

By Randall Bell, MAI

Ashby Building—Leaking Underground Storage Tank (LUST)—Eugene, Oregon
Class VIII—Environmental Contamination Case Study

The Ashby Building is a 240,644-sq.-ft. multitenant industrial building located on the West Coast of the United States. It was sold without the proper disclosure of an illegally installed underground storage tank (UST). The UST had originally been used to store petroleum products but was later abandoned for that purpose and utilized for the storage of hazardous fiberglass resins by a custom speedboat manufacturer. Without proper governmental disclosure, the UST was later removed, but the contents of the UST had leaked into the soil and groundwater.

Because the tank had been illegally installed and removed, there were no records of its existence in the city's files. The problem went undetected by the property's buyer and the contracted environmental engineer until ground settlement problems arose in the area where the UST had been located. Apparently, the soils had not been properly compacted when the UST was removed. The soil settlement led to an investigation whereby the new property owner learned of the UST's history from prior tenants who had occupied other units within the industrial complex.

A lawsuit was filed against the prior property owner in 1989. The scope of the appraisal assignment was to determine the actual market value of the subject property inclusive of the UST. In other words, while the property owner paid $6.5 million for the property, what was the real market value when it was purchased? As the property owner had thought he was purchasing an environmentally clean property, the actual purchase price of $6.5 million was accepted by both the plaintiff and defendant as the value as if not contaminated.

In order to determine the value as contaminated, construction and remediation estimates were obtained from the respective consultants. The property assessment costs included all the costs associated with assessing the environmental damages, such as Phase I and II studies, soil and geotechnical studies, well monitoring, and other costs. These costs were provided by the engineering firms. In this situation, the site assessment costs totaled $50,542.

The remediation costs involve all costs associated with the actual cleanup and correction of the site contamination. This could include a vast spectrum of costs, depending on the remediation method chosen. In this case, the remediation method chosen was the excavation of the most problematic contaminated soils, treatment of some of the soil by incineration, and disposal of some soil in an approved landfill. These costs included agency oversight, engineering, legal review, permits, sampling and analysis, backfill, and the actual remediation, totaling $331,188. Again, these costs were provided by the engineers of the firm contracted to conduct the remediation.

As stated, remediation costs can exceed their original estimates. For this reason, a contingency was required to adjust the remediation costs to reflect a truly reasonable worst-case scenario. The premise for this adjustment was that the real estate market must have a sensible assurance that *all* possible remediation costs will be accounted for in the estimates provided. In this case, upon investigation it was determined that the remediation costs were estimated on an expected-case basis. In a deposition, the engineers and technical experts stated that these costs could reasonably increase by $75,000. Based on this information, a $75,000 contingency was applied to the remediation costs to reflect what costs may actually be incurred. It is important to note that the contingency applied to the remediation costs relates to the hard costs of remediation and should not be confused with intangible losses, such as market resistance or stigma. Informed potential buyers must have reasonable assurance that they have a clear indication of their potential cash liability. Therefore, it is essential that the total remediation costs accurately reflect the total maximum reasonable cleanup costs, not just a cursory and optimistic estimate.

During environmental remediation, the property may experience a significant down time while the cleanup process is carried out. In these situations, there may be considerable carrying costs, such as interest payments, lost rents, property taxes, security, etc. These various user-related costs were analyzed and estimated to be $325,000.

Under the conditions of market value, a knowledgeable prospective buyer would not likely purchase a property in a contaminated state unless there was a financial incentive to do so. This is much like the profit required by a developer who purchases vacant land and builds a structure. The buyer must be enticed through a lower price or a discount. Without such an incentive, the prospective buyer would likely just buy another similar property that is not contaminated, and thereby avoid the risks and trouble associated with purchasing a contaminated site. In order to determine what the incentive should be, various investors who specialize in purchasing contaminated properties were contacted and interviewed. In addition, properties that sold in a contaminated state were located, and the buyers were interviewed as to the discount they received in purchasing an environmentally contaminated property. This information was compiled and ranged from 5% to 45% (exclusive of market resistance) of the value of the property in an uncontaminated state. This particular property was located in an area where contamination was not uncommon, and there was a very good assurance as to the reliability of the remediation estimates. Based upon the interviews, market data, and subsequent analysis, a project incentive of from 10% to 15% was considered likely, and a 12.5% project incentive was considered reasonable.

Contaminated or formerly contaminated sites may incur difficulty in obtaining financing or insurance. Lenders and insurance carriers may not even consider financing a site that is yet to have contamination remedied and may be reluctant to finance a property that has been remedied. This is usually due to the concerns related to governmental agencies not permanently certifying a site as "clean." This could result in an environmental review of the property, additional loan points, a higher interest rate, or a lower loan-to-value ratio. The net result is that the property owner may pay additional financing costs. In this case, a survey was conducted with numerous lenders, and based on site-specific characteristics and the prevalent attitudes in 1989, an additional financing fee of $13,442 was considered appropriate.

A contaminated site may also incur restrictions in use. For example, a commercial site could be limited to an industrial use. In this case, the highest and best use went unchanged, so no adjustment was required for this factor.

At this point, an adjustment was made for the market resistance related to a formerly contaminated property. This reflected the market's resistance to purchase a property after remediation, but with a history of contamination. In this case, market data and interviews with such buyers indicated that a 5% discount would be appropriate in this situation involving a "source property." This rate is applied to the overall property value to indicate a final value "as contaminated." Again, this reflected the attitudes in 1989.

The total diminution in value was $1,932,672, which reflected a market value as contaminated of $4,567,328. The total losses attributable to the contamination are approximately 30% of the Class I value. This figure is cross-referenced for reasonableness and is comparable with the percentage losses of other similar contaminated properties. As this case study illustrates, the remediation costs ($331,188) are often just a portion of the overall diminution in value ($1,932,672). A summary of the calculations used in the valuation process follows:

Value undamaged		$6,500,000
Less:		
Assessment costs		$50,542
Repair process		
Remediation costs	$331,188	
Contingency costs	75,000	
Use-related costs	325,000	
Project incentive (risk) @12.5%	812,500	
		$1,543,688
Ongoing costs		13,442
Market resistance (risk) @ 5%		325,000
Value as damaged		$4,567,328

CHAPTER 9

Class IX—Natural Conditions

Class IX detrimental conditions involve curable natural conditions that may be economically and physically repaired. These would include earthquakes, naturally occurring geotechnical problems, landslides, floods, wetlands, volcanoes, infestation, and other natural disasters.

Many areas that are susceptible to natural disasters have incredible scenery, which is very enticing, and may even command a premium within the real estate market. Some sites that have risks associated with natural disasters often "come with the view," and there is an interesting resilience among a portion of the home buying market that is almost drawn to these dangers. That is why some of the most prime real estate may be located in areas susceptible to hurricanes, wave damage, flooding, firestorms, and the like. Of course, areas that are prone to natural disasters and that do not have any particular view or location amenity may not fall into this category. For these reasons, it is necessary to study the local market data before drawing any general conclusions about the impact that natural disasters have on property values.

Class IX detrimental conditions may involve a significant safety issue to the occupants of the property. If the detrimental condition can be fully assessed and repaired, the property value may return to the previous level prior to the condition having occurred. However, if a reasonable question remains as to the effectiveness of the repair or remediation or the possibility of future disasters that target a particular property, there may be a residual loss of value due to the market resistance. Again, the impact on value involves the costs to clean up or fortify the site, incidental costs, any residual conditions, and market resistance.

As illustrated in Exhibit 9.1, Class IX natural conditions reflect a drop in value and then a return to full value upon the assessment and repair of the condition. However, in many Class IX conditions there are justifiable uncertainties regarding the effectiveness of the repairs, or there may be ongoing naturally occurring conditions.

Exhibit 9.1 Class IX—Natural Conditions

The primary graph for DC Class IX has been highlighted here; however, DCs have a variety of impacts which, upon analysis, vary on a case-by-case basis. Ultimately any graph may be applicable based on a case-specific facts.

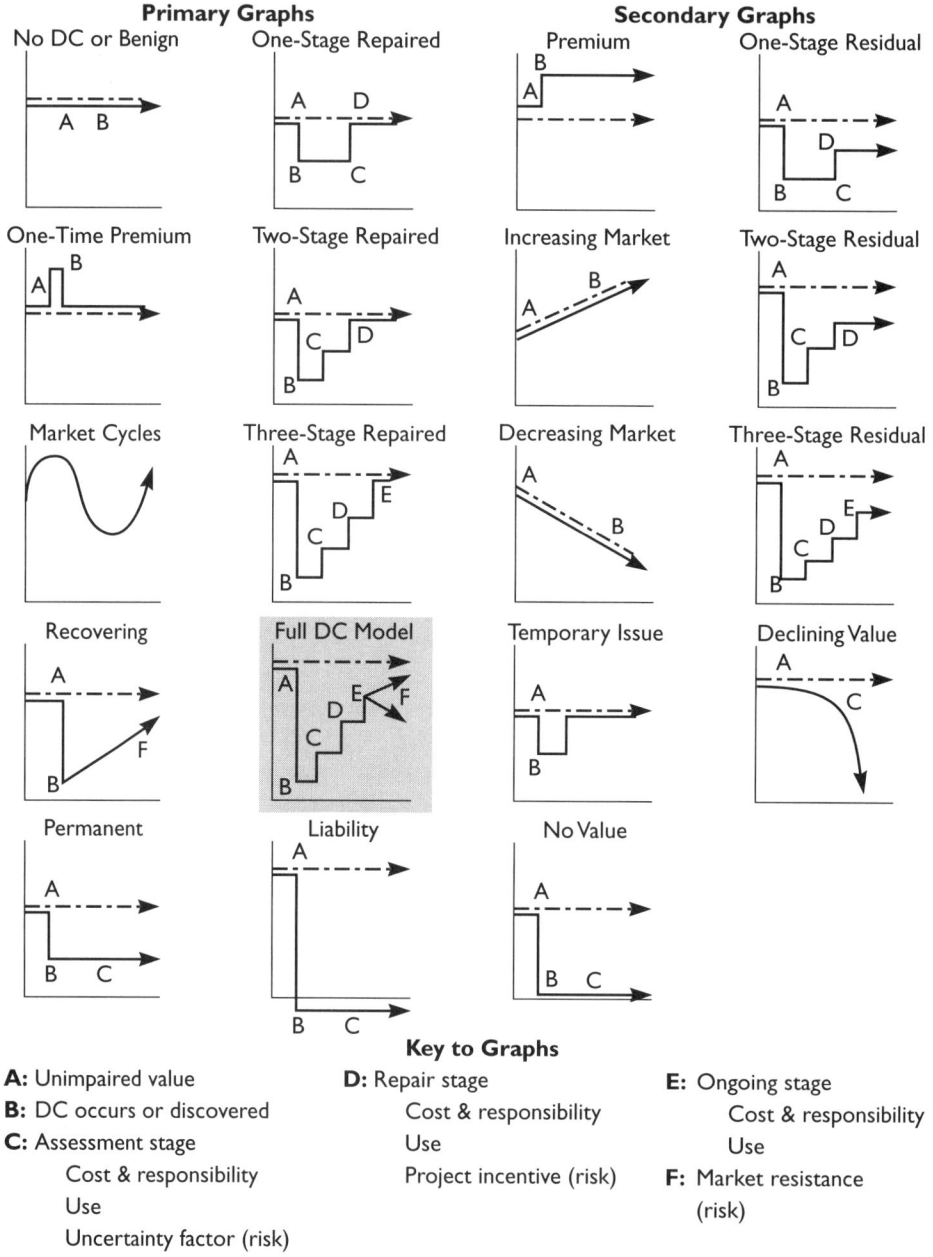

Key to Graphs

A: Unimpaired value
B: DC occurs or discovered
C: Assessment stage
    Cost & responsibility
    Use
    Uncertainty factor (risk)
D: Repair stage
    Cost & responsibility
    Use
    Project incentive (risk)
E: Ongoing stage
    Cost & responsibility
    Use
F: Market resistance
    (risk)

Source: *Bell's Guide: The Real Estate Encyclopedia*

Earthquakes

An earthquake is a shaking, rolling, or sudden shock of the earth's surface generated by the movement of the earth's crust or upper mantle as a result of a buildup of stress. Failure occurs at a point or in a fairly small zone, known as the *focus*, with the *epicenter* being the point on the earth's surface directly above this focus. However, once failure has occurred, movement may persist along a zone of weakness, known as a *fault*, for a considerable distance, as long as hundreds of miles. On average, thousands of earthquakes occur every week around the world, and there can be more than 1 million in a year. However, most are mild, occur in remote areas or under the ocean, and are not noticeable. Severe earthquakes can be expected every 8 to 10 years, but many smaller earthquakes occur annually that are also capable of destruction.

Earthquakes show a marked spatial distribution. The vast majority are located within narrow zones that correspond to the boundaries of the lithospheric plates. These plates are blocks of the earth's crust that are in continuous movement relative to each other. This movement is thought to be driven by the connective processes in the earth's mantle (i.e., the region of rocks beneath the crust that are heated to the point of becoming plastic). The energy released by a large earthquake may equal that of about 200 million short tons of TNT, and its energy may be 10,000 times as great as that of the first atomic bomb.

Richter Scale

The strength of an earthquake is measured on a system called the *Richter Scale*, which was developed by American seismologist Charles F. Richter in 1935. Scientists calculate Richter magnitude by using information obtained from a seismograph, an instrument that records ground motion. Each number on the Richter scale represents an earthquake 10 times as strong as one of the next lower magnitude. For example, an earthquake of magnitude 8 is 10 times stronger than one of magnitude 7. Further, an earthquake of magnitude 7 is 100 times as strong as one of 5. There are approximately 1,000 earthquakes daily with a magnitude of 2.0, and those under 5.0 are considered to be minor as they cause little if any damage. Earthquakes with a magnitude of 7.0 or greater can cause serious damage. Other measurements of intensity can be made, as an earthquake of one given magnitude may cause different damage from place to place. The Modified Mercalli Intensity Scale classifies earthquakes into 12 categories ranging from those barely felt to ones that cause incredible damage.

Property Issues

While certain areas are more prone to earthquakes than others, seismic events cannot be accurately predicted. For example, California can expect a catastrophic earthquake once every 50 to 100 years, but unlike many natural disasters there is no warning as to when they will occur. When an earthquake does hit, the damage is terrifying. During an earthquake, the ground shakes violently, buildings crack and topple, electric transformers explode, windows break, and power lines snap. Because of their unpredictability and intense damage, many areas prone to earthquakes have strict building codes to resist damages. The building codes are not an assurance that a property will withstand any earthquake damage but are designed to prevent the collapse of a building, sparing human life.

At 4:31 a.m. on Monday January 17, 1994, the most expensive earthquake, and one of the most expensive natural disasters in U.S. history, shook the Southern California region. Although this earthquake is considered moderate with a magnitude of 6.8 on the Richter Scale, with the epicenter in the highly populated Northridge suburb of Los Angeles, the quake caused 57 deaths, injured approximately 1,500 people, and caused more than $10 billion in damage. Of the 66,546 buildings inspected, 6% were "red tagged" (severely damaged) and 17% were "yellow tagged" (moderately damaged). Some of the most traveled freeways in the nation were closed for several months, and 11 major roads providing access to Los Angeles were damaged. Many residents and businesses were displaced to adjacent (less damaged) areas while repair projects were completed.

From its outward appearance, this condominium complex looks to be another trendy development in Encino, California. However, closer inspection reveals that tremendous damage was incurred from the Northridge earthquake, which forced the residents of the property to vacate.

Earthquake damage is indiscriminate. Older buildings may withstand earthquakes for decades while newly constructed buildings nearby are completely destroyed. Despite the almost random nature of earthquake damage, properties that have been constructed to code may be worth more than an otherwise similar building that was not. Similarly, older properties that have been retrofitted may be of more value.

When the Northridge earthquake occurred, real estate values in the San Fernando Valley were generally declining due to a regional economic downturn. Immediately following the earthquake, most pending sales of real estate sales in the San Fernando Valley were postponed until damage assessments could be completed. Values of damaged properties were negatively impacted for a short-term period while they were repaired. Nondamaged properties experienced no long-term loss in values. Adjacent areas, such as the Conejo Valley to the east, experienced an upsurge in occupancy for short-term housing (apartments and rental homes) while displaced home owners sought temporary residences as repair projects were completed.

Residential buyer confidence experienced a short downturn with little or no long-term implications. The investor market of large commercial properties required more time to reinstate buyer confidence. Marketing time was extended during repair efforts, yet no permanent effect has been observed. Research indicates that the negative impacts on real estate directly from the Northridge earthquake were short-lived and were related to costs of repairs (and related costs, if any). The market generally reacts on the basis that earthquakes are random in nature and impact Southern California as a whole. The perceived likelihood of an earthquake reoccurring in Northridge are the same as any other community in Southern California.

Landslides

Landslides, sometimes called *landslips* or *mass wasting* by geologists, are one of the most serious and yet most unsensationalized of natural disasters. Although large landslides occur infrequently, they have the potential for enormous loss of life, property, and resources. For example, in 1959 a rock landslide occurred in British Columbia where debris reached speeds up to 360 kilometers per hour. During a 1903 rock landslide at Frank, Alberta, 90 million tons of limestone detached from Turtle Mountain and buried part of the coal mining town of Frank, resulting in the deaths of about 75 people. In the United States, it is estimated that landslides cause in excess of $1 billion in damages and result in about 25 to 50 deaths each year. Globally, landslides are the cause of hundreds of billions of dollars in damages annually and have been responsible for hundreds of thousands of deaths and injuries.

Landslides can be doubly costly and dangerous in that they are usually accompanied by, or even caused by, another major natural disaster. Excessive precipitation can cause landslides in sloped areas where vegetation is scarce as a result of wildfires. Avalanches caused by heavy snows and lava flows resulting from volcanic eruptions are both forms of landslides. Oceanic landslides can result in tsunamis.

Types of Landslides

Some more common terms describing different types of landslides include *avalanches, lava flow,* and *mudslides*. However, geologists have a seemingly endless list of terms describing the different types of landslides. They differentiate between the composition of the landslide (soil, lava, snow, etc.), speed, volume, and cause as well as many other factors. A change in one of those factors affects the behavior of the landslide and thus the term geologists use to describe it. At the macro level, the most common landslides are creep, slump, earthflow, slope failure, and debris flow.

Creep is the indiscernibly slow movement of soil and near-surface rock materials downslope. As is implied by this definition, the process is generally not directly observed. Instead, the movement can be best detected through the movement or response of objects affected by the process, such as walls, utility poles, fences, and concrete slabs. When under the influence of a creep, fence posts will tilt downslope and, if enough time passes, will approach a horizontal position. Small trees on a slope experiencing creep likewise display the effects of the landslide, as their trunks are progressively tilted over by creep, their new growth responds phototropically upwards towards the sun, leading to curvature of the trunk. Doors or windows may stick or jam for the first time. New cracks may appear in plaster, tile, brick, or foundations. Outside walls, walks, or stairs may pull away from the building. Slowly developing, widening cracks may appear on the ground or on paved areas such as streets or driveways. Underground utility lines may break or bulging ground may appear at the base of a slope.

A much quicker type of landslide is described as a *slump*. A slump is the movement of a block of earth material through downward rotation along a curved surface of failure, similar to a snowball rolling downhill. Slumps are especially common where clay-rich materials are exposed on oversteepened slopes, such as on river cutbacks or on highway roadcuts.

A slump with little or no rotation of the mass involved is called an *earthflow*. An earthflow represents the downslope movement of water-saturated, clay-rich materials. In contrast to a slump, the mass "slides" downhill as opposed to "rolling" downhill. However, many slumps terminate in earthflows. The sliding mass moves along a shear surface that generally parallels the slope surface.

Slope failure is a term used to describe a landslide with properties of both a slump and an earthflow. In a slope failure there will be some rolling of the mass downhill and some sliding. As is true of most landslides, heavy snowmelt or rains will contribute to the magnitude of the landslide. Fast-moving landslides commonly start out as a coherent mass but may break up into a debris flow if enough distance is covered and enough water is present. The term *debris flow* implies that a fluid mass is moving down a slope. Debris flows look and act like wet, flowing concrete and contain about 30% water. Velocities of large debris flows can reach more than 110 miles per hour on the steepest slopes. The velocities of smaller debris flows (i.e., the small, narrow flows that descend steep slopes after a heavy rain) are commonly in the range of 10 to 20 miles per hour.

Contributing Factors

Although gravity acting on an overly steep slope is the primary reason for a landslide, there are other contributing factors:

- Erosion by rivers, glaciers, or ocean waves helps to create steep slopes that increase the chance of a landslide. Rock and soil slopes can be weakened through saturation by snowmelt or heavy rains. When slope materials become saturated with water, a debris flow or mudflow may develop. The resulting slurry of rock and mud may pick up trees, houses, and cars, thus blocking bridges and tributaries, causing flooding along its path.
- Earthquakes can create stresses that make already weak slopes fail or cause weaknesses in slopes where there were none previously. Vibrations from machinery, traffic, blasting, and even thunder can, to a lesser degree, have the same effects as an earthquake, causing weak slopes to fail.
- Volcanic eruptions produce loose ash deposits, heavy rain, and debris flows as the force of the eruption throws vast amounts of earth into the air. Additionally, excess weight from the accumulation of rain or snow, stockpiling of rock or ore, from waste piles, or from man-made structures may stress weak slopes to failure causing landslides of varying magnitude.

As weathering and erosion play a major part in the risk of landslides, the prevailing rock type in an area determines how susceptible an area is to erosion. In general, quartzite is the most resistant rock to weathering. Granite will weather faster than quartzite. Basalt tends to weather faster than granite. Limestone tends to erode faster than quartzite, granite, or basalt, and sedimentary evaporates (salt rock) tends to weather fastest of all. Although the physical causes of many landslides cannot be removed, geologic investigations, good engineering practices, and effective enforcement of land-use management regulations can reduce landslide hazards.

In general, any area composed of very weak or fractured materials resting on a steep slope can and will likely experience landslides, which occur in every state and U.S. territory. The Appalachian Mountains, the Rocky Mountains, the Pacific Coastal Ranges, and some parts of Alaska and Hawaii have severe landslide problems. Additionally, there are certain other areas that are more prone to landslides, which include existing old landslides, areas on or at the base of slopes, areas in or at the base of minor drainage hollows, areas at the base or top of an old fill slope or of a steep cut slope, and developed hillsides where leach field septic systems are used. In contrast, there are also certain areas that inherently possess a lower risk of landslides, including areas on hard, non-jointed bedrock that have not moved in the past, sites on relatively flat-lying areas away from sudden changes in slope angle, and areas at the top or along the nose of ridges, set back from the tops of slopes.

As an example of potential effects, two landslides, the Paty-Alani and the Hulu-Woolsey, damaged and destroyed approximately 150 homes in a large residential neighborhood of Honolulu, Hawaii, known as Manoa, which was originally developed in 1951. It is considered a premier area, with many of the homes having an outstanding view of downtown Honolulu and the ocean. The ground movement was first noticed in approximately 1981 and continues today. The slow-moving slippage has caused the ground to heave or sink several feet over a period of several months or even years. As a result, many homes have slowly sunk, tilted, crumbled, or fallen down the hillside, and some streets have a dramatic "rollercoaster" effect. The city began remediation efforts in 1986.

What was once a covered carport is now a crumbled section of walls.

With the foundations undermined from the Manoa landslide, some homes require bracing to avoid their collapse.

At first, the city considered condemning numerous homes at a cost of $10 to $15 million, but it later opted to attempt to repair and reinforce the soils. This effort is ongoing. Most agree that the slippage is due to water-saturated soils; however, the source of the water is disputed. Some contend that the soils saturation was caused by heavy rains, which in turn caused water and sewer lines to burst. Others feel that the water and sewer lines were not installed and maintained properly, causing them to burst and thereby saturating the soils.

When evaluating a property in a landslide area, consideration should be made as to risk of a landslide, the magnitude of that landslide, and the possible effects the landslide could have to that area. Basic information on landslide risks can be obtained from the county geologist or county planning department in the area. Additionally, the United States Geological Survey (USGS) produces landslide susceptibility

Class IX—Natural Conditions

maps for many areas in the country, which can be helpful in assessing the risk of landslides in a specific area.

To mitigate the losses of properties being threatened by a landslide, there are steps that can be taken to reduce the risk of landslide damage, such as to plant ground cover on slopes and build retaining walls. In mudflow areas, channels can be built to deflect the flow around buildings. Caisson and piles, discussed in Chapter 7, can also be used. If a property is impacted by landslide threat, a paired sales analysis is typically utilized to measure any losses in these instances.

In Manoa, many homes collapsed completely, and the sites are considered unbuildable. Therefore, they suffered a total loss of value. Many more homes have suffered a variety of damages, from cracked walls, fallen carports, sunken fences, cracked foundations, and tilting. While many homes have not been impacted, most residents have found it virtually impossible to sell their properties. However, there have been seven home sales from 1989 to 1997. These sales reflected deep discounts, with prices ranging from $150,000 to $398,500 in an area that would normally command prices of from $500,000 to $1 million.

Tsunamis

A tsunami is a series of waves traveling quickly across the ocean with wavelengths up to hundreds of miles between wave crests. *Tsunami* is a Japanese word that translates as "harbor wave." Tsunamis are also called *tidal waves,* although there is a distinction. Tidal waves are simply the periodic movement of water associated with the rise and fall of the tides produced by gravitational attraction of the sun and moon.

The waves seen at the beach are generated by wind blowing over the sea surface. The size of these waves depends on the strength of the wind creating them and the distance over which the wind blows. Tsunamis, on the other hand, are caused by activity that displaces large amounts of water, such as submarine volcanic explosions, submarine landslides, or, most commonly, by earthquakes along the seafloor. Under most circumstances, submarine earthquakes must have a magnitude of 7 or greater on the Richter Scale to create a significant tsunami. Tsunamis created by volcanic activity or landslides are much less energetic than those caused by earthquakes. The size and energy of these tsunamis dissipates rapidly as it moves farther away from the source, thus resulting in more local devastation.

Tsunamis travel approximately 300 miles an hour, though they have been known to reach speeds of 500 to 600 miles an hour. In the open ocean, their amplitude is usually less than four feet, and tsunamis look like nothing more than the gentle rise and fall of the sea surface. This makes detection extremely difficult. For example, the Sanriku tsunami that struck Honshu, Japan, on June 15, 1896, killed 28,000 people and destroyed 170 miles of coastline, yet fishermen 20 miles out to sea did not notice the wave pass under their boats because it only had a height at the time of about 15 inches. They were totally unprepared for the devastation that awaited them when they returned to the port of Sanriku. While tsunamis are generally confined to the Pacific basin, they have been recorded in all of the major oceans of the world. Early records of other destructive tsunamis include one caused by the Krakatoa volcano explosion in 1833, which drowned some 36,000 people in Java and Sumatra.

Many people visualize an enormous wave breaking on the shore when considering the image of a tsunami. Actually, tsunamis appear as an advancing tide without having a developed wave face, resulting in rapid flooding of low-lying coastal areas. Normally the first signs of a tsunami are a receding water level caused by the trough of the wave. Between wave crests the tide has been known to expose up to 500 feet of seafloor in the seaward direction. The incoming wave will approach much like the incoming tide, though at a much faster speed.

The impact of a tsunami is devastating. Both personal and real property can be submerged, broken, or washed further inland or out into the ocean. Power and phone lines are highly vulnerable to tsunamis. Even underground utilities such as sewer and water facilities can be affected, as a tsunami may also result in soil erosion and sedimentation. It is common for widespread fires to erupt if tank farms for fuel are damaged. Boats docked at sea often are damaged by pounding against one another or against the docks. The economy of a coastal community can be greatly disrupted if it depends heavily on shipping, fishing, and water transportation.

After a 1946 tsunami in Hawaii, scientists and governmental agencies established the Pacific Tsunami Warning System for the Hawaiian Islands and U.S. territories in the Pacific. The system involves submarine earthquake detection and a close watch of unusual changes in water level at tide-gauging stations located throughout the Pacific, to predict a time of arrival to allow time for evacuation. Unfortunately the system has not proven to be completely reliable. Seventy-five percent of all warnings issued since 1948 have been false. In 1948, Honolulu was evacuated on a false alarm that cost more than $30 million. Fortunately, today's technology for monitoring the earthquakes that generate tsunamis provides some warning, although nothing can ever be done to prevent tsunamis from occurring, leaving that possibility of mass destruction to coastlines.

Snow Avalanches

An avalanche is a large mass of snow, ice, earth, rock, or other material in swift motion down a mountainside or over a precipice. Soil and mud avalanches are caused when water-saturated soils break loose and ooze down a mountainside. Ice avalanches contain some snow but are primarily made up of glacier ice. Snow avalanches are those most commonly spoken of and have caused death and destruction at mining and transportation facilities in the past. Today, though, the properties primarily at risk are mountain cabins.

Snow avalanches require three factors:

1. sufficient snow
2. sufficient slope of generally greater than 30 degrees
3. instability within the snowpack

Unless all of these conditions exist, there is no risk of an avalanche.

There are two types of avalanches: loose snow and slab avalanches. Loose snow avalanches begin from a single point and expand as they descend. The slide path looks much like an upside-down **V**. Loose snow avalanches are usually fairly minor, but in exposed climbing situations or late in the spring they can be very serious. Slab avalanches are a greater threat to skiers, climbers, and snowmobilers. A slab is a cohesive layer of snow that has not bonded well with the layer below it. As a result, it is under stress as it is supporting its own weight on a slope. When the stress within the snow layer exceeds the strength of the snow, the slab releases much like a pane of glass when it shatters under its own weight. The trigger may be another storm, a change in temperature, or the weight of a person.

The most devastating snow avalanches occur when triggered by earthquakes. One of the most destructive took place in Peru. First, on January 10, 1962, a hanging glacier on the summit of Mount Huascaran broke off at the approximate altitude of 6,300 meters. It traveled 16 kilometers, falling 4,000 meters in elevation, and destroyed everything in its path. More than 4,000 human lives were lost and nine small towns were destroyed. A small hill protected the city of Yungay, but it too fell victim to another destructive avalanche eight years later. On May 31, 1970, a large earthquake shook Peru and released another monstrous avalanche from Mount Huascaran. This time, the avalanche spilled over the hill, buried Yungay, and took 20,000 lives.

An average avalanche of snow is two to three feet deep at the fracture line and 100 to 200 feet wide, and it will fall 300 to 500 feet in elevation. The speed of an avalanche of this size is roughly 49 to 60 miles an hour, if the snow is dry. If the snow is wet, either from heavy rain or from thaw, the speed will be slower, probably in the range of 20 to 40 miles an hour. In general, the larger the avalanches the higher the speeds, and the fastest avalanches measured have traveled at around 230 miles per hour.

In the winter of 1976 an avalanche in Utah's Rocky Mountains destroyed the "Grizzly Adams" cabin used in the filming of the film *Jeremiah Johnson*. The cabin was located in an exclusive area associated with the Sundance Ski Resort, owned by the actor Robert Redford. Numerous subsequent avalanches have occurred in this area, including one 1986 Class 4 Avalanche (Class 5 is the worst). The only residence damaged in this incident was to a 6,500-sq.-ft. cabin owned by Robert G. Allen, author of the real estate book *Nothing Down*. The cabin was condemned.

This cabin, located at the base of a mountain in Sundance, Utah, was destroyed by a snow avalanche in 1996.

Due to destruction of trees and other natural defenses, the avalanches continued with increased frequency and impact. In 1996, another avalanche (Class 3) impacted a total of four cabins within the "Nothing Down" finger, or path (named after the 1986 slide). One house was not hit by the avalanche but by the shock waves. The house was blown off its foundation and ended up in a pile of rubble. The area is now considered a "frequent return interval," with imminent future exposure to avalanche hazard.

The cabins ranged in value from approximately $1 million to $3 million and were either completely destroyed or significantly damaged. All four cabins have been condemned. Sales in the area are very limited. The insurance company that owned one condemned cabin recently sold the damaged property for a substantial discount. The new owner received a building permit in 1997 for a "three-season residence." Utah County has placed the site within the "modified procedural or operational" classification. In other words, the residence may not be occupied in the winter, and the property must be rebuilt if it is destroyed.

The county has yet to implement an avalanche hazard zone classification, similar to flood zone maps, that would alert buyers of the danger. Utah County is currently considering implementing the international hazard zoning for this area.

- Red zones would not permit any new structures nor the rebuilding of existing structures.
- Blue zones would permit limited construction for private residences.
- Yellow and white zones would permit public and private improvements.

There are currently no disclosure laws in Utah regarding avalanches. However, prudent agents are notifying potential purchasers if information is available.

Tornadoes

Tornadoes are one of nature's most fascinating and devastating events. The word *tornado* originated from the Spanish word *tronada,* meaning thunderstorm, although a thunderstorm is only a component of a tornado. Tornadoes are the result of great instability in the atmosphere. Most tornadoes form along a front between cool, dry air from the north and warm, humid air to the south. A narrow zone of cumulonimbus (thunderstorm) clouds develops along such a front. This zone of clouds, called a *squall line,* produces violent weather when a mass of warm, humid air rises extremely rapidly. As this air rises, more warm air rushes in to replace it. The inrushing air also rises and may begin to rotate. These strong storm updrafts, sometimes coupled with the dragging effect of falling rain or hail, results in a further tightening in a rotational motion. The rotating funnel cloud extends downward from the mass of dark storm clouds. Some funnels do not reach the ground, but others dip down and strike the earth.

Tornadoes can occur in many areas of the world, in any month, and at any time, but certain patterns and characteristics do exist. The winds of a tornado spin in a counterclockwise direction in the Northern Hemisphere and clockwise in the Southern Hemisphere. This is in part due to recurring weather patterns in each hemisphere. Most occur in the spring and early summer and most frequently occur during the middle and late afternoon. The greatest incidence of the world's tornadoes occurs in the Mississippi River Valley in the U.S., but Australia, Sweden, Russia, Italy, New Zealand, and the United Kingdom also have a high incidence rate. Within the United States, Texas has had the most reported tornadoes, with an average of 139 per year, as shown in Exhibit 9.2. Most tornadoes last less than an hour and travel at 10 to 25 miles per hour with an approximate distance of 20 miles, yet in extreme cases, a tornado can last a few hours and travel 200 miles at a speed of up to 60 miles per hour. The U.S. National Weather Service constantly gathers weather information from all parts of the country and issues tornado warnings. These warnings include the anticipated intensity of the tornado as well as the location and the path.

The winds of a tornado are the most violent that occur on earth and may whirl at speeds of more than 300 miles per hour. Most tornadoes measure several hundred yards in diameter, but they can measure as far across as a mile and a half and can destroy anything in their path. Tornadoes are capable of lifting entire homes and other structures out with their foundations and completely demolishing them. Where foundations remain, the winds can literally strip floors of their tile and linoleum. Mature trees can be pulled out by the roots.

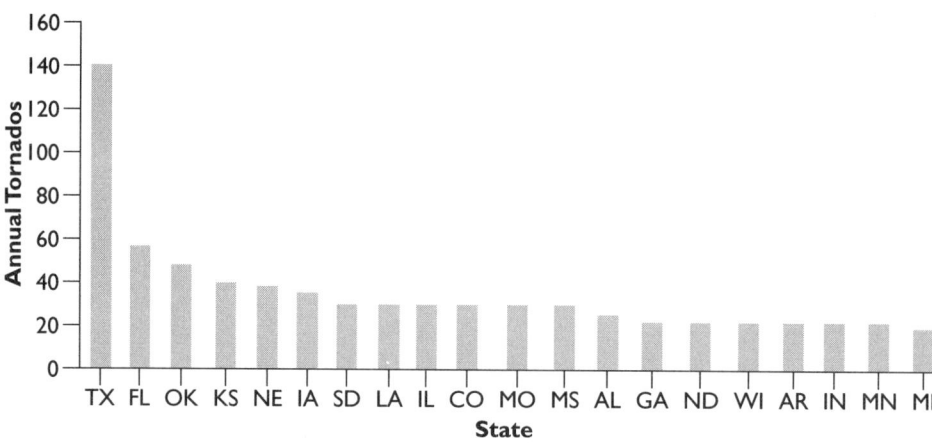

Exhibit 9.2 20 Largest Annual Tornado Distributions by State for 1962–1991

Source: www.geocities.com/Vienna/3885/occur.htm

Fujita Scale

The Fujita Scale is used to measure a tornado's intensity and is named after Dr. T. T. (Ted) Fujita, who made the first systematic study of tornado forces. Dr. Fujita devised a classification scheme based on the damage on a scale from F0 to F6, F0 being the weakest and F6 the most intense, as seen in Exhibit 9.3. The majority of tornadoes of record have been of class F0 to F1.

Following a tornado warning at 3:30 p.m. on May 27, 1997, a tornado hit Jarrell, Texas, with winds of 261 miles per hour at 3:42 p.m. This was an extremely rare event, with an F5 Fujita Scale ranking. The disaster caused 27 deaths, and virtually everything in the path of the tornado was destroyed. Trees were debarked and uprooted, grass was pulled from the ground, 300 head of cattle were lost, and dozens of cars were thrown over one-half mile.

Strong tornadoes are not a new event in Jarrell. On May 17, 1989, a tornado destroyed many properties, including a local market and diner called "Doc's." The tornado in 1997 passed just west of downtown Jarrell and struck the Double Creek residential subdivision. The destroyed homes lost the value of the structure, or incurred the cost of repairs. Much of the damage was paid for by volunteers, insurance claims, and governmental disaster relief funds.

Tornado Risk

Typically with tornado damage, aside from the costs of repairs or replacement, properties do not suffer any extended diminution in value. The prevalent perception within "Tornado Alley" (an area from Illinois down to Texas that is prone to tornadoes) is that acts of nature are random and are an inherent risk associated with the many benefits of living in the area. As a result, property owners generally have the attitude that impacted areas stand no greater risk of being destroyed again in the future than any other properties in the region. In other words, as the entire region is perceived to have a risk of tornadoes,

Exhibit 9.3 The Fujita Scale

F0	Gale tornado	40–72 mph	Some damage to chimneys, breaks branches off trees, pushes over shallow-rooted trees, damages sign boards.
F1	Moderate	73–112 mph	The lower limit is the beginning of hurricane wind speed: peels surface off roofs, mobile homes pushed off foundations or overturned, moving autos pushed off the roads, attached garages may be destroyed.
F2	Significant tornado	113–157 mph	Considerable damage: roofs torn off frame houses, mobile homes demolished, boxcars pushed over, large trees snapped or uprooted, light object missiles generated.
F3	Severe tornado	158-206 mph	Roof and some walls torn off well-constructed houses, trains overturned, most trees in forest uprooted.
F4	Devastating tornado	207-260 mph	Well-constructed houses leveled, structures with weak foundations blown off some distance, cars thrown, and large missiles generated.
F5	Incredible tornado	261-318 mph	Strong frame houses lifted off foundations and carried considerable distances to disintegrate, automobile-sized missiles fly through the air in excess of 100 meters, trees debarked, steel reinforced concrete structures badly damaged.
F6	Inconceivable tornado	319-379 mph	These winds are very unlikely. The small area of damage they might produce would probably not be recognizable along with the mess produced by F4 and F5 winds that would surround the F6 winds. Missiles, such as cars and refrigerators would do serious secondary damage that could not be directly identified as F6 damage. If this level is ever achieved, evidence for it might only be found in some manner of ground swirl pattern, for it may never be identifiable through engineering studies.

there is no discount applied to areas that have been impacted as opposed to those that are not. As Jarrell has been subjected to particularly harsh and repeated tornado damage, research is ongoing as to the long-term impact on real estate values.

Properties can be constructed with tornado safety in mind. In some areas, homes are constructed from concrete that is engineered to withstand 200 mile per hour winds. A storm cellar provides the best protection against a tornado, and a basement is considered the next best place to take shelter. Mobile homes that are not anchored should always be vacated if a tornado is approaching. They provide almost no protection and can be overturned very easily by strong winds. A high water table in some areas precludes construction of basements and makes residents more vulnerable.

The center of a tornado is an area of remarkably low pressure, which may cause buildings to explode if they are not sufficiently ventilated for rapid adjustment to the change in pressure. That is why some recommend that a window be opened to allow for the inside of the house to adjust to the rapid changes in air pressure.

This concrete foundation and a few water lines are all that remained after the Jarrell tornado destroyed the home on this site.

Many homes are being rebuilt with special concrete wall systems that will resist future tornado destruction.

Floods

In terms of human hardship and economic loss, floods are the most frequent and costly of natural disasters. Excluding droughts, approximately 90% of the damage related to natural disasters is caused by floods and associated mud and debris flows. Within the United States from 1985 to 1994, floods caused an average of $3.1 billion in losses annually, and from 1925 to 1988 floods caused an average of 95 deaths annually. (Most flood-related deaths do not involve flooded properties, but rather 80% occur in vehicles trying to navigate flood waters.) No place is entirely safe from the threat of floods, as they occur in all 50 states. Communities exceptionally at risk are those located in low-lying areas, near water, or downstream from a dam. However, any area is susceptible following spring rains, massive thunderstorms, or winter snow thaws.

Floods can rise quickly or develop over many days, depending on the watershed, which is a large area of land that drains into a waterway such as a drainage sewer, river, or stream. A small river will drain a watershed of several thousand or hundreds of thousands of acres. Floods are caused when a watershed takes on so much water from rain or dam failure that its waterways cannot drain suitably. Excess rain or melting snow pack within a watershed will cause increased water levels downstream. Levees may be constructed to contain flooding, but, as more communities construct levees, the river water is forced to run at higher levels because it cannot extend outward. During a deluge, the water runs at a higher level, deposits sediment, and raises the riverbed. During prolonged periods of rain or runoff, a levee may give way because it is under pressure from the swollen river and is being undercut by water seepage. Dam failures are often the most harmful fast-rising flood events, which can result from carelessness, insufficient design, or structural damage caused by a superior event such as an earthquake. When a dam fails, a mammoth amount of water is released on the watershed.

Often properties located on rivers and streams command a premium price, as they provide recreation, fishing, view amenities, and irrigation or drinking water. However, minimal amounts of excess water can cause significant damage to these same properties and threaten the lives of occupants. For example, six inches of rapidly moving flood water can knock a person down, and a few feet of water can float a large vehicle or destroy a structure, entire towns, or even regions. The Mississippi River flood of 1993 covered an area 500 miles long and 200 miles wide. More than 50,000 homes were damaged, and 12,000 acres of farmland were washed out.

If a property is flooded, a variety of damage can occur. Foundations may be cracked and utilities may be destroyed. Basement flooding can cause structural damage to the entire building. Septic tanks, cesspools, pits, and leaching systems may be damaged and actually cause a health hazard. Roads and infrastructure may be weakened to the point that they may even collapse under the weight of a vehicle.

Federal Emergency Management Agency (FEMA)

The Federal Emergency Management Agency (FEMA) is a government program that was designed to help people affected by disasters such as floods. Flood-impacted property owners may be eligible to receive rental payments for temporary housing or grants to make repairs. Additionally, special loans may be available to replace damaged homes, farms, or businesses.

FEMA also publishes flood zone maps, which delineate those areas susceptible to flooding. The 100-year flood standard was developed primarily to estimate flood frequencies in floodplain mapping. The term *100-year flood* does not mean that a flood will occur once every hundred years, rather it is a statistical tool used to estimate the risk of certain flood levels. A 100-year flood has a 1% chance of happening within a given year. Within the span of a 30-year mortgage, a home owner can expect about a 25% chance of the property being flooded. For the same 30-year cycle, the more frequent 10-year flood has a 96% chance of occurring. Statistically, properties located within a 10-year floodplain are virtually certain to flood within a 30-year mortgage term.

Flood Insurance Coverage

There are about 11 million buildings located in designated flood hazard areas in the United States, yet less than 23% are insured against floods. As flooding is the leading cause of property loss from natural disasters, flood insurance issues may be important in calculating any diminution in value. Standard home owners insurance policies do not compensate for flood damage. Special flood insurance coverage is available for residential and nonresidential buildings, and details of flood insurance is available through any licensed property and casualty insurance agent.

Droughts

A drought is a deficiency of water in the ground, streams, lakes, and reservoirs resulting from a prolonged deficiency of rain and snow melt, or an imbalance of water vapor entering the atmosphere by evaporation. Most of the moisture for rain and snow on the land surfaces of the world comes originally from the oceans. Warm ocean waters yield great quantities of moisture to the atmosphere by evaporation. Cooler waters yield much less, especially when water temperatures are cooler than the air above. There are two different kinds of droughts. The first is a *meteorological drought,* which is a period of abnormally low rainfall. The other is an *agricultural drought,* a reduction in soil moisture. The first can be detected by rainfall figures, but the other relies more heavily on the region affected. While it may be assumed that these go hand-in-hand, it is not always true. The difference between them is a measure of the dryness or wetness of a climate. In desert regions, where drought conditions are perpetual, the rate of evaporation and transpiration is much greater than its precipitation.

Aside from the fact that droughts result from a lack of precipitation, they may be intensified by high temperatures, strong winds, and low humidity, all of which increase from the loss of moisture by evapotranspiration (i.e., evaporation and transpiration). Many times, low-pressure storm systems will shift tracks across a region, leaving some areas without their normal precipitation levels. Low sea-surface temperatures are another cause of drought. For example, off the west coast of Peru, low sea-surface temperatures stabilize the atmosphere so that the vertical air currents needed to produce appreciable precipitation are suppressed. As a result, the region normally only receives a small amount of drizzle. However, when warmer water from equatorial regions moves southward along the coasts of Peru, the rainfall becomes abundantly heavy.

In desert regions throughout the world, the lack of rain may be attributed to the amount of dust in the air. Particles in the atmosphere are necessary in order for raindrops to form; however, if there is an abundance of dust particles in the lower atmosphere, a phenomenon called *supernucleation* occurs in which too little water condenses around each particle and clouds do not form properly. Because of this factor, areas such as east-central Australia, China, southern Africa, India, Central and North America, and northeast Brazil all predictably have frequent drought-like conditions.

The actual impact and denotation of a drought varies from region to region, depending on the normal rainfall. A drought in Cairo, Egypt, where the normal annual precipitation is 1.1 inches, is vastly different from a drought in New Orleans, Louisiana, where 64 inches is expected annually. In Britain, a drought is described as a period of at least 15 consecutive days without rain. In the United States, it is a period of 21 days when rainfall is 30% less than the average for the place and time.

The impacts of drought are commonly referred to as *direct* or *indirect*. Examples of direct impacts include reduced crop and forest productivity, increased fire hazards, reduced water levels, increased livestock and wildlife mortality rates, and damage to wildlife and fish habitat. The consequences of these direct impacts have residual effects, or indirect impacts. For example, a reduction in crop, rangeland, and forest productivity may result in reduced income for farmers and agribusiness, increased prices for food and timber, unemployment, reduced tax revenues because of reduced expenditures, increased crime, foreclosures on bank loans to farmers and businesses, migration, and disaster relief programs. As these effect the economy in general, they tend to impact all the real estate in the region, rather than a specific property or neighborhood.

Hurricanes

Hurricane are large, rotating tropical cyclones of extraordinary violence. They can be found in all tropical and subtropical oceans except the South Atlantic and eastern Pacific. They are not as violent as tornadoes, but the combination of size and intensity makes them the most dangerous and destructive of all storms, and they frequently cause flooding and other damage. Hurricanes generally develop between June and November, which coincides with changes in the general circulation of the earth's atmosphere and the increase in the temperature of seawater. When the water reaches a temperature of about 80° F, which is warm even for tropical seas, hurricanes may begin to form. The storm mass moves forward at a rate of 5 to 15 miles per hour. Wind speeds reach from 75 to over 150 miles per hour near the center of a storm, although the maximum speeds are rarely recorded because few anemometers can withstand such conditions. The total rainfall in the course of an average storm ranges from 3 to 6 inches, depending on the speed of the storm.

Hurricanes are part of a family of weather systems known as *tropical cyclones.* A hurricane begins as a disorganized storm system formed over warm, tropical waters. When the storm system becomes more organized, it is classified as a *tropical depression.* If winds then grow in intensity to 40 miles per hour, it is reclassified as a *tropical storm* and receives a name. When winds in the storm reach 75 miles per hour, the storm is up-graded to a hurricane.

The winds of a hurricane are structured around a central *eye,* which is an area that is free of clouds and is relatively calm. Winds blow around this eye in a counterclockwise motion. The *eyewall*—the portion containing clouds, wind, and rain—is the most destructive part of the storm. The eye on average is about 14 miles in diameter, but it can be twice that size. Including the eyewall, the hurricane may cover an area of more than 100 miles in diameter and extend over thousands of square miles. While most storms have a short life span, hurricanes may live for weeks.

The impact of a hurricane can be disastrous. Over the oceans, the human activities at risk are primarily oil rigs, shipping, and air traffic. The state of the sea is chaotic and monstrous waves may develop. In November 1985, Hurricane Kate, located in the eastern Gulf of Mexico, created wave heights greater than 38 feet. Of course, hurricanes mostly pose a threat to life and property over land. They can cause a rapid rise of sea level when a storm approaches the coastline, and excessive rainfall may cause landslides and flooding. The strong winds can produce considerable structural damage to improvements, ruin vegetation, and cause risk to life from flying debris.

There are an average of eight tropical cyclones in the North Atlantic area per year, of which about five usually are intense enough to be classified as hurricanes. The Gulf areas and all of the southern states lining the Atlantic Ocean have experienced hurricanes. Over the past eight years, three major hurricanes have caused a total of over $40 billion in damage in these areas (Andrew in 1992, Hugo in 1989, and Opal in 1995). While some believe that global warming has resulted in increased hurricane activity, research shows that over the last 25 years the number of hurricanes has actually declined from previous decades. In reality, there have simply been more homes built by the sea, thereby putting more properties at risk. In the 1970s and 1980s, almost half of all new construction in the United States took place in coastal areas.

Volcanoes

Throughout time, volcanic eruptions have come unwarned and have destroyed entire cities. Approximately 430 volcanoes in the world have erupted within recorded history. A volcano is defined as a place on the earth's surface from which gases, molten rock, and fragmentary materials are extruded. A vent or chimney connects a reservoir of molten matter, known as *magma,* found deep within the earth's crust, with the surface of the earth. When the magma nearly reaches the earth's surface, the name of the molten rock is then changed to *lava*. Lava is by far the greatest volume of materials that volcanoes erupt, and it moves at speeds ranging from less than 1 mile per hour up to 60 miles per hour. While some associate a volcano with a burning mountain of smoke and fire, there is no actual "burning" in the sense of combustion. The so-called "smoke" is condensed steam, which is frequently mixed with dust particles that make it dark in color. The "fire" is the reflection of the red-hot material on the vapor clouds above the volcano.

The movement of plates across the earth's crust cause volcanoes in two ways. First, separating plates, normally in the middle of the ocean, open a seam that allows magma to well up. Secondly, when plates crash into one another and the heavier one plunges beneath the lighter, the resulting increase in pressure squeezes molten rock up through fractures in the overlying plate. In southern California, the plates grind past one another or butt together without ever overriding. These produce strong earthquakes but no lava. The explosion of a volcano is comparable to the opening of a soda can that has been shaken up. First, when water changes its state from a liquid to a solid, such as ice, it expands by about one-ninth of its volume. However, when water changes to the gaseous state, the volume increases 1,000 times. This is what happens as the magma heats up and bubbles beneath the earth's surface. At some point the pressure of the gas becomes so great that it pushes up and through the surface of the earth. The explosion, or eruption, is similar to that of a cork being released from a champagne bottle.

Dormant since 1857, Mount St. Helens erupted on May 18, 1980, at 8:32 a.m., after a 5.0 magnitude earthquake. It had the most destructive force of any volcano in the history of the United States and caused the world's largest recorded landslide. The eruption was equivalent to 27,000 atomic bombs, and the blast blew 1,300 feet of the mountain down the Toutle River Valley below. Volcanic ash towered 16 miles above the mountain, and the explosion was heard over 700 miles away. Widespread destruction, encompassing 150,000 square miles, was caused by hot gasses, glacier and debris avalanches, mud-flows, and flooding. The majority of damage occurred in about 10 seconds.

There are two different types of volcanoes, *shield* and *composite*. In the shield volcano, the mountain is a gently sloping dome composed of a series of lava flows, and each flow rarely exceeds 25 feet in thickness. Fragmented materials are erupted from these volcanoes but in very small quantities. An eruption of lava takes place not only through the central vent but also through lateral fissures, which makes the volcano increase in diameter but not in height. Examples of shield volcanoes are those found in Hawaii. The composite volcano is characterized by rock fragments exploding from the throat, interspersed with lava flows from the vent or from fissures along the side of the mountain. This type of volcano is normally steeply sloping and symmetrical, with a small crater in the top. The crater is a funnel-shaped depression that rarely exceeds a mile or so in diameter. Many composite volcanoes rise 10,000 feet or move above their base. Some of these volcanoes are found in the Philippines and, Italy, as well as Fuji in Japan and Mount

St. Helens.

Until the eruption of Mount St. Helens, only two known casualties within the United States (one in Hawaii and one in Alaska) had been attributed to volcanoes. This disaster, though, caused 57 deaths. Some who perished simply ignored warnings to stay out of the 6- to 10-mile "Red Zone," while others were in areas that were destroyed by the unexpected lateral blast of the mountain and resulting floods. Ninety-eight cabins at the base of the mountain and around Spirit Lake, along with Boy Scout and Girl Scout camps, the YMCA camp, and other resorts and campgrounds were covered by debris as much as 400 feet deep. Mudflows and flooding completely or partially destroyed 221 homes along the Toutle River. One hundred eighty-five miles of highways and 15 miles of railroads were destroyed or irreparably damaged, and 4 billion board feet of lumber was lost. The loss to wildlife was staggering, including nearly 7,000 deer, elk, and bears and 12 million salmon fingerlings. The property damage and cleanup costs totaled $1.1 billion.

Mount St. Helens, the largest landslide in the history of the world, caused damage for a radius of 18 miles from its north face.

While the damages from the Mount St. Helens eruption were immense, they have been at least partially offset by the tourism that the site of the eruption now attracts. This playground, at a visitors center, is fashioned after a scaled-down version of the volcano.

The immediate destructive areas of the eruption, called the blast zone, spanned north 18 miles from the mountain, far beyond the 6- to 10-mile Red Zone initially predicted. Every property within the blast zone was completely destroyed. Even though these homes and cabins were buried under 400 feet of debris, some of them later sold for $500 to $750, which was considered a "novelty value." The government eventually condemned these properties and paid the owners the market value for the land but not the improvements. Some of these improvements were insured, and those that were not were a complete loss. The downriver areas were impacted by the flooding and dramatic changes in the flood zones. When the floods subsided, many homes had been lifted from their foundations, and the changes in topography created a land surveyor's nightmare. River courses were completely altered, and elevations were altered considerably over thousands of acres. Many property owners simply did not know where their property boundaries were. Other properties that were well outside of the floodplain were now within two-year floodplains. These properties, while still standing after the explosion and flooding, lost much or nearly all of their value because of the risk of future flooding. Some homes are gone, some have been rebuilt, and others still stand partially buried in mud.

The impact from this natural disaster on real estate varied greatly. For some, there was a complete loss of value, as their properties were completely buried. In some of these cases, the property owners were reimbursed for the value of their land by the government, but the value of improvements was covered only by insurance, if at all. For others, the damage amounted to the cost of cleanup and related costs. Some areas actually benefited somewhat from the eruption, as the volcanic ash added nutrients to some agricultural lands located east of the volcano. Other commercial properties along the highway route to the volcano actually benefited by the tourism that the eruption site now attracts.

For those areas that are buildable, there is no measurable market resistance over the fear of another eruption. Although there have been 14 minor eruptions since 1980, and more are inevitable, the general consensus amongst the scientific community is that there is not enough mass left of the mountain to facilitate another major event. In addition, there is no new development, other than tourist centers, within the blast zone.

Modern technology allows for warnings of volcanoes on the edge of an eruption. Researchers have at their disposal an arsenal of newly developed volcanology hardware, ranging from satellites to acoustical sensors to highly sensitive gas sniffers. For example, in 1991, scientists took the pulse of Mount Pinatubo in the Philippines, predicted it was about to erupt, and persuaded officials to evacuate 35,000 people two days before it did. Unfortunately in 1985 the Colombian government did not listen to warnings given by seismologists who warned that the Mount Ruiz volcano was smoldering dangerously. The data were considered "too spotty" by the government, thus nothing was done. One month later, the mountain erupted, claiming 23,000 lives. Close watch is kept on Mount Rainier, 50 miles southeast of Seattle. Some consider it the most dangerous volcano in the U.S., as it appears that it is ready to erupt in the near future.

One of the phenomena of natural disasters was illustrated by the Mount St. Helens explosion, which the media called the "barrier wars." Within a real estate market threatened by a natural disaster, it is common for some property owners to go into a state of denial and believe that "it can't happen to me," and even try to defy nature. Despite warnings and police blockades, many property owners forced their way past police roadblocks and barriers to go to their properties. One man who lived on Spirit Lake, Harry Truman, became a local folk hero for refusing to listen to repeated warnings and leave his resort. He, along with many others, was killed.

Wetlands and Other Environmentally Significant Real Estate

Environmentally significant real estate comprises properties with geographical, biological, ecological, archaeological, paleontological, cultural, or historical significance to society. Over the years, many land owners have lost some or all of the available economically productive uses of their properties, realizing one day that their land was also the home to an endangered species. Some have learned that "the old swimming hole" is now classified as a wetland or that an entire property was once an aboriginal burial site. For example, many citizens, ranchers, and oil speculators were upset when President Bill Clinton used an executive order to declare several million acres of southern Utah an environmentally sensitive area and therefore protected. In effect, these properties have been additionally encumbered by regulation and use requirements that can drastically alter the highest and best use of a property and the developability of the land.

On the other hand, the past few decades have brought a noticeable cognitive shift in the way property owners comprehend and respond to their environmental surroundings. Typically, land has been perceived as valuable for its ore and mineral resources, its agricultural and timber productivity, its connection to water rights, and as real estate for development. These activities define the land's utility on the basis of consumptive and exploitive needs. There is an increasing awareness, however, of land's utility in a natural, preserved context. As the demand for environmentally sensitive property increases for nonconsumptive and nonexploitive purposes, the value of those uses will increasingly compete with development uses.

This "shift" in society's response to its surroundings has sometimes led to political changes in land uses, causing periodic disagreements and conflicts between those who wish to preserve a unique, scarce, or environmentally sensitive resource and private land owners wishing to exploit the marketable economic value of a property. While all, or politically significant portions, of society may place great value on an endangered species habitat or an archaeologically sensitive, historically significant, or similar area, rarely is the land owner able to capitalize upon those uses (which often require that portions of an impacted property remain undeveloped), thereby resulting in a divergence between the private and social utility of a property.

An example of this divergence would be a land owner who wants to fill a wetland near a prime intersection in order to build a strip retail center. This wetland may serve various nonmarket purposes such as providing duck habitat, absorbing some of the spring run-off discharges that help reduce flooding, and helping purify the water that soaks into the aquifer, as well as others. Yet even if the parties who benefit from the presence of the wetlands (e.g., duck hunters, potential downstream flood victims, users of the local aquifer) had adequate funds and valued the benefits at an aggregate level to justify paying for them, the land owner would still find it nearly impossible to get the interested parties to pay an amount large enough to offset the private benefits resulting from building a shopping center.

When market mechanisms do not exist to ensure the protection of a particular property that society deems to be significant, a government entity will sometimes purchase the property. If the property is one of many that exhibit the characteristic deemed worth protecting, the government may regulate the use of all properties that share that characteristic. The most notable examples of these laws include the Endangered Species Act of 1973 (ESA) and Section 404 of the Clean Water Act, which regulates the use and development of wetlands. The federal agencies that enforce these laws have also adopted various rules and opinions that further define these and other laws. In addition, many state and local governments have adopted laws to protect various species and habitats from degradation. In some cases, state and local requirements exceed those at the federal level. In fact, the different federal, state, and local agencies sometimes have conflicting and confusing regulatory objectives and lack the mechanisms to reconcile those objectives. These multilayered regulatory and permitting processes are viewed as a multiple-veto process by much of the development community. In addition, lack of a consistent and coherent set of policy objectives leads to greater uncertainty and higher development costs. In other words, the value of the encumbered, undeveloped land is diminished.

There are several types of properties that are impacted by preservation uses, various limits upon the development of these properties, and a variety of market reactions to these trends. In general, the existence of environmentally significant characteristics reduces the utility of encumbered properties, and therefore impacts its value and marketability.

Wetlands

Wetlands are defined by the Emergency Wetlands Resources Act of 1986 as

> land that has a predominance of hydric soils and that is inundated or saturated by surface or groundwater at a frequency and duration sufficient to support, and that under normal conditions does support, a prevalence of hydrophytic vegetation typically adapted for life in saturated soil conditions

These areas are generally open-water habitats and seasonally or permanently waterlogged land areas. Wetland areas are naturally occurring systems where the exposure of the soils to water at or near the surface on a frequent and prolonged basis creates the type of soil conditions where specific types of vegetation and fish and/or wildlife communities thrive. These areas are often characterized by bogs, marshes, swamps, and tidal areas. Wetlands can also appear seasonally as vernal pools (pools that form in spring but are dry the rest of the year), playas (the bottoms of undrained desert basins that are sometimes covered with water), and prairie potholes. Wetland areas, especially marsh and bog areas, are among the most vulnerable to disturbance because they can easily be drained and reclaimed for agriculture or forestry, drained for pest control (e.g., eliminating the breeding grounds for mosquitoes), or modified for water supply, flood control, hydroelectric power schemes, waste disposal, and other uses.

Over the past few years, members of the scientific community, government agencies, and an increasing majority of the public have become more aware of issues surrounding the ecological role wetlands and habitat play in the environment. Wetlands filter and recharge aquifers, improve the quality of water in rivers and streams, and often provide habitat for threatened and endangered species. In addition, there are a number of economic benefits to society, including helping furnish a variety of valuable products such as fish, timber, wild rice, and furs. Wetlands also help absorb heavy rains and snowmelts, reducing or slowing the run-off that often causes devastating floods, and the wetland vegetation often slows floodwaters. The loss of large amounts of wetlands throughout the Midwest and in California's Central Valley certainly increased the severity of flooding and damage to communities in those areas during the major floods of the mid-1990s.

The identification and general valuation of wetlands is covered in *Valuation of Wetlands* by David Michael Keating, MAI. More important to the current discussion is an examination of the costs associated with environmentally sensitive land and the restrictions placed upon its use.

Legal Issues

Section 404 of the Clean Water Act is the primary federal program regulating activities in wetlands. The Section 404 program is administered by both the U.S. Army Corps of Engineers and the EPA. The act states that the Corps has primary responsibility for the permit program and is authorized, after notice and public hearing, to issue permits for the discharge of dredged or fill material into the "waters of the United States," which has been interpreted to include wetlands. The EPA is responsible for reviewing and commenting on the applications and has veto power over permits. It should be noted that Section 404 regulates only the discharge of dredged or fill material and does not explicitly prohibit drainage or excavation unless those activities involve the discharge of dredged or fill material. Permits to fill or dredge wetlands are only issued if mitigation is possible:

1. There is no available, practical alternative with fewer effects on the aquatic ecosystem.
2. Dischargers will neither violate other applicable regulations or laws (e.g., state water quality standards, toxic effluent standards, the Endangered Species Act) nor significantly degrade the waters into which they discharge.
3. All appropriate and practical steps have been taken to minimize and otherwise mitigate the impacts on the aquatic ecosystem.

Many state and local governments also regulate development activities in wetland areas, as well as the drainage and excavation of wetlands.

In August 1991, President George Bush signed an executive order establishing a national goal of "no net loss" of wetlands. President Bill Clinton has taken up this as an interim goal, while establishing a long-term goal of increasing the quantity and quality of the country's wetlands.

Habitat

While the definition and categorization of wetlands is relatively easy (although the practical identification may be more difficult), the categorization of habitat is substantially more complicated. *Habitat* is the physical and biological environment used by an individual, a population, a species, or perhaps a group of species. Habitat can be discussed at the species level, such as the spotted-owl habitat, the snail darter habitat, or the blue-fin tuna habitat. This can be compared to an *ecosystem,* which is a group of organisms and their physical environment.

Habitat is a complex and chaotic web of relationships between plants, animals, soils, and the climate. While plants and animals have evolved over millions of years, their habitats and communities are always in a process of flux. A habitat will go through a youth-to-maturity process similar to that of a living organism, usually in a period of less than 1,000 years. The process of maturation involves a series of habitat successions until a mature, balanced ecosystem becomes established. These systems are sometimes knocked out of balance by fires, volcanic eruptions, floods, and other periodic catastrophes. The resulting ecological succession is also the process of healing a habitat. Human-induced stress is becoming more and more a cause of *habitat degradation*—that is, the process whereby the quality and quantity of a given species' habitat or a given wetland area is diminished. *Ecosystem degradation* results from changes to an ecosystem that destroy or degrade habitat for several of the species that constitute an ecosystem. When a habitat or ecosystem is severely degraded over a long period of time, the land or water that is the basis for the habitat becomes so damaged that natural succession cannot occur without explicit efforts to help restore them, often by adopting laws that restrict habitat degradation.

The Endangered Species Act (ESA) sets forth a strong mandate to protect and manage the habitats of endangered and threatened species. Section 9 of the act prohibits the "taking" of an endangered or threatened species. In addition, criminal and civil penalties can be brought against individuals who take a species—i.e., "harass, harm, pursue, hunt, shoot, wound, kill, trap, capture, or collect or attempt to engage in any such conduct." Real estate development projects in sensitive areas often impact a species in a manner that is legally construed to consist of a taking. Section 10 of the ESA, however, allows for the U.S. Fish and Wildlife Service to issue an "incidental take" permit following the successful completion of a habitat conservation plan (often referred to as an HCP). The HCP must specify

1. The impact that will result from the taking
2. The steps that will be taken to minimize and mitigate the steps—including the identification of the sources of funding
3. The available alternative actions to the taking and the reasons for not selecting those options
4. Other measures required by the Secretary of the Interior as being necessary or appropriate

Such a permit is to be issued only if

1. The taking is incidental to an otherwise lawful activity
2. The applicant minimizes and mitigates the impacts of the taking to the maximum extent practical
3. The applicant ensures that adequate funding will be provided
4. The taking will not appreciably reduce the likelihood of the survival and recovery of the species in the wild

One problem that has plagued planners and government agencies is the identification of the habitats of various species that have been designated as threatened or endangered. Much of the debate surrounding the northern spotted owl in the Pacific Northwest dealt with the appropriate size of the habitat. Early studies indicated that a nesting pair of northern spotted owls required a minimum of 300 acres of old growth forests surrounding the nest. Although such an observation appears to lead to an obvious solution, many questions still need to be answered. For example, is the minimum size enough for each of the nesting pairs? And even if all of the nesting pairs were to survive, would there be adequate opportunities for the offspring to breed and continue the species, or would the habitat become an island, so fragmented that the species would inevitably die out? Another problem is that the concentration upon one species in a preservation plan ignores the interrelatedness of species in the survival of plants and animals. These types of issues continue to plague development in areas identified as containing the habitat of an endangered species.

Past Trends in Development in Sensitive Areas

In the past, property owners and developers were rarely constrained by legal obstacles in land development, and the highest and best use was generally a function of financial feasibility and maximum net return. A property owner was relatively sovereign in the use of her or his property, so if a property was inhabited by an endangered species such as the spotted owl, logging could continue unabated, and if a property had a wetland, it could be reclaimed by draining or filling it.

In terms of market perceptions most environmentally significant real estate could be used for the private use that represented the greatest net return to a property owner. In other words, any diminution in value that was perceived by the market was the result of overcoming a natural obstacle. For example, some environmentally significant real estate, such as wetlands, was considered by many market participants as a nuisance, and often added little or no contributory value to a given property. If a wetland area did have a substantial market value, it was because the wetland offered an amenity such as a view to a residential use or it was a source of raw materials such as the hardwood forests located in the swamps of the Southeast. In some cases, the cost of draining or filling a wetland area was lower than the resulting value of the filled, usable site. As the population increased and developable land became scarce, many entrepreneurs filled and drained wetlands as a profitable activity. The reclamation of wetlands further increased by virtue of government subsidy programs that promoted the draining and filling of wetlands for agricultural use.

Current Trends in Development in Sensitive Areas

Currently, the market for many of these properties is in flux. Although laws impacting environmentally sensitive real estate are being enforced more vigorously, mitigation is being perceived as a viable tool in the development process. In addition, groups such as the Audubon Society, the Nature Conservancy, the Trust for Public Lands, Ducks Unlimited, and other groups, individuals, and government entities are competing to purchase some of the most sensitive of these properties, thereby creating somewhat of a market.

The protection of both wetlands and habitat areas have similar impacts on the ability to develop and use real estate. If a property is impacted by a wetland or by a habitat of a species listed as threatened or endangered, a permit will most certainly be required for development to proceed. While builders have been frustrated by the resulting delays and headaches, conservation interests are frustrated that the case-by-case permitting process can degrade an ecosystem and thereby severely damage the habitat of a sensitive species. Furthermore, it is difficult for conservationists to monitor the extensive, multi-permitting process, and they face the prospect that if a development is defeated, it may be replaced with a variety of other proposals, thereby increasing their uncertainty.

In some areas of the country, developers and conservationists have acknowledged a common interest in increased predictability and long-term assurances. They have begun to act together, in conjunction with regulatory agencies, in devising regulations and mitigation plans that are acceptable to both sides while meeting the legal requirements. The promising result of these multiconstituency pilot programs has been the development of focused special-area programs such as wetland mitigation banks and multispecies habitat reserves. These two types of programs are similar in that they mitigate impact on a wetland or a species habitat resulting from a particular development project by effectively joining together several developers who are required to mitigate to protect a sizable, unfragmented wetland or habitat area.

Wetland Mitigation

Government regulations permit a property owner to develop a property if the potential impact on a wetland or sensitive habitat area can be mitigated. Mitigation requires that a developer buy a property that has had its naturally occurring habitat damaged or destroyed, and enhance or restore it prior to placing it under protective status. In some cases, the very expensive option of wetland creation is required. In some cases where mitigation was deemed feasible and was permitted, the required mitigation was never performed or the monitoring was haphazard.

As an example of this type of wetland mitigation, consider the Bolsa Chica Wetlands in Huntington Beach, California. Bolsa Chica used to be the mouth of the Santa Ana River. The river changed course during the flood of 1820, and the river mouth moved southeast along the coast to the border of Huntington Beach and Newport Beach. Bolsa Chica has vegetation that is typical of southern California coastal wetlands: pickleweed (salcornia) and cordgrass. It is home to a number of endangered species. There are also archeological sites.

The combined ports of Los Angeles and Long Beach were recently involved in the creation and enhancement of habitat in order to mitigate for the destruction and degradation of marine habitat that will accompany the enlarging of a harbor. To enlarge the port by hundreds of acres, the port must place fill on the ocean floor, destroying or degrading habitat. In 1996, the port paid for 880 acres of wetlands, which was conveyed to the state, and financed both the restoration and maintenance of the habitat. In return for these considerations, the port received mitigation credits sufficient to offset the filling of 454 acres of outer harbor sea floor. In addition, the port is entitled to acquire mitigation credits for the filling of an additional 80 acres of sea floor, at the rate of $150,000 per acre.

Bolsa Chica sits astride the Newport/Inglewood fault zone. This is a very active earthquake fault that caused the Long Beach quake in the 1930s. The fault has created geological structures that hold significant amounts of oil. Petroleum production has occupied much of Bolsa Chica throughout the twentieth century. There is some contamination, mostly from crude oil. Pipeline easements and undocumented pipelines crisscross the property.

The port elected to pay for land and restoration work in Bolsa Chica for several reasons:

- Proximity (only a few miles southeasterly along the coast)
- Deep water habitat (when restored, able to support the young of deep water species)
- Degraded wetland (fill, oil production, pipelines, contamination, etc.)

The proximity of Bolsa Chica to the ports ensures that the same or similar fish species will be enhanced. The degraded state of the wetlands assures that a lot of mitigation credit is available. If the habitat were in a less degraded state, then less work would have to be done and less mitigation credit would be available. When it comes to wetland mitigation, "bad is good."

The creation and enhancement of habitat will be overseen by the state Department of Fish and Game. The only role played by the port was to pay for the land and restoration project. Payment of the money alone secured the rights to enlarge the harbor. It also secured the right to acquire an additional 80 acres of outer harbor landfill mitigation credits for $12 million, or $150,000 per acre. The port may also pay for any restoration cost overruns and accumulate more credits at the same rate. The cost breakdown is as follows:

Purchase 880 acres of degraded wetlands	$25,000,000
Restore and manage wetlands	$41,750,000
Acquisition and restoration (provides 454 acres of sea floor landfill credit)	$66,750,000
Optional acquisition of additional 80 acres of credit	$12,000,000
Total cost of 534 acres of sea floor landfill credit ($147,472/acre of credit)	$78,750,000

Instead of requiring developers to create and maintain wetlands, a task they are not well trained for, the development of mitigation banks is an option. Mitigation banks are wetland areas that have been restored by a government agency or an investor who "transfers" restored, preserved wetlands (in the form of credits) to a developer. The developer can then use these mitigation credits to offset the impact of wetland or habitat destruction resulting from development. Although these banks are often owned and operated by the government or large corporations, there is a growing trend toward private, entrepreneurial mitigation banks, which are being developed to sell mitigation credits on the open market. The formation of mitigation banks requires special permits, and such properties must be owned by competent and adequately funded parties. Examples of mitigation banks are as follows:

1. Single owner/user banks—the most common form. Usually established by a large company or public agency whose future development plans call for filling numerous small wetlands over several years. The company or agency may create a large wetland from which it can later use to withdraw "credits" as compensation for future wetland fills, rather than create a small wetland at each site on a case-by-case basis.

    The Walker Ranch in Florida is an example of a single-owner bank. This bank was created to mitigate the effects of ongoing development at Disney World by the Disney Corporation.

2. Entrepreneurial banks—very few exist. Similar in principle to single-owner banks except that the bank is established by a landowner and/or investor and the credits can be purchased by anyone.

    While entrepreneurial banks are highly touted, only a few such developments are in operation. One entrepreneurial bank is the Milhaven Mitigation Bank operated by Wetlands Environmental Technology in Screven County, Georgia. This is a 350-acre bank, although only the first phase (100 acres) has been completed. The bank has sold credits for $15,000 per acre.

3. Joint projects—common in California. Usually do not involve establishing a bank of credits for future use. Typically, a consortium of developers agree to fund a mitigation project to compensate for specific, future losses of wetlands or endangered species habitat.

Species Habitat Mitigation

Although many wetlands also contain species habitat, if the primary goal of a habitat mitigation project is to offset the negative impacts on a sensitive species habitat, the process generally follows a slightly different path. Using the habitat conservation plan (HCP) process, interested parties get together and negotiate an agreement whereby a preservation area is created and monitored, prior to being set aside in perpetuity. These projects vary on a case-by-case basis in terms of size, number of species to be protected, funding mechanisms, and the desire of participants to be involved.

A particularly well-documented example of an HCP in action is the Balcones Canyonlands Conservation Plan (BCCP) enacted in Austin, Texas. This plan was created by developers, environmentalists, and government agencies. It is based upon obtaining a 30-year Section 10(a) HCP permit for a conservation area of approximately 30,000 acres, including several areas in the city of Austin. The conservation area, which is designed to protect around 43 plant and animal species, consists of five separate preserves (in close proximity) in which any further development will be prohibited. It includes known habitat as well as land not currently suitable for habitat that may be regenerated as habitat over time.

The goal of the BCCP is to assemble preserve lands through land purchases from voluntary sellers, dedications, donations, conservation easements, and leases from public entities, nonprofit organizations, and private owners. The major part of the committed funding is from public sources, although there is belief that substantial funding will come from private sources. In addition, the plan requires the assessment of mitigation fees from landowners for authorization to develop either land confirmed to contain endangered species *or* land that is likely, if developed, to adversely affect land containing habitat. These mitigation fees are voluntary, in that developers are allowed to establish their own mitigation plan and apply for their own permits. The voluntary mitigation permits cost around $2,000 per acre, which is less than the estimated cost of $9,000 per acre for individual mitigation.

Some developments have gone outside of the HCP. For example, the 3M Company planned to clear 11 acres of golden-cheeked warbler habitat. The mitigation offered in the extensive permit process included the acquisition of 215 acres of warbler habitat and the donation of $50,000 to monitor the site, a cash donation of $15,000 to the BCCP, a three-year golden-cheeked warbler census, and a three-year cowbird trapping program. The company also agreed to minimize impacts by controlling the timing of land alteration and revegetation of altered areas caused by development.

Another good example of habitat mitigation is the Moorpark Wetlands, located between the cities of Moorpark and Simi Valley, California, both suburbs of Los Angeles. Land was acquired and a wetland was manufactured in order to mitigate for damage done to an adjacent stream by highway construction. The California State Department of Transportation (Caltrans) had two freeways that were never completed to their original destinations. Ramps were to be constructed to connect these two freeways and close a loop in the local circulation system. Some of the columns of the transition ramps had to be placed in the Arroyo Simi, a local stream that is part of the Pacific Flyway. Birds routinely use the stream and its adjacent floodplain fringe. The work that Caltrans was going to do would destroy or degrade approximately six acres of the stream.

The mitigation approach that was finally selected was to acquire neighboring land somewhere along the stream and to manufacture a wetlands area. The productivity of the stream was measured with a habitat equivalency program (HEP). The HEP score for a wetland manufactured on adjacent land was approximately half of the HEP score for the stream bed. This meant that 12 acres of wetlands had to be manufactured in order to mitigate for the 6 acres of more productive wetlands that were to be destroyed. In addition, there had to be a buffer strip to ensure that the species occupying the habitat are not unduly disturbed. The overall project size was approximately 19 acres.

Caltrans acquired a 48-acre parcel for $20,000 per acre, or $960,000. It included steep uplands of little value and a level area for the project along the Arroyo Simi. The wetlands were built for another $900,000 (construction contract only). Thus, even before indirect costs, Caltrans paid more than $300,000 per acre to mitigate for the destruction of 6 acres of highly productive habitat. The 9-acre manufactured habitat and buffer strip are now managed by neighboring Moorpark College.

Value Patterns

Based upon the ability to mitigate a wetland or habitat area, there are five possible valuation scenarios, depending upon where the project is in the development process.

1. Once the property is identified as being impacted by a wetland or habitat area, the nature of the sensitive area prohibits development of the impacted portion of the property. In this case the market value of the property declines and the value tends to remain level.
2. The habitat impact can be mitigated. The market value declines to reflect the cost of permitting and mitigation, and then increases back toward market value. A subset of this model is the example of an obvious wetland. Oftentimes a wetland is a fairly obvious characteristic of a property, in which case the pre-mitigation market value remains level. However, it is lower than the value of the site after reclamation by the dollar amount required to perform the permitting and mitigation costs.
3. The property is purchased for perpetual preservation by a conservation-minded group or individual. This case is similar to that of the first scenario, but evidence suggests that these groups are willing, or are required, to pay a slight premium for an impacted property, an additional cost that would not be necessary for a party that did not intend to place the property in perpetual protection.
4. A restorable wetland or multispecies habitat can be developed for purposes of off-site mitigation. This requires that the property be of adequate size to meet the mitigation requirements and that the mitigation results in the protection of the same number of quality units as is to be disturbed.

    As mitigation can take several forms, the initial market value of the environmentally significant property is directly related to the costs of preservation, enhancement, restoration, or creation of the wetland or habitat. These costs include regulatory approval and permitting, site design and engineering, construction, operations, and retirement. As the final value of the entire site will be as a preserve (Scenario 3), market value of the property in the initial stages will be inversely related to the expense of the mitigation (i.e., creation is more expensive than enhancement, therefore property purchased for creation would be less valuable on a per unit basis). An additional caveat is that it is generally perceived that a created or restored mitigation property is inferior to the original, natural, undisturbed state of the property. This could affect the market value of the property after the wetland was regenerated should the owner attempt to sell or donate the property to a conservation group. As a final cautionary note, although individual parties buy impacted properties for motivation, a particular developer's willingness to pay for a site for mitigation is directly related to the increase in utility for the project site to be disturbed. It must therefore be remembered that what a developer is willing to pay in a thin market may not reflect market value. Therefore, as the market becomes more complex, the motivations of the participants need to be fully researched.

5. The fifth scenario is similar to the fourth, with the exception that the mitigation is performed as part of creating a mitigation bank that is undertaken to exchange development credits. As more mitigation banks are created and the market matures, the market value of a potential mitigation bank site would likely be bid upward, as a large-scale project may have lower enhancement, restoration, or creation costs, in addition to lowering the transaction costs for the buyers of mitigation credits. In this case, the business of selling credits is also tied directly to the real estate. Therefore, the market value would increase as the significant characteristic is restored. However, until the market matures the estimation of market value will be difficult and challenging. The market value of a for-profit mitigation bank after its creation could theoretically increase to the difference between the market values of the project sites before and after the disturbance of the significant characteristics, less costs to disturb the wetland—discounted for monitoring, risk, and projected sellout period. Of course, typical market pressures such as substitution and competition will drive the market toward its equilibrium. As the development credits are sold, the market value of the mitigation bank will decline, eventually approaching the final market value of the fourth scenario.

Highest and Best Use Analysis

The four standard feasibility tests of highest and best use (physical possibility, legal permissibility, financial feasibility, and maximum productivity) need to be analyzed for any property. However, the existence of a wetland and/or protected species habitat usually requires additional analysis. In effect, this creates a two-stage highest and best use analysis. In the first stage, the proposed mitigation must be analyzed in terms of the four criteria of highest and best use to ascertain whether mitigation of the site is permitted, is feasible, and represents the greatest net return to the site in its original encumbered condition. If the mitigation is warranted, then a traditional highest and best use analysis can be performed.

The first test and often the most important is an examination of the legally permissible uses as well as the agencies that have jurisdiction. In addition to zoning, building codes, and deed restrictions, agencies as diverse as the U.S. Army Corps of Engineers, Department of the Interior, Department of Agriculture, or Department of Commerce (at the federal level alone) could have legal jurisdiction over a given property. State and local governments will also likely have restrictions on development, again through a variety of agencies. As pointed out in the example of the BCCP, the existence of a habitat conservation plan may restrict or permit development. Furthermore, a given property may have deed restrictions that are imposed for purposes of habitat preservation.

It is important for the appraiser to research the legal restrictions impacting development of an environmentally sensitive property. Often, the property owner seeking the appraisal already has researched and applied for the necessary permits required for proposed development, and the developer's attorney is a good source for determining the legal status. Legal restrictions may or may not eliminate the possibility of traditional private property uses. According to *National Geographic,* during one year, "of some 90,000 [wetland] projects under the Corps's jurisdiction, 80,000 were placed in a category that required 'little or no individual review.' And of the 10,000 applications that were put through the full regulatory process, only 6% were denied by the Corps." Based upon current trends, the existence of a wetland or an endangered species habitat on a property usually does not mean that the property cannot be developed, but rather that the development must meet a variety of restrictive requirements.

If a property meets the federal, state, and local regulations indicating that it is possible to gain the appropriate development permits, then development is considered to be legally permissible. It could be debated whether this would include cases where the permits could be obtained at great costs of monitoring and development. For purpose of analysis, these scenarios are considered under financial feasibility.

Once the legal ability to mitigate a wetland or habitat is established, the next step is evaluating the physical possibility of any mitigation. For example, is there adequate room on-site to mitigate the wetland or habitat? Is it possible to buy mitigation credits from a mitigation bank, or is there an HCP in effect that permits developing habitat? If neither of these are available, is it possible to mitigate the sensitive area off-site?

The process of mitigation often requires in-kind preservation—i.e., the destruction of a wetland must result in the creation of at least an equal amount of wetland or habitat area. If the desirable form of mitigation is the restoration or enhancement of a wetland or habitat, then several acres may need to be restored for every acre developed. Thus, the ability to locate and develop restorable wetland areas is crucial in evaluating the physically possible uses. As the number of projects requiring mitigation increases, a comprehensive inventory of restorable properties or mitigation alternatives should become available. However, as more properties are approved for mitigation, the number of restorable properties will decline.

The third test is that of financial feasibility. If the resulting value of a project is greater than its costs, then its development is considered to be financially feasible. Government regulation almost always increases the cost of doing business. The expense of hiring experts, applying for permits, and responding to lawsuits by interested third parties has stopped many real estate developments. Nevertheless, many projects still get built in ecologically sensitive areas indicating that traditional market activities can still be feasible even with increased costs from regulation.

The maximally productive use is the one that produces the highest residual land value (pre-mitigation) consistent with the rate of return warranted by the market for that use. In other words, this test requires that the appraiser determine the residual value of a site by estimating its value after mitigation and subtracting all of the costs. This process is to be performed for each of the financially feasible uses.

As an example, assume that there are three uses that have passed the test of financial feasibility: on-site mitigation, off-site mitigation, and selling the parcel for preservation purposes. For the first two cases, the costs associated with the mitigation should be deducted. The resulting values can then be compared with the value under preservation use. Whichever resultant value is greatest represents the maximally productive use and is the highest and best use. It should be recognized that if the costs are substantially large, mitigation may not represent the highest and best use.

Exhibit 9.4 summarizes the essential questions applicable to highest and best use analysis.

Exhibit 9.4 Wetlands Highest and Best Use Analysis

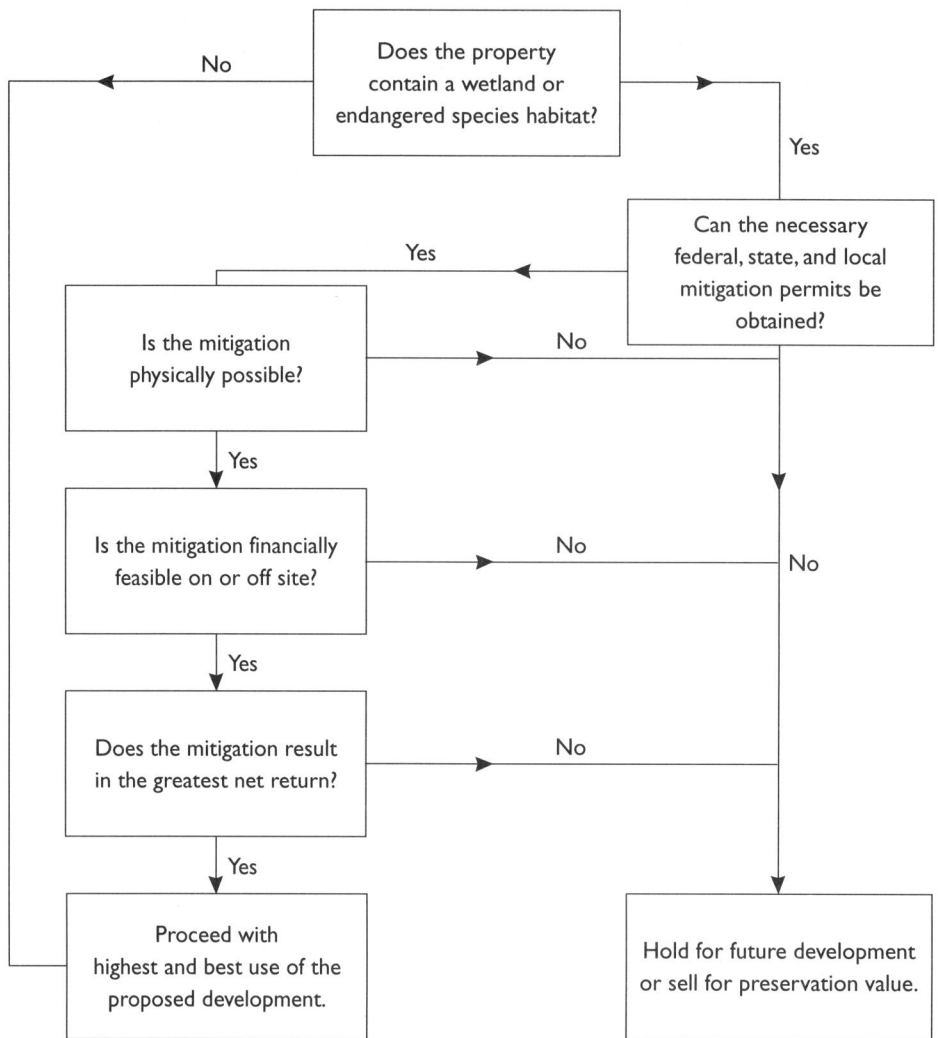

Further Reading

Endangered Species

Guidry, Krisandra A., and A. Quang Do. "Appraisal Assignments Involving Endangered Species." *The Appraisal Journal* (January 1994).

McKenzie-Smith, Robert H. "Endangered Species Habitat and Urban Development." *The Appraisal Journal* (January 1994).

Want, William L. *Law of Wetlands Regulation*. New York: Clark Boardman Co., 1989.

Chapter 9 Case Study

By Randall Bell, MAI

Alaskan Good Friday Earthquake—Alaska
Class IX and X Detrimental Conditions—Earthquake and Tsunami

Over the past 200 years, over 1,000 "strong" earthquakes have been recorded in Alaska. Of these, 14 have been catastrophic. On Good Friday, March 27, 1964, at 5:36 p.m., a 9.2 Richter Scale earthquake centered west of Valdez hit Alaska. It was the largest earthquake in North American history, the second largest in the recorded history of the world, and the most violent in the recorded history of the world. Thousands of square miles of Alaska rose and fell as much as 13 feet, and large cracks in the earth opened up. A 35,000 square mile area sank between 1 and 5½ feet, causing serious flood damage to numerous coastal towns. Thirty-three people were missing and presumed dead, and 78 people were killed, for a total of 111 lives lost. The earthquake lasted approximately four minutes and caused large tidal waves, as high as 90 feet, that greatly amplified the destruction of some coastal towns and villages. The earthquake lasted so long that some local residents recall going into the streets and taking bets on which side of the street various buildings would fall and crumble on. Numerous boats and barges were destroyed, and the vast Alaskan fishing industry was virtually wiped out, as was much of the transportation infrastructure. The earthquake and subsequent tidal wave caused approximately $1 billion in damage. Of this, $400 million was in real estate damages.

The Alaskan earthquake of 1964 shifted ground levels by over 10 feet. These homes were once located in an area well above sea level, but the entire area fell and is now considered a wetland area.

Some structures survived the 1964 earthquake and tidal waves and were later moved to a new town site. This liquor store was once a home on the old town site.

Although 150 miles from the epicenter, Anchorage suffered the most extensive damage, as the city straddles the fault line. Deep crevasses and fissures occurred throughout the city, entire city blocks broke off towards the coastline, and many homes tumbled into the ocean. In Anchorage, 215 homes were totally destroyed, and 157 commercial buildings were destroyed or condemned. Fifty to sixty percent of the water lines, 15% of the sewer lines, and 50%

Class IX—Natural Conditions

Not all disasters mean devastation for everyone. The home to the right did not have an ocean view prior to the 1964 Alaskan earthquake, as this area was once developed with the town's commercial business district. The tidal waves destroyed this business district, and now the home has an unobstructed ocean view.

of the city's streets, curbs, gutters, and sidewalks were severely damaged. Two major slides occurred. One dropped a full block of Fourth Avenue, the main business street, 20 to 30 feet down into the earth. The other landslide destroyed Turnagain by the Sea, a high-priced housing area that overlooked Knik Arm, throwing the homes into the Cook Inlet. This area was never rebuilt and is now called Earthquake Park. Large cracks in the earth are still visible there today.

The earthquake caused what is called the *bathtub effect*, where inlets, or *ocean fingers*, would "swish" back and forth, like the water in a tub, causing major and recurring tidal waves. In Seward, an oceanfront community south of Anchorage, the earthquake ignited several oil storage tanks. The town lost 95% of its railroad, which impacted all of Alaska as it served as the rail head of the Alaskan railroad. The city had a mile-long area collapse into the sea. On top of the earthquake damage, the town suffered enormous destruction from subsequent tidal waves. Numerous homes and businesses were swept away into the ocean, and one family clung to their roof to for 14 hours as recurring tidal waves ripped the house from the foundation and floated it over the neighborhood. That residential area is vacant today, as is much of the destroyed downtown area, which is used for recreational parking.

This disaster has shown a variety of impacts. The only residential development within the damaged tidal wave zone has been housing that is rented to low-income occupants. Some homes located off the coastline now enjoy outstanding oceanfront views, and as a result of the tragedy their values were enhanced. Although the same risk for another tidal wave exists today as in 1964, a $60 million ocean research and aquarium facility began construction in 1996 on lower-risk areas of the coast.

The tidal waves also hit Valdez (a small town later made famous by the Exxon Valdez oil spill, which also occurred on Good Friday). The largest tidal waves occurred here, where they reached 70 meters. Much of the town was destroyed, yet several homes and businesses did survive the waves. Later, the entire town was uprooted and moved to a new town site that was not impacted, just a few miles away. Nearly every building that was not destroyed was eventually moved to the new town, and the old original town site is currently vacant with only some concrete remnants. The local visitors center offers tourists a walking tour map of the various homes and businesses that were moved from the old town site.

The entire town suffered a significant loss, through either the cost of destroyed buildings or the cost of relocating to the new town site. Only the few homes and structures that exist near the old town site suffer from market resistance, as they sell for significant discounts because of the very real danger of a recurrence. The moving of entire towns is not an isolated incident. A village was damaged by the earthquake and tidal waves and was moved to an entirely new island, Evens Island.

The destruction resulting from the Alaskan Earthquake and tidal waves was not limited to Alaska alone. States as far away as Florida and Texas had vertical movements of up to 5 to 10 centimeters of earth. California, Canada, Hawaii, and Oregon also incurred damages from the tsunami.

Damages and Fatalities from the 1964 Alaskan Earthquake Tsunami

Location	Fatalities from Tsunami	Damage from Tsunami
Alaska	107	$84,268,000
California	11	$8,939,000–$9,789,000
Canada	0	$10,250,000
Hawaii	0	$67,590
Oregon	4	$716,000

CHAPTER 10

Class X—Incurable Conditions

Some detrimental conditions can render a property useless and without value. Class X represents the most serious detrimental conditions, where the property may not be economically or physically remedied and as a result the property has lost considerable or all value. In addition, there may be a risk of physical harm if the property is occupied. In some conditions, a property may be a liability to own if the condition creates a serious hazard or if the cost of repair exceeds the property's value. Examples of Class X detrimental conditions include sites of massive natural disasters that are perceived to reoccur, or toxic or hazardous waste issues where the contamination is so serious that it poses a serious health hazard or where the costs to remediate the site exceed the property's unimpaired value.

For example, on April 1, 1946, a tsunami that originated in the Aleutian Islands struck the island of Hawaii and killed over 170 people, mostly in Laupahoehoe and Hilo, where the wave heights averaged 30 feet. The maximum wave height was 55 feet at Pololu Valley on the northern tip of the island. Much of downtown Hilo was demolished, and a schoolyard clock, frozen at 1:05 and now a memorial, marks the exact time of the destruction. (Another tsunami hit Hilo on May 23, 1960. Warning systems were more advanced then, though, and only six people were killed.)

The eastern areas of downtown Hilo have never been rebuilt. Remnants of many empty blocks of old streets, gutters, and sidewalks still exist. A major tourist attraction, Lili'uokalani Gardens replaces an area that was once improved with various structures. After the 1946 tidal wave, the debris was bulldozed into large piles, soaked with kerosene, and burned. Over the years, the buried burnt debris has decomposed and caused considerable soil subsidence problems throughout the area. For example, many parking lots have large open holes and depressions. A civil defense warning system and evacuation routes are located throughout the area, and the threat of another tidal wave still exists today.

In addition to the continuing threat of tidal waves, Hilo is also in a Zone 2 Volcano Area (1 is most dangerous and 9 is least). Recent lava flows came within four miles of Hilo. Further inland, a 1987 lava flow from the Kilauea Volcano within the Hawaii Volcanoes National Park buried much of the Royal Gardens Subdivision in Kapa'ahu under 40 feet of lava. The volcano destroyed numerous homes and a newly constructed multimillion-dollar Park Visitor Center and Museum near the Poupou-Kauka ancient villages (1275 A.D.). The 1987 lava flows spared an ancient temple used for human sacrifices, but it was subsequently destroyed by 1997 lava flows. The lava flowed slowly, and the destruction occurred over several weeks or even months. Efforts to divert the lava flow with concrete berms were entirely ineffective.

A clock, set at 1:05, the exact time of the April Fools' Day tsunami, is all that remains of an elementary school that was entirely destroyed by the disaster.

The subdivision is located in a Zone 2 Volcano Area. Housing in the area has always been inexpensive by Hawaiian standards, and people were able to buy a house with an ocean view for about the price of a car. While some homes were spared, the area's infrastructure was destroyed by the lava flows. Some people still reside in these homes, but they have no water, electricity, gas, or telephone. The roads are partly over old lava flows. Lots in the subdivision sell for nominal amounts of approximately $500, although there is little chance of ever rebuilding on them.

Despite being in a tidal wave zone, Hilo still draws many tourists. This restaurant has gone so far as marking the water levels from two of this century's tsunamis.

In some situations, the detrimental condition issue may be curable, but it would still be considered a Class X condition because the problem cannot be cured by the property owner. For example, if a landslide originates in an adjoining canyon, this may be a Class X situation because the property owner cannot make repairs on a condition stemming from a property belonging to another person or entity, which is thereby out of the control

Lava flows are still active today on the big island of Hawaii and are unpredictable. Here, lava flows literally surround some homes.

of the owner of the subject property.

In Exhibit 10.1, Class X incurable conditions reflect a total or overwhelming loss in value upon the discovery of the condition. These situations are so severe that the property becomes virtually worthless, or even a liability if the cost to correct the detrimental condition exceeds the property's unimpaired value.

Consider another illustration of a Class X detrimental condition. The Robinson home is located in Alaska at the bottom of a canyon that has been stable for all recorded history. The house, without any detrimental condition issues, is worth $250,000. In 1995, an adjacent land owner graded several roads on the ridge tops without any engineering studies or permits. During subsequent winters, rains flooded the canyon, and rock and debris partially buried the Robinson home. City engineers determined that the erosion was so enormous that the situation was virtually impossible to repair and that future landslides were likely. Landslides have occurred each winter for the last three years and have caused approximately $50,000 in damages per incident. The Robinsons are concerned for their safety, as well as their property's value.

While the value of the home may justify its initial repair, the continued threat to life and property puts the Robinsons' home in the Class X category. Class X detrimental conditions can involve virtually any detrimental condition classification if the situation is extreme. However, the analysis should consider if there is any residual value to the property, such as the land being used for open space or a storage area for an agricultural use.

Exhibit 10.1 Class X—Incurable Conditions

The graphs for DC Class X have been highlighted here; however, DCs have a variety of impacts which, upon analysis, vary on a case-by-case basis. Ultimately, any graph may be applicable based upon the case-specific facts.

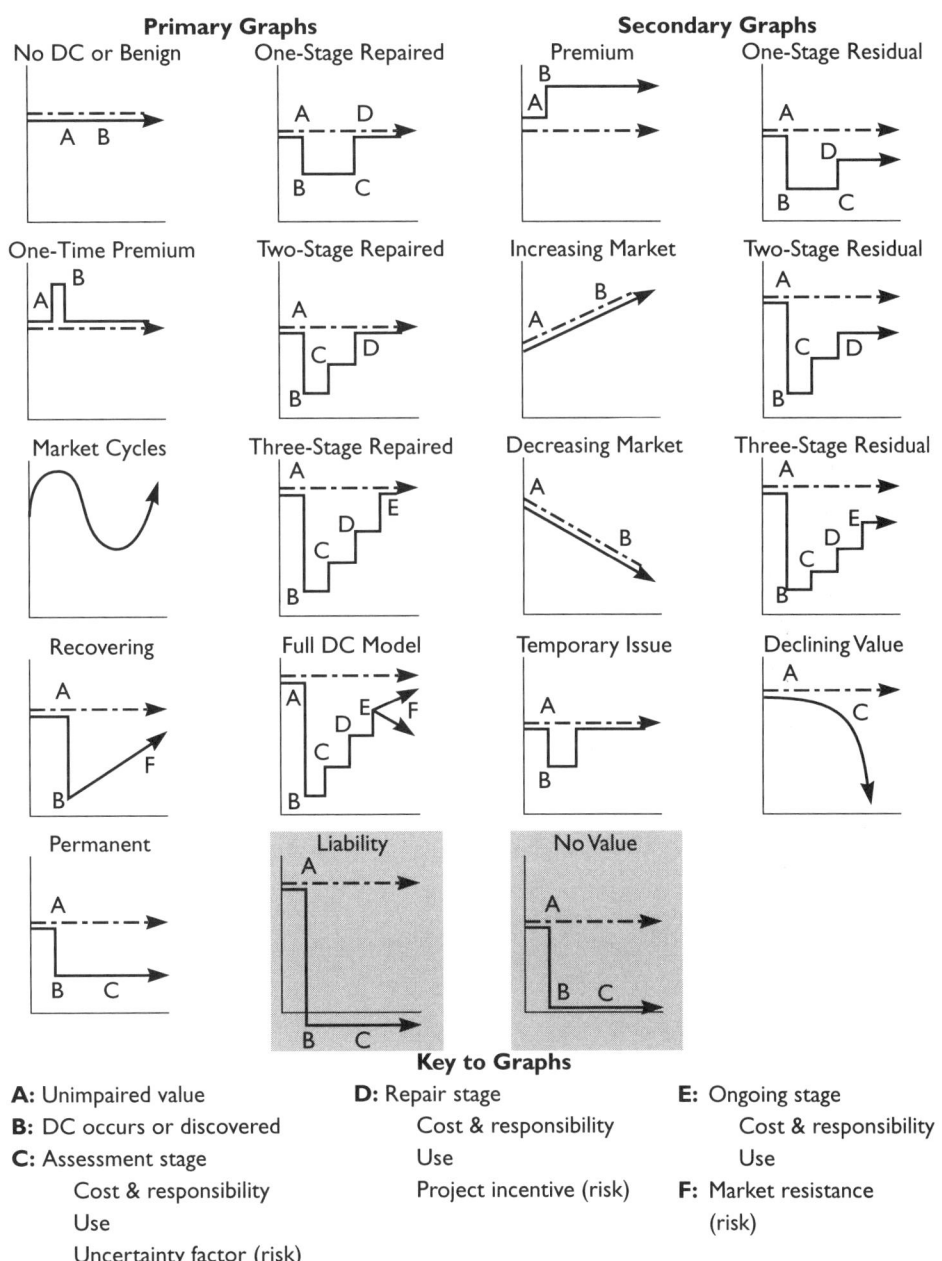

Key to Graphs

A: Unimpaired value
B: DC occurs or discovered
C: Assessment stage
  Cost & responsibility
  Use
  Uncertainty factor (risk)

D: Repair stage
  Cost & responsibility
  Use
  Project incentive (risk)

E: Ongoing stage
  Cost & responsibility
  Use
F: Market resistance
  (risk)

Source: *Bell's Guide: The Real Estate Encyclopedia*

Chapter 10 Case Study

By Randall Bell, MAI

Benedict Canyon Landslide—Los Angeles, California
Class X—Incurable Conditions

The subject property is a single-family residence containing 3,946 square feet of living area, four bedrooms, three bathrooms, and a pool on 6.23 acres of land in the Benedict Canyon area of Los Angeles, California. This area is well-located and has proximity to schools, shopping, employment, and other amenities. The area generally has very good appeal. The subject property was purchased by the current owners, David J. and Anita B. Lowd, on January 4, 1979, for $1,130,500. The property sits at the base of a large canyon, and the mountains to the rear rise approximately 1,500 feet above the grade of the subject property.

A revetment is a structure constructed to hold back mud or debris flows. While they can be effective, they are also very expensive and require tremendous upkeep with each incident.

On four occasions during winter rain storms over the prior three years, the property was damaged by large volumes of mud, rock, and debris that flooded the home and general area. The debris came from the canyon walls above, which had been stable for all recorded history until the local fire department graded fire roads at the ridge of the mountains. These fire roads were installed without any engineering and have caused tremendous erosion, which has funneled down the canyon into the subject property. On multiple occasions, the house was partially destroyed by debris measuring over eight feet in height. The pool was filled with mud and rock debris, and part of the house was flooded. The property underwent extensive refurbishment by the owner. The property also has an extensive revetment (a fenced area with multiple dams), which is designed to retain mud, rock, and debris in the event of another landslide.

Market Value as if no Detrimental Condition

The value as if no detrimental condition was determined by the traditional appraisal process using the sales comparison approach and the cost approach and estimated at $1.5 million. In its current condition, the subject property is an attractive single-family residence. However, the revetment distracts from the canyon characteristics and location.

Market Value as is

In completing the report, the appraiser inspected the subject property, reviewed an engineering geologic report prepared by Anderson Geo-Soils, Inc. (dated August 1, 1993), researched, inspected, and photographed various improved comparables, and spoke with 12 brokers who have been involved with similar Class IX and X detrimental condition situations specifically involving flooding and landslides. Additionally, research was conducted regarding numerous sites involving flooding and landslides throughout the Southern California area to estimate the loss in property values as a result of flood damage.

Upon the inspection of the subject property, a review of photographs and videos showing the flood and landslide damages, and an inspection of adjoining canyon areas, the appraiser concluded that the subject property has no value in its current condition. The subject property is considered a Class X detrimental condition in its existing state and would be considered a Class IX detrimental condition in a repaired state.

This conclusion was drawn for the following reasons:

1. The condition that originally caused the flood and landslide damage is located off the subject site, thereby preventing the current owner from making the repairs necessary to prevent future damages.
2. The cause of the damages requires very significant repairs and at a high cost in relationship to the value of the subject property.
3. The historical damages were severe, resulting in damage to the structure of the residence (over $50,000 per incident).
4. The costs of removing debris for each incident is high (over $75,000), and the costs of installing and maintaining the revetment is also high, in relationship to the overall property value.
5. A risk to life and personal property exists for occupants of the residence. The piles of debris have exceeded eight feet and could seriously injure or kill a person within its path.
6. There may be a liability, or perceived liability, if future landslides pass over the subject property and onto adjoining properties.

Based upon these factors, it is concluded that a reasonable buyer would not purchase the property at any price, as the costs, inability to make repairs, risks to life and property, and possible liability exceed the value of the residence.

Value as if Repaired and Indemnified

In the event that the causes of the flood and landslide damage are repaired to the satisfaction of qualified engineering professionals, a residual loss to property value may remain due to the perceptions of the market.

Because of the severity of the historical problems, a potential buyer would likely be hesitant to purchase the property at its full market value when other properties are available that do not have any past incidence of severe flooding and landslides. This hesitancy would likely be due to perceived risks of human judgment in making the repairs, as well as the general unpredictability of nature and related natural disasters.

In order to entice a potential buyer upon the completion of repairs, a discount to the market value would be warranted. In order to quantify this market resistance, various homes and areas involving flooding were studied, and local brokers were surveyed. These areas included Blue Bird Canyon, Mystic Canyon, and Laguna Canyon in Laguna Beach, Temecula, Murrietta, Anaheim Hills, and Malibu.

Of those areas studied, the loss in value ranged from 0% to 50.2%, based upon the severity of the problem and the value of the property. In extreme cases, where repairs were yet to be completed, homes were considered "not marketable." Following is a summary of market data:

Market Resistance—Flood Damaged Homes Sold Repaired

Study	Market Resistance*	Comments
Blue Bird Canyon, Laguna Beach		
Property A	6.4%	Minor damage
Property B	2.2%	Minor damage
Property C	32.4%	Major damage, no warranty
Mystic Canyon, Laguna Beach		
Property A	9.8%	Minor damage
Property B	50.2%	Major damage, no warranty
Property C	5.0%	Minor damage
Property D	22.3%	Major damage, warranty
Laguna Canyon, Laguna Beach		
Property A	18.7%	Major damage, warranty
Property B	19.9%	Major damage, warranty
Temecula		
Property A	12.0%	Moderate damage
Property B	4.2%	Minor damage
Murrietta		
Property A	14.5%	Reflooding unlikely
Anaheim Hills		
Property A	27.1%	Major damage, unsure slope
Property B	25.5%	Major damage, unsure slope
Malibu		
Property A	0%	On ocean, accustomed to storm damages
Property B	7%	Minor damage from landslide
Property C	0%	On ocean, accustomed to storm damage

* Market resistance is computed as the estimated loss, as a percentage of its value unimpaired, of a fully repaired property that has sold with a history of landslide or flood damage.

Based upon these interviews and other information, it is estimated that a 20% loss in value would be applicable to the subject property, located in Benedict Canyon, in the event that repairs were made. This assumes that the property owner is fully indemnified by those making the repairs against any future damages. This loss in value would not likely diminish significantly for several years, and then only after several heavy rains to demonstrate to potential buyers the true effectiveness of any repairs.

Conclusion

Market value as if no detrimental condition	$1,500,000
Market value as is	No value—liability
Market value as if repaired and indemnified	$1,200,000

Additional Case Studies

Case Study 1

By Joe Haeussler, MAI

Hill View Development—Adjoining a Two-Story House to the Rear
Class 1 Detrimental Condition—Benign Condition

The Hill View residential subdivision is an upper-middle class neighborhood in a suburban area northwest of Los Angeles. Within the development is a property that was the subject of litigation. The case involved a 1,784-sq.-ft. single-family home built in 1971. The house is of good-quality, wood-frame and stucco construction, and the floorplan is the "Plan Three" of the Montego Plan within the Hill View Development. The single-story house was built on a 6,565-sq.-ft. site, which is typical for the homes in the development.

The property is located in an area undergoing revitalization, and many homes are being remodeled, being substantially reconfigured, or undergoing additions. The subject property is level and abuts the surrounding residences at grade with the properties to the rear being above grade approximately four feet.

An appraiser was retained by the sellers of the subject property, Ken and Linda Gattenio, and their attorney. The subject property sold in August 1993 to Gregory and Sherrie Connor for the sum of $407,000. After the close of escrow, a complaint ensued. The buyers asserted that prior to the start of escrow, the adjacent property owner to the rear, Oscar and Ann Andersen, at 1802 Arlow Place, began the approval process for a second-story add-on. The community association required the Andersens to have a *Neighborhood Awareness Form* signed by all surrounding neighbors affected by the proposed project. Mr. Gattenio signed the form.

Weeks after Mr. Gattenio was made aware of the Andersens' plans to construct a second-story add-on, he sold the property to Mr. and Mrs. Connor. After buying the property, the Connors removed mature trees to add sunlight into the backyard, unaware of the plans of the adjacent property owner to build an addition. Weeks later Mrs. Connor observed construction activity at the Andersen property. She asked the construction personnel about the construction project and the time of its completion. According to the Connors, once the construction was completed, the loss of privacy and light would permanently impact the property. The Connors filed a complaint for rescission and damages, fraudulent failure to disclose, and intentional infliction of emotional distress.

The appraiser was hired to assess the damage, if any, to the apparent imposed condition of a second-story add-on to the adjacent property. One of the Connors' complaints was that the value of their property would be permanently diminished due to the loss of privacy from the second-story add-on of the adjoining property.

Given the full line of complaints that the Gattenios were required to deal with, the appraiser's focus of attention was to interpret the market's opinion as to a two-story residence existing to the rear of a property versus a single-story home existing to the rear of a property. Data was sought to test if an imposed condition existed or to test if a benign condition existed.

In addressing the appraisal problem, two tests were employed. The first involved the analysis of the market's reaction of a home having an adjoining two-story home versus an adjoining one-story home to the rear. A paired sales analysis was employed to study the impact on similar homes with the distinguishing characteristic of a one- or two-story home to the rear of the property.

The second test was a study of the subject property and the surrounding homes. The complaint was that the buyers were buying the home with "privacy," and after they had purchased the home, the adjacent second-story addition negatively impacted the perceived privacy. This study of the subject property addresses the privacy of the subject property, before and after the completion of the second-story addition to the property to the rear.

The initial study involved a search of recent sales of homes in the area of the subject property. The homes were categorized into, first, size of home and, second, whether a home had a one-story home to the rear or a two-story home to the rear. All of the homes compared were in the same development and were in similar condition when compared to the subject property. The quality of construction and location are all similar, as they were built in a similar time frame and by the same developer. Exhibit CS 1.1 sets forth the market data used for analysis.

The market data in Exhibit CS 1.1 was then paired to establish market support as to whether an impaired condition existed or a benign condition existed. Exhibit CS 1.2 sets forth the market data used for the paired data analysis. The indicated adjustments are a result of the various pairings of homes with adjoining one-story homes and homes with adjoining two-story homes. The percentage adjustment is the indicated adjustment for a home with an adjoining two-story home.

By comparing the two types of data sets, no correlation was found as to the appropriate adjustment. From a slight negative property attribute of having an adjoining two-story home, the next two pairings indicate a positive value. From the data set used and the mixed indicated adjustments, it was clear that there is no correlation between home prices that do or do not adjoin homes to the rear that looks into the backyard. This is a market indication of a benign condition.

The second study was the analysis of the existing privacy of the backyard before the sale took place. During the property inspection, it was noted that the site did not have privacy as of the date of sale because other two-story homes were already visible from the subject backyard. If an imposed condition was created by the addition to the adjoining rear property, then it would not be a condition that existed prior to the start of the project. It was also a condition that existed between many homes in the development.

The market data and the paired sales showed that no correlation exists between homes with a two-story home adjoining to the rear or a one-story home adjoining to the rear. The Connors claimed that an imposed condition would permanently impair or diminish the value of the subject property. From a test of the market data, it was apparent that there was no impact to property value. To further support this claim, the analysis of the subject property's rear yard privacy showed that if an imposed condition existed, it was in place prior to the Andersen's plans to construct a second-story add-on. Therefore, it was the conclusion of the analyst that the market interprets this condition as being benign.

Exhibit CS 1.1 Hill View Development Market Data

Sale No.	Address	Sale Price	Sale Date	Year Built
Plan 1 (1,475 square feet) Sales Adjoining One-Story Home to the Rear				
1	1859 Abbey Street	$390,000	3/93	1969
2	1979 Albans Place	$430,000	3/93	1970
3	1933 Bridge Avenue	$467,000	9/93	1970
4	2041 Vince Place	$385,000	1/94	1969
Plan 1 (1,475 square feet) Sales Adjoining Two-Story Home to the Rear				
5	1936 Sea Place	$435,000	7/94	1969
6	2021 Bridge Avenue	$390,000	5/93	1969
7	2045 Bridge Avenue	$425,000	9/94	1969
8	1806 Gart Place	$425,000	3/94	1970
9	1859 Berly Place	$380,000	8/94	1970
10	1843 Leigh Place	$405,000	4/93	1971
Plan 2 (1,659 square feet) Sales Adjoining One-Story Home to the Rear				
1	1700 Charles Place	$405,000	7/94	1969
2	1800 Bourne Place	$410,000	7/93	1969
3	1800 Wheel Place	$406,000	1/93	1970
4	1982 Albans Place	$425,000	5/93	1971
Plan 2 (1,659 square feet) Sales Adjoining Two-Story Home to the Rear				
5	1942 Bourne Place	$389,000	3/94	1970
6	1960 Digan Place	$445,000	6/93	1971
7	1930 Rant Place	$410,000	6/93	1971
8	1950 Bish Place	$490,000	7/94	1971
9	1974 Ward Place	$580,000	2/93	1971
10	1967 Bourne Place	$437,000	1/93	1970
Plan 3 (1,784 square feet) Sales Adjoining One-Story Home to the Rear				
1	1964 Vince Place	$385,000	12/93	1970
2	1801 Berly Place	$445,000	7/93	1970
3	1942 Ward Place	$480,000	8/94	1971
Plan 3 (1,784 square feet) Sales Adjoining Two-Story Home to the Rear				
4	1723 Heff Place	$407,000	5/94	1968
5	2018 Sea Place	$535,000	7/94	1969

Exhibit CS 1.2 Paired Data Analysis

Adjoining One-Story		Adjoining Two-Story		Indicated Adjustment
Sale No.	Sale Price	Sale No.	Sale Price	
Plan No. 1				
1	$390,000	5	$435,000	
2	$430,000	6	$390,000	
3	$467,000	7	$425,000	
4	$385,000	8	$425,000	
		9	$380,000	
		10	$405,000	
Average	$418,000		$410,000	-1.9%
Plan No. 2				
1	$405,000	5	$389,000	
2	$410,000	6	$445,000	
3	$406,000	7	$410,000	
4	$425,000	8	$490,000	
		9	$580,000	
		10	$437,000	
Average	$411,500		$458,500	11.42%
Plan No. 3				
1	$385,000	1	$407,000	
2	$445,000	2	$535,000	
3	$480,000			
Average	$436,667		$471,000	7.9%

Case Study 2

By Randall Bell, MAI

Durham Woods—Edison, New Jersey
Class IV Detrimental Condition—Gas Pipeline Explosion

Today a playground sits in an area that was destroyed by the Durham Woods pipeline explosion. The charred trees in the background are a constant reminder of the damage that was caused years ago.

On March 23, 1994, a 36-inch diameter, underground methane gas pipeline exploded in Edison, New Jersey. The pipeline was operated by Texas Eastern Transmission Corporation and had last been inspected in 1986. The explosion created a crater 60 feet deep and sent a 300-foot fireball into the air that could be seen by residents of New Jersey, New York, and Pennsylvania. Homes shook for a 10-mile radius, and the blast was likened by many to a nuclear disaster. Workers needed 2½ hours to turn off the gas flow. Fifteen hundred tenants were forced to flee their homes, the Red Cross intervened, and the area was declared a federal disaster area. The disaster prompted new federal legislation regarding pipeline operations. While the tragedy occurred near midnight, there was only one related death (a heart attack suffered by a fleeing person), and the balance of the victims successfully escaped.

The Durham Woods apartment complex contains 63 buildings, of which eight (containing 128 units) were completely destroyed. A total of 96 units in six buildings were damaged. Insurance proceeds paid for the reconstruction of the damaged and destroyed units at a cost of $12.25 million. The apartment building owners eventually were able to re-lease the rebuilt units. An adjoining condominium development, called Talmadge Village, was in the approved planning stages at the time of the disaster. As it is generally much easier to rent properties associated with tragedies as opposed to selling them, the development was converted to an apartment complex in order to keep the project progressing.

Case Study 3

By Randall Bell, MAI

Simpson Condominium—West Los Angeles, California
Class IV Detrimental Condition—Crime Scene

From the air, the Bundy Drive condominium can be seen to be really more of a duplex rather than part of a large condominium complex.

The murders of Nicole Brown Simpson and Ron Goldman occurred on the walkway to a West Los Angeles condominium on Bundy Avenue in June 1994. The property is a well-designed, tri-level condominium, which contains 3,405 square feet, four bedrooms, three bathrooms, and a rooftop patio.

The property was purchased in January 1994 by Nicole Simpson for an effective price of $652,000. Shortly thereafter she listed the property for rent for $4,800 per month in an effort to relocate.

The condominium was listed for sale shortly after the crime for $795,000. Over the last two years, various written offers have been presented, but none were consummated. The property suffered from an extended marketing period of approximately 2½ years, far beyond the typical six-month time frame for residential properties in the area. The property was scheduled to be auctioned in January 1997, but it was sold prior to the public auction for a price less than the $595,000 asking price.

Case Study 4

By Randall Bell, MAI, and Orell C. Anderson, MAI

Luby's Cafeteria—Killeen, Texas
Class IV Detrimental Condition—Crime Scene

Today the Luby's Restaurant enjoys business as usual and is considered by many to be a textbook example of how to manage a tragedy.

In October 1991, a man drove his truck through the window of a cafeteria-style restaurant called Luby's, shot and killed 23 people, and then turned the gun on himself.

As a result of Luby's management style and in spite of the tragedy, the City of Killeen petitioned Luby's to not abandon the site but rather to reopen the facility. The restaurant management extensively remodeled the property and approximately five months later reopened the restaurant. Employees were compensated for the down time of the restaurant. Both the local and corporate management maintains an open and cooperative attitude towards the media and other inquiries, and today the restaurant enjoys business as usual. According to a company spokesperson, the key to this situation was that they were not focused on stock values, but rather on how they could genuinely help the community. The company's CEO, Pete Erben, flew to the site within hours of the incident and immediately put $100,000 towards assisting the victims and their families. Luby's management indicated that they have no intention of selling the property. While there is no memorial on the site, there is a memorial commemorating those who died in this incident at a nearby community center. The Luby's incident is considered by many to be a textbook case on properly handling a tragedy.

Case Study 5

By Orell C. Anderson, MAI

Pacific Motel—California
Class V Detrimental Condition—Eminent Domain Partial Taking

The Pacific Motel is a 100-room budget motel in California, comprising five buildings totaling approximately 25,000 square feet on a 75,000-sq.-ft. site. Current occupancy is 70% and the average daily room rate (ADR) is $30. Amenities include a gift shop, a breakfast room with complimentary continental breakfast, a video arcade, laundry, a popcorn, juice, and soda room, a complimentary heated swimming pool, luggage storage, free cable television, and concierge service in the lobby. In the before condition, the subject property had good freeway exposure with fair access.

The subject property was partially condemned by the State of California Department of Transportation for the expansion of the local freeway. Because the motel improvements currently utilized as the Pacific Motel sit on a portion of the Part Taken Parcel, a portion of these improvements are to be demolished by the Department of Transportation in the process of the road widening. Finally, there are various site improvements that will also be acquired, demolished, or relocated for this acquisition.

The scope of the appraisal assignment was to address the effect of the proposed acquisition by the condemning agency, any damages incurred, and any benefits attributable to the condemnation. The purpose of the assignment was to estimate total just compensation as supported by fair market value. As this is considered a permanent imposed condition, the value of the Remainder Parcel will be negatively impacted in perpetuity.

Larger Parcel

Methodology utilized in this analysis includes the three standard approaches: the cost approach, the sales comparison approach, and the income capitalization approach.

The cost approach indicated a value of $2,250,000. The cost of building the subject improvements was in excess of the value of the subject property indicated through the income capitalization approach as well as the sales comparison approach. It became apparent that the difference was attributable to external obsolescence, as the income generated by the subject motel cannot justify the cost to construct the improvements. External obsolescence in the form of economic obsolescence was estimated. Land was concluded to be valued at $15 a square foot for the 75,000-sq.-ft. site.

The sales comparison approach indicated a value on a per-room basis of $22,000 a room for 100 rooms, indicating a $2.2 million estimate.

The income capitalization approach indicated a value of $2 million. The ADR of the subject property was considered to be normal as compared to rental comparables within the subject property neighborhood. Therefore, the existing ADR for the subject property as well as its current occupancy was concluded to be appropriate for the analysis.

In the reconciliation of the various approaches to value, major consideration was given to the sales comparison approach, which was supported by the income capitalization approach. The cost approach was considered a secondary indicator of value primarily due to the presence of external obsolescence and the difficulty of estimating accrued depreciation.

Based on the above factors, it is concluded that the fair market value of the fee simple estate of the Pacific Motel as the Larger Parcel in the before condition is $2,200,000, allocated $1,125,000 to land and $1,075,000 to the improvements.

Part Taken Parcel

Two parcels are being acquired, one at fee and one temporary construction easement. The total land area of the Part Taken Parcel is 5,000 square feet. The Part Taken Parcel is irregular in shape, generally comprising a long strip of land. Improvements located within the Part Taken Parcel include portions of Buildings A and B used for both guest rooms and a manager's unit used for additional office space and storage. Additional improvements within that area include a gift shop, a breakfast room converted from three motel rooms in Building A, and various site improvements including concrete and asphalt paving, concrete block wall, landscaping and irrigation with six large trees, one pole sign, and one wall-mounted sign (to be relocated). The number of parking spaces in the before condition was 108 with 100 rooms.

The severance of the Part Taken Parcel will effectively result in the loss of five motel rooms. Additionally, cut and reface work will result in the reconfiguration of areas affected by the part taken, including the reconfiguration of the breakfast room, the gift shop area, as well as the lobby area, storage, and the office area. In summary, five motel rooms are located in the part taken area, and five rooms will be lost in cut and reface and remodel for a total room loss of ten.

The subject site in the before condition had three points of egress and ingress. During the demolition and construction, the center access point will be temporarily eliminated. The loss of on-site circulation is not considered significant in terms of passenger cars or tour buses; however, 18-wheel trucks will be hindered in their ability to drive completely around the motel. Access to the front desk, which will be relocated into temporary office trailers during remodeling of the lobby building, will be available at a northerly driveway. In the after condition, all three driveways will be re-graded as a part of construction contract work by the highway department, and full on-site circulation will be restored. Finally, the existing wall and pole signs will be relocated.

The area encompassed by the temporary construction easement (TCE) is effectively located at the front of the subject property, adjacent to the frontage road. The total area is 1,500 square feet. Improvements located within the TCE include various site improvements, such as paving and landscaping. No additional motel rooms are affected by the temporary construction easement. Duration of the TCE is 12 months.

The construction of the public improvements in the manner proposed is anticipated to significantly disrupt motel operations. In the severing, removing, and remodeling of a portion of the two motel buildings, it is anticipated that there will be a reduction in income from operating the motel. The income loss is associated primarily with reduction of all rentable rooms in both Building A and Building B during remodeling. General overall occupancy reduction due to the on- and off-site construction is also anticipated. The reduction in occupancy will also result in the possible loss of a portion of various motel market segments. The administrative office will be required to be relocated into portable office trailers during the remodeling. Motel operations are anticipated to resume on-site within these portable office trailers.

Value of the Part Taken as Part of the Whole
Land

The land value of the Part Taken Parcel is based upon the unit value of the entire larger parcel. Having previously calculated the value of the whole, the value of the Part Taken Parcel is as follows:

5,000 square feet at $15 a square foot equals $75,000.

Improvements

The value of the five motel units located within the Part Taken Parcel, net of land value, is $10,750 per room. This yields an indicated value of the motel improvements for five rooms of $53,750. The value of the site improvements is based upon the unit value of the components as previously calculated in the cost approach of the Larger Parcel section, which included paving, landscaping, block walls, and relocation cost of the pole and wall signs. The total depreciated value of the motel improvements and site improvements is $114,750. The value of the part acquired as part of the whole is therefore $189,750. Landscaping was not depreciated but was given a contributory value only.

Valuation of the Temporary Construction Easement (TCE)

Ground lease rates and interviews were obtained for use in this analysis. The lease rates and interviews of individuals familiar with ground lease rates range from an annual payment equivalent to 8-10% of the fee simple value of the land. Based upon these leases as well as interviews, the land rate has been estimated to be 9%. Upon termination of the construction period, the easement area will be reverted to the Remainder Parcel and will be otherwise unaffected.

The value calculation of the temporary construction easement is as follows:

1,500 square feet at $15 a square foot at 9% for 12 months equals $2,025.

Valuation of the loss of total income and site improvements associated with the TCE was estimated as a cost to cure damage and is presented in the Curative Work and Cost Estimate section.

Description of the Remainder Parcel

The Remainder Parcel is smaller in size by 5,000 square feet, or a remaining total of 70,000 square feet. In the after condition, it will continue to have an irregular shape. It will be reduced by 10 motel rooms within the Part Taken Parcel. The manager's unit/office area will be incorporated with the entire ground floor of Building A, which contained the original lobby/front desk area and offices. The breakfast room and gift shop will be relocated into Building B. The wall-mounted sign as well as the pole sign will have been relocated onto the subject property outside the area of the Part Taken Parcel. Access as well as exposure and visibility will be similar in the after condition. As indicated previously, parking will have been reduced from 108 spaces to 100 spaces. Current zoning requirements are one space per motel room. Therefore, the remaining parking ratio is conforming to existing zoning.

Project Impact

There are several project impacts related to the fee taking in the TCE that are considered significant. Temporary project impacts related to the TCE include the following:

- There will be a temporary loss of mature landscaping and pavement for a 12-month period during the construction phase of the freeway widening. These site improvements will be removed and later replaced.
- There will be a temporary loss and removal of an existing wall sign mounted on Building A during construction.
- There will be temporary noise, dust, and fumes related to the freeway and frontage road construction as well as from demolition and construction of the subject motel and site improvements.
- There will also be a temporary loss of the front desk lobby area and also a blocking of the motel rooms in Buildings A and B during demolition and construction for cut and reface.

The collective project impact associated with temporary construction is anticipated to result in the reduction of the motel's occupancy level for a 12-month period. Cut and reface is estimated to be set for only a six-month period.

Permanent Project Impacts

There will be a loss of landscaping, paving, and 10 motel rooms. The cost to demolish the existing improvements within this part taken area and the remodel of the remaining motel room improvements is addressed in the Curative Work and Cost Estimate section.

Finally, the freeway will be three feet further away from the subject property's ultimate right-of-way line as compared to the before condition. The frontage road will have been widened from 33 feet in the before condition to 36 feet in the after condition (net effect). As the freeway is further away from the subject property in the after condition, no sound/noise study was necessary. Prior to the analysis of the highest and best use of the Remainder Parcel and evaluation of the Remainder Parcel, an analysis of curative work to restore utility to the Remainder Parcel is necessary.

Curative Work and Cost Estimate

A brief discussion follows of each of the curative features required to restore the utility to the Remainder Parcel in the after condition, addressing the temporary project impacts related to the temporary construction easement and the respective cost estimates.

Demolition and remodeling cost estimates. To determine the costs associated with this construction work, attempts were made to obtain a summary of estimated costs from the subject property owner. However, they were not made available for this analysis. Therefore, the associated costs were estimated by a team of motel/hotel developers, investors, and managers who had extensive experience in building and remodeling motel facilities. Based on their estimates, the concluded cost to cure was $200,000.

Occupancy. While the majority of the frontage road and the freeway construction work will occur at the perimeter of the subject site, construction will clearly impact normal operation of the motel. It was concluded that there will be a loss of occupancy revenue due to the temporary construction easement for a 12-month period. The on- and off-site construction for the public improvements is anticipated to occur over a 12-month period. The remodel of the motel is estimated to last approximately six months. In addition, 13 rooms in Buildings A and B would be blocked during the cut and reface period. Furthermore, the gift shop would also be closed for this period. No income would be derived from the blocked rooms or the gift shop during this period.

To address the occupational impacts of construction, the motel owner (from the appraiser's perspective) has two options: 1) continue to operate the motel to the best of their ability during the construction period, or 2) close the motel on a temporary basis and re-open upon the completion of construction. Based upon interviews of both the subject property management company as well as surveys of other motels that had been impacted by freeway widenings in the area, it was concluded that the best option was for the continued operation of the subject motel during the construction period. The loss of room revenue is estimated through analysis to be a 40% reduction in occupancy. This was based upon accounts of loss of occupancy of other motel operators in the area who have been impacted by construction.

The total loss of income is calculated by adding the loss of income resulting from the motel operation and gift shop during the construction period plus the income that would have been generated from the blocked rooms. This is based upon a stabilized occupancy. The net overall loss of *NOI* during the TCE and the income loss to the blocked rooms and gift shop during the construction period was estimated at $175,000.

Temporary office facility. The subject property will require the leasing of portable office trailers to operate its office and front desk facilities during the remodel of the impacted office in Building A for a six-month period. The cost to lease two trailers was estimated by a professional office trailer rental company at approximately $2,000.

Replacement of landscaping and pavement. During construction, the majority of these improvements will be lost as they are located in a temporary construction easement, therefore requiring their replacement in the after condition. Price and cost of these items have been estimated using a cost publication service. The concluded estimate is $7,000.

Banners (installation of temporary sign). Disruptions due to the construction work will require the placement of a temporary sign on the office trailer to inform prospective patrons that the facility is open during construction and that the trailer is the location of the front desk area. A temporary sign could be attached to the trailer if a custom vinyl sign is used and professionally installed. The cost of one banner, approximately 5 by 20 feet, including installation is approximately $500, as provided by a professional banner sign company.

Summary. In summary, curable severance damages include the demolition and remodel of two motel buildings at $200,000. Income lost during the temporary construction easement and blocked rooms for cut and reface is at $175,000. Replacement of paving and landscaping is at $7,000. The temporary sign is at $500, and the temporary office trailer for a six-month rental period is at $2,000, for a total of $384,500.

Highest and Best Use of the Remainder Parcel

The highest and best use of the Remainder Parcel resulting from the Part Taken Parcel is for the continued use of the lodging improvements after curative work is performed. The subject property includes all the necessary amenities for a competitive budget scale motel and is considered competitive with most other budget motel properties in the market area. Parking ratios in the after condition also appear to be well within the range of parking ratios of other motels in the area, as well as conforming to current zoning ordinances.

Valuation of the Remainder Parcel

For the valuation of the Remainder Parcel, the sales comparison approach was applicable in determining the value of the lodging facility in the after condition. The income capitalization approach was considered secondary support. The cost approach was not utilized due to the substantial accrued depreciation including external obsolescence and the effects of a property with improvements that have significantly different chronological and effective ages within the same structure.

Sales comparison approach

The Remainder Parcel in the after condition will be reduced by 10 rooms. The total number of rental units will be 90. The sales comparison approach is based upon the same conclusions as set forth in the Larger Parcel sales comparison approach. The value on a per-room basis for the Remainder Parcel after the acquisition and in a cured condition but before any benefits is $22,000 per room. Therefore, 90 rooms at $22,000 per room equals $1,980,000.

Income capitalization approach

Using the income capitalization approach and measuring any loss of value as a result of a decrease of 10 motel rooms caused by the Part Taken cut and reface and relocation of the breakfast room, gift shop, and lobby office, the subject's motel revenues and expenses were analyzed and adjusted accordingly. The estimate of fair market value as indicated by the capitalization method is $1,895,000.

Reconciliation

The strength of the sales comparison method is its simplicity, and it is a method utilized by many buyers who simply compare properties on a total price basis. Based upon market conditions and various transactions of similar lodging facilities that have occurred on a price per room basis, primary weight was given to the sales comparison approach with secondary weight to the income capitalization approach. The value of the remainder after the acquisition (cured condition) and before benefits is therefore $1,980,000.

Incurable Severance Damages and Benefits

Based on the highest and best use analysis in valuation of the Remainder Parcel, it was concluded that severance damages do apply to the Remainder Parcel as a result of the partial taking and are estimated to be $30,250 (due to the additional loss of five rental units lost to remodeling and cut and reface issues). This is the difference between the value of the remainder as a part of the whole ($2,000,000), less the concluded value of the remainder after the acquisition (cured condition) and before benefits ($1,980,000). The Remainder Parcel was also analyzed for any benefits as a result of proposed construction of public improvements, and none were found. Therefore the value of the remainder after the acquisition and after considering benefits is also $1,980,000. The indicated total just compensation for the subject property due to the Part Taken Parcel is therefore $604,500. A summary of value calculations is provided on the following page.

Summary of Severance Damage and Benefits

		Amount
Value of the whole before acquisition		$2,200,000
Land	$1,125,000	
Improvements	$1,075,000	
Value of the part acquired as part of the whole		$189,750
Land	$75,000	
Improvements	$114,750	
Value of the remainder as part of the whole		$2,010,250
Land	$1,050,000	
Improvements	$960,250	
Value of the remainder after the acquisition (cured condition) and before benefits		$1,980,000
Land	$1,050,000	
Improvements	$930,000	
Severance damages (incurable)		$30,250
Land	$0	
Improvements	$30,250	
Value of the remainder after the acquisition and after considering benefits		$1,980,000
Land	$1,050,000	
Improvements	$930,000	
Special benefits		$0
Land	$0	
Improvements	$0	
Net damages or net special benefits		$30,250
Value of the part acquired as part of the whole		$189,750
Severance damages (incurable)		$30,250
Curable severance damages		
Partial demolition and remodel of two motel buildings	$200,000	
Income loss during TCE and blocked rooms (cut and reface)	$175,000	
Replace paving and landscaping	$7,000	
Temporary sign	$500	
Temporary office trailer, 6 month rental	$2,000	
Total		$384,500
Total compensation		$604,500

Case Study 6

By Randall Bell, MAI

Airport Noise Impact Study—Irvine, California
Class V Detrimental Condition—Imposed Condition

The subject properties consist of a subdivision of single-family residences in Irvine, California. The nearby El Toro Marine Base will be closed by the year 1999, and the County is considering developing an international airport in its place. The occupants' homes adjoin the flight corridor of the proposed airport. The home owners and some local business owners are concerned that a proposed international airport will cause a diminution in value to their properties located under or near the flight corridors.

The environmental impact report published by the County states that the proposed airport will serve 38.3 million passengers annually. This would be the fifth largest airport in the United States. By comparison, the Los Angeles International Airport currently serves 54 million passengers annually. At peak operations, the proposed airport will have 116 takeoffs and landings per hour, or approximately one every 30 seconds. So far, the County has not conducted any studies as to the impact that the airport will have on property values, yet airport proponents contend that the airport will have no impact on values. The property owners question this position and desire to know the general impact that airports have had in other Southern California locations.

The fact that the military base will close is a foregone conclusion; therefore, the scope of this assignment included simply studying the effects of the noise associated with an international airport compared with no airport noise, as related to single-family residences. Noise pollution, like any nuisance, may have a significant impact on property values, although if the loss in property values are real, they may be derived from the market. Class V detrimental conditions typically show a value "as if unimpaired" as compared to "as impaired." This difference may be expressed as a dollar amount or as a percentage. This comparison may be made by simply comparing properties that are otherwise similar, except for the issue being studied, which in this case is proximity to an airport.

A paired sales analysis was used comparing sales of homes that were under or near flight corridors with otherwise similar homes that were not, as shown in Exhibit CS 6.1. If a real loss in property value exists, a distinct and pronounced difference in price levels should be apparent.

This study is accomplished by a paired sales analysis, whereby paired sets of data are compared to each other. The objective was to examine sale comparables that are similar in all respects except for their airport proximity.

In this study, sales of single-family residences, primarily from 1,500 to 2,000 square feet, that had similar lot sizes and sold within a six-month period were studied. Further, the homes were all located in the same or similar nearby communities. By using these search parameters, virtually all non-airport elements of value are eliminated, such as the size of the improvements, location, market conditions, etc. In all, 190 sales comparables were studied.

This study indicated that in this location airport proximity consistently has a negative impact on value. These market data indicate that single-family residences located in proximity to an airport are worth less than an otherwise similar property that is not located by an airport. This impact on value ranges from -15.1% to -42.6% and averages -27.4%.

As part of this study, secondary market data related to the LAX office market were reviewed. It is well-known within the local real estate community that the LAX market has

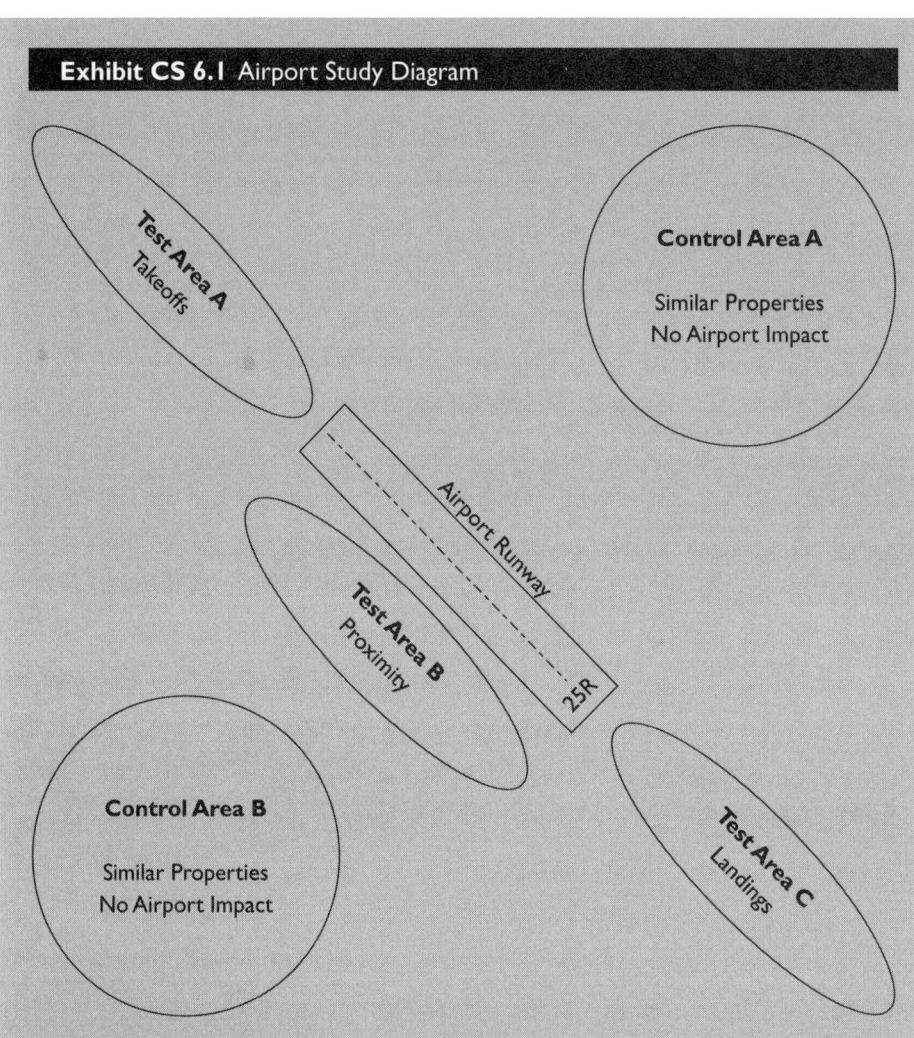

Exhibit CS 6.1 Airport Study Diagram

the lowest rental rates of any office market in the region despite the facts that the office market has outstanding freeway and airport access and the office improvements themselves are comparable with other office buildings in the area.

The LAX office market is distinct from other markets within the area in that many of the office buildings are located on Century Boulevard under the airport's final landing approach. These office buildings have similar features and amenities and are otherwise comparable with other office buildings throughout Southern California, except these office buildings are subjected to considerable noise and related airport issues.

The LAX office market has an average actual rental rate of $0.85 per square foot per month. Other office buildings within the South Bay office market have average actual rental rates ranging from $1.05 per square foot to $1.50 per square foot. The rental rates for the LAX office market range from 19.1% to 43.3% lower than any other market in the surrounding South Bay area. Combined with the effects of also having the highest vacancy rate of 38.1%, the negative net impact on value is further amplified, as shown in Exhibit CS 6.2.

Exhibit CS 6.2 South Bay Office Building Market

1995 Vacancy and Absorption

Square Feet in thousands

Submarket	Rentable sq. ft.	Vacant sq. ft.	% Vacant Direct	Avg. Net Absrp.	Effective Rent $/sq. ft. FSG
El Segundo/Manhattan Beach	9,295	1,933	20.8%	-330	$1.50
Torrance Freeway	3,291	1,070	32.5%	-266	$1.35
Torrance Central	3,255	629	19.3%	80	$1.40
Carson	1,621	330	20.4%	45	$1.05
LAX/Century Blvd.	**4,198**	**1,599**	**38.1%**	**-70**	**$0.85**
Long Beach Suburbs	4,278	615	14.4%	458	$1.35
Long Beach Downtown	3,826	996	26.0%	-120	$1.40
South Bay Total	29,763	7,172	24.1%	-203	$1.28

Source: Grubb & Ellis

Conclusions

The market data from this study indicated that national and international airports impact the values on properties in close proximity to flight corridors. The impact on single-family residences located in proximity to an airport was consistently negative, as compared to otherwise similar properties not located near an airport. The impact on single-family residences ranged from -15.1% to -42.6% and averaged -27.4%. This did not include the costs of noise mitigation measures that individual home owners may incur.

Additional studies could address issues that this study did not address. For example, are properties in closer proximity to an airport more significantly impacted as opposed to those properties located further away. Additionally, there may be distinctions between locations on the final landing, takeoff, and side-proximity that this study did not address.

The LAX office market enjoys outstanding transportation access, and the improvements are comparable with other office buildings in the area. However, this market is distinct in that it is located under the final landing approach to an international airport. The rental rates for the LAX office market are from 19.1% to 43.3% lower than any other office market in the surrounding South Bay area. Combined with the effects of also having the highest vacancy rate of 38.1%, the negative net effects on value are further amplified. These figures do not include any special noise mitigation costs incurred by the property owners.

The market data clearly and consistently indicate that as of the date of value and within the local regional market, homes that are under or near a flight corridor did sell for less than an otherwise similar home in the area that was not located under or near a flight corridor. This is supported by a study published by the FAA indicating that the diminution in value would be expected to exceed 19% for upper-middle class homes.

Based upon the market data, it was concluded that the diminution in value on a mid- to high-value single-family residence under a flight corridor of an international airport would experience a significant loss in property value of over 25%.

Case Study 7

By Orell C. Anderson, MAI

Hollywood Boulevard Sinkhole and Subsidence—Hollywood, California
Class V and VII Detrimental Condition—Tunneling

The Los Angeles Metropolitan Transit Authority broke ground in 1983 for the construction of the Red Line, a commuter train line that will connect downtown Los Angeles with North Hollywood. The first phase was completed January 30, 1993, with the second phase completed on July 13, 1996, at Western and Wilshire Boulevards. The next scheduled opening was for November 1998 at Hollywood and Vine. In August 1994, the construction crew punched through one of two tunnel segments, 80 feet below Hollywood Boulevard. Ground subsidence was anticipated to be one-half inch, but 2 inches resulted. The second tunnel segment was punched through 21 days later, which resulted in 5 inches to 6 inches of subsidence, with a maximum subsidence of 10 inches. The cause was attributed to a variety of factors, including water content in the soil and the alleged use of improper materials in the support shield of the tunnel.

Portions of the Hollywood Walk of Fame crumbled when the underlying soils subsided as a result of the tunneling project. Situations such as these may cause public skepticism towards engineers' assurances of project safety.

The most significant damage occurred in the 6500 block of Hollywood Boulevard, between Vine and the El Capitan Theater, with several buildings incurring severe damage such as storefronts separating from the main portion of the structures and on Hudson Street involving an apartment building and a three-story retail/office building. On June 22, 1995, allegedly faulty and "unrealistic" design work triggered the dramatic 80-foot-wide sinkhole within the 6300 block of Hollywood Boulevard. Transit officials were forced to shut down the street again on June 27 after discovering a cluster of serious cracks in the tunnel near the giant sinkhole. The problem was brought under

The soil subsidence underneath Hollywood Boulevard literally pulled buildings towards the center of the street, as depicted by the large crack along the side face of this retail building.

control within a few months after it occurred, but it left visible signs, such as boarded-up buildings, for a longer period. As of September 1997, the apartment and retail/office buildings in the 6500 block area continue to require structural bracing.

This area was impacted by an economic recession, which accounted for some of the declines in value, but the dramatic decline exceeded the typical market declines. In 1992, prior to the tunneling event, ground-level retail rents were $1.50 to $2.50 per square foot triple net; in 1997 they ranged from $0.50 to $1.25 per square foot. Second-story office space leased for $1.00 per square foot gross previously and dropped to approximately $0.50 per square foot. Ground-floor retail values were approximately $175 to $200 per square foot in 1992, and in 1997 they were approximately $125 per square foot. Land values were approximately $100 per square foot in 1992, and in 1997 they ranged from a low of $40 per square foot to $60 per square foot. In 1992, retail occupancy was approximately 90%, but in 1997 it dropped to 25% for ground-floor retail and 50% for second-floor office.

Case Study 8

By Mark W. Smith, MAI

Desert Resort Subdivision
Class V Detrimental Condition—Imposed Loss of Access

Inadequate or inappropriate planning of a development opportunity can have a pronounced negative impact on a property. In cases where the property is in an area with an ample supply of developable land, the effects of poor planning can linger for many years, and in the most severe instances indefinitely.

The following case study involves a residential subdivision in a desert resort community. As both the climate and the geography of the area have had a dramatic impact on local development patterns, a short description of both is helpful.

The community is in a valley bordered by mountain ranges on the north and south. The valley has narrow openings at the northwest and southeast. Very high winds constantly blow through these openings from northwest to southeast along the lower slopes of the northern mountain range. The crescent-shaped southern mountain range offers protection from the constant high winds. Winter temperatures typically range from about 65° to 80° F, but summer temperatures routinely exceed 100°, and frequently soar to well above 110°.

Over the last four decades, the mild winter weather has attracted a large number of relatively affluent vacation home buyers. The areas best sheltered from constant winds have been developed with hotels, restaurants, upscale shopping, museums, and private golf course-oriented residential communities.

As the entire valley is closely associated with winter golfing activities, it is not surprising that the areas best protected from the wind are in the highest demand by the most affluent buyers. Areas impacted by high winds are generally populated by the considerably less affluent year-round residents who work in the local service industries. This being the case, construction quality and property values generally increase as one travels from the north to the south.

The subject of this case study is a 10-acre parcel in the far northern, or less affluent, sector of the community. In contrast to virtually all of the surrounding neighborhoods, the subject's developer chose to improve the site as a private (walled and gated) 67-lot residential subdivision with private streets and a private park. A plat map (Exhibit CS 8.1) of the subdivision has been reproduced on the following page.

The homes in the subject development are of good to very good quality. The quality of the homes is similar to homes found in some of the valley's most desirable neighborhoods. The subdivision is, however, in a neighborhood only marginally protected from the high winds. In short, the area is only attractive to the most price-sensitive local service industry employees. Given the price sensitivity of the typical buyer in the area, the homes immediately surrounding the subject site are of only fair quality.

Construction of the backbone infrastructure was completed early in the development process, including the installation of underground utilities and construction of perimeter walls, gates, and the private park. All of the 67 lots were rough-graded and the streets were cut. Construction of the first two phases of homes was begun simultaneously. The first phase consisted of 11 homes, while the second phase consisted of 17 homes.

As the homes in the subject development are vastly superior to the homes in the surrounding neighborhood, the developer would have to sell the homes for some 50% more per square foot than the prevailing market values in the area just to break even. Market acceptance of the project, and therefore absorption, was considerably weaker than the developer anticipated. Fifteen of the homes were completed and sold before the developer was forced into bankruptcy. Thirteen of the homes were about 95% complete at the time of bankruptcy.

It is quite common in the area to have a set of conditions, covenants, and restrictions (CC&Rs) for enforcing rules and regulations in a planned community similar to the subject. These CC&Rs usually work to the benefit of the owners within the community. Unfortunately, the subject's history as a failed subdivision created some unusual circumstances for the individual lots.

The CC&Rs required the developer to set up the association prior to the close of the first escrow. Once the first escrow within each phase was closed, the association was to collect assessment fees for each lot within the phase. In other words, once the first escrow of a lot in phase one was closed, assessments would be levied on all the lots within that phase. Each property owner is responsible for the payment of assessment fees. In the case of lots not yet sold, the developer was to pay the assessment fees until the lot was sold.

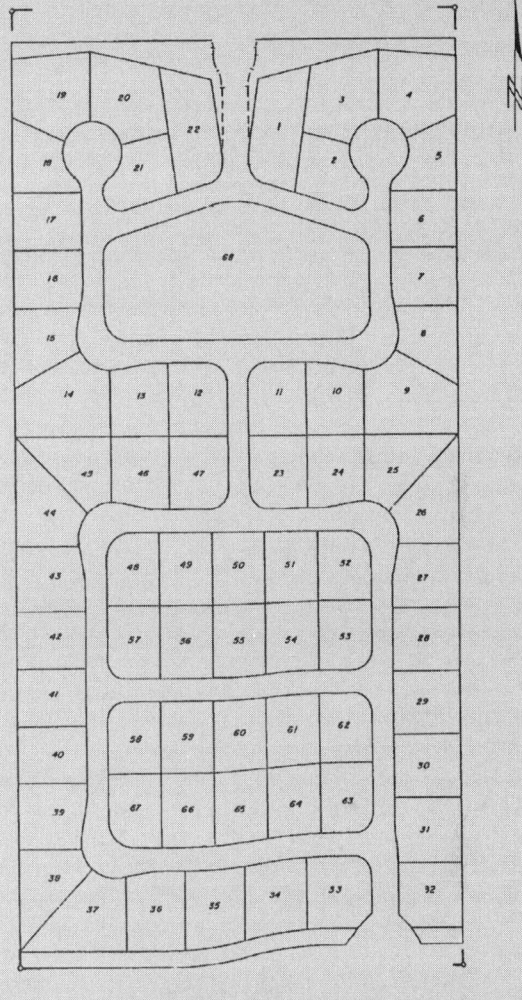

Exhibit CS 8.1 Plat Map of Subdivision

In an effort to limit the fees they would have to pay for unsold homes, the developer intended to build the project in several phases. To further limit their liability for assessment fees on unsold homes, the developer decided to encumber only those lots in the initial construction phases with the original declaration of the CC&Rs for the community. The recorded document provided the means for annexing the remaining lots in the tract into the association as construction proceeded, thereby encumbering the annexed lots with the CC&Rs.

Only the phase one lots were initially encumbered by the CC&Rs. This included Lots 1 through 7 inclusive, Lots 19 through 22 inclusive, Lot 68 (the community park), common area landscaped lots fronting to the primary access point, and various private street lots as shown in the plat map.

To ensure the project would be completed as originally intended, the CC&Rs gave the developer certain benefits not granted to others. Among these benefits was the right to annex the remaining lots in the tract into the home owners association without a majority vote from the members of the association. Another benefit granted to the developer was the right to cast three votes for each lot it owned. These benefits had expiration dates specified within the original declaration of CC&Rs.

Prior to the bankruptcy, the developer annexed Lots 8 through 18 inclusive, 23 through 25 inclusive, 45 through 47 inclusive, and the remaining street lots into the association. This declaration encumbered these lots with the CC&Rs and transferred title to the private streets to the home owners association.

The 13 unfinished homes and 39 rough-graded vacant lots were foreclosed upon by the construction lender subsequent to the developer's bankruptcy. The owner's right to cast three votes for each lot it owned expired shortly thereafter, prior to the completion of the subdivision and annexation of the 39 vacant lots into the home owners association. Likewise, the home owners no longer has the right to annex additional property into the association, thereby encumbering the added lots with the terms of the CC&Rs, without a 67% majority vote of the members of the association.

The expiration of these rights created a problem for the development of the 39 vacant lots. These unimproved lots are wholly within the walls and gates of the community and are accessed by the private streets now owned by the home owners association. Technically, because the owner of the 39 vacant lots no longer has the right to annex the lots into the association and because the access streets to the vacant lots are owned by the association, the owner of the 39 lots no longer has legal access to the lots.

Even if the association agrees by majority vote to annex the vacant lots into the association, development of the 39 vacant sites may not be possible. When the developer's special privileges expired, control over what could be built on each site was turned over to the association's architectural committee. The homes within the development are vastly superior to virtually every other product in the immediate neighborhood. The developer's failure to sell all of the existing homes provides adequate proof that the original product line is economically infeasible in the subject neighborhood. Unfortunately, the owners of the existing homes have made it abundantly clear to local building officials they will not allow the construction of a product materially different from the existing one. In short, the association will only allow the construction of the existing product, a product proven to be economically infeasible even if the land value is zero.

The circumstances outlined above created a conflict between the existing home owners and the owner of the vacant lots. To make matters worse, there is an abundant supply of vacant land in the immediate neighborhood and in more upscale neighborhoods to the south to satisfy virtually all development requirements well into the foreseeable future. This being the case, there is virtually no incentive for anyone to take control of the subject lots and bring them to a buildable status. Conversations with numerous local developers, investors, and agents revealed that the subject lots have been rendered virtually unmarketable and actually represent a liability from a property tax standpoint. Control of the lots has since been turned over to a federal agency. Five years after the foreclosure transferred title to the construction lender, the sites remain unsold and undeveloped, with the property taxes seriously in arrears.

Case Study 9

By Randall Bell, MAI

Beverly Hills Estate—Beverly Hills, California
Class VI Detrimental Condition—Building Construction Defects and Water Damage

The subject property is a 6,544-sq.-ft. house in the city of Beverly Hills, California. The scope of this assignment was to

1. Inspect the subject property referenced above.
2. Determine if the sales price of $2,750,000 on January 4, 1994, was considered to be the market value.
3. Determine the diminution in value, if any, resulting from undisclosed construction defects.

The subject property was thoroughly inspected by appraisers, contractors, and a licensed land surveyor. The subject property contains a pool, indoor spa, tennis court, terraced grounds, and a panoramic view of the Los Angeles basin. Several areas of water damage throughout the house were also noted during the subject property inspection.

In order to determine if the sales price was commensurate with the market value, a search was made for other luxury home sales in the same time frame. The subject property is large and does not lack any of the amenities expected in a luxury home. Additionally, the subject site is particularly private and enjoys an exceptional view amenity. As would be expected, market data were limited for single-family residences of a similar caliber, yet five comparable sales were identified and field inspected. All five sale comparables sold at similar prices, ranging from $2,250,000 to $3 million. The subject property is most similar to the sales comparable located at 755 Parker Lane, which sold for $2.7 million in December 1994. Based upon these factors, it is concluded that the subject property did sell for an appropriate market value, assuming that the property suffered from no detrimental conditions.

It was represented that the subject property was sold without the proper disclosure of construction defects and water intrusion problems. Not being a licensed contractor or engineer, the appraiser relied upon information and figures provided by construction experts. However, the appraiser reviewed the information provided by other professionals in an effort to determine its reasonableness. The appraiser's inspections indicated that there have been severe water intrusion problems at the subject property. Further, these problems occurred in various parts of the residence, so apparently the problem is not isolated to one particular issue or area. It appears reasonable that significant construction problems do exist; however, the valuation analysis is based upon the assumption that the cost to repair the damage as provided by the contractors is accurate and correct.

The subject property is categorized as Class VI, which is the classification given to detrimental conditions involving above-grade construction defects. Typically, Class VI detrimental conditions are relatively easy to assess, while Class VII (below grade) are more difficult. When construction defects are severe, as they are in this case, the Detrimental Condition Model is applicable.

The basic premise of this model is to answer the question, "What would the market value have been if the detrimental conditions were known to the buyer at the time the property was purchased?" This model basically indicates that there are four considerations that must be made when quantifying the diminution in value due to a detrimental condition.

These are

1. The costs to assess the situation
2. The costs to repair and remediate the problems
3. The costs of any ongoing conditions or monitoring (i.e., additional financing charges, insurance costs, etc.)
4. The market resistance, which is the discount or incentive to entice a prospective buyer to purchase a previously damaged property

To calculate the damages, the costs of damage assessment, repairs, remediation, and carrying costs provided on the Record of Defect/Damage Issues were assumed to be correct. When purchasing a severely damaged property, a typical buyer will not occupy the premises until the repairs are completed. In this situation, it has been represented that the owners purchased the property without knowledge of the detrimental conditions. As a result, they have or will incur moving costs that would not have otherwise been incurred. According to the owner's legal counsel, the moving-out costs were $4,560. It was assumed that this same cost will be incurred to move back into the premises.

Some detrimental conditions will incur ongoing costs, even after the condition is repaired. For example, a flood-damaged property may incur the costs of maintaining a revetment or levee, and a contaminated property may require ongoing monitoring. Construction defects do not typically incur such costs. The appraiser was not made aware of any such ongoing costs, and as such costs are not typically applied in construction defect situations, no such deduction has been made.

The final consideration in quantifying a diminution in value issue is the discount to reflect the risks, contingencies, and trouble to which a buyer is exposed when purchasing a damaged property. This is termed, the "project incentive" to a damaged property. A typical buyer will not simply deduct the costs of repair from the normal sales price. Otherwise, there is an incentive to just purchase an undamaged property and avoid the considerable risks and trouble. In an effort to quantify this "discount" or project incentive, market data were studied in the local market for similar discounts when damaged properties were purchased, as shown in Exhibit CS 9.1.

These market data reflect a discount ranging from 4% to 33%, typically 15% to 25%. This reflects the risks, carrying costs, and entrepreneurial profit that one requires to be enticed to purchase a damaged property. It was noted that when repairs are relatively minor there is little or no project incentive. Less expensive homes also generally have a lower project incentive as compared with more expensive homes. Considering the high value of the asset, the significant carrying costs, the significant damage, and the limited number of buyers who are financially capable and willing to purchase a damaged property of this type, the most similar market data is in the range of 15% to 25%, and is estimated to be most likely 20%.

All of the costs and losses set forth within the Detrimental Condition Model were considered, and based upon the analysis, the value of the subject property, as of January 4, 1994, was $1,900,000, which represents an overpayment of $850,000 for the undisclosed construction defects and related costs. A summary of value calculations follows on page 224.

Exhibit CS 9.1 Summary of Damaged Property Sales

Project Incentive of Homes with No Market Resistance

Single-Family Residences—Bel Air, Holmby Hills, Westwood

Study	Value Undamaged	Value Damaged	Detrimental Condition	DC Class	Assessment Repairs Carrying Costs Contingencies	Project Incentive (Dollars)	Project Incentive (Percentage)	Broker Opinion of Project Incentive	Market Resistance/ Ongoing Costs	Comments
1	$600,000	$420,700	Site Damage	VII	N/A	N/A	N/A	N/A	None	Buyers were end users
2	$1,800,000	$1,400,000	Earthquake Damage	IX	$150,000	$250,000	13.89%	N/A	None	House shifted
3	$1,500,000	$1,000,000	Earthquake Damage	IX	$200,000	$300,000	20.00%	N/A	None	Interior finish and décor needed
4	$400,000	$155,000	Earthquake Damage	IX	$150,000	$95,000	23.75%	N/A	None	House shifted
5	$800,000	$537,500	Soil Subsidence	VII	$200,000	$62,500	7.81%	N/A	None	Sub-floor buckling
6	N/A	$328,000	Earthquake Damage	IX	N/A	N/A	N/A	25.00%	None	Exterior cracking and leaking
7	$625,000	$460,000	Site Drainage	VII	$55,000	$110,000	17.60%	N/A	None	Electric, roof, and plumbing
8	$560,000	$455,000	Soil Subsidence	VII	N/A	N/A	N/A	25.00%	None	Sinkhole on site
9	$2,000,000	$1,275,000	Site Drainage	VII	$250,000	$475,000	23.75%	20.00%	None	High-end property needs high incentive
10	$400,000	$295,000	Earthquake Damage	IX	$30,000	$75,000	18.75%	15.00%	None	Foundation damage
11	$4,750,000	$2,800,000	Incomplete Construction	VI	$800,000	$1,150,000	24.21%	25.00%	None	Buyer is contractor
12	$300,000	$240,000	Site Drainage	VII	$30,000	$30,000	10.00%	20.00%	None	Buyer is end user
13	$325,000	$229,000	Earthquake Damage	IX	$55,000	$41,000	12.62%	10.00%	None	Low-end property for area
14	$2,500,000	$1,425,000	Incomplete Construction	VI	$500,000	$575,000	23.00%	25.00%	None	High-end property needs high incentive
15	$1,400,000	$630,000	Incomplete Construction	VI	$300,000	$470,000	33.57%	25.00%	None	10% incentive is not worth the risk
16	$1,700,000	$1,185,000	Construction Defect	VI	$145,000	$370,000	21.76%	25.00%	None	Problems with second-story addition
17	$2,700,000	$2,100,000	Incomplete Construction	VI	$500,000	$100,000	3.70%	20.00%	None	Needs flooring and certificate of occupancy
Average							18.2%	21.4%		

Case Study 9

Value "As Of" 1-4-94—Without Detrimental Conditions		$2,750,000
Less:		
Assessment stage		
Contractors assessment and report		$18,000
Repair stage		
Repair costs (from contractor)		$193,626
Contingencies (from contractor)		$13,232
Carrying costs (mortgage and taxes @ 4 months)		$60,276
Project incentive (see market data)	20%	$550,000
Incidental costs to repairs and remediation		
Moving costs (out only)		$4,560
Moving costs (back)		$4,560
Ongoing stage (post-remediation)		
None known		0
Market resistance		
Incentive to purchase previously defective property		0
Total diminution in value		$844,254
Value "as is"		**$1,905,746**
Rounded		**$1,900,000**

Case Study 10

By Joseph Haeussler, MAI

Krantz House—Suburban Boston, Massachusetts
Class VII Detrimental Condition—Subsurface Construction Condition

The Krantz House is located in an upper-class neighborhood in a suburb of Boston, Massachusetts. The property is a custom single-family residence comprising 6,716 square feet of livable area. The home is a two-story structure built in 1989, with a concrete foundation, wood-frame and stucco construction, and Colonial-style architecture. The 5-bedroom, 5¾-bathroom house was constructed on a 0.85-acre site with a pool and spa. The property is located in a small development of custom single-family homes. In the extended area, the homes range from middle to upper-middle price properties.

As of the date of the initial inspection, the subject property had evidence of subsurface construction defects. The area of the subject property is known to have expansive soils in the natural state. Soils engineers had conducted studies and determined that prior to the construction of the subject property and during the site preparation phase substandard fill soils were transported and used on a portion of the site.

At some point after the completion of construction, the subject property began to have signs of subsurface failure in the southwest wing of the home. After the assessment was conducted by engineers, it was found that the property had poor fill material in the immediate area of the failure. The faulty soil material on the subject property included "silty gravelly sand fill, loose black silty gravelly sand topsoil with organic materials, and silty gravelly alluvium," according to the geotechnical reports. The material could not hold the load-bearing capacity of a portion of the improvements. The engineering reports indicated that a portion of the subject property had a distressed foundation as evidenced by a ⁵⁄₁₆-inch-wide slab crack running across the southwest end of the house. The foundation also had indications of depressions of one-half to one inch in the same area. Further engineering tests indicated that the southwest corner of the home was constructed on an area with relative soil compaction of 75%, which is less than the 90% typically required.

The damage was located in only one portion of the subject property, in a bedroom and a bathroom on the southwest end of the home. The remediation and repair efforts of the subject property would be concentrated in this portion of the house only, an area that is approximately 20% of the total area of the home.

The current owners of the subject property purchased the subject property from the original owners of the home in July 1996. The current owners claim that the construction defect preexisted the purchase contract, and that the former owners and the selling real estate agent did not disclose the known defective construction issues. The scope of the assignment was to

1. Inspect the subject property
2. Determine if the sales price of $899,000 was considered to be market value as if no defect existed
3. Determine the diminution in value, if any, resulting from undisclosed construction defects

The diminution in value study focused on a) the assumption of the entrepreneurial incentive to purchase and assume responsibility of a defective property and b) the market resistance relating to owning a home with a history of a construction defect. Both of these issues are addressed as a percentage of the total sale price. Costs to assess, remediate, and monitor the repair project were compiled by soils and structural experts and were not within the scope of the assignment.

Valuation as if Not Damaged

The sales comparison approach was used to value the subject property as if no construction defects existed. The sale of the subject property itself was a strong indication of its market value. This indication of value reflects the value of the subject property with no defect or damage because the buyers of the subject property were not aware of the defective condition of the property at the time of sale. Additionally, a search was conducted for other custom homes in the area in an undamaged condition. Five sales, one of which was the sale of the subject property, were considered. The sale prices were from $750,000 to $1,025,000. In the comparison process, the sale of the subject property is well supported by the market data. Therefore, the best indication of value is the sale of the subject property at $899,000.

Exhibit CS 10.1 Undamaged Sales Comparables

No.	Address	Date	Area (Sq. Ft.) Bed/Bath	Site Area (Acres)	Sale Price	Other Features
SP	1034 Abbey Lane	7/96	6,716 5/5.75	0.85	$899,000	Pool
1	1048 Lamon Street	10/95	4,756 5/4.5	1.17	$1,025,000	Pool, tennis, guest house
2	394 Pend Street	11/95	6,900 5/4.5	0.80	$860,000	Pool
3	3742 Hollins Street	2/96	7,018 5/4.75	0.81	$815,000	Pool
4	852 Penin Place	1/96	5,010 4/4.5	0.67	$750,000	Pool

Valuation as Damaged

The second analysis, based on the Detrimental Condition Model, involved conducting a search for properties that have sold with similar construction defects or detrimental condition issues in place at the time of sale. The sales were relatively similar to the subject property in size and type of improvements. But most importantly the purchasers were able to quantify the costs of repair, the entrepreneurial incentive, and the market resistance.

Exhibit CS 10.2 Comparable Sales with Soils Issues

No	Undamaged Value	Damaged Value	Class VII Remediation	Project Incentive	Market Resistance
1	$1,000,000	$700,000	$100,000	$150,000 (15%)	$50,000 (5%)
2	$700,000	$525,000	$60,000	$115,000 (16%)	$0 (0%)
3	$450,000	$215,000	$85,000	$100,000 (22%)	$50,000 (11%)
4	$1,750,000	$900,000	$450,000	$300,000 (17%)	$100,000 (6%)

While market data were limited, four sales of properties with Class VII soils issues were located and verified. Sales 1 and 4 were most similar to the subject property. Based upon these factors, an entrepreneurial incentive of 15% and market resistance of 5% were considered applicable to the subject property.

By applying the factors to the normal market value of the subject property, a value conclusion with the existing detrimental condition can be concluded as follows:

Normal market value: $899,000

Less:
    Entrepreneurial incentive @ 15% (rounded): $135,000
    Market resistance @ 5% (rounded): $45,000
Value, as of July 1996, with detrimental condition: $719,000 less assessment costs and repair process

The above conclusion is the value of the subject property as of the date of value, with consideration given to the market resistance and the assumption of entrepreneurial incentive of a damaged property. A potential buyer of this property in a damaged state would likely retain an engineer to assess the problem and seek an estimate of costs to repair the defects.

Case Study 11

By Randall Bell, MAI

Kangaroo Hill Slope Instability—Anaheim Hills, California
Class VII—Geotechnical Construction

The subject property is a 3,500-sq.-ft. tract house located in Anaheim Hills, California. While the surrounding areas are geotechnically stable, the subject property was built on a former small canyon, which required 57 feet of fill soil. During heavy rains in 1992, the subject property experienced some differential settlement, at a ratio of 1.6 inches over a 60-foot span. While this degree of tilting is visually imperceptible, it caused the water level within the backyard pool to be offset by about 1¼ inches. Additionally, there was a one-quarter inch separation between the kitchen cabinets and the ceiling. No cracking of the patios, driveway, garage, or patios was noted.

Soil borings were completed, and a soil engineer was dropped by a rope and harness to inspect the inside of the hole. The soil engineer estimated that the soils have likely settled to their maximum levels, although they may settle up to another one-half inch over time.

The builder agreed to repair the pool's water level and the kitchen cabinets, but the property owners were concerned that they will suffer from a diminution in value when the property is eventually sold, as they will be required to fully disclose the condition and history of the house to all potential buyers. They felt that they will need to discount the price in order to entice a potential buyer to purchase the home. The appraisal assignment included making a market study to see if the home owners' concerns were justified and, if so, what would be an appropriate discount.

To complete the assignment, numerous historical newspaper articles were reviewed that pertained to properties with geotechnical problems. An ideal housing tract was identified called Kite Hill. This tract of approximately 600 single-family residences includes several homes that experienced differential settlement and slope creep. Additionally, the entire tract has expansive soils. Some home owners filed lawsuits against the developer of the tract, which resulted in various articles appearing in local papers. As a result of this situation, some local real estate agents would not list or show their clients' homes within the tract. While the problems actually affected less than 10% of all the homes in the tract, in essence, the entire tract was stigmatized as having geotechnical problems. This tract provided a good source of market data, as home owners within the tract experienced the same difficulty in selling their homes as would be expected in the case of the subject property.

A paired sales analysis was conducted whereby the average price per square foot of the Kite Hill tract was compared with other similar tracts that did not have any known geotechnical problems. (This same paired sales analysis was completed over three different points in time, and the results were similar in all three instances.) The Kite Hill homes sold for an average price of $103 per square foot, while similar homes in surrounding tracts sold at an average price of $117 per square foot, reflecting a 12% difference. These market data reflect that local buyers required an approximate 12% discount in order to purchase a home associated, or perceived to be associated, with geotechnical problems.

Case Study 12

By Michael V. Sanders, MAI, SRA

Geotechnical Issues
Class VII Detrimental Condition—Declining Market Resistance Over Time

Properties impacted by geotechnical problems often experience residual stigma or market resistance after completion of repairs, a psychological reflection of perceived risk or uncertainty. While the market may reasonably fear a recurrence of the original problem, the passage of time often lessens the impact of residual stigma, as market participants become more confident that repairs were adequate and the problem will not recur.

The following case study involves a tract of single-family homes in a master-planned community constructed during the late 1970s. Homes reflect good quality construction, with five standard floor plans ranging from approximately 1,800 to 2,800 square feet. Because of hillside topography, many dwellings enjoy average to good area views.

During the mid-1980s, it was discovered that three homes in the tract were constructed on expansive fill material, resulting in slab cracks and associated structural distress. One of these (Property A) was repurchased by the original builder, repaired, and immediately resold at a significant discount of nearly 20%. The adjacent home (Property B) with a similar history sold at about the same time, except that repairs had been made six years before the sale. The indicated discount for stigma was less than 10%, suggesting that while the market still recognized some risk, the probability of recurrence was perceived to be lessening over time.

Property A was originally purchased new in early 1979 for $219,000. When difficulties related to the expansive soils became apparent during the 1980s, the builder agreed to repurchase the home at fair market value, paying the owner $620,000 in mid-1990. After repairs, the property was listed for sale in late 1991 for $629,000 and finally sold in September 1992 for $475,000, including a 10-year warranty relative to future settlement or soils problems. Sales of comparable unaffected properties during 1992 indicated an appropriate value range of $562,500 to $580,000, with the most comparable property reflecting a value of $575,000. This figure is lower than the price paid by the builder in mid-1990, consistent with a declining market trend over this period. In the opinion of the builder/seller, stigmatization accounted for a 20% discount relative to otherwise comparable properties without a similar history, even with the 10-year warranty. Empirical data is generally supportive, with the most relevant transaction indicating that the property sold for a discount of $100,000, or approximately 17.4%.

Property B was purchased new in late 1978 for $206,000 and sold in 1982 for unknown consideration. After discovery of soils problems, repairs were undertaken in 1986, including removal and replacement of foundation and expansive fill, costs of which were paid by the builder. Six years later, the property was listed for $675,000 and sold for $629,000 in August 1992. In the opinion of the listing agent, disclosure of the property's history negatively impacted marketability, suggesting that the sales price would have otherwise been closer to $700,000. Comparison with unaffected properties that sold at about the same time indicated a range of $663,000 to $700,000, which was correlated towards mid-range at $680,000, a discount of about $50,000, or 7.5%.

This case study illustrates a situation where market resistance was clearly a factor for single-family residential properties with a history of soils problems. In this case, residual stigma was higher for a property that sold immediately after completion of repairs, reflecting considerable market uncertainty as to their adequacy and probability of recurrence. An adjacent property with similar problems was repaired several years prior to sale, and while some discount was still apparent, it was demonstrably lower, suggesting that the market perceived less risk and/or uncertainty regarding future problems. The market value of a stigmatized property may or may not eventually equal the market value of an undamaged property.

Case Study 13

By Richard A. Neustein, MAI, SRA

Degrees of Indemnification—Thousand Oaks, California
Class VIII Detrimental Condition—Environmental Contamination

This contamination case illustrates that the amount of value diminution varies with the degree of indemnification. Ordinary indemnifications for this detrimental condition are usually limited to the cost to monitor and remediate the contamination. This is known as a Level 1 indemnification. Level 0 is no indemnification, while Levels 2 and 3 successively add indemnification of acquisition financing and then development financing. A Level 2 indemnification was involved in this case.

This case involves a 39,587-sq.-ft. concrete tilt-up industrial building on 3.68 acres of land in Thousand Oaks, California. The 14-foot clear building had heavy power and contained 90% office. The buyer intended to remove much of the office and renovate the rest. At the same time, the roof cover was to be replaced. The rehabilitation work was expected to take four months and to cost approximately $500,000.

The seller of this property had at one time also leased an adjacent property on which there was an underground solvent tank that leaked. The solvents, trichloroethane (TCA) and trichloroethylene (TCE), reached groundwater. In addition, chloroform was also found in the groundwater. Neither this property nor the adjacent one is a likely source of the chloroform contamination.

In 1988, the property had gone into escrow at $2.5 million. The buyer withdrew when contamination was found. In the following years, as values in the local market rose and then fell, a number of interested buyers turned away when contamination was disclosed or when their lenders declined to finance the property. In November 1992, after five months of negotiations, the property entered escrow for sale at $1.2 million with a $200,000 cash down payment. The seller indemnified the buyer against costs of monitoring, remediation, consequential damages, and loss of the ability to finance the property. This is the only sale that has been found with a Level 2 indemnification. This sale is summarized and analyzed in Exhibits CS 13.1 and CS 13.2.

The reason that this sale went together at all was that the seller, a division of Communications Satellite Corporation, had the financial muscle to effectively stand behind its indemnification. During this same time frame, properties that were not backed by such strength were not selling. This points out the need for indemnification from an entity with virtually doubtless financial strength in order to return marketability to a property with a serious contamination problem.

Exhibit CS 13.1 Summary of Sale of Contaminated Property

Newbury Park (Thousand Oaks), California

Land:	160,284 square feet
Building:	39,587 square feet, 14-foot clear, CTU manufacturing building, 90% office area with HVAC, 1600 amps @ 480/277 VAC
Sale dates:	Negotiation since 6/92
	Agreed 11/92
	Recorded 12/31/92
Sale price:	$1,200,000
Cash down:	$200,000
Trust deed:	$1,000,000 seller T.D.
	9.0%, 30-year amortization, 5-year call
Indemnification:	• Seller pays for all future monitoring, including wells already on the property.
	• Seller pays for cleanup of problems that existed before the sale.
	• Seller indemnifies against future consequential damages in the amount of $1.2 million (the price of the property).
	• Seller indemnifies buyer's ability to borrow by providing for extension of the note and T.D. if contamination by the seller prevents conventional financing. Any extended loan would be based upon the value of the property at the time of extension.
Deferred maintenance:	Buyer is to repair or replace the roof and water-damaged interior elements, most partitioning, HVAC, etc., and to modify the driveway to lessen its slope. Estimated direct cost is $500,000.

Exhibit CS 13.2 Analysis of Contaminated Sale

Sale price (as though contaminated, but with indemnifications)		$1,200,000
Cash 16.67%		$200,000
Seller financed T.D. (9%, 30-year amortization/5-year call; indemnified by seller)		$1,000,000
Property value as though in good condition and never contaminated		
Supported by market evidence and opinion of listing broker, $50/sq. ft.:		$1,979,350
Rounded to:		$1,975,000
Less cost to monitor and remediate prior contamination (indemnified)		$0
Less cost of rehabilitation		
Property rehabilitation	$500,000	
Financing cost @ 9%, 4 months construction time		
$500,000 × 0.09 × 4 / 12 =	$15,000	
Holding cost @ 9%, 4 months construction time		
$1,200,000 × 0.09 × 4 / 12 =	$36,000	
Total rehabilitation cost	$551,000	
Rounded to:		− $550,000
Property value as though unrehabilitated and never contaminated		$1,425,000
Less sale price		− $1,200,000
Decline in value		$225,000
Value decline as percentage of uncontaminated value		15.79%

Case Study 14

By Gregory D. Trimanche and Craig A. Moyer

Three Brownfield Case Studies
Class VIII Detrimental Condition—Large-Scale Contamination

1. Solutions Emerge for the Port of Seattle

In Seattle, strategic planning for the Port of Seattle's restoration of a 200-acre contaminated industrial property led to a fast-track expansion of its existing marine terminal facilities. As a result, an international shipping firm relocated its headquarters there.

Although remediation occurred at many levels, two properties were particularly challenging. One was an existing marine terminal that contained contamination from petroleum hydrocarbons deposited in the soil and groundwater during 70 years of operation. The other was a 25-acre site that housed a wood-preserving facility. The 25-acre property had been designated as a Superfund site during property negotiations. Spills, leaks, drips, and on-site waste disposal of organic and inorganic preservatives used in the wood treatment process had impacted soil and groundwater. The risk exposure analysis indicated that petroleum hydrocarbons were leaching to the groundwater and subsequently through and around the bulkhead to the ocean.

Through the cooperative efforts of the Port Authority, the property owner, and the state environmental agency, a risk management plan was proposed that protected human health and the environment through the implementation of key remediation strategies:

- Removal of soils with high concentrations of petroleum hydrocarbons.
- Construction and operation of a biologically stimulated zone (or "biobarrier") near the bulkhead to prevent impacted groundwater from migrating to the ocean.
- Construction and operation of a bioventing/sparging system to degrade the petroleum hydrocarbons.

The Environmental Protection Agency (EPA) estimated that at least $50 million would have to be spent to remediate the site, a sum the property owners did not have. The owners' liability problem presented the Port Authority with an opportunity to design a win-win proposal, which all interested parties accepted.

Approval of this plan enabled the Port Authority to purchase the property, negotiate consent agreements with various state authorities, and specify the conditions of sale that would absolve the former property owner of continued liability.

Under the plan, the EPA agreed to relieve current property owners from future liability if in exchange they agreed to go out of business and place the business assets and acquisition funds from the Port Authority into a cleanup trust. This provided the Port Authority with the basis for productive negotiation with the EPA for a prospective purchaser agreement and covenant not to sue under CERCLA. This in turn absolved the Port Authority of any liability for existing contamination.

In exchange for the covenant not to sue, the Port Authority agreed either to pay money into a cleanup fund or to conduct remedial work. The Port Authority was willing to do both. It agreed to place an amount equivalent to what it would cost to acquire the property, if it were clean, into the trust and to perform "in kind" work—a pledge valued at close to $17 million.

The Port Authority implemented a risk-based remediation plan that could be integrated with new construction. Its plan utilized the EPA's presumptive remedies for wood-treating sites under the Superfund Accelerated Cleanup Model (SACM). The remedy selection focused on

1. Removal of soil and debris that contained only the greatest concentrations of contamination
2. Construction of barriers that would prevent physical contact with a migration of hazardous constituents into nearby waters

This approach limited potential exposure to human health and the environment. The EPA and the Port Authority estimated that this approach saved approximately $8 million in disposal costs.

2. Another City Learns a Tough Brownfields Lesson

One eastern city took a revolutionary step when it crafted and successfully negotiated a voluntary cleanup agreement for a contaminated 200-acre site. A multidisciplinary team of city planners, lawyers, and environmental consultants had advised the city to reject a traditional investigation and cleanup approach. The city's innovative approach led to a voluntary agreement with the state's environmental agency. The agreement promoted cooperation instead of conflict among property owners, developers, lenders, and regulatory agencies. It encouraged the innovative and mutually beneficial approach to problem solving that is necessary for brownfield projects.

Once a flourishing industrial complex, the multi-owner site had become blighted with derelict factory buildings, an unused fuel tank farm, and neglected empty lots. In the post-World War II period, more than 10,000 people worked there; that number had decreased to less than 1,000 by 1996. Known and suspected contamination, and the liability that went with it, kept property owners, developers, and lenders from participating in what otherwise would be considered a prime site for industrial and commercial development.

The city initially negotiated a Letter of Intent with the state agency. The letter provided for a phased approach, with the city acting as an intermediary between the state and property owners, lenders, and developers. It described in advance what each of these stakeholders could expect from the process. Its foundation was an areawide, risk-based, site-specific determination of remediation goals, which took into account

- Future land use
- The risk of human exposure to existing contamination in the context of the proposed land use
- The use of engineering and institutional controls to contain and control contamination and exposure
- Relief of liability for past contamination through prospective purchaser agreements issued by the city to future landowners

Through this strategy, the letter agreement consolidated what otherwise would have been separate but substantially similar efforts in regulatory compliance, site investigation, and remediation. By setting common standards and goals for all property owners, the agreement was intended to remove much of the regulatory, technical, and liability uncertainty that can paralyze restoration. It was also intended to prevent potential adversarial relationships between property owners and the state.

The letter agreement was to be followed by Consent Orders that would allow demolition of abandoned structures and construction of a new access road and a factory. With the cooperation of the site's responsible parties, the city would take the lead in the overall site investigation, focusing on defining a cost-effective, sitewide, risk-based remedial strategy. By participating in the program, responsible parties would obtain releases from certain environmental liabilities, take advantage of risk-based cleanup standards and solutions, and convert economic liabilities into assets. To facilitate the city's efforts, the city was awarded a pilot grant of $200,000 from the EPA under the Brownfields Economic Redevelopment Initiative.[1]

However, despite the federal support and the considerable effort by the stakeholders, the city's innovative cleanup and redevelopment plans soon became stuck in the quagmire of the traditional regulatory regime, which threatened to make the project technically and economically infeasible. The Letter of Intent, the city's crowning achievement, was scrapped.

As this book goes to press, the stakeholders and their representatives continue their efforts to achieve an innovative solution. They continue to work with the state's voluntary cleanup program in an effort to negotiate a feasible cleanup plan, and they continue to pursue an areawide, risk-based investigation and remediation strategy. They remain committed to consolidating the various efforts in regulatory compliance, site investigation, and remediation. They also have established a dialogue directly with the Governor's office and various regulatory agencies to promote regulatory reform.

There are important lessons to be learned from this city's experience. Perhaps most significant is that responsible agency staffers, at every level, must embrace the project. They must accept the brownfields concepts of flexible cleanup standards based on future land use, of balancing the needs of the community and the interests of the project proponents against the actual risks posed at the site, and of breaking with the tradition of tunnel-visioned "command and control" regulatory oversight. This process of forging a common vision among project proponents, regulators, and the public is essential to a successful brownfields project.

3. Cleanup Plan for Koppers Site Based on Ultimate Use

In 1988, EPA Region IX announced that it would amend the cleanup plan for the Koppers wood treatment and storage facility located south of Oroville, California. The site, owned by Beazer East, Inc., is heavily contaminated with hydrocarbons, dioxins, heavy metals, and other wood treatment chemicals. A 1989 cleanup plan for the site assumed that future use would be for residential purposes. Since that time, Region IX has reevaluated the soil cleanup standards and the technology available to meet those standards, and determined that the available remediation techniques could not reduce the contaminant levels to residential standards.

In a somewhat surprising move, Region IX then decided to change the cleanup standards. The amended cleanup plan is based on future industrial use of the site. This may be the first time that EPA has amended an existing cleanup plan for a National Priorities List (NPL) site to retroactively change cleanup standards to reflect future land use. The amended plan changed both the cleanup standards and the technology to be used. To reflect the assumption of future industrial use, the amended plan requires deed restrictions be placed on the property to prevent residential use.

The move came after considerable negotiations with local planning authorities, other local officials, and the community. Clearly, this type of integrated approach, particularly when it incorporates risk-based cleanup standards, goes a long way toward solving the brownfields puzzle.

---

1. The Brownfields Economic Redevelopment Initiative is a cornerstone of the federal government's effort to encourage redevelopment of contaminated industrial sites nationwide.

Case Study 15

By Randall Bell, MAI
Exxon Valdez Oil Spill—Bligh Reef—Prince William Sound, Alaska
Class VIII Detrimental Condition—Oil Spill

At 12:04 a.m. on March 24, 1989, an oil tanker loaded with 1,264,155 barrels of North Slope crude oil ran aground on Bligh Reef in the northeastern portion of Prince William Sound, Alaska. Approximately one-fifth of the cargo, 11.2 million gallons, spilled into the ocean. In 1981, at the approval of the State of Alaska, and in order to save money, the company's emergency response team had been disbanded. Despite this, containment efforts were started soon after the accident. However, after three days of calm seas, strong northeasterly winds arose and dispersed the oil beyond any hope of containment. Some oil formed a floating sheen, while some mixed with sea water, creating a thick emulsion known as *mousse*, which does not burn and is very difficult to clean up. The sheen and mousse spread over a 470-mile trajectory from Prince William Sound to the Alaska Peninsula. Seven hundred ninety miles of Prince William Sound coastline were oiled, of which 200 miles were heavily oiled. In the Kenai Peninsula-Kodiak region, more than 2,400 miles of coastline were oiled.

Much of the areas along Alaska's coastline are dark-colored rocks, which makes the presence of spilled oil difficult to discern.

The damage to wildlife was high. From 100,000 to 300,000 birds and 2,650 sea otters were killed, and fishing was severely impacted. The cleanup efforts took three years, involving more than 11,000 people and 1,400 marine vessels. On June 10, 1992, the federal government issued a letter officially stating that the cleanup effort was concluded. The cleanup effort cost $2.1 billion, of which $95 million was spent in just the first six weeks.

The Exxon Valdez spill caused enormous wildlife destruction, but the direct impact on real estate values was less severe. The vast majority of impacted coastlines were uninhabited wilderness areas, and inhabited areas were quickly "boomed off" so damage to these areas was minimal or nonexistent. Unlike many environmental disasters, the spill did not impact subterranean soils or the groundwater. As such, property remediation efforts were limited to the coastline surfaces, which were easily accessed, and the verification of complete cleanup was much more assured. Additionally, because the contamination involved crude oil on the surface rather then refined petroleum with chemical additives in the soils, bioremediation (natural disintegration) and evaporation assisted greatly in restoring the coastline surfaces. As nearly all the impacted coastline was wilderness, the real estate damages related to the temporary disruptions of logging, recreational uses, fishing, subsistence lifestyles (living off the land), and mining. The impact on property values was computed on a case-by-case basis, determined by the level of oil on the coast and the disruption (if any) to each of the above uses. The large amounts of money spent in the cleanup efforts actually created a stronger demand for some real estate, as many people came from out-of-state to live and work in the many new remediation-related jobs created by the spill.

Case Study 16

By Randall Bell, MAI

Love Canal—Niagara Falls, New York
Class VIII and X Detrimental Condition—Environmental Contamination

The Love Canal was christened by a nineteenth century industrialist named William T. Love. In 1893, Love started construction of a 10-mile canal from the Lake Erie side of the Niagara River to the Lake Ontario side to the north. The plan was that the 110-foot drop would bypass Niagara Falls and the hydro-power from the running water would produce electricity to power the "model city" he envisioned. Only about a mile of the canal was ever dug, and the project was abandoned due to the discovery of alternating current, which could travel long distances over power lines. The abandoned canal filled with rain and runoff water and became a local swimming hole in the summer and an ice rink in the winter.

From 1942 to 1953, Hooker Chemical Company and others disposed of 21,800 tons of toxic chemicals, including acid chlorides, sulfur compounds, trichlorophenol (TCP), and bentyl alcohol, in the canal. The site was later covered with a clay "cap" and sod, and it was sold for $1 to the local school board. It was common knowledge that the site harbored dangerous chemical contaminants, yet the school board built the 99th Street elementary school directly on top of the old covered canal. In the 1950s, hundreds of middle-class homes were built in the immediate area. Little or nothing was ever done by either the school board or local developers to monitor or maintain the property.

In the 1970s local residents became alarmed at health problems, sludge, fumes, and phosphorous rocks, which would make a fiery impact when thrown by children. By the mid and late 1970s, chemicals were found seeping into basements of homes surrounding the old landfill property. The Love Canal Homeowner's Association became very vocal, and the situation received high-profile media attention, which grew and grew. On August 7, 1978, President Jimmy Carter declared a Federal State of Emergency for the area, and the government offered to pay full-price for all homes in the impacted areas, referred to as Rings 1, 2, and 3. (Ring 1 was the worst area, directly on or near the canal, Ring 2 was not considered fit for residential use and was eventually enclosed within Ring 1, and Ring 3 surrounded the canal and was the least impacted.)

The Love Canal Area Revitalization Agency (LCARA) was created to facilitate the buying of over 789 homes. This high-profile incident was the epicenter of the explosion of environmental legislation, particularly CERCLA, the $1.6 billion "Superfund act" passed on December 12, 1980. The school was demolished, as were all the homes in the immediate area of the old canal (Rings 1 and 2). The canal area itself is currently covered and fenced-off, and a remediation unit treats the underlying areas. Many homes to the east (a portion of Ring 3) still stand but are mostly abandoned, and there are plans to demolish all of them and build light-industrial buildings and a retail power center. The Lasalle public housing project to the west was demolished, and the site is currently vacant.

Houses to the north (a portion of Ring 3) were largely abandoned, but many were eventually refurbished and resold by the LCARA. This area is currently called Black Creek Village and, in retrospect, never posed much, if any, real environmental danger. The homes in Ring 3 began sales on August 15, 1990, at a 20% discount under the appraised value. The first home was sold on November 28, 1990. The discount required to entice buyers has gradually

Love Canal in 1978

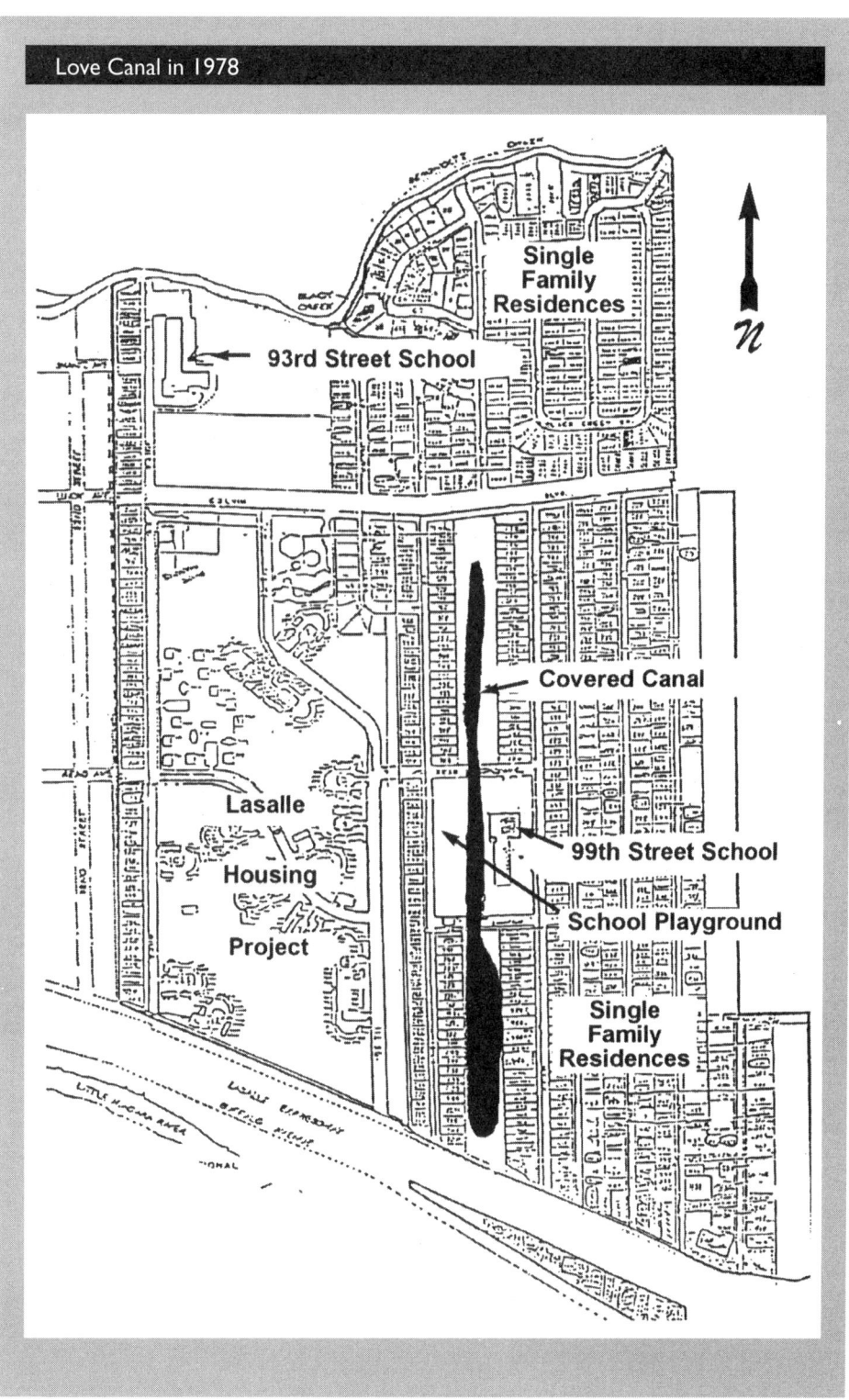

Case Study 16

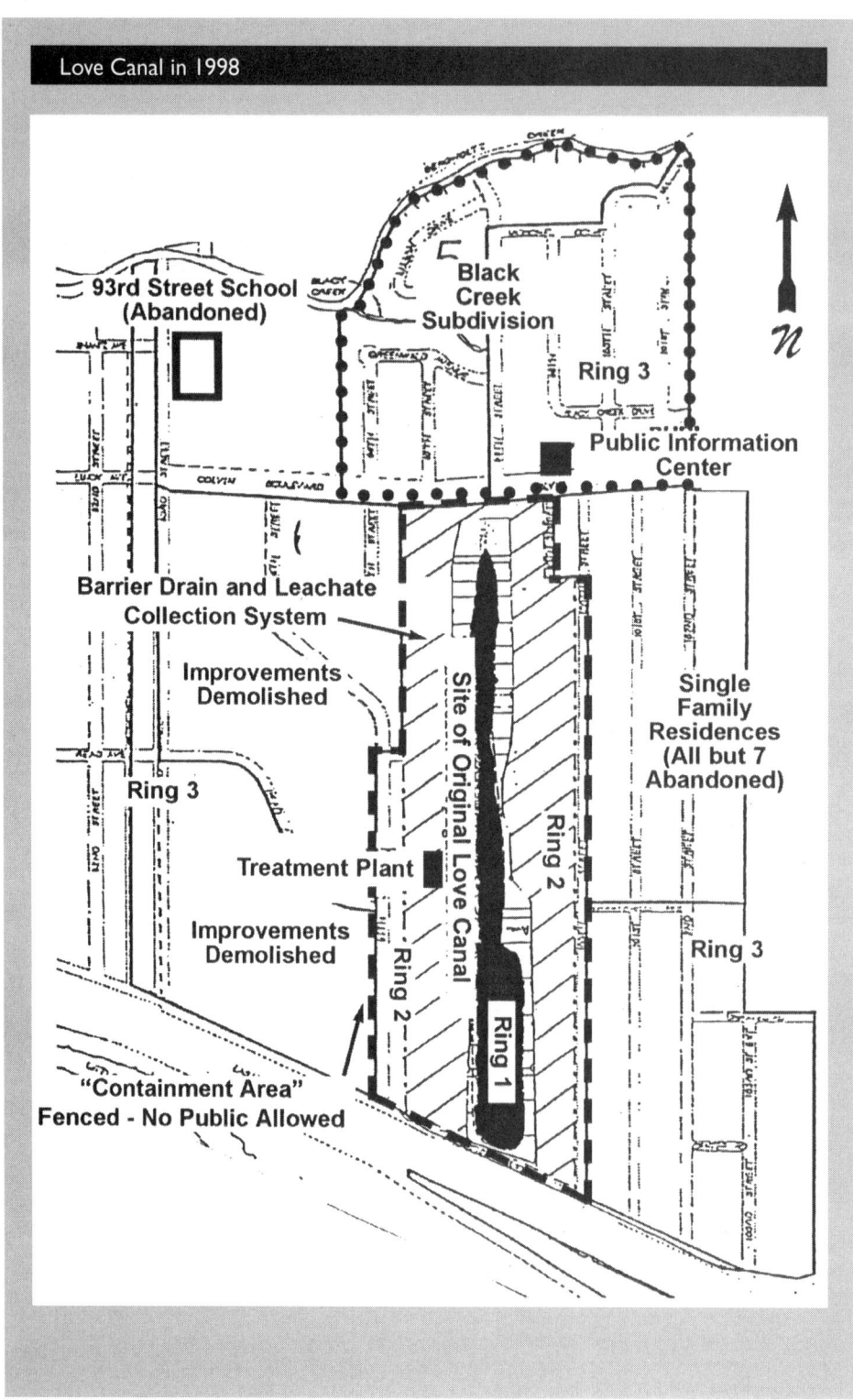

Real Estate Damages: An Analysis of Detrimental Conditions

been reduced, and after seven years the remaining homes were sold for their full value. Homes outside of the EPA study area (Rings 1, 2, and 3) were not considered impacted in value. While hundreds of families made an exodus, seven families in the eastern portions of Ring 3 never left the area and still reside there today, although there are rows of homes within this area that are abandoned.

Major litigation arose from the Love Canal, and much can be learned from the Court's decision, reported at 850 F. Supp. 993 (W.D.N.Y. 1994). Superfund claims by the United States and New York, along with personal injury and property damage claims by area residents, were filed against Occidental Chemical, the successor to Hooker Chemical. The government's claim ultimately totaled $865 million, and personal injury, property damage, and punitive claims totaled $25 billion. Related insurance claims totaled hundred of millions.

Hundreds of deserted and boarded up homes that were once a thriving neighborhood are all that remain of much of the area east of the Love Canal treatment area. Despite the hazards associated with the site, a few residents chose to remain, even after the disaster was discovered.

An eight-month trial ensued, and dozens of expert witnesses, public officials, toxicologists, risk assessors, engineers, chemists, and hydrologists testified. Senior Federal Judge John T. Curtin rejected the state's claims. Basically, the decision stated that the practices and science of the 1940s and 1950s could not be measured against the science and technology of the 1990s. The Court rejected much of what it called "junk science," and further found that only 8 to 10 homes were in fact contaminated. Further, Court documents showed that Hooker Chemical had actually been very reluctant to sell the site to the school district, and the company donated it only after providing strong warnings not to build on the site of the canal, which the school district ignored.

The Love Canal situation illustrates a spectrum of numerous important issues related to damaged real estate. On one hand, it awakened society to the dangers of environmental contamination, yet in some circumstances it illustrated the over-reaction, hysteria, fear, and anxiety that can be generated by junk science. Nevertheless, hundreds of homes were, in fact, abandoned, and many areas surrounding the canal area remain vacant today. In those areas that were shown to not be environmentally impacted, the homes still sustained a 20% discount for market resistance, but after seven years this discount was eliminated, and they now sell for full value. Clearly, those areas directly over and immediately adjacent to the canal have no value, or are even a liability, as they can never be built upon or developed.

Case Study 17

By Randall Bell, MAI
Three Mile Island—Susquehanna River, Pennsylvania
Class VIII Detrimental Condition—Nuclear Power Plant Disaster

Some residents near Three Mile Island have stated that while their concerns about the power plant are diminishing their concerns about airport noise from the nearby Harrisburg International Airport are increasing.

Despite the accident, homes located in close proximity to Three Mile Island do sell. The accident has had a variety of impacts on the surrounding real estate, ranging from the increased demand for workers hired to clean up after the accident, to developers who had to discount their properties in order to sell them, to some local farmers who stated that the accident had no impact on their property values.

Construction began on the Three Mile Island (TMI) nuclear power plant in 1968 on a 382-acre island located on the Susquehanna River in Londonderry Township, about 10 miles south of Harrisburg, Pennsylvania. The plant has two units. Commercial operation of Unit 1 began on September 2, 1974, and Unit 2 began commercial operation in December 1978. The reactor buildings are 200 feet high and have a wall thickness of four feet. They are designed to withstand a strike by a 200,000 pound aircraft and earthquakes up to 6.5 on the Richter scale. The cooling towers have a flow of 222,000 gallons per minute. The plant is capable of generating 870 megawatts of electricity, enough to supply approximately 500,000 homes. Unit 1 cost $400 million to construct, and Unit 2 cost $700 million. It would cost approximately $4 billion today to construct a plant comparable to Unit 1. The plant is owned by GPU, Inc., a utility holding company.

On March 28, 1979, a valve within Unit 2 malfunctioned, and river water used to cool the nuclear core flowed out of the reactor's system. Due to inadequate operator training, the stuck valve went unnoticed for 2 hours 20 minutes. The core overheated and some radioactive material (within prescribed limits) was released into the atmosphere. The core temperature reached 5,000° F. TMI came within one hour of a "Group 1" accident—a complete meltdown with failure of the backup safety system, a near impossibility calculated at 1 chance in 200 million reactor years. (The nuclear disaster at Chernobyl, Russia, was a Group 1 accident.) Local residents were advised to evacuate the area. The full extent of damage was not known until mid-1982 when a remote camera showed that about 90% of the 37,000 fuel rods were damaged. Cleanup was completed 14 years after the accident. The subsequent cleanup took the efforts of over 1,000 people and cost $973 million. The radioactive core debris was shipped by railroad to Idaho.

Reactor Unit 1 was never damaged and still operates today. A report issued by The President's Commission on the Accident at Three Mile Island concluded that there will be no significant health effects to the public as a result of the accident; however, some researchers allege that cancer levels are up for people living downwind of the reactor. Clearly, the health risks issue is controversial.

The areas immediately around TMI predominately comprise scarcely populated farmlands. More populated areas are located about five miles away, and Harrisburg is 10 miles away. Interviews with numerous local residents indicated that there are mixed reactions related to real estate values. In fact, a spectrum of impact has occurred on real estate values, ranging from losses to no impact to even a positive impact.

The local farms are owned predominately by families who have long-term ties to the area. Many of these residents indicated that they never left the area, even during the period of the initial accident. Many of these farmers indicated that the accident did not disrupt their farming activities or their property values. However, one developer indicated that it was virtually impossible to sell property in the immediate area, and only after waiting approximately 1½ years after the accident were they able to sell a spec-built home at a 30% discount. In other nearby urban areas, particularly Harrisburg, real estate values remained level or even increased. This phenomenon was attributed to the fact that only 200 workers were displaced by the accident and new demand was created by over 1,000 new workers employed for the 14-year cleanup. At the time of the last field inspection, in 1997, virtually all parties agreed that the incident no longer impacted real estate values. Some people stated that their concerns with TMI are receding, while their concerns over the noise from the local airport (Harrisburg International) is increasing.

Prompted by the Three Mile Island accident, emergency planning became a federal requirement in 1979. The U.S. Nuclear Regulatory Commission (NRC) retained jurisdiction of emergency planning for nuclear plant sites. By 1980, all nuclear utilities were required to coordinate with local, state, and federal officials every other year. These delineated areas nearby a nuclear power plant have ongoing monitoring and civil warning sirens throughout the area.

The NRC established the following four levels of emergency classification for the nuclear power industry, which impact properties within the emergency planning zone.

1. Unusual Event

There is a minor problem at the plant. No release of radioactive material is expected. Public officials will be notified. Residents within the emergency planning zone will not have to do anything.

2. Alert

Also a minor problem. It is not expected to seriously affect the safety of the plant. Any releases of radioactivity are expected to be limited to small fractions of federal exposure limits. Officials will be notified. Most likely, residents will not have to do anything. Public officials may, at their discretion, sound a steady siren tone for three minutes. This means turn on your radio or television to an emergency broadcast station and listen for official information.

3. Site Emergency Area

A more serious event has occurred. Major plant systems might be affected, but releases of radioactivity would not be expected to exceed any federal limits outside the site boundary. Public officials may, at their discretion, sound a steady siren tone for three minutes. This means turn on your radio or television to an emergency broadcast station and listen for official information.

4. General Emergency

Such an emergency would involve serious damage at the plant and the release of radioactivity beyond the site boundary. Public officials may, at their discretion, sound a steady siren tone for three minutes. This means turn on your radio or television to an emergency broadcast station and listen for official information.

Case Study 18

By Burrell E. Montz and Graham A. Tobin

Yuba River Floods—Ten Year Study on Residential Values—Yuba County, California
Class IX Detrimental Condition—Flooding

In February 1986, the communities of Linda and Olivehurst in Yuba County, California, were flooded when a levee broke along the Yuba River. Research following that flood centered on two lines of inquiry to evaluate the immediate impacts of flooding on residential property values:

1. Identification of relationships that may exist between characteristics of the flood event and changes in house values over time.
2. Determination of the extent to which house prices are influenced by the flood hazard.[1]

The findings of that research demonstrated spatial and temporal impacts of flooding on house values. Not only was there a significant decline in property values throughout the floodplain over a two-year period, including non-flooded properties in the area, but the degree of impact was also directly related to the depth of flooding. Those properties flooded in excess of 10 feet clearly experienced the greatest decline in sale prices. By the end of the research period, properties flooded to lesser depths (18 inches) were beginning to increase in value, even relative to non-flooded properties, a fact explained in part by the improvements made to such properties because of the flooding. Thus, the effects of the flood were felt throughout the entire residential real estate market and not just in submarkets defined by flood depths. Further, the flood made a significant contribution to explaining differences in selling prices, as greater flood depths meant lower selling prices. A particularly important result of this research, therefore, was the identification of real estate submarkets based on flood experience.

The foregoing discussion presents the situation in Linda and Olivehurst within two years following the 1986 flood and documents the immediate post-flood impacts. However, in order to determine if and how long it takes a residential real estate market to recover to pre-flood levels, it is necessary to examine house prices over a longer period. It is such a longitudinal analysis of the residential property values in Linda and Olivehurst that is the focus of current research, the results of which are reported here. Three general research questions were addressed in this phase of the research:

1. What is the length of the recovery period for the residential real estate market following catastrophic flooding?
2. Do the flood depth submarkets continue to exhibit differences in property values more than six years after the flood?
3. To what extent do variables associated with flooding continue to explain differences in selling prices for houses?

---

1. Montz and Tobin, 1988; Tobin and Montz, 1988; Tobin and Montz, 1994. See case study bibliography for complete citation.

Related Literature

Studies on both long- and short-term responses of housing markets to a natural event, or to the threat of an event, have been undertaken, with most of this research focusing on earthquakes and floods. The premise on which most of these studies are based suggests that the existence of a hazard or the occurrence of an event will have a negative effect on house values because of a decrease in utility that is associated with the hazard/event. For instance, in a theoretical examination of the earthquake hazard, researchers suggested that house values would fall in high-risk areas and they would rise in low-risk areas,[2] an argument that has been supported empirically in a study of Los Angeles and San Francisco.[3] In these cities, houses in areas designated as Special Studies Zones, and thus particularly prone to earthquakes, sold for less than houses outside those zones. Studies of the flood hazard have shown similar results, although there have been some contradictory findings in different communities.[4]

This research theme is not limited to the United States. Studies in Australia[5] and New Zealand[6] demonstrated an immediate depreciating effect following disaster events with some continued impact over the longer term. However, these studies also pointed out problems associated with trying to separate flood-related market impacts from market impacts relating to other socioeconomic and environmental variables.

Furthermore, there is another, more indirect impact that has been found by this research, and that relates to the existence of housing submarkets. Earlier research by the authors identified discernible submarkets associated with flood depths,[7] and submarkets were also identified in the communities studied in Australia and New Zealand. Again, the earthquake hazard also illustrates the importance of submarkets, wherein older brick buildings that do not meet building standards regarding earthquake safety comprise a submarket.[8]

What remains to be documented is the longevity of these submarkets—that is, whether they are a short-term response to a hazardous situation or whether they continue over the long term. Part of this may be explained by the expectation model proposed by Yezer and Rubin (1987). This model relates economic change to anticipation of events. If an event is unanticipated, then economic change will follow; if anticipated, no change occurs or there is no lasting impact. Certainly flooding from a levee break, as in Linda and Olivehurst in 1986, was unanticipated, so economic impacts might have been expected and were, in fact, documented.[9] The extent to which these economic impacts can be seen 10 years later is under study here.

The Theoretical Foundation

The conceptual framework for this work was presented in Tobin and Newton (1986) and is depicted in Exhibit CS 18.1. Briefly, the graph presents three scenarios following a flood (or other event).

Immediately following a flood, property values decrease because the utility that can be derived from that parcel of land is reduced. Depending upon the nature of the flood, in terms

---

2. Scawthorn, et al., 1982.
3. Brookshire, et al., 1985.
4. MacDonald, et al., 1987; Muckleston, 1983; Shilling, et al., 1985.
5. Lambley and Cordery, 1991.
6. Montz, 1992.
7. Tobin and Montz, 1994.
8. Alesch and Petak, 1986.
9. Montz and Tobin, 1988.

of frequency and magnitude, recovery can follow any of several paths, three of which are presented here. Line A represents a situation where frequent flooding may keep land prices low relative to non-flood areas. While the trend in property values may not be entirely flat, any increases that may occur are negated by the next flood. Line C represents the opposite situation, that of extreme flooding, either a very infrequent, perhaps "once-in-a-lifetime" event or extremely catastrophic flooding, or both. In this case, it is expected that property values will decrease immediately after the event but will recover eventually to pre-flood levels and perhaps rise even higher. Under other circumstances, property values might recover somewhere in between these two extremes (line B).

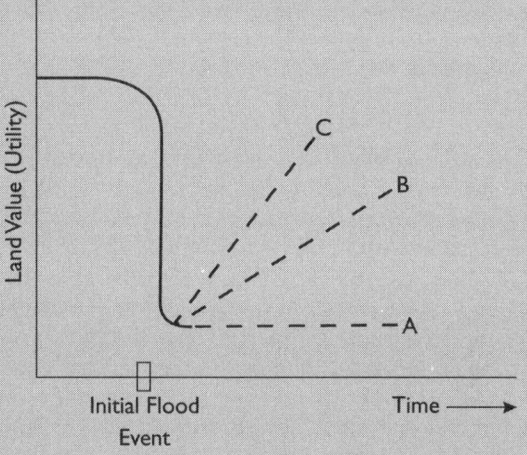

Exhibit CS 18.1 Theoretical Framework Depicting Utility Following Flooding. Lines A, B, and C represent different flood hazard scenarios.

Research to date has verified this model, to a certain extent. For instance, the community of Des Plaines, Illinois, experiences relatively frequent flooding. Although other dynamics of the real estate market had a significant impact in this Chicago suburb, capitalization of flooding was apparent after the community experienced two floods within a 10-month period and five floods within 50 years.[10] Similarly, in Wilkes-Barre, Pennsylvania, trends in sale prices for properties flooded more than 9 feet in a catastrophic event in 1972 virtually replicate line C on the graph in Exhibit CS 18.1. However, properties flooded less than 9 feet (the mid-range depth for this event) recovered rather quickly, and prices exceeded pre-flood values within one year of the flood. Thus, empirical evidence from several study areas tends to support the theoretical base, though there are variations from what was expected in some submarkets.

Previous work in Linda and Olivehurst also served to validate the model. The decrease in sale prices immediately following the flood was followed by recovery to almost pre-flood prices for those properties flooded to 18 inches, in keeping with the model. Properties flooded to 10 feet or more experienced some recovery after the initial drop, but prices never got higher than 80% of pre-flood levels and they then experienced another decline.[11] Of course, the time periods examined in the initial study may have reflected short-term market fluctuations unrelated to the flood, as well as impacts of the flood. Nonetheless, it appeared at the time that the flood was indeed capitalized in property values, as hypothesized, and the data on the non-flooded property supported this contention. Examination of a longer time period, therefore, permitted further evaluation of the extent to which the model continues to apply and provided a longitudinal test of the concept of capitalization of the flood.

---

10. Tobin and Montz, 1990 and 1994.
11. Montz and Tobin, 1988.

Study Area And Methods

As mentioned earlier, the 1986 flood in Linda and Olivehurst, California, was triggered by a levee break along the Yuba River (Exhibit CS 18.2). Prior to this event, flooding in this area had affected the communities of Marysville and Yuba City, on the other side of the Feather and Yuba Rivers, while Linda and Olivehurst received only localized storm damage. The 1986 flood was devastating, affecting approximately 6,500 buildings in the two communities, which in 1990 had a combined population of approximately 22,000. The floodplain in this area is extensive, with levees virtually ringing the two towns along the Feather, Yuba, and Bear Rivers. Because of the levee break, water flowed rapidly into the towns. Because of the level topography it slowed in velocity but increased in depth, up to 12 feet in places. In addition, the level topography caused the water to remain in some places for more than two weeks. Thus, damage resulted from both rapid water velocities and from the long duration of saturation. In the end, more than 3,000 homes were damaged and 895 destroyed. Total public and private losses were estimated at $22.5 million.[12]

In order to evaluate any relationship between flood experience and impacts on house prices, the communities were divided into three spatial areas: those neighborhoods flooded to 18 inches, those flooded to 10+ feet (the eaves of the single-story houses), and non-flooded areas. For all houses in these areas, data on house listings and sales were obtained from the multiple listing service records of the Sutter-Yuba Board of Realtors, for the period January 1983 (to establish the pre-flood market) until December 1996. Unfortunately, the Board of Realtors was unwilling to make available pre-flood data on non-flooded properties, though an estimate of median selling price was offered. The number of properties in each flood area is presented in Exhibit CS 18.3.

All information that was consistently available was collected for each residential listing and sale, including list price, sale price, date listed, date sold, days on the market, number of bedrooms and bathrooms, and square footage of the house. For the most part, the flooded houses were located in tract developments and had similar sizes and configurations. Indeed, chi-square analysis of housing characteristics between and within the flooded neighborhoods, undertaken for the earlier studies, showed no significant differences among the flooded neighborhoods, thus verifying the homogeneity of the tract developments.[13] Consequently, controls on differences in housing type and size are embedded in the sample. Non-flooded houses were more dispersed throughout the communities and therefore not as uniform, but chi-square analysis of housing characteristics (number of beds and baths, and square footage) resulted in no significant difference for pre-flood conditions between the flooded and non-flooded areas. All list and sale prices were converted to 1984 dollars, using the CPI housing index.

Analysis of the data was divided into three parts, reflecting the research questions presented earlier. First, percentage change in mean house values, as manifested by the sale price, was graphed by flood zone at yearly or several-year intervals to depict market patterns over time. This graph allowed for comparison of trends as they varied between spatial areas, that is, with flood depths. Changes in sale prices were then compared within flood groups using "t-tests," such that each floodplain category was defined by its own mean price, and temporal changes within groups were evaluated. Two sets of analyses were presented. The first compared pre-flood mean sale prices to post-flood sale prices for successive periods after the flood, thus providing an analysis of the impact of the flood on house prices. A significant difference between pre- and post-flood prices indicated a possible impact of the flood. The second set compared immediate post-flood prices to sale prices for

---

12. Teets and Young, 1986.
13. Montz and Tobin, 1988.

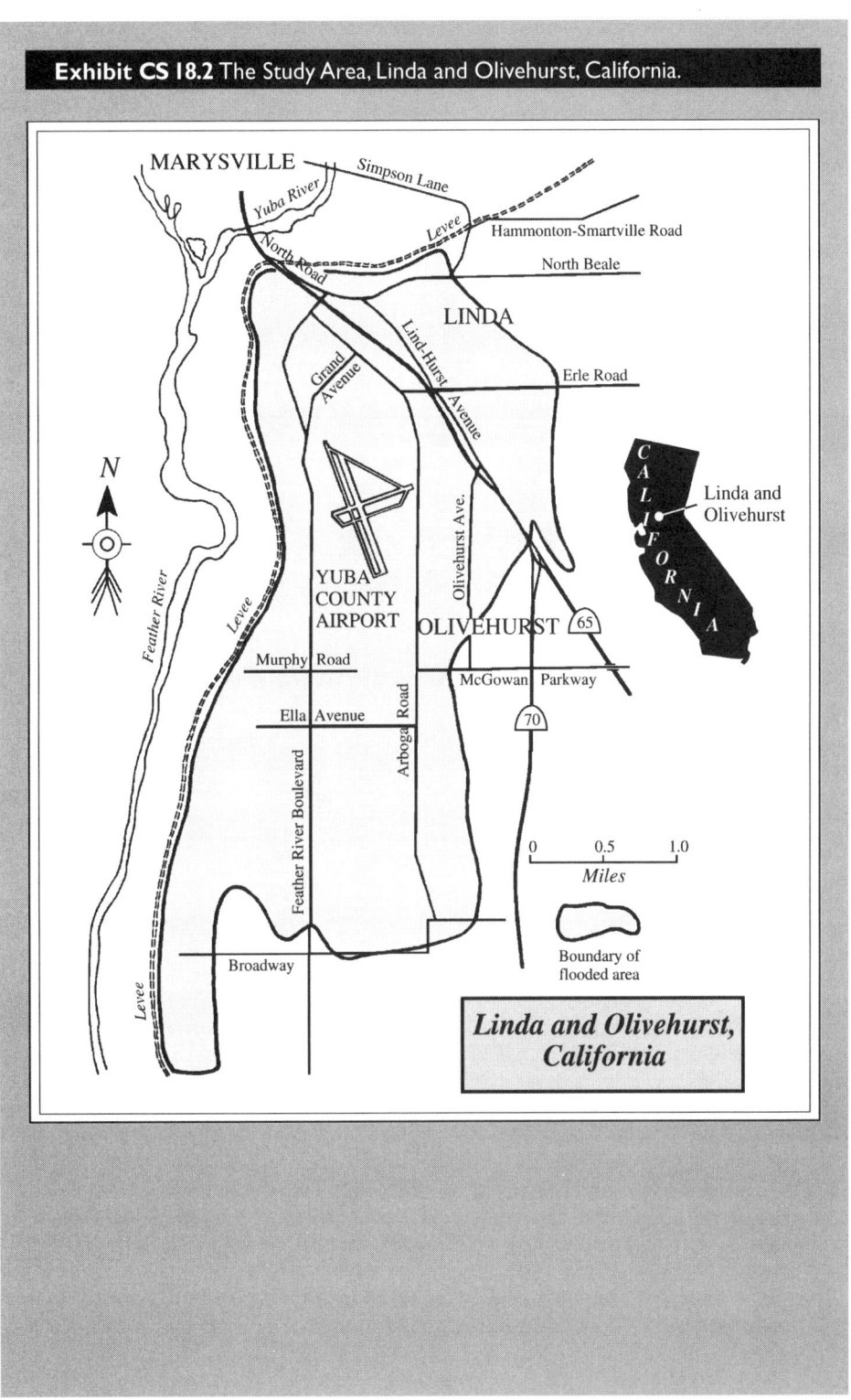

Exhibit CS 18.2 The Study Area, Linda and Olivehurst, California.

Exhibit CS 18.3 Number of Properties by Flood Category

Flood Category	Number of Sales
Non-flood	108
Flooded 1.5 feet	107
Flooded >10 feet	71

successive years. Here, a significant difference between immediate post-flood prices and later post-flood prices indicated a recovery of the market in that flood area.

Finally, the extent to which location, in this case flood zone, influences selling prices of houses was analyzed using a form of hedonic modeling. Because hedonic models have been found to be useful in determining significant differences in prices due to specific factors, they have direct application to the third research question. Earlier research showed that flood depth was a significant contributor to explaining sale prices such that greater flood depth meant lower house prices. Whether that relationship holds over the 10-year period considered here was an important question.

Temporal Changes in Selling Prices

The graph in Exhibit CS 18.4, depicting the different experiences of each flood zone, indicates that the flood did indeed have an impact on sale prices that varied depending upon depth of flooding. Properties flooded to more than 10 feet experienced a significant, immediate post-flood decline in sale prices, such that even after one year, prices were almost 30% lower than pre-flood levels. An increase by the end of the second year probably reflected investments in repairs and the resale of houses. But this did not last, as prices fell again over the next two years, only rebounding somewhat at the end of the 10-year period. In contrast, the sale prices for houses flooded to 18 inches reproduced the theoretical pattern presented by line B in Exhibit CS 18.1. Prices fell immediately following the flood but then increased gradually over time and ended the period with the highest proportional increase. Non-flooded houses also experienced a post-flood decline, perhaps contrary to what might be expected, although this may have reflected a general lack of interest in the housing market of Linda and Olivehurst after such a catastrophic event.

Although indicative of temporal trends and differences among submarkets, the changes presented in the graphs do not necessarily represent statistically significant differences in recovery. Therefore, t-tests were used to evaluate the statistical significance, if any, and directions of impacts over different time periods. The comparison of pre- and post-flood mean sale prices is presented in Exhibit CS 18.5. As noted earlier, data on pre-flood, non-flooded properties were not available. Nevertheless, the flood clearly had a differential impact on sale prices over the long term. For example, properties flooded to the greatest depths continued to elicit a significant difference between pre- and post-flood means throughout the 10-year study period, whereas a different pattern emerged regarding properties flooded to lesser depths. While pre- and post-flood sale prices for these properties were significantly different at the end of 12 months, the degree of difference waned over time, and within two years no significant difference was found. Thus, the flood depressed property values throughout the flooded areas, but the significance of impact differed depending upon flood depth.

Given that a significant change from pre-flood values had been documented, the next step was to determine if there was a significant difference in the recovery of property values in the different areas. Once again, t-tests were used, this time to compare immediate post-flood sale prices to sale prices for successive years after the flood. A significant difference between the means would indicate a measure of recovery with later values higher than immediate post-flood values. The results of these analyses are presented in Exhibit CS 18.6. There was no significant difference for either flood area until more than six years after the flood, when sale prices for those properties in the lesser flooded area eventually rebounded. In addition, there was no significant recovery in the area flooded to greater depths over the same period. Therefore, not only was the impact of flooding most severe in areas of greatest flood depths, but recovery was also extended. While the first result may appear to be obvious, the second is not. One might have expected that those houses flooded to the eaves would be worth more after five years because of subsequent repairs and upgrades made to properties. These data suggest that this is not the case. This issue is discussed later in the conclusions.

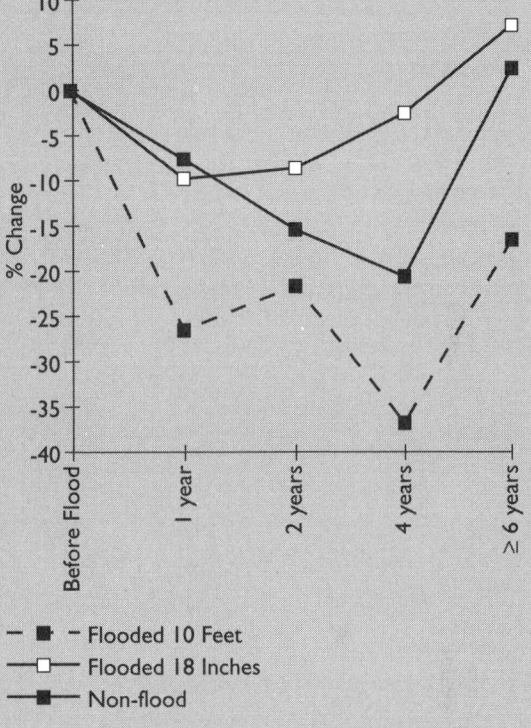

Exhibit CS 18.4 Trends in Sale Prices for Three Submarkets Following the 1986 Flood. Changes are proportional to pre-flood house prices for each submarket.

Flooding as a Variable in Selling Price

To examine the extent to which flooding contributed to variations in selling prices, a hedonic model was used, as follows:

Sale price = f (house size, # of bedrooms, # of bathrooms, square footage of the house, listing date, sale date, days on the market, and flood depth)

Two multiple regression analyses were undertaken to test the model. One utilized the full data set, and the other included only those properties sold after February 1990 (four years after the flood). The results of the first model are presented in Exhibits CS 18.7 and CS 18.8. Variations in sale prices were explained in part by four variables:

1. number of bathrooms
2. square footage
3. flood depth
4. date listed

Exhibit CS 18.5 Impact of the Flood on Property Values by Time Period

	N	Difference* (1984 $)	T-Value	Probability
1 Year After				
Flooded 1.5 ft.	26	-4,730	2.12	.044†
Flooded >10 ft.	21	-14,550	2.26	.035†
2 Years After				
Flooded 1.5 ft.	49	-4,369	1.90	.062
Flooded >10 ft.	34	-13,482	2.42	.021†
4 Years After				
Flooded 1.5 ft.	71	-3,227	1.72	.09
Flooded >10 ft.	42	-14,927	2.41	.021†
> 6 Years After				
Flooded 1.5 ft.	107	-561	0.30	.77
Flooded >10 ft.	71	-12,351	2.1	.04†

* Difference = post-flood sale price − pre-flood sale price
† Significant at 0.05

Although these account for only 44% of the variation in prices, the results support earlier findings. As expected, some of the variation in prices can be attributed to housing characteristics. More importantly for the questions raised here, though, is the significance of flood experience, represented directly by flood depth and more indirectly by listing and sale dates. The results of the regression model demonstrate that greater flood depths translate into lower sale prices. Listing dates emerged as a significant variable, though this raises some questions. Immediately following the flood, listing dates were significant, indicating that houses listed after the flood tended to sell for less, as had been hypothesized. However, as time from the flood increased, one would expect that the effect of this variable would diminish as recovery proceeds. The results here suggest otherwise. Clearly, however, the flood has had a continuing negative influence on house values in Linda and Olivehurst.

Conclusions

The empirical evidence from this research validates, to a large extent, the theoretical model depicted in Exhibit CS 18.1. The effects of flooding remained long after a catastrophic event, and, while recovery was evident, the effects varied with flood experience. The results of this work, then, serve to provide answers for the research questions presented earlier.

Length of the Recovery Period

Properties that experience flooding did eventually recover to near pre-flood levels, but the length of time that this recovery took varied with depth of flooding. More than six years after this flood, properties experiencing flood depths greater than 10 feet had not yet returned to pre-flood values, while those flooded to 1.5 feet showed evidence of recovery. When compared to immediate post-flood values, houses with lower flood levels recovered more quickly and exhibited a greater increase in sale prices. For houses experiencing greater depths, recovery was not yet evident 10 years after the flood.

Earlier research showed that repairs to flooded properties may influence recovery such that properties with greater flood depths would perhaps recover more quickly because there were more extensive repairs and thus upgrading and updating of houses.[14] This did

---

14. Tobin and Montz, 1994.

not appear to be the case, over the longer term. Indeed, the different recovery rates and times for different flood levels confirmed that the flood had been capitalized into property values in spite of repairs. That is, the rebound in prices documented earlier did not last, as the market continued to reflect differences related to flood depths. Therefore, despite the once-in-a-lifetime nature of this flood, the spatial variations in recovery demonstrated that the effects are long-lasting. Part of this may be due to the fact that not all properties in the areas with the greatest flood depths were repaired. Indeed, many years after the flood, some houses remained abandoned. Certainly this is a constant reminder of the flood for potential buyers, in addition to the depreciating effect such properties can have on surrounding property values. Hence, although the expectation of flooding is probably low, given the nature of this flood, the reminders that exist in the communities influence recovery.

Exhibit CS 18.6 Significance of Post-flood Recovery by Time Period

	N	Difference* (1984 $)	T-Value	Probability
1 Year: 2 Years				
Flooded 1.5 ft.	34	534	-0.17	.865
Flooded >10 ft.	29	2,383	-0.58	.567
1 Year: 4 years				
Flooded 1.5 ft.	33	3,268	-1.86	.072
Flooded >10 ft.	24	-5,616	0.93	.365
1 Year: 6+ Years				
Flooded 1.5 ft.	47	8,317	-4.26	.000†
Flooded >10 ft.	45	5,485	-1.51	.140

* Difference = later sale price − immediate post-flood sale price
† Significant at 0.05

Flood Submarkets

In keeping with the recovery trends documented above, flood submarkets remained identifiable over the long term. The areas experiencing differences in flood depths continued to have different market recovery trends. Throughout the 10-year study period, trends in sold prices verified that the flood was having a significantly negative impact with greater flood depths having more difficulty recovering to pre-flood levels. Results from the earlier research indicated that the differences among flood areas were waning, perhaps in response to the relative homogeneity of the housing stock and the timing and extent of repairs. Indeed, some houses in the area with higher flood depths were repaired and remodeled rather quickly, considering the amount of damage incurred. Thus, they were on the market with those properties flooded to lower depths, and they competed well, perhaps given the once-in-a-lifetime perception of this flood event. However, this did not last over the long term. There remain reminders of the extent of devastation, and flood submarkets have become more distinct.

Flooding as a Variable in Selling Price

The results of the hedonic model supported the continued significance of flood submarkets, as flood-related variables surfaced as significant contributors to variations in sale prices, no matter what time frame was considered. In fact, as time from the flood progressed, the proportion of explanation related to these flood-related variables increased. This provided further evidence of the long-term negative effect that flooding can have on property values

Exhibit CS 18.7 Model Results (All Data)

Variable	B	Beta	T-ratio	Probability
No. of Bathrooms	11779.911	.421040	7.024	.0000
Square Footage	12.356	.409926	8.640	.0000
Days on Market	4.288	.023065	.487	.6263
Flood Depth	4555.610	.410451	8.892	.0000
Sale Date	-69.886	-.020127	-.354	.7239
List Date	-691.250	-.157739	-2.627	.0090
No. of Bedrooms	-2277.970	-.107449	-1.729	.0848
Constant	20728.003		6.994	.0000

Adjusted $R^2 = .44362$

Standard Error of the Estimate = 13899.05

Exhibit CS 18.8 Model Results (After February 1990)

Variable	B	Beta	T-ratio	Probability
No. of Bathrooms	23312.857	.481332	7.054	.0000
Days on Market	14.421	.050368	.871	.3854
List Date	-2412.437	-.134448	-2.328	.0214
Flood Depth	4714.560	.366189	6.290	.0000
Square Footage	7.898	.124601	1.943	.0541
No. of Bedrooms	409.846	.008306	.129	.8980
Constant	19874.187		1.184	.2383

Adjusted $R^2 = .53829$

Standard Error of the Estimate = 15871.69

and for the differentiation of the community into flood submarkets. The results were consistent over time, with the strength of the model increasing as time since the flood lengthened.

The results of this longitudinal study are in line with the theoretical model. Recovery of residential property values was dependent on the extent of flooding, and the impacts of floods on the market remained long after repairs had been made. It had been suggested that the expectation of future flooding has an influence on the nature of change that occurs in a community,[15] and early results tended to verify this idea.[16] However, over the long-term this does not appear to hold. The levee was repaired and "protection" was back, thus providing

---

15. Yezer and Rubin, 1987.
16. Tobin and Montz, 1994.

once again a sense of security from floods and decreasing expectations of future floods. However, either the losses were so significant or faith in flood protection so lost that this once-in-a-lifetime event continued to have lasting impacts on the residential real estate market.

Epilogue

In January 1997, Olivehurst was flooded twice within a two-week period. The areas affected are not the same ones as those flooded in 1986, but the cause was the same—two levee breaks. Two issues arise from these more recent floods. First is the question of what impact, if any, these floods will have on the submarkets in Linda and Olivehurst that are the subject of this study. The related second issue concerns the extent to which the 1997 floods will affect expectations of flooding for areas spared in 1997 but flooded in 1986. The answers to these questions remain to be seen and are the focus of further research.

Literature Cited

Alesch, D. J., and W. J. Petak. *The Politics and Economics of Earthquake Hazard Mitigation: Unreinforced Masonry Buildings in Southern California.* Program on Environment and Behavior Monograph #43. (Boulder, Colo.: Institute of Behavioral Science, University of Colorado, 1986).

Brookshire, D. S., M. A. Thayer, J. Tschirhart, and W. D. Schulze. "A test of the expected utility model: Evidence from earthquake risks," *Journal of Political Economy,* vol. 93, no. 2: 369–389.

Lambley, D. B., and I. Cordery. "Effects of floods on the housing market in Sydney," *Proceedings of International Hydrology and Water Resources Symposium, 1991* (Perth, Australia: 1991): 863–866.

MacDonald, D. N., J. L. Murdoch, and H. L. White. "Uncertain hazards, insurance, and consumer choice: Evidence from housing markets," *Land Economics,* vol. 63, no. 4: 361–371.

Montz, B. E., and G. A. Tobin. "The spatial and temporal variability of residential real estate values in response to flooding," *Disasters: The Journal of Disaster Studies and Management,* vol. 12, 1988: 345–355.

Montz, B. E. "The effects of flooding on residential property values in three New Zealand communities," *Disasters: The Journal of Disaster Studies and Management,* vol. 16, no. 4, 1992: 283–298.

Muckleston, K. W. "The impact of floodplain regulations on residential land values in Oregon," *Water Resources Bulletin,* vol. 19: 1–7.

Scawthorn, C., H. Iemura, and Y. Yamada. "The influence of natural hazards on urban housing location," *Journal of Urban Economics,* vol. 11: 242–251.

Shilling, J. D., J. D. Benjamin, and C. F. Sirmans. "Adjusting comparable sales for floodplain location," *The Appraisal Journal* (July 1985): 429–436.

Teets, B., and S. Young. *Rivers of Fear: The Great California Flood of 1986.* (Terra Alta, W.Va.: C.R. Publications, Inc., 1986).

Tobin, G. A., and B. E. Montz. "Catastrophic flooding and the response of the residential real estate market," *The Social Science Journal,* vol. 25, no. 2, 1988: 167–177.

____. "Response of the real estate market to frequent flooding: the case of Des Plaines, Illinois," *Bulletin of the Illinois Geographical Society,* vol. 32, no. 2, 1990: 11–21.

____. "The flood hazard and dynamics of the urban residential land market," *Water Resources Bulletin,* vol. 30, no. 4, 1994: 673–685.

Tobin, G. A., and T. G. Newton. "A Theoretical Framework of Flood Induced Changes in Urban Land Values," *Water Resources Bulletin,* vol. 22, 1986: 67–71.

Yezer, A. M., and C. B. Rubin. *The Local Economic Effects of Natural Disasters.* Natural Hazard Research Working Paper #61. (Boulder, Colo.: Institute of Behavioral Science, University of Colorado, 1987).

Case Study 19

By Randall Bell, MAI

Oklahoma Federal Building—Oklahoma City, Oklahoma
Class X Detrimental Condition—Terrorist Bombing

In April 1995, the Alfred E. Murrah Federal Building in Oklahoma City, Oklahoma, was destroyed by a powerful bomb left in a rented vehicle. This tragedy took the lives of 168 people, injured 600 others, and irreparably damaged the nine-story building.

Although the Federal Building received the focus of media attention, the blast destroyed numerous other buildings to the north, east, and west, including the YMCA, the Regency Towers Apartments, several churches, and the post office. Many of these buildings were later demolished, repaired, or rebuilt.

Soon after the rescue efforts were completed the balance of the Federal Building was demolished, the site was fenced, and a grass lawn was planted. Traffic on Fifth Street has been permanently closed, and plans have been made to erect a memorial on part of the site. The parking structure and terrace were not damaged, and the parking structure is still used today by the courthouse located south of the site.

The Oklahoma bombing affected many properties beyond the Federal Building. The post office across the street was destroyed, and the two buildings seen here were also damaged.

The blast zone from the Oklahoma bombing expanded for many blocks. This structure collapsed, although it was located several blocks away from the explosion.

The incident fundamentally altered the future building plans of the federal government. The government purchased numerous destroyed properties to the north and are planning a low-rise building complex that will be a model for future government buildings, all having permanent barriers to prevent any similar delivery of a large-scale explosive.

Case Study 20

By Sandra Laudone, MAI, SRA

Sinkholes—Northampton County, Pennsylvania
Class X—Incurable Subsurface Condition

This assignment involved the valuation of a 1,600-sq.-ft. suburban tract house, circa late 1960s, located in Northampton County, Pennsylvania. When a water main broke, the soils became saturated and sinkholes developed, significantly damaging the subject property. Ultimately, the real estate was condemned as "uninhabitable." The report developed the *before* and *after* value of the real estate to determine the total damages to the property value.

A *before* value, or unimpaired value, immediately prior to the occurrence of the sinkhole was estimated to be $143,000, using a standard sales comparison approach. This value established a benchmark from which all of the costs and losses associated with the detrimental condition were based. Next, the three stages of a detrimental condition were considered (assessment stage, repair stage, and ongoing stage inclusive of market resistance).

From both a physical and financial standpoint, the detrimental condition had a major impact on the subject property. Even assuming that the building could be repaired and the land could be remediated, several factors still adversely impacted the market value. Since December 26, 1995, the local municipality has condemned the house, and the home owner's insurance carrier has canceled the fire insurance policy.

The primary factors that were considered in estimating damages included the following:

- The property was uninhabitable and had been condemned.
- Mortgage financing was not available.
- Fire and home owner's insurance was not available and would be unavailable in the future due to the history of the site.
- Local real estate agents would not market the property.

During the assessment stage, independent contractors and engineers estimated the cost of repairs to be $135,121. This would cure the site damage and make the structure inhabitable. This figure includes all direct and indirect costs, but not the points and interest that must be paid to finance the repairs, which were estimated to be $10,000. Nor does that cost to cure estimate provide for the time it will take to complete the repairs, estimated at approximately six months to one year. As reported in the sales comparison approach, the estimate of market value before the water main break was $143,000, of which 28% is attributed to the land. Thus, the $145,121 cost of repairs for the site and the improvement, plus the interest and loss of use, exceeds the unimpaired value of the subject property.

The appraisal problem included analyzing the general effects of post-repair market resistance. The perceived risk of ownership was high within the local market because over the past 12 years there had been two separate water main breaks at the same location. Although independent studies stated that the land had the potential of being stabilized, apparently there were no guarantees against a reoccurrence, and the site could not be insured. Serious questions remained as to the integrity of the site. Based upon interviews with local brokers, there was no market for the site as if vacant. With more than an adequate inventory of building lots readily available, no prudent buyer would purchase the lot and then spend a considerable amount to improve it. Based upon these factors, market resistance would exist, even after remediation, thereby severely limiting future development. There was no market demand for "open space" lots, and there was no market created by neighbors, who were concerned about the costs of maintaining a lot with a history of sinkholes.

Based upon these factors, the value of the subject property, as if unimpaired, was $143,000. The subject property had no value as impaired. There is no economic justification to repair the subject property. Nevertheless, if it were repaired, the improved property would suffer from significant market resistance due to the site's history.

Case Study 21

By Orell C. Anderson, MAI

Dahmer Apartment Building—Milwaukee, Wisconsin
Class X Detrimental Condition—Crime Scene

Jeffrey Lyle Dahmer was arrested on July 22, 1991, for suspicion of murder. Dahmer stored and consumed his victim's remains within his apartment unit. He was subsequently convicted of murder and sent to prison, where he later died in a prisoner attack.

The 24-unit apartment where he had lived and committed his crimes was owned by a private party. After the discovery of Dahmer's crimes, most of the renters in the other units quickly moved, and within a year the vacancy within the apartment building rose to 83%. Although the owner realized the building had diminished in value, he did not want to demolish it, nor did he want to discount the apartment for liquidation.

The apartment was located in a blighted urban area where the crime rate was high and drug houses and absentee landlords were common. These neighborhood conditions negatively impacted nearby Marquette University, which has an enrollment of 10,000 students. In 1991, the neighborhood became part of a revitalization program under a nonprofit organization called Campus Circle, which was in the start-up process at the time of Dahmer's arrest. Within a year of its inception, Campus Circle had acquired approximately 100 properties ranging from abandoned single-family residences to a 59-unit apartment building. By 1994, it had constructed a $35 million retail and residential development two blocks from the university, and a community-oriented police station was constructed on 21st

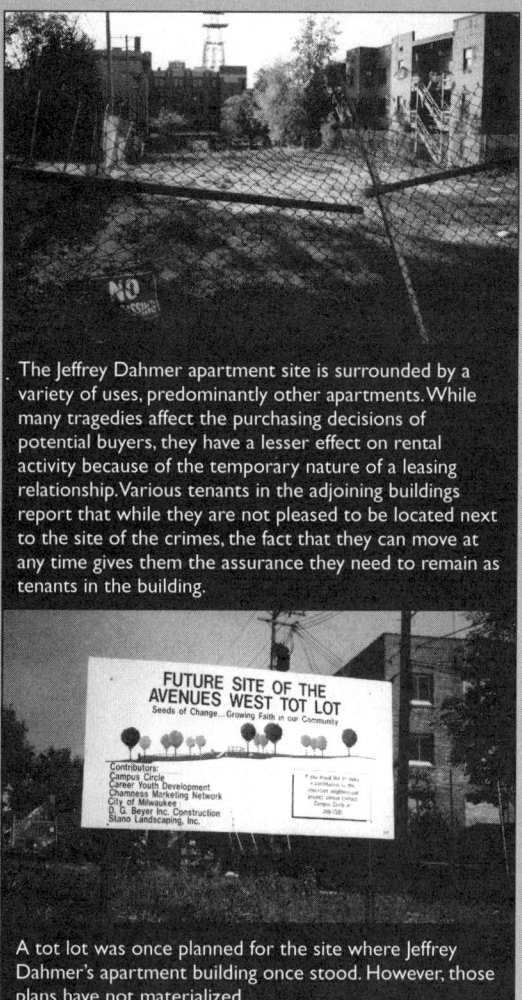

The Jeffrey Dahmer apartment site is surrounded by a variety of uses, predominantly other apartments. While many tragedies affect the purchasing decisions of potential buyers, they have a lesser effect on rental activity because of the temporary nature of a leasing relationship. Various tenants in the adjoining buildings report that while they are not pleased to be located next to the site of the crimes, the fact that they can move at any time gives them the assurance they need to remain as tenants in the building.

A tot lot was once planned for the site where Jeffrey Dahmer's apartment building once stood. However, those plans have not materialized.

Street. As a result of this redevelopment activity, the drug houses disappeared and crime rates dropped 44%. The enrollment at the university increased notably. Despite the progress made in this redevelopment activity, the apartment building where Dahmer had lived was a daily reminder to the local residents and the university of the crimes that were committed there. As would be expected, its presence had a significant negative impact upon the Campus Circle project and the university. Many members of the community, the victims' families, and Campus Circle desired to demolish the Dahmer apartment building and build a small playground.

Similar apartment buildings in the area had sold for $9,000 to $10,000 per unit. The apartment building owner was aware of the surrounding redevelopment and the special motivations of Campus Circle. It was finally sold to Campus Circle on August 7, 1992, for $325,000, or $13,500 per unit. This is reportedly $3,000 to $4,000 per unit above market rate. This premium was paid due to their major financial investment in the neighborhood and school, as well as to address the desires of the victim's families. In November 1992, the improvements were demolished. The planned "tot-lot" development had a cost of $150,000, and the city was to maintain the park. However, for various reasons the park was never started, and the site remains vacant. Current plans include the use of the site as a parking lot for the telephone company's offices across the street. There are no plans for a memorial on the site.

This situation is unusual and stands in contrast to most crime scene situations. Technically, the property sold for a premium, although it was purchased in an effort to demolish the building and thereby enhance the neighborhood. In recognizing the high vacancy rate caused by the crimes and the special motivations of the buyer to acquire the property and promptly demolish it, it is apparent that the apartment building was negatively impacted by the crime scene stigma, yet in this instance the prior owner profited from the situation.

To this day, the site is a negative reminder to the community of the tragedy. The site has apartment buildings on both sides of the vacant lot. One tenant commented that he rented his apartment without knowing about the history of the vacant lot next door, and now places a large picture in the window sill to shut off the view. Generally the tenants commented that they rent their apartment knowing that they can leave at any time. This case study illustrates that, while it is difficult to sell stigma-impacted properties, it is generally easier to rent them. It also illustrates that market resistance can have a powerful effect on property values.

APPENDIX I

Detrimental Conditions and Typical Classification

Note that the impact of detrimental conditions may vary over time and place. Any detrimental condition can be so insignificant that, upon analysis, it is ultimately a Class I. On the other hand, many conditions may be so severe that they fall into the Class X category. A proper analysis must be performed in order to determine the specific impact, if any, of a detrimental condition in a particular situation.

1. Abortion clinic (IV)
2. Absorption loss (IV)
3. Access diminution (V)
4. Accident (I-X)
5. ADA compliance (V)
6. Adverse possession (V)
7. Air and light diminution (V)
8. Air disaster (IV)
9. Airport noise (V)
10. Airport proximity (V)
11. Alteration of free trade zone (V)
12. Alteration of traffic pattern (V)
13. Anchor tenant closes and pays rents (IV)
14. Anchor tenant merges with local competitor (IV, V)
15. Ancient burial ground (V)
16. Archeological site (V)
17. Asbestos (VIII)
18. Ash from neighboring incident (IV, V, VIII)
19. Assemblage (II)
20. Atomic bomb (IV, V)
21. Auction (I)
22. Avalanche (IX)

23. Ballot initiative (IV)
24. Bankruptcy (IV)
25. Benign condition (I)
26. Black carbon from neighboring use (IV, V)
27. Blast zone (V)
28. Blight (IV, V)
29. Bombing site (IV)
30. Bond assessment (V)
31. Bond default (IV)
32. Brownfield (VIII)
33. BTEXs (VIII)

34. Build-to-suit (I)
35. Building not to code (VI)
36. Building permit expired (IV)
37. Building permit lacking (IV)
38. Business included (I)
39. Bulk sale (I)
40. Burial ashes (V)

41. Calamity (IV)
42. Carbonaceous sediment (IV, V)
43. Catastrophe (I-X)
44. Cemetery proximity (V)
45. CERCLA (VIII)
46. Chlorinated solvents (VIII)
47. Civil unrest (IV)
48. Clear title (I)
49. Collapse of building (IV)
50. Collapse of soil (VII, IX)
51. Concert noise (V)
52. Condemnation (V)
53. Conditional use permit (II, V)
54. Conditional use permit expiration (IV, V)
55. Construction defect (VI, VII)
56. Construction material or procedure change (V)
57. Construction material shortage (II, IV)
58. Construction noise (IV)
59. Construction not to code (VI, VII)
60. Contaminated public wells (VIII)
61. Contamination (VIII)
62. Contraction (V)
63. Coral in cement (VI)
64. Corporate dissolution of credit tenant (IV)
65. Covenant (V)
66. Covenant not to compete (V)
67. Cracking (VI, VII, IX)
68. Crime scene (IV)
69. Crude oil spill (VIII)
70. Cut and fill (VII)
71. Cyclone (IX)

72. Dam proximity (V)
73. Dam spillage or bursting (IV)
74. Death in property (IV)
75. Debris compost (VIII)

76. Deed restriction (V)
77. Deed restriction unenforceable (I)
78. Deferred maintenance (IV)
79. Deluge (IX)
80. Depression (III)
81. Design flaws (VI, VII)
82. Destruction of legal nonconforming use (V)
83. Differential settlement (VII)
84. Dike proximity (V)
85. Dike spillage or bursting (IV)
86. Direct condemnation (V)
87. Disaster (I-X)
88. Disease (IV)
89. Disinflation (III)
90. Disintermediation (III)
91. Distress sale (IV)
92. Double escrow (I)
93. Downzone (V)
94. Drainage (VII, IX)
95. Drought (IX)
96. Drug activity (IV)
97. Dump (VIII)
98. Dust from neighboring use (V)

99. Earthquake damage (IX)
100. Earthquake fault zone (IX)
101. Earthquake retrofit (VI, VII)
102. Easement (V)
103. Easement by necessity (V)
104. Easement by prescription (V)
105. Economic depreciation (V)
106. Economic depression (III)
107. Economic disaster (III)
108. Economic obsolescence (V)
109. Economy (III)
110. Egress diminution (V)
111. El Nino (IX)
112. Electric lines (V)
113. Electric plant (V)
114. Electromagnetic fields (V)
115. Eminent domain (V)
116. Encroachment (V)
117. Endangered species (IX)
118. Engineering standards altered (V)
119. Enterprise zone exclusion (V)
120. Entitlements expired (V)

121. Entitlements incomplete (IV)
122. Environmental contamination (VIII)
123. Environmental impact report (I-X)
124. Environmental lien (VIII)
125. ERNS list (VIII)
126. Estate sale (I)
127. Excavation collapse (VII)
128. Exercise of option (I)
129. Expansion (II)
130. Expansive soil (IX)
131. External depreciation (IV, V)
132. External obsolescence (IV, V)

133. Fault zone (IX)
134. FDIC sale (IV)
135. Feng shui (II)
136. Fill dirt (VII)
137. Fire (IV)
138. First right of refusal (I)
139. Flash floods (IX)
140. Flood damage (IX)
141. Floodplain (IX)
142. Foreclosure (IV)
143. Formaldehyde (VIII)
144. Foundation issues (VII)
145. Fractional interests (V)
146. Franchise included (IV)
147. Fraud (IV)
148. Full-take (V)
149. Functional depreciation (VI)
150. Functional obsolescence (VI)
151. Freeway noise (V)
152. Freeway relocation (V)

153. Gang activity (IV, V)
154. Garbage dump (V)
155. General plan (V)
156. Gentrification economics infeasible (IV)
157. Geotechnical issues (VII, IX)
158. Government incentives (II)
159. Government mandates (V)
160. Grading (VII)
161. Graffiti (IV)
162. Graveyard proximity (V)
163. Ground lease (V)
164. Groundwater contamination (VIII)
165. Groundwater seepage (IX)

166. Gun club proximity (V)

167. Hazardous waste (VIII)
168. Highway relocation (V)
169. Highway widening (V)
170. Historical site designation (V)
171. Homestead (V)
172. Hurricane (IX)

173. Illegal activity (IV)
174. Illegal use (IV)
175. Imposed condition (V)
176. Inadequate funding (IV)
177. Incurable condition (X)
178. Indoor air quality problem (VIII)
179. Infestation (IX)
180. Inflation (III)
181. Infrastructure incomplete (IV)
182. Ingress diminution (V)
183. Invasion (IV, V)
184. Inverse condemnation (V)

185. Jail proximity (V)
186. Judicial foreclosure (IV)

187. Kangaroo rat (IX)

188. Labor dispute (IV)
189. Land contract (I)
190. Landfill (VIII)
191. Landing pattern proximity (V)
192. Landscape damage (IV)
193. Landslide (IX)
194. Lead (VIII)
195. Lead paint (VIII)
196. Leaks (VI, VII)
197. Lease option (I)
198. Legal issues (IV)
199. Lender special motivation (II)
200. Liquefaction (IX)
201. Lis pendens (IV)
202. Litigation pending (IV)
203. Litter (IV, V)
204. Low income housing mandated (V)
205. LUST (leaking underground storage tank) (VIII)

206. Market conditions (III)
207. Mass suicide (IV)
208. Metals (VIII)
209. Military base proximity (V)
210. Monsoon (IX)
211. MRI release (IV, V)
212. MTBEs (VIII)
213. Murder site (IV)

214. National Priority List (VIII)
215. Natural condition (IX)
216. Nature preserve (V)
217. Neighborhood blight (V)
218. Neighborhood disturbance (IV, V)
219. Neighborhood nuisance (IV, V)
220. Neighboring construction (IV)
221. Non-compete clause in lease (IV, V)
222. Nonconforming use (V)
223. Nonmarket motivation (II)
224. Nuclear disaster (VIII)
225. Nuclear fallout (VIII)
226. Nuclear plant proximity (V)
227. Nuisance in area (IV, V)

228. Obstruction (IV, V)
229. Odors in area (V)
230. Oil seepage (VIII, IX)
231. Oil spill (VIII)
232. Option (I)

233. Parking monopolized (V)
234. Partial interests (V)
235. Part-take (V)
236. PCBs (VIII)
237. PCEs (VIII)
238. Petroleum spill (VIII)
239. Pipeline easement (V)
240. Pipeline explosion (IV, V)
241. Poison (VIII)
242. Poisonous gas (VIII)
243. Political uncertainty (IV)
244. Pollution (VIII)
245. Ponding (VII)
246. Poor workmanship (VI, VII)
247. Portfolio sale (IV)
248. Power lines (V)

249. Power outage (IV)
250. Power plant (V)
251. Prescriptive easement (V)
252. Prison proximity (V)
253. Probate sale (IV)
254. Protected species or vegetation (V)
255. Privacy loss (V)
256. Puddling (VII)

257. Quicksand (IX)

258. Radioactive waste (VIII)
259. Radon (VIII, IX)
260. Rail easement (V)
261. Receivership (IV)
262. Recession (III)
263. Reciprocal parking easement (V)
264. Redevelopment zone (II, V)
265. Reduction in permissible business operating hours (V)
266. Refuse disposal site (VIII)
267. Rent control (V)
268. REO (real estate owned) (IV)
269. Reputation of listing price/rate too high (IV)
270. Retaining slope (VII)
271. Retaining wall (VII)
272. Retrofit (VI)
273. Riot (IV)
274. Rodent infestation (IX)
275. Rolling option (I)
276. RTC sale (IV)

277. Sale-leaseback (I)
278. Sales arrangement at market (I)
279. Septic system malfunction (IV, VII, VIII)
280. Settlement (VII, IX)
281. Sewage discharge (VIII)
282. Sewage treatment plant proximity (V)
283. Shore wall collapse (VII)
284. Short sale (IV)
285. Short-term condition (IV)
286. Sick building syndrome (VIII)
287. Signage diminution (V)
288. Sinkhole (VII, IX)

289. Site grading (VII)
290. Slope creep (IX)
291. Slope instability (IX)
292. Soil compaction (VII)
293. Soil contamination (VIII)
294. Soils subsidence (VII, IX)
295. Solid waste disposal proximity (V)
296. Solvent contamination (VIII)
297. Soot from neighboring use (IV, V, VIII)
298. Special buyer motivation (II)
299. Special tax assessment (V)
300. Special use permit (II)
301. Specific plan amendment (V)
302. Spillage (VIII)
303. Storm (IX)
304. Street noise (V)
305. Subsidence (VII, IX)
306. Subsurface construction defect (VII)
307. Suicide on premises (IV)
308. Sulfates (IX)
309. Superfund site (VIII)
310. Super-surface construction defect (VI)
311. Supply and demand (III)
312. Surging soil (IX)

313. Takedown (III)
314. Tax assessment (V)
315. Tax lien (V)
316. TCEs (VIII)
317. Temporary condition (IV)
318. Temporary construction easement (IV)
319. Temporary easement (IV)
320. Tenant purchase (I, II)
321. Tenant relocation (IV)
322. Termites (IX)
323. Threat of condemnation (I, IV)
324. Tidal wave (IX)
325. Title dispute (IV)
326. Tornado (IX)
327. Torrent (IX)
328. Toxic contamination (VIII)
329. Toxic waste (VIII)
330. TPHs (VIII)
331. Traffic congestion (IV, V)
332. Traffic diminution (V)
333. Traffic noise (V)

334. Traffic pattern alteration (V)
335. Traffic signal installation (V)
336. Tragedy (I-X)
337. Trash dump proximity (V)
338. Treatment storage and disposal facility proximity (V)
339. Trespass (V)
340. Tsunami (IX)
341. Tunnel collapse (VII)
342. Tunneling (V)

343. U.S. Marshal sale (IV)
344. Unchlorinated solvents (VIII)
345. Unenforceable deed restriction (I)
346. Urban decay (V)
347. Utility deregulation (I)
348. Utility disruption (IV)
349. Utility easement (V)
350. Utility upgrade required (IV)

351. Vacancy problems (IV)
352. Vandalism (IV)
353. Variance (II)
354. Variance discontinued (V)
355. View diminution (V)
356. Volcano (IX)

357. War (IV)
358. Waste site (V, VIII)
359. Waste water discharge (VIII)
360. Water contamination (VIII)
361. Water intrusion (VI, VII, IX)
362. Water leaks (VI, VII)
363. Water shortage (IV)
364. Wetlands (IX)
365. Woodrot (IX)

366. X-ray release (IV)

367. Yazoo clay (IX)
368. Youth hostel proximity (V)

369. Zoning change (V)
370. Zoning variance (II)

APPENDIX 2

Americans with Disabilities Act (ADA) Overview

Congress passed the Americans with Disabilities Act (ADA) in 1990 with the objective of bringing persons with disabilities into mainstream life. The law is actually an extension of the 1964 Civil Rights Act. That law states that an employer cannot discriminate on a basis of race, color, sex, national origin, or religion. Simply stated, the ADA adds "disability" to that list. The ADA involves employment issues as well as physical building features.

The ADA Accessibility Guidelines regarding real estate are issued by the Architectural and Transportation Barriers Compliance Board, and they have been adopted by the Justice Department. The ADA affects the following places of public accommodation:

- Places of lodging: hotels, motels, inns, unless the building in which establishment is located contains no more than five rooms for rent or hire and the proprietor resides on the premises, e.g., small boarding houses.
- Establishments serving food or drinks: bars, nightclubs, restaurants, etc.
- Places of exhibition or entertainment: concert halls, movie and live theaters, stadiums, etc.
- Places of public gathering: auditoriums, convention centers, lecture halls, etc.
- Sales or rental establishments: bakeries, bookstores, car rental establishments, clothing stores, grocery stores, hardware stores, jewelry stores, pet stores, shopping centers, videotape rental stores, etc.
- Service establishments: banks, barber/beauty shops, funeral parlors, hospitals, insurance offices, laundromats, offices of lawyers, accountants and health care providers, pharmacies, travel services, etc.
- Stations used for specified public transportation: depots, terminals, etc.
- Places of public display or collection: galleries, libraries, museums, etc.
- Places of recreation: amusement parks, parks, zoos, etc.

- Places of education: colleges, nurseries, private schools, trade schools, etc.
- Social service center establishments: adoption agencies, day care centers, food banks, halfway houses, homeless shelters, rape crisis centers, senior citizen centers, substance abuse treatment centers, etc.
- Places of exercise or recreation

Summary of ADA Regulations

Space Allowance
Minimum clear width is 32 inches at a point (doorways) and 36 inches continuously. Wheelchairs to be able to pass at least every 200 feet. The width for two wheel chairs to pass is 60 inches. For turning is 60 inches.

Accessible Route
Minimum clear width of accessible route shall be 36 inches, except at doors. Maximum level change is ½ inch.

Protruding Objects
Objects, such as telephones, over 27 inches high may protrude on the accessible walkway a maximum of 4 inches.

Ground and Floor Surfaces
Changes up to ¼ inch may be vertical. From ¼ inch to ½ inch must be beveled. Gratings must have spaces no larger than ½ inch in direction of travel. Maximum carpet pile of ½ inch.

Parking and Passenger Loading Zones
Accessible parking is to be located at the shortest distance from the parking area to the accessible entrance. Accessible spaces to be designated with a sign.

Curb Ramps
Maximum slope of 1:12. Minimum width of 36 inches. If no hand rails, the curb ramp must have flared sides with a maximum slope of 1:10.

Ramps
Ramps are needed on any part of an accessible route with a slope greater than 1:20. Maximum ramp slope of 1:12. Maximum rise of 30 inches. Minimum clear width of 36 inches. If rise is greater than 6 inches, handrails are required on both sides.

Stairs
Stair tread minimum of 11 inches. Handrails required on both sides.

Elevators
Call buttons raised or flush. Up button to be on top. Minimum fully open response time is three seconds. Braille required for buttons.

Platform Lifts (Wheelchair Lifts)
Must comply with ASME Safety Code for elevators and escalators.

Windows
The ADA has reserved this category for possible further guidelines.

Doors
Minimum clear opening of 32 inches. Threshold maximum of ¾ inch for exterior sliding doors and ½ inch for other doors, and to be beveled. Hardware to not require tight grasping, twisting of wrist. Lever and push-types are acceptable.

Entrances
One to accompany each accessible route.

Drinking Fountains and Water Coolers
Spouts no higher than 36 inches. Water flow at least 4 inches high.

Water Closets
Height of seat to be 17 inches to 19 inches.

Toilet Stalls
Minimum depth of 56 inches for wall-mounted toilets. Minimum depth 59 inches for floor-mounted toilets. Grab bars to be provided.

Urinals
Rim a maximum of 17 inches above the finished floor.

Lavatories and Mirrors
Rim or counter 34 inches maximum above floor. Hot pipes and drains to be insulated. Faucets to be lever-operated, push-type, or electronic. Bottom of mirror to be a maximum of 40 inches high.

Bathtubs
In-tub seat provided. Grab bars provided. Controls that do not require twisting of wrist. A shower unit with a minimum of 60 inches of hose.

Shower Stalls
Stall to be minimum of 36 inches by 36 inches. Seat to be provided. Grab bars provided. Controls that do not require twisting of wrist.

Toilet Rooms
Provided on accessible route.

Sinks
Maximum of 34 inches to counter or rim. Knee clearance of 27 inches minimum. Sink to be 6½ inches deep maximum. Exposed hot pipes and drains to be insulated. Faucets to be lever-operated, push-type, or electronically controlled.

Storage
Fixed storage such as cabinets, shelves, closets, and drawers to have a clear floor space of 30 inches by 48 inches minimum, with maximum height of 48 inches.

Handrails, Grab Bars, and Tub and Shower Seats
Diameter of grab bar to be 1¼ inches to 1½ inches. Grab bars may not rotate in their fittings. Structural strength to meet ADA guidelines.

Controls and Operating Mechanisms
Controls, such as light switches, must be operable with one hand. Controls must not require tight grasping, pinching, or twisting of the wrist. Maximum forward reach of 48 inches. Wall-mounted electrical and communication receptacles must be at least 15 inches high.

Alarms
Audible and visual alarms to be provided.

Detectable Warnings
Warnings required at hazardous vehicular areas and reflecting pools.

Signage
Character height a minimum of 3 inches. Raised and Braille characters and pictorial signs to comply with ADA standards.

Telephones
Clear floor space of 30 inches by 48 inches minimum. Maximum height to highest operable portion of phone to be 48 inches. Push-button controls where available. Telephone handset cords to be 29 inches minimum. Hearing aid and TDD as required by the ADA.

Fixed or Built-in Seating and Tables
Knee space of 27 inches minimum. Tabletops to be 28 inches to 34 inches above finished floor or ground.

Assembly Areas
Wheelchair location requirements (area of 30 inches by 48 inches). An accessible route shall connect wheelchair seating with performing areas and dressing rooms. Seating areas to be within 50 feet of stage or playing area and have a complete view.

Automated Teller Machines
To be provided on an accessible route. Controls, clearances, reach range, and vision impairment equipment to comply with ADA standards.

Dressing and Fitting Rooms
Must allow a 180 degree wheelchair turn. Doors may not swing inward. Benches required that are 24 inches by 48 inches and 17 inches to 19 inches above the finished floor. Mirrors provided with a minimum of 18 inches wide and 54 inches high.

Special Categories
The ADA has additional specific guidelines for

- restaurants and cafeterias
- medical care facilities
- businesses and mercantile
- libraries
- accessible transient lodging
- transportation facilities

Refer to the ADA guidelines for details. This description of ADA Guidelines is to be considered to be only a brief overview of selected issues. It is not designed or intended to be comprehensive. For current and detailed information, contact the U.S. Department of Justice, Civil Rights Department, Washington, D.C. 20530, or visit the ADA home page at www.usdcj.gov/crt/ada/aadahom1.htm. The Civil Rights Deppartment may be contacted through the ADA Information Line at 202/514-0301 (voice) or 202/514-0381 (TDD) or 202/514-0383 (TDD). The ADA Accessibility Guidelines are issued by the Architectural and Transportation Barriers Compliance Board at 202/272-5434 (voice).

ADA Accessible Parking

Total Spaces	Required Minimum Number of Accessible Spaces (Spaces 96 inches wide, 60-inch access aisle)	Required Minimum Number of "Van Accessible" Spaces (96-inch access aisle)
1–25	1	1
26–50	2	1
51–75	3	1
76–100	4	1
101–150	5	1
151–200	6	1
201–300	7	1
301–400	8	1
401–500	9	1
501–1000	2% of Total	1 in Every 8 Accessible Spaces
1001+	20, +1 for Each 100 Over 1000	1 in Every 8 Accessible Spaces

Note: The designated Van Accessible spaces are not required of all the accessible spaces to comply with the Universal Parking Design. The Universal Parking Space Design has parking spaces 132 inches wide and 60-inch aisles at every other parking stall.

APPENDIX 3

Federal and State Agencies

Federal Agencies

Department of Transportation
Hazardous Materials Hotline
202/366-4488

Emergency Planning and Community
Right to Know
800/535-0202

Department of Transportation
400 Seventh Street SW
Washington, DC 20590

Office of Energy and Safety
202/366-4220

Federal Highway Administration
202/366-0650

Federal Highway Administration
Office of Environment and Planning
202/366-2951

Federal Highway Administration
Environmental Operations Division
202/366-0106

Federal Highway Administration
Environmental Analysis Division
202/366-6221

Federal Highway Administration
Office of Right of Way
202/366-0342

Federal Highway Administration
Hazardous Materials Programs
Division
202/366-6121

Department of Transportation
2100 Second Street SW
Washington, DC 20593

Office of Safety and Environment
202/267-1883

Office of Marine Technology and
Hazardous Materials
202/267-2967

Marine Environmental Protection
Division
202/267-2767

Department of Transportation
800 Independence Avenue SW
Washington DC 20593

    Federal Aviation Department
    202/267-3576

Environmental Protection Agency (EPA)

    EPA Public Information Center
    202/260-2080

    RCRA/Superfund/UST Hotline
    800/424-9346

    Safe Drinking Water Hotline
    800/426-4791

Mail Drop 12
Research Triangle Park, NC 27711

    Air Act Hotline
    Clean Air Technology
    919/541-0800

    Air RISC Hotline
    Air Risk Information Support Center
    919/541-0888

EPA—Region 1
1 Congress Street, Suite 1100
Boston, MA 02114-2023

    Region 1 Headquarters
    617/918-1111

    Air Toxics
    617/918-1656

    Waste Management Division
    RCRA Bureau
    617/573-5770

    Waste Management Division
    Superfund I
    617/573-9610

    Waste Management Division
    Superfund II
    617/573-9650

    Water Management Division
    Water Compliance Bureau
    617/565-3493

    Water Management Division
    Waste Water Management Bureau
    617/565-3560

    Water Management Division
    Water Quality Branch
    617/565-3531

    Water Management Division
    Groundwater Management and Water Supply
    617/565-3531

EPA—Region 1
60 Westview Street
Lexington, MA 02173

    Environmental Services Division
    Emergency Planning and Response
    617/860-4368

    Environmental Services Division
    Technical Support Bureau
    617/860-4368

    Environmental Services Division
    Oil and Hazardous Waste Materials Hotline
    617/860-4368

EPA—Region 2
290 Broadway
New York, NY 10007

    Region 2 Headquarters
    212/637-3000

    Office of Regional Council
    New York/Carribbean Superfund Bureau
    212/637-3152

    Office of Regional Counsel
    New Jersey Superfund Branch
    212/637-3118

    Office of Regional Counsel
    Air/Waste/Toxic Sub Branch
    212/637-3196

    Office of Regional Counsel
    Water/Grants/General Law
    212/637-3225

Air and Waste Management Division
Hazardous Solids Waste Programs
Bureau
212/637-4126

Air and Waste Management Division
Hazardous Waste Compliance Bureau
212/637-4144

Air and Waste Management Division
Hazardous Waste Facilities Branch
212/637-4109

Air and Waste Management Division
Air Compliance Branch
212/637-4080

Air and Waste Management Division
Air Programs Branch
212/637-3951

Water Management Division
Water Permits/Compliance Branch
212/637-3767

Water Management Division
Marine/Wetlands Protection Branch
212/637-3779

Water Management Division
Surface Water Quality Branch
212/637-3705

Water Management Division
Drinking Groundwater Protection
Branch
212/637-3880

Emergency and Remedial Response
Division
New York Caribbean Programs
212/637-4261

Emergency and Remedial Response
Division
New Jersey Superfund Branch I
212/637-4480

Emergency and Remedial Response
Division
New Jersey Superfund Branch II
212/637-4418

Emergency and Remedial Response
Division
New York Caribbean Superfund
Branch I
212/637-4262

Emergency and Remedial Response
Division
New York Caribbean Superfund
Branch II
212/637-4285

EPA—Region 2
Woodbridge Avenue
Edison, NJ 08837

Emergency and Remedial Response
Division
Removal Action Branch
908/321-6621

Environmental Services Division
Pesticides/Toxics Sub Branch
908/321-6765

Environmental Services Division
Technical Support Branch
908/321-6706

EPA—Region 3
841 Chestnut Building
Philadelphia, PA 19107

Region 3 Headquarters
215/597-9800

Water Management Division
Drinking/Groundwater
215/597-8911

Water Management Division
Permits Enforcement Branch
215/597-6511

Water Management Division
Municipal Wastewater Construction
Grants
215/597-9966

Hazardous Waste Management
Division
Superfund Programs Branch
215/597-9401

Hazardous Waste Management Division
Superfund Pennsylvania Remediation Branch
215/597-8334

Hazardous Waste Management Division
RCRA
215/597-6632

Hazardous Waste Management Division
RCRA Programs Branch
215/597-9401

Hazardous Waste Management Division
RCRA Enforcement/Underground Storage Tanks
215/597-8125

Hazardous Waste Management Division
Superfund Removal Branch
215/597-0992

Air, Radiation, and Toxics Division
Air Programs Branch
215/597-9075

Air, Radiation, and Toxics Division
Air Enforcement Branch
215/597-3989

Air, Radiation, and Toxics Division
Toxics and Pesticides Branch
215/597-8598

Environmental Services Division
Environmental Assessment Branch
215/597-1181

EPA—Region 4
345 Courtland Street NE
Atlanta, GA 30365

Region 4 Headquarters
404/347-4727

Water Management Division
Municipal Facilities Branch
404/347-2207

Water Management Division
Groundwater Protection Branch
404/347-3379

Water Management Division
Water Permits and Enforcement Branch
404/347-2019

Water Management Division
Groundwater and Facilities Branch
404/347-4450

Water Management Division
Wetlands, Oceans, and Watersheds Branch
404/347-3379

Waste Management Division
North Superfund Remediation Branch
404/347-7791

Waste Management Division
South Superfund Remediation Branch
404/347-2643

Waste Management Division
Waste Programs Branch
404/347-5059

Waste Management Division
RCRA/Federal Facilities Branch
404/347-3016

Waste Management Division
Office of Municipal Solid Wastes
404/347-2091

Waste Management Division
RCRA Permit/Compliance Branch
404/347-3433

Waste Management Division
Emergency Response/Removal
404/347-3931

Air, Pesticides, and Toxics Division
Air Programs Branch
404/347-2864

Waste Management Division
Air Enforcement
404/347-2904

Waste Management Division
Pest/Toxic Substances Branch
404/347-5201

EPA—Region 4
960 College Station Road
Athens, GA 30605

  Environmental Services Division
  Environmental Compliance Branch
  706/546-3118

  Environmental Services Division
  Ecological Support Branch
  706/546-2294

EPA—Region 5
77 West Jackson Boulevard
Chicago, IL 60604

  Region 5 Headquarters
  312/353-2000

  Great Lakes National Program Office
  Remedial Program Staff
  312/353-3576

  Great Lakes National Program Office
  Surveillance/Research Staff
  312/353-3612

  Regional Counsels
  Air/Water/Toxics/General Law
  312/886-0703

  Regional Counsels
  Solid Waste/Emergency Response
  312/886-0556

  Air and Radiation Division
  Air Enforcement Branch
  312/353-2088

  Air and Radiation Division
  Air, Toxics, and Radiation Branch
  312/353-8559

  Environmental Services Division
  Pest/Toxic Substances Branch
  312/886-6018

  Environmental Services Division
  Monitoring/Quality Assurance Branch
  312/353-2306

  Waste Management Division
  Office of Superfund
  312/353-9773

  Water Division
  Water Quality Branch
  312/353-2079

  Water Division
  Water Compliance Branch
  312/353-2121

  Water Division
  Safe Drinking Water Branch
  312/353-2151

  Water Division
  Water Protection Branch
  312/886-1490

EPA—Region 6
1445 Ross Avenue
Dallas, TX 75202

  Region 6 Headquarters
  214/665-6444

  Hazardous Waste Management
  Division
  RCRA Enforcement Branch
  214/665-6726

  Hazardous Waste Management
  Division
  RCRA Programs Branch
  214/665-6656

  Hazardous Waste Management
  Division
  Superfund Management Branch
  214/665-2241

  Hazardous Waste Management
  Division
  RCRA Permits Branch
  214/665-6770

  Hazardous Waste Management
  Division
  Superfund Programs Branch
  214/665-6664

  Air, Pesticides, and Toxics Division
  Air Programs Branch
  214/665-7205

  Air, Pesticides, and Toxics Division
  Air Enforcement Branch
  214/665-7220

Air, Pesticides, and Toxics Division
Pesticides and Toxics Branch
214/665-7235

Environmental Services Division
Emergency Response Branch
214/665-2270

Environmental Services Division
Emergency Response Branch/24-Hour Hotline
214/665-2222

Environmental Services Division
Quality Assurance
214/665-2217

Environmental Services Division
Surveillance Branch
214/665-2284

Water Management Division
Enforcement Branch
214/665-6468

Water Management Division
Municipal Facilities Branch
214/665-7110

Water Management Division
Permits Branch
214/665-7170

Water Management Division
Water Quality Branch
214/665-7135

Water Management Division
Water Supply Branch
214/665-7150

Water Management Division
Criminal Investigation Division
214/665-6600

EPA—Region 7
726 Minnesota Avenue
Kansas City, KS 66101

Region 7 Headquarters
913/551-7000

Regional Counsel
Air/Water/Toxics/General Law
913/551-7010

Regional Counsel
Hazardous Waste/RCRA Emphasis
913/551-7010

Regional Counsel
Hazardous Waste/CERCLA Branch
913/551-7010

Air and Toxics Division
Air Branch
913/551-7020

Air and Toxics Division
Toxics/Pesticides Branch
913/551-7020

Waste Management Division
RCRA Branch
913/551-7051

Waste Management Division
Superfund Branch
913/551-7052

Water Management Division
Drinking Water Branch
913/551-7032

Waste Management Division
Groundwater Protection
913/551-7033

Waste Management Division
Water Compliance Branch
913/551-7034

Waste Management Division
Criminal Investigation Division
913/551-7060

Waste Management Division
RCRA Branch
913/551-7051

EPA—Region 7
25 Funston Road
Kansas City, KS 66115

Environmental Services Division
Emergency Planning and Response
913/551-5064

Environmental Services Division
Support Branch
913/551-5183

Environmental Services Division
Environmental Monitoring/Compliance Branch
913/551-5002

EPA—Region 8
999 18th Street
Denver, CO 80202

Region 8 Headquarters
303/293-1603

Hazardous Waste Management Division
Superfund Remedial Branch
303/294-7630

Hazardous Waste Management Division
RCRA Implementation Branch
303/293-1663

Hazardous Waste Management Division
RCRA Management Branch
303/293-1513

Hazardous Waste Management Division
Emergency Response Branch
303/294-7129

Hazardous Waste Management Division
Superfund Management Branch
303/293-1293

Air and Toxics Division
Air and Technical Operations Branch
303/293-1750

Air and Toxics Division
Radiation Indoor Air Programs Branch
303/293-1440

Water Management Division
Drinking Water Branch
303/293-1652

Water Management Division
Environmental Assessment Branch
303/293-1701

Water Management Division
Groundwater Branch
303/293-1164

Water Management Division
Municipal Facilities Branch
303/293-1545

Water Management Division
Water Quality Branch
303/293-1565

EPA—Region 9
75 Hawthorne Street
San Francisco, CA 94105

Region 9 Headquarters
415/744-1305

Air Toxics Division
Air Planning Branch
415/744-1210

Air Toxics Division
Stationary Source Branch
415/744-2140

Air Toxics Division
Air Compliance Branch
415/744-1198

Air Toxics Division
Pesticide/Toxic Branch
415/744-1090

Hazardous Waste Management Division
Facilities Branch
415/744-2138

Hazardous Waste Management Division
Waste Compliance Branch
415/744-2120

Hazardous Waste Management Division
RCRA Programs Branch
415/744-2090

Hazardous Waste Management Division
Superfund Remedial Action Branch
415/744-2261

Hazardous Waste Management
Division
Superfund Enforcement Branch
415/744-2421

Water Management Division
Watershed Protection Branch
415/744-1953

Water Management Division
Permits and Compliance Branch
415/744-2001

Water Management Division
Drinking Water Protection Branch
415/744-1870

EPA—Region 10
1200 Sixth Avenue
Seattle, WA 98101

Region 10 Headquarters
206/553-1200

Water Division
Drinking Water/Groundwater Branch
206/553-4092

Water Division
Surface Water Branch
206/553-0966

Water Division
Waste Water Management/Enforcement Branch
206/553-1728

Environmental Services Division
Risk Evaluation Branch
206/553-1597

Environmental Services Division
Investigation and Technical Evaluation Branch
206/553-1567

Air and Toxics Division
Air and Radiation Branch
206/553-1152

Air and Toxics Division
Pesticides and Toxics Substances Branch
206/553-1198

Hazardous Waste Division
Program Management Branch
206/553-1088

Hazardous Waste Division
Waste Management Branch
206/553-7151

Hazardous Waste Division
Superfund Remediation Branch
206/553-7151

Hazardous Waste Division
Superfund Response/Investigation Branch
206/553-1677

Department of Labor
Occupational Safety and Health Administration
OSHA Information
202/693-4999

OSHA—Region 1
(CT, MA, ME, NH, RI, VT)
JFK Federal Building, Room E340
Boston, MA 02203
617/565-9860

OSHA—Region 2
(NJ, NY, Puerto Rico, Virgin Islands)
201 Varick Street, Room 670
New York, NY 10014
212/337-2378

OSHA—Region 3
(DC, DE, MD, PA, VA, WV)
Gateway Building, Suite 2100
3535 Market Street
Philadelphia, PA 19104
215/596-1201

OSHA—Region 4
(AL, FL, GA, KY, MS, NC, SC, TN)
61 Forsyth Street SW
Atlanta, GA 303033
404/562-2300

OSHA—Region 5
(IL, IN, MI, OH, WI)
230 South Dearborn Street
32nd Floor, Room 3244
Chicago, IL 60604
312/353-2220

OSHA—Region 6
(AR, LA, NM, OK, TX)
555 Griffin Street, Room 602
Dallas, TX 75202
214/767-4731

OSHA—Region 7
(IA, KS, MO, NE)
City Center Square
1100 Main Street, Suite 800
Kansas City, MO 64105
816/426-5861

OSHA—Region 8
(CO, MT, ND, SD, UT, WY)
1999 Broadway, Suite 1690
Denver, CO 80202-5716
303/844-1600

OSHA—Region 9
(American Samoa, AZ, CA, Guam, HI, HV, Pacific Trust Territories)
71 Stevenson Street, Room 420
San Francisco, CA 94105
415/975-4310

OSHA—Region 10
(AK, ID, OR, WA)
111 Third Avenue, Suite 715
Seattle, WA 98101-3212
206/553-5930

Department of Housing and Urban Development (HUD)
Office of Single Family Housing and Mortgage Activities
451 Seventh Street SW, Room 9282
Washington, DC 20410
202/708-3175

U.S. Environmental Protection Agency
Water Mall
401 M Street SW
Washington, DC 20460

Public Information Center
Room W385
202/260-4048

Environmental Protection Agency
202/260-2090

Small Business and Asbestos Ombudsman
800/424-9300

TSCA Hotline
Office of Pollution Prevention and Toxics
202/554-1404

Office of Enforcement and Compliance Assurance
Office of Compliance
Water Mall
401 M Street SW
Washington, DC 20460

Agriculture and Ecosystem
202/564-2320

Chemical, Commercial Services, and Municipal Division
202/564-2310

Office of Enforcement and Compliance Assurance
Office of Criminal Enforcement
Water Mall
401 M Street SW
Washington, DC 20460

Criminal Enforcement Counsel Division
202/260-9660

Criminal Investigations Division
202/260-5262

Office of Enforcement and Compliance Assurance
Office of Regulatory Enforcement
Water Mall
401 M Street SW
Washington, DC 20460

Air Enforcement Division—Air Toxics
202/564-2285

Air Enforcement Division—Mobile Source
202/564-2255

Air Enforcement Division—SIPS-NSPS-Acid Rain
202/564-2275

RCRA Enforcement Division—Waste Identification and Enforcement
202/564-4002

RCRA Enforcement Division—Waste Management Branch
202/564-4001

Toxics and Pesticides Enforcement Division
202/564-2325

Water Enforcement Division—Industrial Branch
202/564-2245

Water Enforcement Division—Municipal Branch
202/564-2205

Office of Enforcement and Compliance Assurance
Office of Site Remediation Enforcement
Water Mall
401 M Street SW
Washington, DC 20460

Headquarters
202/564-5110

Policy and Program Evaluation Division
202/564-5100

Regional Support Division
202/564-4302

Department of Policy, Planning, and Evaluation
Water Mall
401 M Street SW
Washington, DC 20460

Office of Strategic Planning and Environmental Data
Environmental Statistics and Information Division
202/260-2680

Office of Policy Analysis
Waste and Chemical Policy Division
Toxic and Pollution Policy
202/260-8661

Office of Policy Analysis
Waste and Chemical Policy Division
Pesticide Policy
202/260-7570

Office of Policy Analysis
Waste and Chemical Policy Division
Waste Policy Branch
202/260-2750

Office of Policy Analysis
Water and Agriculture Policy Division
Agriculture Policy
202/260-2753

Office of Policy Analysis
Water and Agriculture Policy Division
Water Policy
202/260-2756

Office of Policy Analysis
Air and Energy Policy Division
Air Policy
202/260-2771

Office of Policy Analysis
Air and Energy Policy Division
Energy Policy
202/260-5492

Office of Water
Office of Groundwater and Drinking Water
401 M Street SW
Washington, DC 20460

Drinking Water Standards Division
Drinking Water Technical Branch
202/260-3022

Drinking Water Implementation Division
Drinking Water Branch
202/260-5526

Groundwater Protection Division
Groundwater Resources Protection
202/260-1894

Office of Water
Office of Wastewater Management
401 M Street SW
Washington, DC 20460

Municipal Support Division
202/260-5859

Office of Water
Office of Wetlands, Oceans, and Watersheds
401 M Street SW
Washington, DC 20460

Assessment and Watershed Protection Division
Monitoring Branch
202/260-7046

Assessment and Watershed Protection Division
Nonpoint Source Control
202/260-7100

Assessment and Watershed Protection Division
Watershed
202/260-7074

Oceans and Coastal Protection Division
Coastal Management Branch
202/260-6502

Oceans and Coastal Protection Division
Marine Pollution Control Branch
202/260-6502

Wetlands Division
Wetlands/Aquatic Resources
202/260-1799

Office of Solid Waste and Emergency Response
401 M Street SW
Washington, DC 20460

Office of Emergency and Remedial Response (Superfund)
703/603-8960

Office of Program Management
Emergency Response Division
703/603-8760

Office of Program Management
Hazardous Site Control Division
703/603-8800

Office of Program Management
Hazardous Site Evaluation Division
703/603-8850

Office of Solid Waste
Municipal and Industrial Solid Waste Division
703/308-8254

Office of Solid Waste
Waste Management Division
703/308-8254

Office of Underground Storage Tanks
703/308-8850

U.S. Coast Guard
National Response Center Hotline
800/424-8802

State Agencies

Alabama
Department of Environmental Management
1751 Congressman W. L. Dickinson Drive
Montgomery, AL 36130

Air Quality
334/271-7861

Emergency Response Commission
334/271-7700

Environmental Protection
334/271-7700

Hazardous Waste
334/271-7700

Solid Waste Management
334/271-7761

Underground Storage Tanks
Leaking Underground Storage Tanks
334/271-7700

Waste Minimization and Pollution Prevention
334/271-7700

Water Quality
334/271-7826

**Coastal Zone Management
Water Division**
2204 Perimeter Road
Mobile, AL 36615-1131
334/450-3400

Department of Conservation and Natural Resources
64 North Union Street, Room 567
Montgomery, AL 36130

Fish and Wildlife
334/242-3465

Natural Resources
334/242-3486

**Department of Labor
Occupational Safety**
100 North Union Street
Suite 620
Montgomery, AL 36130
334/242-3460

**Department of Agriculture and Industries
Pesticide Registration**
P.O. Box 3336
1445 Federal Drive
Montgomery, AL 36109
334/240-7171

**Department of Environmental Management
State Used Oil Recycling**
P.O. Box 870203
Tuscaloosa, AL 35487-0203

**Department of Environmental Management
State Waste Reduction Program**
University of Alabama
P.O. Box 6373
Tuscaloosa, AL 35487-6373

Alaska
Department of Environmental Conservation
410 Willoughby Avenue
Suite 105
Juneau, AK 99801-1795

Air Quality
907/465-5103

Coastal Zone Management
907/465-5010

Emergency Preparedness and Community Right-to-Know
800/478-2337

Environmental Protection
907/465-5010

Solid Waste Management
907/465-5162

Underground Storage Tanks
Leaking Underground Storage Tanks
907/465-5200

State Recycling
907/465-5010

State Used Oil Recycling
907/465-5010

Water Quality
907/465-5308

Pesticide Services
500 South Alaska Street
Palmer, AK 99645
907/745-3236

Watershed Development
610 University Avenue
Fairbanks, AK 99709-3643
907/451-2101

Department of Fish and Game
Fish and Wildlife
P.O. Box 25526
Juneau, AK 99802-5526
907/465-4100

Department of Natural Resources
Natural Resources
400 Willoughby Avenue
Fifth Floor
Juneau, AK 99801
907/465-2400

Department of Labor
Occupational Safety
P.O. Box 21149
Juneau, AK 99802-1149
907/465-4855

Department of Environmental Conservation
555 Cordova Street
Anchorage, AK 99501

> Compliance Assistance Office
> 907/269-7586
>
> Hazardous Waste and Pollution Prevention
> 907/269-7586
>
> Drinking Water and Wastewater
> 907/269-7647

Arizona
Department of Environmental Quality
3033 North Central Avenue
Phoenix, AZ 85012

> Air Quality
> 602/207-2308
>
> Environmental Protection
> 602/207-2300
>
> Statewide Watershed Approach
> 602/207-4582
>
> State Recycling
> 602/207-4133
>
> State Used Oil Recycling
> 602/207-4140
>
> Solid Waste Management
> 602/207-4117
>
> Underground Storage Tanks
> Leaking Underground Storage Tanks
> 602/207-4345
>
> Water Quality
> 602/207-4630
>
> Pollution Prevention
> 602/207-4235

Department of Emergency Management
Emergency Preparedness and Community Right-to-Know
5636 East McDowell Road
Phoenix, AZ 85008
602/244-0504

Department of Game and Fish
2221 West Greenway Road
Phoenix, AZ 85023-4399
602/942-3000

State Land Department
Natural Resources
1616 West Adams
Phoenix, AZ 85007
602/542-4626

Industrial Commission of Arizona
Occupational Safety
800 West Washington
Phoenix, AZ 85007
602/542-4411

Arizona Department of Agriculture
Pesticide Registration
1688 West Adams
Phoenix, AZ 85007
602/542-4373

Arkansas
Department of Environmental Quality
8001 National Drive
P.O. Box 8913
Little Rock, AR 72209-8913

> Air Quality
> 501/682-0730

Emergency Preparedness and Community Right-to-Know
501/682-0716

Environmental Preservation
501/682-0019

Hazardous Waste Management
501/682-0833

Solid Waste Management
501/682-0600

Underground Storage Tanks
Leaking Underground Storage Tanks
501/682-0999

State Recycling
501/682-0812

State Used Oil Recycling
501/682-0744

Water Quality
501/682-0660

Department of Labor
Occupational Safety
10421 West Markham
Little Rock, AR 72202
501/682-9091

Game and Fish Commission
Fish and Wildlife
#2 Natural Resources Drive
Little Rock, AR 72205
800/364-4263

Department of Arkansas Heritage
Natural Heritage
1500 Tower Building
323 Center Street
Little Rock, AR 72201
501/324-9619

State Plant Board
Pesticide Registration
One Natural Resources Drive
Little Rock, AR 72205
501/225-1598

Pollution Control and Ecology Commission
One State Capitol Mall
Little Rock, AR 72201
501/682-7890

California
California Environmental Protection Agency
Headquarters
555 Capitol Mall
Sacramento, CA 95814
916/445-3846

Air Resources Board
P.O. Box 2815
Sacramento, CA 95812
916/445-3745

Office of Emergency Services
2800 Meadowview Road
Sacramento, CA 95832

Emergency Preparedness and Community Right-to-Know
916/464-3230

Chemical Emergency Planning and Response
916/464-3230

**California Environmental Protection Agency
Department of Toxic Substances Control**
400 P Street
P.O. Box 806
Sacramento, CA 95812

Hazardous Waste Management
916/324-7193

State Waste Reduction Program
916/324-1815

1416 Ninth Street, Room 1320
Sacramento, CA 95814

Resources Agency
Natural Resources
916/653-5656

Department of Fish and Game
Fish and Wildlife
916/653-7664

Department of Industrial Relations
Occupational Safety
45 Fremont Street, Room 1200
San Francisco, CA 94105
415/972-8500

Department of Pesticide Regulations
Pesticide Registration
830 K Street
Sacramento, CA 95814-3510
916/445-4400

Integrated Waste Management Board
8800 California Center Drive
Sacramento, CA 95826

    Solid Waste Management
    916/255-2341

    State Used Oil Recycling
    916/255-2891

Water Resources Control Board
Underground Storage Tanks
Leaking Underground Storage Tanks
P.O. Box 944212
Sacramento, CA 94244-2120
800/999-8844

California Environmental Protection Agency Department of Toxic Substances Control
Waste Minimization and Pollution Prevention
P.O. Box 806
Sacramento, CA 95812-0806
916/322-8322

Department of Conservation
State Recycling
801 K Street, MS 20-50
Sacramento, CA 95814
916/323-5778

Water Resources Control Board
Water Quality
901 P Street
Sacramento, CA 95814
916/657-1247

Colorado
Department of Public Health and Environment
4300 Cherry Creek Drive S
Denver, CO 80246-1530

    Air Quality
    303/692-3190

    Emergency Preparedness and Community Right-to-Know
    303/692-3020

    Hazardous Waste Management
    303/692-3320

    Pollution Prevention
    303/692-3028

    State Recycling
    303/692-3017

    State Used Oil Recycling
    303/692-3300

    Solid Waste Management
    303/692-3445

    Water Quality
    303/692-3584

Environmental Protection Info Center
999 18th Street
Denver, CO 80202
303/312-6312

Department of Natural Resources
Fish and Wildlife
6060 Broadway
Denver, CO 80216
303/692-1192

Department of Natural Resources
Natural Resources
1313 Sherman Street
Room 718
Denver, CO 80203
303/866-3311

Department of Agriculture
Pesticide Registration
700 Kipling Street
Suite 4000
Lakewood, CO 80215-5894
303/239-4100

Colorado State Oil Inspection Office
Underground Storage Tanks
Leaking Underground Storage Tanks
1515 Arapahoe Street
Tower 3, Suite 610
Denver, CO 80202-2117
303/620-4300

Connecticut
Department of Environmental Protection
79 Elm Street
Hartford, CT 06106-5127

   Air Quality
   860/424-3027

   Coastal Zone Management
   860/424-3034

   Emergency Preparedness and Community Right-to-Know
   860/424-3001

   Emergency Response Commission Right-to-Know Program
   860/424-3373

   Environmental Protection
   860/424-3002

   Fish and Wildlife
   860/424-3011

   Groundwater Management
   860/424-3705

   Hazardous Waste Management
   860/424-3375

   Natural Resources
   860/424-3010

   Pesticide Registration
   860/424-3000

   Solid Waste Management
   860/424-3666

   Underground Storage Tanks
   Leaking Underground Storage Tanks
   860/424-3376

   Waste Minimization and Pollution Prevention
   860/424-3297

   State Recycling
   860/424-3000

   Used Oil Recycling
   860/424-3000

   Water Quality
   860/424-3704

Department of Labor
Occupational Safety
38 Wolcott Hill Road
Wethersfield, CT 06109
860/566-4550

Hazardous Waste Management Service
State Waste Reduction Program
50 Columbus Boulevard
Fourth Floor
Hartford, CT 06106
860/244-2007

Delaware
Department of Natural Resources and Environmental Control
Richardson and Robbins Building
89 Kings Highway
Dover, DE 19903-1401

   Air Quality
   302/739-4542

   Coastal Zone Management
   302/739-3451

   Air and Waste Management
   302/739-4764

   Environmental Protection
   302/739-5072

   Fish and Wildlife
   302/739-5295

   Groundwater Management
   302/739-6330

Hazardous Waste Management
302/739-3689

Natural Resources
302/739-4403

Pollution Prevention
302/739-4506

State Recycling
302/739-5361

Solid Waste Management
302/739-3820

Water Quality
302/739-6330

Department of Public Safety
Emergency Preparedness and Community Right-to-Know
P.O. Box 527
Delaware City, DE 19706
302/326-6000

Department of Agriculture
Pesticide Registration
2320 South Dupont Highway
Dover, DE 19901
302/739-4811

Facilities Management
Used Oil Recycling
Margaret O'Neill Building
Dover, DE 19903-1401
302/739-5305

District of Columbia
Department of Consumer and Regulatory Affairs
941 North Capitol Street NE
Washington, DC 20460

Air Quality
202/260-5575

Environmental Protection
202/260-2090

Fish and Wildlife
202/260-2090

Groundwater Management
202/260-2090

Hazardous Waste Management
202/260-2090

Natural Resources
202/654-6617

Pesticide Registration
202/654-6080

Water Quality
202/566-7301

Emergency Management Agency
Emergency Preparedness and Community Right-to-Know
2000 14th Street NW
Frank Reeves Center for Municipal Affairs
Washington, DC 20009
202/727-6161

Department of Employment Services
Occupational Safety and Health
950 Upshur Street NW
Washington, DC 20011
202/576-6339

Office of Waste Reduction
Pollution Prevention
Office of Industrial Technology
Washington, DC 20585
202/962-8696

2750 South Capitol Street SE
Washington, DC 20032

Office of Recycling
State Recycling
202/727-5887

Department of Energy
Used Oil Recycling
202/727-5856

Department of Consumer and Regulatory Affairs
Underground Storage Tanks
Leaking Underground Storage Tanks
1235 Jefferson Davis Highway
Arlington, VA 22202
703/603-9900

Florida
Department of Environmental Protection
Air Quality
111 South Magnolia
Suite 23
Tallahassee, FL 32301
850/488-0114

Department of Community Affairs
Emergency Preparedness and Community Right-to-Know
2555 Shumard Oak Boulevard
Tallahassee, FL 32399
850/413-9910
800/635-7179 (in FL)

Department of Environmental Protection
3900 Commonwealth Boulevard
Tallahassee, FL 32399-3000

Environmental Protection
850/488-1554

Hazardous Waste Management
850/488-0300

Natural Resources
850/488-1554

Pollution Prevention
850/488-0300

Recycling
850/488-0300

Used Oil Recycling
850/488-0300

Solid Waste Management
850/488-0300

Water Quality
850/488-0780

2600 Blair Stone Road, MS 4525
Tallahassee, FL 32399-2400

Storage Tank Regulation Section
Underground Storage Tanks
Leaking Underground Storage Tanks
850/488-3935

Department of Environmental Protection
Groundwater Management
850/921-9428

Game and Fresh Water Fish Commission
Fish and Wildlife
620 South Meridian Street
Tallahassee, FL 32399-1600
850/488-2975

Department of Agriculture
Pesticide Registration
3125 Conner Boulevard
Tallahassee, FL 32399-1650
850/488-3731

Georgia
Department of Natural Resources
205 Butler Street SW
Atlanta, GA 30334

Air Quality
404/363-7006

Coastal Zone Management
404/656-4713

Environmental Protection
404/656-4713

Natural Resources
404/656-3500

Solid Waste Management
404/362-2692

Groundwater Management
404/656-2750

Water Quality
404/656-4905

Emergency Preparedness and Community Right-to-Know
404/656-6300
800/241-4113

State Used Oil Recycling
404/656-4713

Hazardous Waste Management
404/656-7802

Department of Natural Resources
Fish and Wildlife
2070 U.S. Highway 278 SE
Social Circle, GA 30025
770/918-6400

Department of Labor
Occupational Safety
148 International Boulevard, #600
Atlanta, GA 30303
404/656-3017

Department of Agriculture
Pesticide Registration
19 Martin Luther King Jr. Drive, Room 550
Atlanta, GA 30334
404/656-9378

Department of Community Affairs
State Recycling
60 Executive Park South NE
Atlanta, GA 30329-2231
404/679-4950

Department of Natural Resources
State Reduction Program
151 Sixth Street
O'Keefe Building, Room 027
Atlanta, GA 30332
404/894-3806

Department of Natural Resources
Underground Storage Tanks
Leaking Underground Storage Tanks
4244 International Parkway, #100
Atlanta, GA 30354
404/362-2687

Environmental Protection Department
Waste Minimization and Pollution Prevention
Georgia Institute of Technology
151 Sixth Street
O'Keefe Building, Room 143
Atlanta, GA 30332
404/894-3806

Hawaii
Department of Health
919 Ala Moana Boulevard
Honolulu, HI 96814

Air Quality
Room 203
808/586-4200

Hazardous Waste Management
Room 212
808/586-4226

Pollution Prevention
Room 312
808/586-4337

State Used Oil Recycling
808/586-4224

Solid Waste Management
Room 212
808/586-4226

Underground Storage Tanks
Leaking Underground Storage Tanks
808/586-4225

Emergency Preparedness and Community Right-to-Know
808/586-4249

Department of Land and Natural Resources
1151 Punchbowl Street
Honolulu, HI 96813

Fish and Wildlife
Room 325
808/587-0166

Groundwater Management
Room 227
808/587-0214

Natural Resources
Room 311
808/587-0077

Labor and Industrial Relations Department
Occupational Safety
830 Punchbowl Street
Room 423
Honolulu, HI 96813
808/586-9100

Office of Environmental Quality Control
Environmental Protection
235 South Beretania Street, #702
Honolulu, HI 96813
808/586-4424

Department of Agriculture
Pesticide Registration
1428 South King Street
Honolulu, HI 96814-2512
808/973-9535

Department of Land and Natural Resources
State Recycling
Recycling Association of Hawaii
808/RECYCLE

Idaho
Department of Health and Welfare
Division of Environmental Quality
1410 North Hilton
Boise, ID 83706

Air Quality
208/373-0502

Environmental Protection
208/373-0502

Groundwater Management
208/373-0502

Hazardous Waste Management
208/337-0502

Pollution Prevention
208/334-5500

Solid Waste Management
208/334-0502

State Recycling
208/334-0502

State Used Oil Recycling
208/334-6558

Underground Storage Tanks
Leaking Underground Storage Tanks
208/334-0502

Water Quality
208/334-0502

Department of Health and Welfare
Emergency Preparedness and Community Right-to-Know
4040 Guard Street
Building 600
Boise, ID 83705
208/334-3263

Department of Fish and Game
Fish and Wildlife
600 South Walnut Street
P.O. Box 25
Boise, ID 83707
800/635-7820

Labor and Industrial Services Department
Occupational Safety
317 Main Street
Boise, ID 83735
208/334-6100

Department of Agriculture
Pesticide Registration
P.O. Box 790
Boise, ID 83701
208/332-8500

Illinois
Illinois Environmental Protection Agency
2200 Churchill Road
Springfield, IL 62794

Air Quality
217/782-7326

Coastal Zone Management
217/782-1654

Office of Emergency Management
217/782-3397

Environmental Protection
217/782-3397

Leaking Underground Storage Tanks
217/782-6762

State Recycling
217/785-2800

State Used Oil Recycling
217/782-2984

Groundwater Management
217/785-4787

Department of Natural Resources
Water Quality
P.O. Box 19276
1021 North Grand Avenue E
Springfield, IL 62794-9276
217/782-1654

Emergency Management Agency
Emergency Preparedness and Community Right-to-Know
110 East Adams Street
Springfield, IL 62701-1109
217/524-1008

Department of Natural Resources
524 South Second Street
Springfield, IL 62701

Fish and Wildlife
217/785-8287

Natural Resources
217/782-6302

1 East Hazelwood Drive
Champaign, IL 61821

Environmental Protection Agency Hazardous Waste Management
217/333-8940

Department of Natural Resources Waste Minimization and Pollution Prevention
217/333-8940

Department of Natural Resources State Waste Reduction Program
217/333-8940

Department of Labor
Occupational Safety
1 West Old State Capitol Plaza
Room 300
Springfield, IL 62701
217/782-9386

Department of Agriculture
Pesticide Registration
P.O. Box 19281
Springfield, IL 62794-9281
217/785-5478

Department of Natural Resources
Solid Waste Management
325 West Adams Street, #300
Springfield, IL 62704-1092
217/785-1997

Office of State Fire Marshal
Underground Storage Tanks
1035 Stephenson Drive
Springfield, IL 62703
217/785-5878

Department of Natural Resources
Industrial Waste Elimination Resources
Illinois Institute of Technology
Alumni Building, Room 103
10 West 33rd Street, Row 127
Chicago, IL 60616
312/567-3535

Indiana
Department of Environmental Management
P.O. Box 6015
Indianapolis, IN 42606-6015

Air Quality
317/233-0178

Waste Reduction and Pollution Prevention
317/232-8172

State Recycling
317/232-8172

State Used Oil Recycling
317/232-8941

Solid and Hazardous Waste Management
317/233-3656

Underground Storage Tanks
Leaking Underground Storage Tanks
317/233-5530

Coastal Zone Management
317/232-4221

Department of Natural Resources
402 West Washington Street
Indianapolis, IN 46204

Natural Resources
317/232-4200

Fish and Wildlife
317/232-4080

Department of Labor
Occupational Safety
317/232-2693

Department of Natural Resources
Groundwater Management
105 South Meridian Street
Indianapolis, IN 46225
317/305-3322

Department of Agriculture
Pesticide Registration
Office of Indiana State Chemist
Purdue University
1154 Biochemistry Building
West Lafayette, IN 47907-1154
765/494-1492

Department of Environmental Management
Waste Minimization and Pollution Prevention
Clean Manufacturing, Technology, and Safe Materials Institution
School of Civil Engineering
Purdue University
2655 Yeager Road
Suite 103
West Lafayette, IN 47906-1337
765/463-4749

Iowa

Department of Natural Resources
Air Quality Bureau
7900 Hickman Road, Suite 1
Urbandale, IA 50322
515/281-8852

Department of Natural Resources
Wallace State Office Building
502 East Ninth Street
Des Moines, IA 50319-0034

Emergency Preparedness and Community Right-to-Know
515/242-6346

Environmental Protection
515/281-8973

Fish and Wildlife
515/281-3474

Hazardous Waste Management
515/281-8934

Natural Resources
515/281-5385

Solid Waste Management
515/281-8934

Underground Storage Tanks
Leaking Underground Storage Tanks
515/281-8135

Waste Minimization and Pollution Prevention
515/281-4367

State Used Oil Recycling
515/281-5859

State Recycling
915/281-8176

Water Quality
515/281-8877

Department of Agriculture
Pesticide Registration
Wallace Building, First Floor
502 East Ninth Street
Des Moines, IA 50319-0034
515/281-8591

Department of Labor Services
Occupational Safety and Health
1000 East Grand Avenue
Des Moines, IA 50319
515/281-3606

Center for Industrial Research and Services
State Waste Reduction Program
Iowa State University
2501 North Loop Drive
Suite 500
Ames, IA 50011
515/294-3420

Kansas
Department of Health and Environment
Division of Environment
Forbes Field
Building 740
Topeka, KS 66620-0001

Air Quality
913/296-1593

Environmental Protection
913/296-1535

Solid Waste Management
913/296-1600

Underground Storage Tanks
Leaking Underground Storage Tanks
913/296-1685 (UST)
913/296-1684 (LUST)

Waste Minimization and Pollution Prevention
913/296-1600

State Recycling
913/296-1594

State Used Oil Recycling
913/296-1609

State Waste Reduction Program
913/296-1600

Department of Health and Environment
Forbes Field
Building 283
Topeka, KS 66620

Emergency Preparedness and Community Right-to-Know
913/296-1690

Water Quality
913/296-5500

Department of Wildlife and Parks
Fish and Wildlife
512 Southeast 25th Avenue
Pratt, KS 67124-8174
316/672-5911

Department of Human Resources
Occupational Safety
512 Southwest Sixth
Topeka, KS 66603
785/274-1390

Board of Agriculture
Pesticide Registration
109 Southwest Ninth Street
Topeka, KS 66612-1281
913/296-2263

Kentucky
Department for Environmental Protection
Frankfort Office Park
14 Reilly Road
Frankfort, KY 40601

Air Quality
502/573-3382

Emergency Preparedness and Community Right-to-Know
502/564-2150

Environmental Protection
502/564-2150

Groundwater Management
502/564-3410

Hazardous Waste Management
502/564-6716

Solid Waste Management
502/564-6716

State Recycling
502/564-6716

State Used Oil Recycling
502/564-6716

State Waste Reduction Program
502/564-6716

Underground Storage Tanks
Leaking Underground Storage Tanks
502/564-6716

Water Quality
502/564-3410

Department for Environmental Protection
Emergency Response Commission
Boone National Guard Center
Frankfort, KY 40601-6168
502/564-8660

Fish and Wildlife Resources Department
Fish and Wildlife
1 Game Farm Road
Frankfort, KY 40601
502/564-3596

Department of Natural Resources
Natural Resources
663 Teton Trail
Frankfort, KY 40601
502/564-2184

Kentucky Labor Cabinet
Occupational Safety
1047 U.S. 127 South
Suite 4
Frankfort, KY 40601
502/564-3070

Department of Agriculture
Pesticide Registration
500 Metro Street
Seventh Floor
Frankfort, KY 40601
502/564-7274

Department of Chemical Engineering
Waste Minimization and Pollution Prevention
University of Louisville
Ernst Hall, Room 106
Louisville, KY 40292
502/852-6357

Louisiana

Department of Environmental Quality
7290 Bluebonnet Boulevard
Baton Rouge, LA 70810

    Environmental Protection
    225/765-0720

    Air Quality
    225/765-0219

Department of Environmental Quality
P.O. Box 82178
Baton Rouge, LA 70884-2178

    Groundwater Protection
    225/765-0634

    Hazardous Waste Management
    225/765-0355

    Solid Waste Management
    225/765-0249

    State Recycling
    225/765-0355

    State Used Oil Recycling
    225/765-0249

    State Waste Reduction Program
    225/765-2610

    Underground Storage Tanks
    Leaking Underground Storage Tanks
    225/765-0243

Department of Natural Resources
Coastal Zone Management
P.O. Box 44487
Baton Rouge, LA 70804-4487
225/342-1375

Office of State Police
Emergency Preparedness and Community Right-to-Know
P.O. Box 66614
7901 Independence Boulevard
Baton Rouge, LA 70896-6614
225/925-6113

Wildlife and Fisheries Department
Fish and Wildlife
P.O. Box 98000
Baton Rouge, LA 70898-9000
225/765-2800

Department of Natural Resources
Natural Resources
P.O. Box 94396
Baton Rouge, LA 70804-9396
225/342-4500

Department of Labor
Occupational Safety
P.O. Box 94094
Baton Rouge, LA 70804-9094
225/342-3111

Department of Agriculture and Forestry
Pesticide Registration
P.O. Box 3596
Baton Rouge, LA 70821-3596
225/925-3789

Maine
Environmental Protection Department
17 State House Station
Augusta, ME 04333-0017

Air Quality
207/287-2437

Environmental Protection
207/287-7688

Groundwater Management
207/287-7725

Pollution Prevention
207/287-7767

State Recycling
207/287-5300

State Used Oil Recycling
207/287-2651

Solid Waste Management
207/287-2651

Underground Storage Tanks
Leaking Underground Storage Tanks
207/287-2651

Water Quality
207/287-3901

Environmental Protection Department
Coastal Zone Management
38 State House Station
Augusta, ME 04333-0038
207/287-3261

Environmental Protection Department
Emergency Preparedness and Community Right-to-Know
72 State House Station
Augusta, ME 04333
207/287-4080
800/452-8735 (in ME)

Department of Inland Fisheries and Wildlife
Fish and Wildlife Commissioner
41 State House Station
Augusta, ME 04333
207/287-5202

Department of Labor
Occupational Safety
82 State House Station
Augusta, ME 04333-0045
207/624-6400

Department of Agriculture
Board of Pesticide Control
Pesticide Registration
28 State House Station
Augusta, ME 04333-0028
207/287-2731

Maryland
Department of the Environment
2500 Broening Highway
Baltimore, MD 21224

Air Quality
410/631-3265

Emergency Preparedness and Community Right-to-Know
410/631-3800

Environmental Protection
410/631-3000

Groundwater Management
410/631-3590

Hazardous Waste Management
410/631-3343

Solid Waste Management
410/631-3314

Underground Storage Tanks
Leaking Underground Storage Tanks
410/631-3442

Waste Minimization and Pollution Prevention
410/631-3441

State Recycling
410/631-3315

State Waste Reduction Program
410/631-3343

Water Quality Certification
410/631-3390

Tawes State Office Building
580 Taylor Avenue
Annapolis, MD 21401

Department of the Environment
Coastal Zone Management
410/974-2156

Department of Natural Resources
Fish and Wildlife
410/974-3195

Department of Natural Resources
Natural Resources
410/260-8100

Occupational Safety and Health
Licensing and Regulation Department
1100 North Ewtaw Street
Baltimore, MD 21201
410/767-2215

Department of Agriculture
Pesticide Registration
50 Harry S. Truman Parkway
Annapolis, MD 21401
410/841-5710

Department of the Environment
State Used Oil Recycling
2011 Commerce Park Drive
Annapolis, MD 21401
410/974-7281
800/4RECYCLE

Massachusetts
Department of Environmental Protection
One Winter Street
Boston, MA 02108

Air Quality
617/292-5630

Environmental Protection
617/292-5856

Groundwater Management
Seventh Floor
617/292-5500

Hazardous Waste Management
Third Floor
617/292-5589

Solid Waste Management
Fourth Floor
617/292-5939

Leaking Underground Storage Tanks
Fifth Floor
617/556-1044

Source Reduction Program
Seventh Floor
617/292-5870

State Recycling
Fourth Floor
617/292-5962

State Used Oil Recycling
Fifth Floor
617/556-1022

Water Quality
Ninth Floor
617/292-5857

100 Cambridge Street
Boston, MA 02202

Coastal Zone Management
Room 2000
617/727-9530

Department of Fisheries, Wildlife, and Environmental Law Enforcement
Fish and Wildlife
Room 1902
617/727-3151

Department of Environmental Management
Natural Resources
19th Floor
617/727-3180

Department of Labor and Workforce Development
Division of Occupational Safety
617/727-3567

Department of Food and Agriculture
Pesticide Registration
21st Floor
617/727-3020, ext. 1147

Department of Environmental Protection
Waste Minimization and Pollution Prevention
617/727-3260

Department of Environmental Protection
State Waste Reduction Program
617/727-3260

Emergency Management Agency
Emergency Preparedness and Community Right-to-Know
P.O. Box 1496
400 Worcester Road
Framingham, MA 01701-0317
508/820-2000

Office of the State Fire Marshal
Underground Storage Tanks
1010 Commonwealth Avenue
Boston, MA 02215
617/351-6010

Michigan

Department of Environmental Quality
Air Quality
Hollister Building
Fourth Floor
P.O. Box 30260
Lansing, MI 48909-7760
517/373-7023

Department of Environmental Quality

P.O. Box 30457
Lansing, MI 48909-7957

Coastal Zone Management
517/335-4056

Emergency Preparedness and Community Right-to-Know
517/373-8481

Environmental Protection
517/373-9278

Department of Environmental Quality

John Hannah Building
608 West Allegan Street
Lansing, MI 48933

Hazardous Waste Management
517/373-2730

Solid Waste Management
517/373-4750

State Recycling Waste Management Division
517/373-4742

State Used Oil Recycling
517/373-4742

State Waste Reduction Program
517/373-4742

Waste Minimization and Pollution Prevention
800/662-9278

Water Quality
517/373-1949

Department of Natural Resources
Stevens T. Mason Building
530 West Allegan Street
P.O. Box 30028
Lansing, MI 48909

Fish and Wildlife
517/373-1263

Natural Resources
517/373-2329

Department of Labor
Occupational Safety
7150 Harris Drive
P.O. Box 30643
Lansing, MI 48909
517/322-1814

Department of Public Health
3423 North Martin Luther King Jr. Boulevard
Box 30195
Lansing, MI 48909
517/335-8022

Department of Agriculture
Pesticide Registration
P.O. Box 30017
Lansing, MI 48909
517/373-1087

Department of Natural Resources
Leaking Underground Storage Tanks
P.O. Box 30157
Lansing, MI 48909-7657
517/373-8168

Minnesota
Pollution Control Agency
520 Lafayette Road N
St. Paul, MN 55155-4194

Air Quality
612/296-7331

Coastal Zone Management
612/296-4800

Groundwater Management
612/296-7333

Hazardous Waste Management
612/297-8502

Solid Waste Management
612/296-7333

Underground Storage Tanks
Leaking Underground Storage Tanks
612/297-8577

Waste Minimization and Pollution Prevention
612/297-8502

State Recycling
612/296-6300

State Waste Reduction Program
612/296-7333

Water Quality
612/296-7202

Department of Natural Resources Emergency Preparedness and Community Right-to-Know
B-5 State Capitol
St. Paul, MN 55155
612/297-7372

Department of Natural Resources
500 Lafayette Road
Saint Paul, MN 55155

Natural Resources
612/296-6157

Fish and Wildlife
612/297-1038

Department of Labor and Industry
Occupational Health and Safety
443 Lafayette Road
St. Paul, MN 55155-4307
612/296-2116

Department of Agriculture
Pesticide Registration
90 West Plato Boulevard
St. Paul, MN 55107
612/296-1161

Office of Waste Management
State Used Oil Recycling
1350 Energy Lane
Suite 201
St. Paul, MN 55108
612/296-3417

Minnesota Technical Assistance Program
University of Minnesota
W-140 Boynton Health Service
Minneapolis, MN 55455
800/247-0015 (in MN)

Minnesota Waste Management Board
10050 Naples Street
Blaine, MN 55428
612/536-0816

Mississippi

Department of Environment Quality
P.O. Box 10385
Jackson, MS 39289-0385

Air Quality
601/961-5171

Solid Waste Management
601/961-5171

Underground Storage Tanks
Leaking Underground Storage Tanks
601/961-5171

Water Quality
601/961-5171

Department of Marine Resources
Coastal Zone Management
1141 Bayview Avenue, Suite 101
Biloxi, MS 39530
228/374-5000

Emergency Management Agency
Emergency Preparedness and Community Right-to-Know
1410 Riverside Drive
Jackson, MS 39296
601/352-9100

Department of Environment Quality
P.O. Box 20305
Jackson, MS 39289-1305

Environmental Protection
601/961-5241

Natural Resources
601/961-5666

Hazardous Waste Management
601/961-5321

Pollution Prevention
601/961-5321

State Recycling
601/961-5036

State Used Oil Recycling
601/961-5036

Department of Wildlife, Fisheries, and Parks
Fish and Wildlife
P.O. Box 451
Jackson, MS 39205
601/364-2123

Department of Labor
Occupational Safety
Mississippi State University
2906 North State Street, Suite 201
Jackson, MS 39216
601/987-3981

Department of Agriculture and Commerce
Pesticide Registration
P.O. Box 5207
Mississippi State University, MS 39762
601/325-3390

Missouri
Department of Natural Resources
Division of Environmental Quality
P.O. Box 176
Jefferson City, MO 65102

Air Quality
573/526-3315

Environmental Protection
800/334-6946

Hazardous Waste Management
573/751-3176

Natural Resources
800/334-6946

Solid Waste Management
573/751-5401

Waste Minimization and Pollution Prevention
573/751-5401

State Recycling
573/751-5401

State Used Oil Recycling
573/751-5401

State Waste Reduction Program
573/751-5401

Underground Storage Tanks
Leaking Underground Storage Tanks
573/751-6822

Water Quality
573/751-1300

Department of Natural Resources
Emergency Preparedness and Community Right-to-Know
P.O. Box 3133
Jefferson City, MO 65102
573/751-3443

Department of Conservation
Fish and Wildlife
P.O. Box 180
Jefferson City, MO 65102-0180
573/751-4115

Department of Natural Resources
Groundwater Management
Illinois Fairground Road
P.O. Box 250
Rolla, MO 65401
573/368-2100

Labor and Industrial Relations Department
Occupational Safety
P.O. Box 504
Jefferson City, MO 65102-0504
573/751-9691

Department of Agriculture
Pesticide Registration
P.O. Box 630
Jefferson City, MO 65102-0630
601/751-5504

Montana
Department of Environmental Quality
Metcalf Building
1520 East Sixth Avenue
P.O. 20091-0901
Helena, MT 59620

Air Quality
406/444-3490

Emergency Preparedness and Community Right-to-Know
406/444-2544

Department of Military Affairs
Emergency Response Commission
406/444-3948

Environmental Protection
406/444-4953

Groundwater Management
406/444-3080

Hazardous Waste Management
406/444-3490

Pollution Prevention
406/444-4643

State Recycling
406/444-2544

State Used Oil Recycling
406/444-2544

Solid Waste Management
406/444-3490

Underground Storage Tanks
Leaking Underground Storage Tanks
406/444-1420

Water Quality
406/444-3080

Fish, Wildlife, and Parks Department
Fish and Wildlife
1420 East Sixth Avenue
P.O. Box 200701
Helena, MT 59620
406/444-2535

Department of Natural Resources and Conservation
Natural Resources
1625 11th Avenue
P.O. 201601
Helena, MT 59620-1601
406/444-2074

Department of Labor and Industry
Occupational Health and Safety
P.O. Box 1728
Helena, MT 59624
406/444-9091

Department of Agriculture
Pesticide Registration
Agriculture/Livestock Building
P.O. Box 200201
Helena, MT 59620-0201
406/444-2944

Nebraska
Department of Environmental Quality
301 Centennial Mall S
P.O. Box 98922
State House Station
Lincoln, NE 68509-8922

Air Quality
402/471-2186

Emergency Preparedness and Community Right-to-Know
402/471-4208 and 402/471-4230

Department of Agriculture
Pesticide Registration
402/471-2394

Pollution Prevention
402/471-2186

Solid Waste Management
402/471-4210

Underground Storage Tanks
Leaking Underground Storage Tanks
402/471-2186

Water Quality
402/471-2186

State Civil Defense Agency
Emergency Response Commission
1300 Military Road
Lincoln, NE 68508-1090
402/471-3241

Department of Environmental Quality
Environmental Protection
1200 N Street
Suite 400
Box 98922
Lincoln, NE 68509-8922
402/471-2186

Game and Parks Commission
Fish and Wildlife
2200 North 33rd Street
P.O. Box 30370
Lincoln, NE 68503-0370
402/471-0641

Department of Environmental Quality
Groundwater Management
P.O. Box 98922
Lincoln, NE 68509
402/471-2186

Natural Resources Commission
Natural Resources
Director
301 Centennial Mall S
Box 94876
Lincoln, NE 68509-4876
402/471-2081

Department of Labor
Occupational Health and Safety
P.O. Box 95024
Lincoln, NE 68509-5024
402/471-2239

Department of Environmental Quality
State Recycling
P.O. Box 81814
Lincoln, NE 68501
402/475-3637

Department of Economic Development
State Used Oil Recycling
County-City Building
555 South 10th Street
Lincoln, NE 68508

State Fire Marshal's Office
Underground Storage Tanks
246 South 14th Street
Lincoln, NE 68508
402/471-9465

Nevada
Department of Conservation and Natural Resources
333 West Nye Lane
Carson City, NV 89706-0851

Air Quality
702/687-4670 ext. 3075

Environmental Protection
702/687-4670

Fish and Wildlife
702/687-4670

Groundwater Management
702/687-4670 ext. 3140

Hazardous Waste Management
702/687-4670 ext. 3001

Natural Resources
702/687-4670

Pollution Prevention
702/687-3137

State Recycling
702/687-3003

State Used Oil Recycling
702/687-3003

Solid Waste Management
702/687-4670 ext. 3001

Underground Storage Tanks
Leaking Underground Storage Tanks
702/687-4670 ext. 3001

Water Quality
702/687-4670 ext. 3098

Emergency Response Commission
Emergency Preparedness and Community Right-to-Know
555 Wright Way
Carson City, NV 89711-0925
702/687-6973

Department of Industrial Relations
400 West King Street
Suite 200
Carson City, NV 89703

Occupational Health and Safety
702/687-5240

Federally Approved State Program
702/687-5240

Division of Agriculture
Pesticide Registration
350 Capitol Hill Avenue
Reno, NV 89502
702/688-1182

New Hampshire
Department of Environmental Services
Air Quality
64 North Main Street
Concord, NH 03302
603/271-1370

Department of Environmental Services
Coastal Zone Management
2½ Beacon Street
Concord, NH 03301
603/271-2155

Office of Emergency Management
Emergency Preparedness and Community Right-to-Know
State Office Park S
107 Pleasant Street
Concord, NH 03301
603/271-2231

Department of Environmental Services
6 Hazen Drive
P.O. Box 95
Concord, NH 03301-0095

> Environmental Protection
> 603/271-3503
>
> Groundwater Management
> 603/271-3406
>
> Hazardous Waste Management
> 603/271-2047
>
> Pollution Prevention
> 603/271-6460 or 800/273-9469 (in NH)
>
> State Recycling
> 603/271-2900
>
> State Used Oil Recycling
> 603/271-2900
>
> Solid Waste Management
> 603/271-2047
>
> Underground Storage Tanks
> Leaking Underground Storage Tanks
> 603/271-2900 or 603/271-3644
>
> Water Quality
> 603/271-3503

Fish and Game Department
Fish and Game
2 Hazen Drive
Concord, NH 03301
603/271-3211

Department of Resources and Economic Development
Natural Resources
172 Pembroke Road
P.O. Box 1856
Concord, NH 03302-1856
603/271-2591

Occupational Safety and Health Administration
55 Pleasant Street
Concord, NH 03301
603/225-1629

Department of Agriculture
Pesticide Registration
P.O. Box 2042
Concord, NH 03302-2042
603/271-3550

New Jersey
Environmental Protection Department
401 East State Street
P.O. Box 402
Trenton, NJ 08625-0402

> Environmental Protection
> 609/292-2885
>
> Hazardous Waste Management
> 609/984-2014
>
> Pesticide Registration
> 609/777-3373
>
> Solid Waste Management
> 609/984-2080
>
> Underground Storage Tanks
> Leaking Underground Storage Tanks
> 609/292-3131
>
> State Recycling
> 609/984-3438
>
> State Used Oil Recycling Control
> 609/984-3438

Environmental Protection Department
Air Quality
P.O. Box 027
Trenton, NJ 08625-0027
609/984-3023

Environmental Protection Department
P.O. Box 404
Trenton, NJ 08625

    Coastal Zone Management
    609/777-3373

    Natural Resources
    609/633-2765

Fish, Game, and Wildlife
P.O. Box 400
Trenton, NJ 08625
609/292-9450

Environmental Protection Department
Emergency Preparedness and Community Right-to-Know
22 South Clinton
Third Floor
Trenton, NJ 08625
609/292-6714

Environmental Protection Department
Groundwater Management
P.O. Box 409
Trenton, NJ 08625
609/292-1623

Department of Health
Occupational Safety and Health
John Fitch Plaza
Trenton, NJ 08625-0110
609/588-7463

Environmental Protection Department
Waste Minimization and Pollution Prevention
28 West State Street
Room 514
Trenton, NJ 08625-0406
609/292-3600

Environmental Protection Department
Water Quality
P.O. Box 029
Trenton, NJ 08625
609/292-4543

New Mexico
Department of Public Safety
Emergency Preparedness and Community Right-to-Know
13 Bataan Boulevard
P.O. Box 1628
Santa Fe, NM 87504-1628
505/476-9600

Department of Environment
1190 St. Francis Drive
Santa Fe, NM 87505-4182

    Air Quality
    505/827-0031

    Occupational Safety and Health Department
    Occupational Safety
    505/827-4230

    Environmental Protection
    505/827-2855

    Groundwater Quality Bureau
    505/827-2919

    Pollution Prevention
    505/827-2855

    State Recycling
    505/827-0197

    State Used Oil Recycling Control
    505/827-0197

    Solid Waste Management
    505/827-2775

    Underground Storage Tanks
    Leaking Underground Storage Tanks
    505/827-0188

    Surface Water Quality Bureau
    Water Quality
    505/827-0187

New Mexico Game and Fish Department
Fish and Wildlife
P.O. Box 25112
Santa Fe, NM 87504
505/827-7911

Department of Environment
Hazardous Waste Management
2044 Galisteo Street
P.O. Box 26110
Santa Fe, NM 87502
505/827-1557

Department of Energy, Minerals, and Natural Resources
Natural Resources
2040 South Pacheco
Santa Fe, NM 87505
505/827-5950

Department of Agriculture
Pesticide Registration
P.O. Box 30005
Department 3AQ
Las Cruces, NM 88003-0005
505/646-3007

New York
Department of Environmental Conservation
50 Wolf Road
Albany, NY 12233

    Air Quality
    518/457-7230

    Emergency Preparedness and Community Right-to-Know
    800/457-7362

    Environmental Protection
    518/457-3446

    Fish and Wildlife
    518/457-5690

    Groundwater Management
    518/457-6674

    Solid and Hazardous Waste Management
    518/457-6934

    Natural Resources
    518/457-2475

    Pesticide Registration
    518/457-7482

    Underground Storage Tanks
    Leaking Underground Storage Tanks
    Room 326
    518/457-5861

    Pollution Prevention
    518/457-2553

    State Recycling
    Room 208
    518/457-6934

    State Used Oil Recycling
    518/457-5861

    State Waste Reduction Program
    518/457-5861

    Water Quality
    518/457-7464

Department of State
Coastal Zone Management
41 State Street
Albany, NY 12231
518/474-6000

State Emergency Management Office
Emergency Response Commission
1220 Washington
Albany, NY 12226-2251
518/457-2222

Department of Labor
Occupational Safety
State Office Building Campus
Building 12
Albany, NY 12240
518/457-3518

North Carolina
Department of Environment and Natural Resources
512 North Salisbury Street
Raleigh, NC 27611

    Air Quality
    P.O. Box 29580
    919/733-3340

    Coastal Zone Management
    P.O. Box 27687
    919/733-2293

Environmental Protection
P.O. Box 27687
919/733-4984

Groundwater Management
P.O. Box 29578
919/733-3221

Hazardous Waste Management
P.O. Box 27626
919/733-4996

Solid Waste Management
P.O. Box 27626
919/733-4996

Water Quality
P.O. Box 29578
919/733-3221

Emergency Response Commission
Emergency Preparedness and Community Right-to-Know
116 West Jones Street
Raleigh, NC 27603-1335
919/733-3867

512 North Salisbury Street
Raleigh, NC 27604-1188

Wildlife Resources Commission
Fish and Wildlife
919/733-3391

Department of Environment and Natural Resources
Natural Resources
919/733-4984

Department of Labor
Occupational Safety
4 West Edenton Street
Raleigh, NC 27603-3432
919/807-2900

Department of Agriculture
Pesticide Registration
P.O. Box 27647
Raleigh, NC 27611-7647
919/733-3556

Department of Environment and Natural Resources
Underground Storage Tanks
Leaking Underground Storage Tanks
441 North Harrington Street
Raleigh, NC 27603
919/733-3221

Department of Environment and Natural Resources
Waste Minimization and Pollution Prevention
P.O. Box 29569
Raleigh, NC 27626-9569
919/715-6600

North Dakota

1200 Missouri Avenue
Bismarck, ND 58506-5520

Department of Health
Air Quality
P.O. Box 5520
701/328-5188

Department of Health
Environmental Protection
Chief, Environmental Health Section
P.O. Box 5520
701/328-5150

Game and Fish Department
Fish and Wildlife
P.O. Box 5520
701/328-6300

Department of Health
Groundwater Management
P.O. Box 5520
701/328-5210

Department of Health
Hazardous Waste Management
P.O. Box 5520
701/328-5166

Department of Labor
Occupational Safety
P.O. Box 5685
701/328-5188

Agriculture Department
Pesticide Registration
P.O. Box 0020
701/328-4756

Department of Health
Pollution Prevention
701/328-5150

Department of Health
State Recycling
Room 302
P.O. Box 5520
701/328-5166

Department of Health
State Used Oil Recycling
P.O. Box 5520
701/328-5166

Department of Health
Solid Waste Management
P.O. Box 5520
701/328-5166

Department of Health
Underground Storage Tanks
Leaking Underground Storage Tanks
P.O. Box 5520
701/328-5166

Department of Health
Division of Water Quality
Environmental Health Section
P.O. Box 5520
701/328-5210

Department of Health
Emergency Preparedness and Community Right-to-Know
P.O. Box 5511
Bismarck, ND 58506-5511
701/328-2121 or 328-3300

Ohio
Environmental Protection Agency
P.O. Box 1049
Columbus, OH 43216-1049

    Air Quality
    614/644-2270

Emergency Preparedness and Community Right-to-Know
614/644-2270

Emergency Response Commission
614/644-2270

Environmental Protection
614/644-3020

Groundwater Management
614/644-2752

Hazardous Waste Management
614/644-2917

Pollution Prevention
614/644-3469

State Used Oil Recycling
614/644-3020

State Waste Reduction Program
614/644-3020

Solid Waste Management
614/644-2621

Waste Minimization and Pollution Prevention
614/644-2917

Water Quality
614/644-3020

Department of Natural Resources
Coastal Zone Management
1952 Belcher Drive
Building C-4
Columbus, OH 43224
614/265-6395

Department of Natural Resources
Fish and Wildlife
1840 Belcher Drive
Columbus, OH 43224-1329
614/265-6300

Department of Natural Resources
Natural Resources
1930 Belcher Drive
Building D-3
Columbus, OH 43224
614/265-6875

Industrial Safety and Hygiene Commission
Occupational Safety
246 North High Street
Columbus, OH 43266
614/466-3564

8995 East Main Street
Reynoldsburg, OH 43068-3399

Department of Agriculture
Pesticide Registration
614/866-6361

Department of Commerce
Underground Storage Tanks
Leaking Underground Storage Tanks
614/752-8200

Oklahoma
Department of Environmental Quality
P.O. Box 1677
Oklahoma City, OK 73101

Air Quality
405/702-4100

Environmental Protection
405/702-6100

Fish and Wildlife
405/702-6100

Hazardous Waste Management
405/702-5100

Natural Resources
405/702-6100

Solid Waste Management
405/702-5100

State Recycling
405/702-5100

State Used Oil Recycling
405/702-5100

State Waste Reduction Program
405/702-5100

Waste Minimization and Pollution Prevention
405/702-5100

Water Quality
405/702-8100

Department of Pollution Control
Emergency Preparedness and Community Right-to-Know
P.O. Box 53504
Oklahoma City, OK 73152
405/271-7363

Department of Agriculture
Pesticide Registration
2800 North Lincoln Boulevard
Oklahoma City, OK 73105
405/521-3864

Oklahoma Corporation Commission
Underground Storage Tanks
Leaking Underground Storage Tanks
Jim Thorpe Building
2101 North Lincoln Boulevard
Oklahoma City, OK 73105
405/521-3107 (UST)
405/521-6575 (LUST)

Oregon
Department of Environmental Quality
811 Southwest Sixth Avenue
Portland, OR 97204-1390

Air Quality
503/229-5359

Coastal Zone Management
503/229-5324 or 541/686-7838

Environmental Protection
503/229-5696

Groundwater Management
503/229-5279

Hazardous Waste Management
503/229-5913

Natural Resources
503/986-4700

Solid Waste Management
503/229-5913

State Recycling
503/229-5913

State Used Oil Recycling
503/229-5913
800/452-4011 (in OR)

State Waste Reduction Program
503/229-5913

Underground Storage Tanks
Leaking Underground Storage Tanks
503/229-5913

Waste Minimization and Pollution Prevention
503/229-5913

Water Quality
503/229-5279

State Fire Marshal
Emergency Preparedness and Community Right-to-Know
4760 Portland Road NE
Salem, OR 97305-1760
503/378-3473

Department of Fish and Wildlife
Fish and Wildlife
5201 Southwest First Avenue
Portland, OR 97207
503/872-5270

Department of Consumer and Business Services
Occupational Safety
350 Winter Street NE
Room 430
Salem, OR 97310
503/378-3272

Department of Agriculture
Pesticide Registration
635 Capitol Street NE
Salem, OR 97310
503/986-4635

Pennsylvania
Environmental Protection Department
400 Market Street
Harrisburg, PA 17105-8468

Air Quality
717/787-9702

Environmental Protection
717/787-5028

Groundwater Management
717/787-9702

Hazardous Waste Management
717/787-9702

State Recycling
717/787-9702

State Used Oil Recycling
717/787-9702

Bureau of Waste Management
717/787-9702

Water Quality
717/787-9702

Bureau of Watershed Conservation
Coastal Zone Management
P.O. Box 8555
Harrisburg, PA 17105-8555
717/787-2529

Emergency Management Council
Emergency Preparedness and Community Right-to-Know
P.O. Box 3321
Harrisburg, PA 17105-3321
717/651-2001

Department of Fish and Wildlife
3532 Walnut Street
P.O. Box 67000
Harrisburg, PA 17106-7000
717/657-4518

Environmental Protection Department
Natural Resources
Harrisburg, PA 17105-2063
717/787-2814

Department of Labor and Industry
Occupational Safety
Room 1529
Harrisburg, PA 17120
717/787-3323

Department of Agriculture
Pesticide Registration
2301 North Cameron Street
Harrisburg, PA 17110-9408
717/787-4843

Bureau of Land Recycling and Waste Management
Solid Waste Management
P.O. Box 8471
14th Floor
Harrisburg, PA 17105-8471
717/787-9870

Department of Environmental Protection
Underground Storage Tanks
Leaking Underground Storage Tanks
3600 Vartan Way
Second Floor
P.O. Box 8762
Harrisburg, PA 17105-8762
717/783-2300

117 Technology Way
University Park, PA 16802

Department of Environmental Protection
Waste Minimization and Pollution Prevention
814/865-0427

State Waste Reduction Program
Pennsylvania Technical Assistance Program
814/865-0427

Rhode Island
Department of Environmental Management
235 Promenade Street
Providence, RI 02908-5767

Air Quality
401/222-2808

Coastal Resources
401/222-3429

Environmental Protection
401/222-6677

Hazardous Waste Management
401/222-2797

Natural Resources
401/222-6605

Ocean State Cleanup/Recycling
401/222-3434

Pesticide Registration
401/222-2782

Solid Waste Management
401/222-2797

State Recycling
401/222-3434

State Used Oil Recycling
401/222-3434

Waste Minimization and Pollution Prevention
401/222-3434

Underground Storage Tanks
Leaking Underground Storage Tanks
401/222-2797

Water Quality
401/222-3961

Department of Environmental Management
Emergency Response Commission
645 New London Avenue
Cranston, RI 02903
401/222-3039

Department of Environmental Management
Fish and Wildlife
4808 Tower Hill Road
Wakefield, RI 02879
401/222-3075

Department of Labor
Occupational Safety
101 Friendship Street
Providence, RI 02903-3740
401/457-1800

Center for Environmental Studies
Brown University
P.O. Box 1943
135 Angell Street
Providence, RI 02912
401/863-3449

South Carolina
Department of Health and Environmental Control
2600 Bull Street
Columbia, SC 29201

Air Quality
803/898-4123

Emergency Preparedness and Community Right-to-Know
803/898-3900

Environmental Protection
803/898-3900

Hazardous Waste Management
803/898-4172

Pollution Prevention
803/898-4201

State Recycling
803/898-4201

State Used Oil Recycling
803/898-4201

Solid Waste Management
803/898-4201

Underground Storage Tanks
Leaking Underground Storage Tanks
803/734-5000

Water Quality
803/734-4300

Department of Natural Resources
Natural Resources
1000 Assembly Street
Columbia, SC 29201
803/734-3888

Department of Wildlife and Marine Resources
Fish and Wildlife
Dennis Building
P.O. Box 167
Columbia, SC 29203
803/734-4007

Department of Labor
Occupational Safety
3600 Forest Lane
P.O. Box 11329
Columbia, SC 29211-1329
803/734-9632

Department of Agriculture
Pesticide Registration
212 Barre Hall
Clemson University
Clemson, SC 29634-2775
864/656-3311

Ocean and Coastal Resource Management
1326 McMillan Avenue
Suite 400
Charleston, SC 29405
843/744-5838

South Dakota
Department of Environmental and Natural Resources
Joe Foss Building
523 East Capitol Avenue
Pierre, SD 57501-3181

Air Quality
605/773-7171

Emergency Preparedness and Community Right-to-Know
605/773-3153

Environmental Protection
605/773-3153 or 605/773-4127

Groundwater Management
605/773-3296

Hazardous Waste Management
605/773-3153 or 605/773-4127

Natural Resources
605/773-5559

Pollution Prevention
605/773-3153

State Recycling Program
605/773-3153 or 605/773-4127

State Used Oil Recycling
605/773-3153 or 605/773-4127

Solid Waste Management
605/773-3153 or 605/773-4127

Underground Storage Tanks
Leaking Underground Storage Tanks
605/773-3296

Water Quality
605/773-3351

Department of Game, Fish, and Parks
Fish and Wildlife
605/773-3381

Department of Agriculture
Pesticide Registration
523 East Capitol
Pierre, SD 57501-3182
605/773-3375

Tennessee
Department of Environment and Conservation
L&C Tower
401 Church Street
Nashville, TN 37243

Environmental Protection
21st Floor
615/532-0554

Solid Waste Management
Fifth Floor
615/532-0780

State Recycling
888/891-8332

State Used Oil Recycling
888/891-8332

Underground Storage Tanks
Leaking Underground Storage Tanks
Fourth Floor
615/532-0945

Water Quality
Sixth Floor
615/532-0625

Department of Environment and Conservation
L&C Annex
401 Church Street
Nashville, TN 37243

Air Quality
Ninth Floor
615/532-0554

Hazardous Waste Management
Eighth Floor
615/532-0554

Department of Environment and Conservation
Waste Minimization and Pollution Prevention
Eighth Floor
615/532-8012

Emergency Management Agency
Emergency Preparedness and Community Right-to-Know
3041 Sidco Drive
Nashville, TN 37204
615/741-0001
800/258-3300 (outside TN)
800/262-3300 (inside TN)

Wildlife Resources Agency
Fish and Wildlife
P.O. Box 40747
Nashville, TN 37204
615/781-6610

Department of Environment and Conservation
Natural Resources
Customs House
First Floor
Nashville, TN 37243
615/742-6747

Department of Labor
Occupational Safety
710 James Robertson Parkway
Third Floor
Nashville, TN 37243
615/741-2793

Department of Agriculture
Pesticide Registration
P.O. Box 40627
Nashville, TN 37204
615/837-5103

Department of Environment and
Conservation
State Waste Reduction Program
University of Tennessee
102 Alumni Building
Knoxville, TN 37966
615/974-2456

Texas
Natural Resource Conservation Commission
P.O. Box 13087
Austin, TX 78711-3087

Air Quality
512/239-5440

Hazardous Waste Management
512/239-6383

Natural Resources
512/239-1000

Pollution Prevention
512/239-1000

State Recycling
512/239-6750

State Used Oil Recycling
512/239-6750

Underground Storage Tanks
Leaking Underground Storage Tanks
512/239-1000

Water Quality
512/239-4473

Natural Resource Conservation Commission
1700 North Congress Avenue
Austin, TX 78701

Coastal Zone Management
512/239-1000

Groundwater Management
512/239-4506

Department of Health
Occupational Safety Program
903 San Jacinto Boulevard, #319
Austin, TX 78756
512/916-5783
800/452-2791 (in TX)

Department of Health
1100 West 49th Street
Austin, TX 78756

Emergency Preparedness and Community Right-to-Know
512/834-6603

Environmental Protection
512/458-7541

Solid Waste Management
512/458-7271

Parks and Wildlife Department
Fish and Wildlife
4200 Smith School Road
Austin, TX 78744
512/389-4800

Department of Agriculture
Pesticide Registration
P.O. Box 12847
Austin, TX 78711
512/463-7476

Utah
Department of Environmental Quality
Air Quality
P.O. Box 144820
150 North 1950 West
Salt Lake City, UT 84114
801/536-4000

Department of Environmental Quality
P.O. Box 144810
168 North 1950 West
Salt Lake City, UT 84114

> Emergency Preparedness and Community Right-to-Know
> 801/536-4100
>
> Environmental Protection
> 801/536-4400
>
> Underground Storage Tanks
> Leaking Underground Storage Tanks
> 801/536-4100

Department of Natural Resources
P.O. Box 144870
288 North 1460 West
Salt Lake City, UT 84114-4870

> Groundwater Management
> 801/538-6146
>
> Water Quality
> 801/538-6146

Department of Natural Resources
P.O. Box 144880
288 North 1460 West
Salt Lake City, UT 84116

> Hazardous Waste Management
> 801/538-6170
>
> Pollution Prevention
> 801/538-6170
>
> State Recycling
> 801/538-6170
>
> State Used Oil Recycling
> 801/538-6170
>
> Solid Waste Management
> 801/538-6170

Department of Natural Resources
1594 West North Temple
Salt Lake City, UT 84114

> Fish and Wildlife
> 801/538-4700

Natural Resources
801/538-7200

Labor Commission
Occupational Safety
P.O. Box 146650
160 East 300 South
Salt Lake City, UT 84111
801/530-6800

Department of Agriculture and Food
Pesticide Registration
350 North Redwood Road
P.O. Box 146500
Salt Lake City, UT 84114-6500
801/538-7187

Vermont
103 South Main Street
Waterbury, VT 05671

> Agency of Natural Resources
> Air Quality
> 802/241-3840
>
> Department of Health
> Department of Public Safety
> 802/244-8721
>
> Agency of Natural Resources
> Environmental Protection
> 802/241-3800
>
> Department of Fish and Wildlife
> Fish and Wildlife
> 802/241-3730
>
> Agency of Natural Resources
> Groundwater Management
> 802/241-3400
>
> Agency of Natural Resources
> Hazardous Waste Management
> 802/241-3888
>
> Agency of Natural Resources
> Natural Resources
> 802/241-3800
>
> Agency of Natural Resources
> Pollution Prevention
> 802/241-3800

Agency of Natural Resources
State Recycling Program
802/244-3800

Agency of Natural Resources
State Used Oil Recycling
802/241-3800

Agency of Natural Resources
Solid Waste Management
802/241-3888

Agency of Natural Resources
Underground Storage Tanks
Leaking Underground Storage Tanks
802/241-3888

Agency of Natural Resources
Water Quality
802/241-3777

Department of Health
Emergency Preparedness and Community Right-to-Know
Essex Police Department
81 Main Street
Essex Junction, VT 05452

Department of Labor and Industry
Occupational Safety
National Life Building, Drawer 20
Montpelier, VT 05620-3401
802/828-2765

Department of Agriculture, Food, and Markets
Pesticide Registration
116 State Street, Drawer 20
Montpelier, VT 05620-2901
802/828-2431

Virginia
Department of Environment Quality
P.O. Box 10009
Richmond, VA 23240

Air Quality
804/698-4424

Groundwater Management
804/698-4043

Underground Storage Tanks
Leaking Underground Storage Tanks
804/698-4297

Water Quality Standards
804/698-4114

Department of Environment Quality
629 East Main Street
Richmond, VA 23219

Coastal Zone Management
804/698-4319

Emergency Preparedness and Community Right-to-Know
804/698-4000

Environmental Protection
804/698-4000

Hazardous Waste Management
804/698-4000

State Waste Reduction Program
804/698-4000

State Recycling
800/698-4000

State Used Oil Recycling
804/698-4000

Solid Waste Management
804/698-4155

Waste Minimization and Pollution Prevention
804/698-4344

Department of Game and Inland Fisheries
Fish and Wildlife
4010 West Broad Street
Richmond, VA 23230
804/367-1000

Department of Natural Resources
Natural Resources
P.O. Box 1475
Richmond, VA 23212
804/786-0044

Department of Labor and Industry
Powers-Taylor Building
13 South 13th Street
Richmond, VA 23219

   Occupational Safety
   804/786-2391

   Headquarters
   804/786-2327

Department of Agriculture and Consumer Services
Pesticide Registration
P.O. Box 1163
Richmond, VA 23209
804/371-6558

Washington
Department of Ecology
P.O. Box 47600
Olympia, WA 98504-7600

   Air Quality
   360/407-6880

   Coastal Zone Management
   360/407-6977

   Department of Ecology
   360/407-6000

   Hazardous Waste Management
   360/407-6702

   Solid Waste Management
   360/407-6103

   State Recycling
   360/407-6103

   State Used Oil Recycling
   360/407-6103

   Underground Storage Tanks
   Leaking Underground Storage Tanks
   360/407-6257

   Waste Minimization and Pollution Prevention
   509/407-6103

   Water Quality
   360/407-6405

Department of Community Development
Community Right-to-Know
Ninth and Columbia Building
Olympia, WA 98504
360/407-6729

Environmental Protection
1200 Sixth Avenue
Seattle, WA 98101
206/553-1200

Department of Fish and Wildlife
Fish and Wildlife
600 Capitol Way
Olympia, WA 98501
360/902-2200

Department of Natural Resources
Natural Resources
1111 Washington Street
Olympia, WA 98504-7000
360/902-1000

Department of Labor and Industries
P.O. Box 44710
Olympia, WA 98504-4710

   Occupational Safety
   360/902-5642

   Federally Approved Program
   360/553-5930

Department of Agriculture
Pesticide Registration
P.O. Box 42560
Olympia, WA 98504-5260
360/902-2010

West Virginia
Division of Environmental Protection
Air Quality
1558 Washington Street E
Charleston, WV 25311
304/558-4022

Capitol Complex
Building 3
1900 Kanawha Boulevard East
Charlestown, WV 25305

Department of Agriculture
Pesticide Registration
304/558-2209

Division of Environmental Protection
Emergency Response Commission
Room EB-80
304/558-5380

Division of Environmental Protection
Environmental Protection
304/558-3315

Department of Natural Resources
Fish and Wildlife
304/558-2771

Department of Natural Resources
304/558-2754

Department of Natural Resources
State Used Oil Recycling
304/558-6350

Department of Industry, Labor, and Human Relations
Occupational Safety
Room 319
304/558-7890

Department of Natural Resources
State Recycling Contact
304/558-3370

Division of Environmental Protection
1201 Greenbrier Street
Charleston, WV 25311

   Groundwater Management
   304/558-2107

   Water Quality
   304/558-2107

Division of Environmental Protection
1356 Hansford Street
Charleston, WV 25301

   Hazardous Waste Management
   304/558-5393

   Pollution Prevention
   304/558-5929

   Solid Waste Management
   304/558-6350

Underground Storage Tanks
Leaking Underground Storage Tanks
304/558-6371

Wisconsin
P.O. Box 7921
Madison, WI 53707-7921

Department of Natural Resources
608/266-2621 or 608/266-2107

Department of Environmental Management
Air Quality
608/264-8887

Department of Environmental Management
Environmental Protection
608/266-1099

Department of Resource Management
Fish and Wildlife
608/266-7025

Department of Natural Resources
Groundwater Management
608/266-2104

Department of Environmental Management
Hazardous Waste Management
608/266-1327

Department of Environmental Management
Solid Waste Management
608/266-1327

Department of Natural Resources
Leaking Storage Tanks
608/266-2621

Department of Natural Resources
State Recycling Contact
608/266-2711

Department of Natural Resources
State Used Oil Recycling Contact
608/266-2711

Department of Environmental
Management
Water Quality
608/266-2104

Department of Environmental Management
Coastal Zone Management
P.O. Box 7868
Madison, WI 53707-7868
608/266-8234

Department of Labor and Human
Relations
Occupational Safety
P.O. Box 7969
Madison, WI 53707-7969
608/266-1816

Department of Agriculture, Trade, and
Consumer Protection
Pesticide Registration
2811 Agriculture Drive
Madison, WI 53708-8911
608/266-7130

Department of Industry, Labor, and
Human Relations
Underground Storage Tank
201 East Washington Avenue
P.O. Box 7969
Madison, WI 53702-7969
608/266-7605

Wyoming

Herschler Building
122 West 25th Street
Cheyenne, WY 82002

Department of Environmental
Quality
Air Quality
Fourth Floor West
307/777-7391

Department of Environmental
Quality
Environmental Protection
Fourth Floor West
307/777-7938

Department of Employment
Occupational Safety
Second Floor East
307/777-7786

Department of Employment
Federally Approved Program
Second Floor East
307/777-7786

Department of Environmental
Quality
Solid and Hazardous Waste Management
Fourth Floor West
307/777-7752

Department of Environmental
Quality
Underground Storage Tanks
Leaking Underground Storage Tanks
Fourth Floor West
307/777-7781

Department of Environmental
Quality
State Recycling
307/777-7752

Department of Environmental
Quality
State Used Oil Recycling
307/777-7752

Department of Environmental
Quality
State Waste Reduction Program
307/777-7752

Department of Environmental
Quality
Water Quality
Fourth Floor West
307/777-7781

Department of Environmental
Quality
Waste Minimization and Pollution
Prevention
Fourth Floor West
307/777-7752

Emergency Management Agency
Emergency Preparedness and Community Right-to-Know
5500 Bishop Boulevard
Cheyenne, WY 82009-3320
307/777-4900

Game and Fish Commission
Fish and Wildlife
5400 Bishop Boulevard
Cheyenne, WY 82006
307/777-4600

Department of Agriculture
Pesticide Registration
2219 Carey Avenue
Cheyenne, WY 82002-0100
307/777-6573

APPENDIX 4

Associations and Periodicals

Acid Rain Hotline
Acid Rain Foundation
1410 Varsity Drive
Raleigh, NC 27606
202/233-9620

Agency for Toxic Substances and Disease Registry (ATSDR) Toxic Profile Information System TOX Information Line
1600 Clifton Road NE
Atlanta, GA 30329
404/639-6000

Air and Waste Management Association
1 Gateway Center
Third Floor
Pittsburgh, PA 15222
412/232-3444
Periodical: *Journal of the Air and Waste Management Association*

American Academy of Environmental Engineers
130 Holiday Court
Suite 100
Annapolis, MD 21401
410/266-3311
Periodicals: *Who's Who in Environmental Engineering/Environmental Engineer/Environmental Engineering Selection Guide*

American Association for the Advancement of Science
1200 New York Avenue NW
Washington, DC 20005
202/326-6400

American Association of Certified Appraisers
800 Compton Road
Suite 10
Cincinnati, OH 45231
800/543-2222

American Bankers Association
1120 Connecticut Avenue NW
Washington, DC 20036
202/663-500

American Chemical Society
1155 16th Street NW
Washington, DC 20036
202/872-4600
Periodical: *Environmental Science & Technology*

American College of Toxicology
9650 Rockville Pike
Bethesda, MD 20814
301/571-1840
Periodicals: *Journal of the International College of Toxicology/International College of Toxicology Newsletter*

American Council on Science and Health
1995 Broadway
Second Floor
New York, NY 10023
212/362-7044
Periodicals: *Priorities for Long Life and Good Health/ACSH Media Update*

American Crop Protection Association
1156 15th Street NW
Suite 400
Washington, DC 20005
202/296-1585

American Hotel and Motel Association
1201 New York Avenue NW
Suite 600
Washington, DC 20005-3931
202/289-3100

American Industrial Health Council
2001 Pennsylvania Avenue NW
Suite 760
Washington, DC 20006
202/833-2131
Periodical: *AIHC*

American Industrial Hygiene Association
2700 Prosperity Avenue
Suite 250
Fairfax, VA 22031-4307
703/849-8888
Periodical: *American Industrial Hygiene Journal*

American Institute of Architects
1735 New York Avenue NW
Washington, DC 20006
202/626-7300

American Institute of Biological Sciences
1444 I Street NW
Suite 200
Washington, DC 20005
202/628-1500
Periodicals: *BioScience/Forum*

American Institute of Biomedical Climatology
1023 Welsh Road
Philadelphia, PA 19115
215/673-8368

American Institute of Chemical Engineers
345 East 47th Street
New York, NY 10017
212/705-7338
Periodicals: *AIChE Journal/Chemical Engineering Progress/Chemical Engineering Faculties Directory*

American Institute of CPAs
1211 Avenue of the Americas
New York, NY 10036-8775
212/596-6200

American Littoral Society
Sandy Hook
Highlands, NJ 07732
908/291-0055
Periodicals: *Coastal Reporter/Underwater Naturalist*

American Meteorological Society
45 Beacon Street
Boston, MA 02108
617/227-2425
Periodicals: *Journal of Applied Meteorology/Journal of Climate*

American Petroleum Institute
1220 L Street NW
Washington, DC 20005
202/682-8000

American Planning Association
122 South Michigan Avenue
Suite 1600
Chicago, IL 60603-6107
312/431-9100
Periodicals: *Planning Magazine/Journal of American Planning Association/Land Use Law Zoning Digest/Zoning News/PAS Reports*

American Public Health Association
1015 15th Street NW
Washington, DC 20005
202/789-5600
Periodicals: *The Nation's Health/American Journal of Public Health*

American Public Works Association
2345 Grand Boulevard
Suite 500
Kansas City, MO 64108
816/472-6100
Periodical: *APWA Reporter*

American Real Estate and Urban Economics Association
Indiana University School of Business
1309 East 10th Street
Suite 461
Bloomington, IN 47405
812/855-7794
Periodicals: *Real Estate Economics*

American Resort Development Association
1220 L Street
Suite 500
Washington, DC 20005
202/371-6700

American Society for Microbiology
1325 Massachusetts Avenue NW
Washington, DC 20005
202/737-3600

American Society of Agricultural Engineers
2950 Niles Road
St. Joseph, MI 49085-9659
616/429-0300
Periodicals: *Resource/ASAE Standards/Transactions of the ASAE/Applied Engineering and Agriculture*

American Society of Agronomy
677 South Segoe Road
Madison, WI 53711
608/273-8080
Periodicals: *Agronomy Journal/Journal of Production Agriculture/Journal of Environmental Quality/Journal of Natural Resources and Life Sciences Education/Agronomy News*

American Society of Appraisers
555 Herndon Parkway
Suite 125
Herndon, VA 20170
703/478-2228

American Society of Civil Engineers
1801 Alexander Bell Drive
Reston, VA 20191
Periodicals: *Civil Engineers/ASCE News*

American Society of Farm Managers and Rural Appraisers
950 South Cherry Street, Suite 508
Denver, CO 80246
303/758-3513

American Society of Golf Course Architects
221 North LaSalle Street
Suite 3500
Chicago, IL 60601-1520
312/372-7090
Periodicals: *Golf Course Development Planning Guide/Remodeling Your Golf Course/Request For Proposal/Selecting Your Golf Course Architects*

American Society of Sanitary Engineering
28901 Clemens Road
Suite 100
West Lake, OH 44145
216/835-3040
Periodicals: *ASSE Yearbook and Newsletter/ Plumbing Standards*

American Water Resources Association
950 Herndon Parkway
Suite 300
Herndon, VA 20170
703/904-1225
Periodicals: *Hydata News/Journal of the American Water Resources Association*

American Zoo and Aquariums Association
Oglebay Park
Wheeling, WV 26003
304/242-2160

Amusement and Music Operators Association
401 North Michigan Avenue
Suite 2200
Chicago, IL 60611
312/644-6610

Appraisal Institute
875 North Michigan Avenue
Suite 2400
Chicago, IL 60611-1980
312/335-4100
Periodicals: *The Appraisal Journal/Valuation Insights and Perspectives/Appraiser News in Brief/MarketSource*

Asbestos Information Association/North America
1745 Jefferson Davis Highway
Suite 406
Arlington, VA 22202
703/412-1150
Periodical: *AIA/NA Newsletter*

Association for the Environmental Health of Soils
150 Fearing Street
Amherst, MA 01342
413/549-5170

Association of American Pesticide Control Officials
P.O. Box 1249
Hardwick, VT 05843
802/472-6956

Association of American Railroads
Bureau of Explosives Hotline
202/639-2222

Association of Local Air Pollution Control Officials
444 North Capitol Street NW
Suite 307
Washington, DC 20001
202/624-7864

Association of Metropolitan Sewerage Agencies
1000 Connecticut Avenue NW
Suite 410
Washington, DC 20036-5302
202/833-2672
Periodical: *AMSA Monthly Report*

Association of New Jersey Environmental Commissions
P.O. Box 157
300 Mendham Road
Mendham, NJ 07945
973/539-7547
Periodical: *ANJEC Report*

Association of State and Interstate Water Pollution Control Administrators
750 First Street NW
Room 910
Washington, DC 20002
202/898-0905

Association of State and Territorial Health Officials
1275 K Street NW
Suite 800
Washington, DC 20005
202/371-9090

Association of State and Territorial Solid Waste Management Officials (ASTSWMO)
444 North Capitol Street NW
Suite 388
Washington, DC 20001
202/624-5828

Black's Guide
818 West Diamond Avenue
Suite 300
Gaithersburg, MD 20878
301/948-0995

Bowling Proprietors' Association
615 Six Flags Drive
Arlington, TX 76011
817/649-5105

Building Owners and Managers Association International (BOMA)
1201 New York Avenue NW
Suite 300
Washington, DC 20005
202/408-2662

Cement Kiln Recycling Coalition
1225 I Street NW
Suite 300
Washington, DC 20005
202/789-1945

Center for Environmental Information, Inc.
55 St. Paul
Rochester, NY 14604
716/262-2870
Periodicals: *CEI Sphere/Global Climate Change Digest*

Center for Environmental Management Information
P.O. Box 23769
Washington, DC 20026-3769
800/736-3282

Chamber of Commerce of the United States
1615 H Street NW
Washington, DC 20062
202/659-6000
Periodicals: *Nation's Business/The Business Advocate*

Chemical Manufacturers Association
1300 Wilson Boulevard
Arlington, VA 22209
703/741-5000
Periodical: *ChemEcology*

Chemical Producers and Distributors Association
1430 Duke Street
Alexandria, VA 22314
703/548-7700
Periodicals: *Executive News/Legislative and Regulatory Journal*

Chemical Waste Transportation Council
4301 Connecticut Avenue NW
Suite 300
Washington, DC 20008
202/244-4700

Chem Trec Center—Non-Emergency Services
1300 Wilson Boulevard
Arlington, VA 22209
703/741-5000
800/CMA-8200

Chlorine Institute, Inc.
2001 L Street NW
Suite 506
Washington, DC 20036-4919
202/775-2790

Center for Health, Environment, and Justice
P.O. Box 6806
Falls Church, VA 22040
703/237-2249

Citizen's Clearinghouse for Hazardous Waste
P.O. Box 926
Arlington, VA 22116
703/276-7070

Coalition for Environmentally Responsible Economics (CERES)
11 Arlington Street
Sixth Floor
Boston, MA 02116
617/451-0927
Periodicals: *CERES Report*

Container Recycling Institute (CRI)
1400 16th Street NW
Suite 250
Washington, DC 20036-2217
202/797-6839
Periodicals: *Container and Packaging Recycling Update*

Council of State Governments
Iron Works Pike
P.O. Box 11910
Lexington, KY 40578-1910
606/244-8000

Council on Economic Priorities
30 Irving Place
Ninth Floor
New York, NY 10003
212/420-1133
Periodical: *Shopping for a Better World: A Quick and Easy Guide to Socially Responsible Supermarket Shopping*

Craighead Environmental Research Institute
P.O. Box 156
Moose, WY 83012
307/733-3387

Consumer Federation of America
1424 16th Street NW
Washington DC 20036
202/387-6121

Ecological Society of America
2010 Massachusetts Avenue NW
Suite 400
Washington, DC 20036
202/833-8773
Periodical: *Bulletin of the Ecological Society of America/Ecology/Ecological Monographs*

Electronic Industries Environmental Association Coalition
Electronic Industries Association
2500 Wilson Boulevard
Arlington, VA 22201
703/907-7500

Employee Relocation Council
1720 N Street NW
Washington DC, 20036
202/857-0857

Entomological Society of America
9301 Annapolis Road
Lanham, MD 20706-3115
301/731-4535
Periodical: *Environmental Entomology*

Environmental Assessment Association
8383 East Evans Road
Scottsdale, AZ 85260-3614
602/483-8100

Environmental Business Association (TEBA)
1150 Connecticut Avenue NW
Suite 900
Washington, DC 20036
202/862-4363

Environmental Careers Organization
286 Congress Street
Third Floor
Boston, MA 12210
617/426-4375

Environmental Defense Fund
257 Park Avenue S
New York, NY 10010
212/505-2100
Periodical: *EDF Letter*

Environmental and Energy Study Institute (EESI)
122 C Street NW
Suite 700
Washington, DC 20001
202/628-1400
Periodical: *EESI Weekly Bulletin*

Environmental Industry Association
4301 Connecticut Avenue NW
Suite 300
Washington, DC 20008
202/244-4700
Periodicals: *Waste Age/Recycling Times/ Infectious Waste News*

Environmental Information Association
4915 Auburn Avenue
Suite 303
Bethesda, MD 20814
301/961-4999
Periodicals: *EIA Technical Monograph Series/ EIA Environmental Choices*

Environmental Law Institute
1616 P Street NW
Suite 200
Washington, DC 20036
202/328-5150
Periodicals: *Environmental Law Reporter/ National Wetlands Newsletter*

Environmental Mutagen Society
11250 Roger Bacon Drive
Suite 8
Reston, VA 20190
703/437-4377
Periodicals: *Environmental and Molecular Mutagenesis/EMS Newsletter*

Environmental Technology Council
734 15th Street NW
Suite 320
Washington, DC 20005
202/783-0870
Periodical: *CSMEE*

ERIC Clearinghouse for Science, Mathematics, and Environmental Education
1929 Kenny Road
Columbus, OH 43210-1080
614/292-6717
800/276-0462

Farm Credit Council
7100 East Belleview
Suite 205
Englewood, CO 80111
303/740-4200

Foundation for Environmental Education Society of Environmental Toxicology and Chemistry (SETAC)
1010 North 12th Avenue
Pensacola, FL 32501
904/469-1500
Periodicals: *Journal of Environmental Toxicology and Chemistry*

Freshwater Foundation
Spring Hill Center
725 County Road 6
Wayzata, MN 55391
Fax: 612/449-0092
Periodical: *Facets of Freshwater Newsletter/ Health and Environment Digest/U.S. Water News*

Government Institutes, Incorporated
4 Research Place
Suite 200
Rockville, MD 20850
301/921-2300

Green Seal
1400 16th Street NW
Suite 300
Washington, DC 20036-2215
202/588-8400

Hazardous Materials Advisory Council
1101 Vermont Avenue NW
Suite 301
Washington, DC 20005
202/289-4550

Hazardous Materials Control Research Institute
1 Church Street
Suite 200
Rockville, MD 20850-4129
301/251-1900
Periodical: *Focus*

Illinois Hazardous Waste Research and Information Center
One East Hazelwood Drive
Champaign, IL 61820
217/333-8940
For a list of periodicals:
www.hazard.uiuc.edu/wmrc

Industrial Biotechnology Association
1625 K Street NW
Suite 1100
Washington, DC 20006-1604
202/857-0244
Periodical: *Biotechnology at Work*

Institute for Environmental Auditing
28 East Ostend
Baltimore, MD 21230
410/706-1849
Periodical: *Working Papers*

Institute for Local Self-Reliance
2425 18th Street NW
Washington, DC 20009
202/232-4108

Institute for Real Estate Management
430 North Michigan Avenue
Chicago, IL 60611
800/837-0706
Periodicals: *Journal of Property Management*

Institute of Clean Air Companies
1660 L Street NW
#1100
Washington, DC 20036
202/457-0911
Periodical: *Clean Air News*

Institute of Environmental Sciences
940 East Northwest Highway
Mt. Prospect, IL 60056
847/255-1561
Periodical: *Journal of Environmental Sciences*

Institute of Hazardous Materials Managers
11900 Parklawn Drive
Suite 450
Rockville, MD 20852
301/984-8969

Institute of Noise Control Engineering
Box 3206, Arlington Branch
Poughkeepsie, NY 12603
914/462-4006
Periodicals: *Noise Control Engineering Journal/Noise News International Newsletter*

Institute of Scrap Recycling Industries, Inc. (ISRI)
1325 G Street NW
Suite 1000
Washington, DC 20005
202/737-1770
Periodicals: *Scrap*

International Association of Assessing Officers
130 East Randolph Street
Suite 850
Chicago, IL 60601
312/819-6100

International Association of Environmental Testing Laboratories
505 Wythe Street
Alexandria, VA 22314
202/434-4547

International Council of Shopping Centers
665 Fifth Avenue
New York, NY 10022-5370
212/421-8181

International Institute for Energy Conservation
750 First Street NE
Suite 940
Washington, DC 20002
202/842-3388

International Right of Way Association
13650 South Gramercy Place
Gardena, CA 90249
310/538-0233

International Society of Chemical Ecology
University of South Florida,
Department of Biology
4202 Fowler Avenue
Tampa, FL 33620
813/974-2336
Periodical: *Journal of Chemical Ecology/ISCE Newsletter*

Interstate Council on Water Policy
1401 I Street
Suite 900
Washington, DC 20005
202/218-4196
Periodical: *ICWP Policy Statement & Bylaws*

Keep America Beautiful, Inc.
1010 Washington Boulevard
Stamford, CT 06902
203/323-8987

Legal Environmental Assistance Foundation, Inc. (LEAF)
1115 North Gadsden Street
Tallahassee, FL 32303-6327
904/681-2591

Lender's Service, Inc.
700 Cherrington Parkway
Coraopolis, PA 15108
412/299-4000

Manufacturers of Emission Controls Association
1660 L Street NW
Suite 1100
Washington, DC 20036
202/296-4797

Mortgage Bankers Association
1125 15th Street NW
Suite 700
Washington, DC 20005
202/861-6500

Mortgage Guaranty Insurance Corporation
270 East Kilbourn Avenue
Milwaukee, WI 53202
800/558-9900
Periodicals: *Prologue*

Mortgage Insurance Companies of America
727 15th Street NW
12th Floor
Washington, DC 20005
202/393-5566

National Apartment Association
1050 17th Street NW
Suite 300
Washington, DC 20036
202/296-3390

National Association of Chemical Recyclers
1200 G Street NW
Suite 800
Washington, DC 20005
202/434-8740
Periodical: *Flashpoint*

National Association of Conservation Districts
509 Capitol Court NE
Washington, DC 20002
202/547-6223

National Association of Environmental Risk Auditors (NAERA)
P.O. Box 53185
Cincinnati, OH 45253
513/681-9900

National Association of Independent Fee Appraisers
7501 Murdoch Avenue
St. Louis, MO 63119
314/781-6688

National Association of Industrial and Office Parks
2201 Cooperative Way
Third Floor
Herndon, VA 20171
703/904-7100

National Association of Manufacturers
1331 Pennsylvania Avenue NW
Suite 600
Washington, DC 20004
202/637-3000
Periodicals: *Briefing/Public Affairs*

National Association of Master Appraisers
303 West Cypress Street
San Antonio, TX 78212
210/271-0781
Periodical: *The Master Appraiser*

National Association of Noise Control Officials
53 Cubberly Road
Trenton, NJ 08690
609/586-2684
Periodical: *Vibrations*

National Association for Plastic Container Recovery (NAPCOR)
100 North Tryon Street
Suite 3770
Charlotte, NC 28202
704/358-8882

National Association of Realtors (DC offices)
700 11th Street NW
Washington, DC 20001
202/383-1000
Periodicals: *Today's Realtor/Real Estate Outlook*

National Association of Realtors (Chicago offices)
430 North Michigan Avenue
Chicago, IL 60611
312/329-8200
Periodicals: *Today's Realtor/Real Estate Outlook*

National Association of State Development Agencies
750 First Street NE
Suite 710
Washington, DC 20002
202/898-1302

National Capital Poison Control Center
George Washington University Hospital
202/625-3333 (Collect calls accepted)

National Council on Radiation Protection and Measurements
7910 Woodmont Avenue
Suite 800
Bethesda, MD 20814
301/657-2652
Periodical: *NCRP Report*

National Council for Urban Economic Development
1730 K Street NW
Suite 700
Washington, DC 20006
202/223-4735
Periodicals: *Economic Developments/Economic Developments Abroad/Commentary*

National Environmental Development Association
1440 New York Avenue NW
Suite 300
Washington, DC 20005
202/289-0966

National Environmental Health Association
720 South Colorado Boulevard, #970
South Tower
Denver, CO 80222
303/756-9090

National Environmental Training Association
3020 East Camelback Road
Suite 399
Phoenix, AZ 85016
602/956-6099
Periodicals: *NETA News/Who's Who in Environmental Training*

National Fire Protection Association
1 Batterymarch Park
P.O. Box 9101
Quincy, MA 02269-9101
617/770-3000

National Golf Foundation
1150 South U.S. Highway 1
Suite 401
Jupiter, FL 33477
561/744-6006

National Governors Association
Hall of the States
444 North Capitol Street NW
Suite 267
Washington, DC 20001-1512
202/624-5300

National League of Cities
1301 Pennsylvania Avenue NW
Suite 550
Washington, DC 20004
202/626-3000

National Materials Exchange Network
509/466-1532

National Mining Association
1130 17th Street NW
Washington, DC 20036
202/463-2625
Periodical: *Mining Voice*

National Oil Recyclers Association
12429 Cedar Road
Suite 26
Cleveland, OH 44106-3172
216/791-7316
Periodical: *NORA News*

National Paint Coatings Association
1500 Rhode Island Avenue NW
Washington, DC 20005
202/462-6272

National Pesticide Telecommunications Network
800/858-7378

National Research Council, National Academy of Sciences, National Academy of Engineering, Institute of Medicine
2101 Constitution Avenue NW
Washington, DC 20418
202/334-2000

National Retail Federation
325 Seventh Street NW
Suite 1000
Washington, DC 20004
202/783-7971

National Technical Information Service
52885 Port Royal Road
Springfield, VA 22161
703/605-6000

National Water Resources Association
3800 North Fairfax Drive, #4
Arlington, VA 22203
703/524-1544
Periodical: *National Water Line*

National Wetlands Technical Council
1616 P Street NW
Suite 200
Washington, DC 20036
202/328-5150

National Wildlife Federation
1400 16th Street NW
Washington, DC 20036
202/797-6800
Periodicals: *International Wildlife/National Wildlife*

Natural Resources Defense Council
40 West 20th Street
New York, NY 10011
212/727-2700
Periodicals: *The Amicus Journal*

North American Association for Environmental Education
1255 23rd Street NW
Suite 400
Washington, DC 20037
202/884-8700
Periodical: *Environmental Communicator*

Northeast Waste Management Officials' Association
129 Portland Street
Fifth Floor
Boston, MA 02114-2014
617/367-8558

Pollution Prevention Information Clearinghouse
202/260-1023

Public Lands Foundation
P.O. Box 10403
McLean, VA 22102
703/790-1988

Real Estate Educators Association
10565 Lee Highway
Suite 104
Fairfax, VA 22030
703/352-6688

Real Estate Research Corporation
2 North LaSalle Street
Suite 730
Chicago, IL 60602
312/346-5885
Periodicals: *Annual Emerging Trends in Real Estate Report/Quarterly Real Estate Report*

Recreational Vehicle Industry Association
1896 Preston White Drive
Reston, VA 20191-4363
703/620-6003

Renew America
1400 Sixteenth Street NW
Suite 710
Washington, DC 20036
202/232-2252
Periodical: *Environmental Success Index*

Savings & Community Bankers of America
900 19th Street NW
Suite 400
Washington, DC 20006
202/857-3100

Sierra Club
730 Polk Street
San Francisco, CA 94109
415/776-2211
Periodicals: *Sierra/National News Report/Energy Report*

Society for Epidemiological Research
c/o American Journal of Epidemiology
111 Market Place
Suite 840
Baltimore, MD 21202-6709
410/223-1600
Periodical: *American Journal of Epidemiology*

Society for Vector Ecology
P.O. Box 87
Santa Ana, CA 92702
714/971-2421, ext. 148
Periodical: *Vector Ecology Newsletter/The Journal of Vector Ecology*

Society of Industrial and Office Realtors
700 11th Street NW
Suite 510
Washington, DC 20001
202/737-1150
Periodical: *Today's Realtor*

Society of Environmental Toxicology and Chemistry
1010 North 12th Avenue
Pensacola, FL 32501-3307
904/469-1500
Periodicals: *SETAC News/Environmental Technology and Chemistry*

Society of Toxicology
1767 Business Center Drive
Suite 302
Reston, VA 22090
703/438-3101
Periodicals: *Fundamental and Applied Toxicology/Toxicology and Applied Pharmacology*

Soil and Water Conservation Society
7515 Northeast Ankeny Road
Ankeny, IA 50021
515/289-2331
Periodical: *Journal of Soil and Water Conservation*

Southern Environmental Law Center
201 West Main Street
Suite 14
Charlottesville, VA 22902-5065
804/977-4090

Southwest Research and Information Center
P.O. Box 4524
Albuquerque, NM 87106
505/262-1862
Periodicals: *The Workbook/Strict News*

State and Territorial Pollution Program Administrators
444 North Capitol Street
Washington, DC 20001
202/624-7864
Periodical: *Washington Update Newsletter*

Steel Recycling Institute
680 Andersen Drive
Pittsburgh, PA 15220-2700
800/876-7274
Periodical: *The Recycling Magnet*

Synthetic Organic Chemical Manufacturers Association
1850 M Street NW
Suite 700
Washington, DC 20005
202/296-8577
Periodical: *SOCMA Newsletter*

Technical Association of the Pulp and Paper Industry
P.O. Box 105113
Atlanta, GA 30348-5113
404/446-1400
Periodical: *TAPPI Journal*

Union of Concerned Scientists
2 Brattle Square
P.O. Box 9105
Cambridge, MA 02238-9105
617/547-5552

United Nations Environment Programme (UNEP)
Regional Office of North America
2 U.N. Plaza
Room 803
New York, NY 10017
212/963-8138

United States-Asia Environmental Partnership (US-AEP)
U.S. Agency for International Development
320 21st Street NW
Suite 3319
Washington, DC 20523-0047

United States Operating Committee on ETAD
1100 New York Avenue NW
Suite 1090
Washington, DC 20005
202/414-4100

U.S. Public Interest Research Group (PIRG)
218 D Street, SE
Washington, DC 20003
202/546-9707
Periodical: *Citizen Agenda*

Urban Land Institute
1025 Thomas Jefferson Avenue NW
Suite 500W
Washington, DC 20007
202/624-7000
Periodicals: *Land Use Digest/Project Reference File/Urban Land*

Washington Workshops Foundation
Global Environment Seminar
3222 N Street NW
Suite 340
Washington, DC 20007
202/965-3434

Water Environment Federation
601 Wythe Street
Alexandria, VA 22314-1994
703/684-2400
Periodical: *Operations Forum/Highlights/ Water Environment and Technology/Water Environment Research/Industrial Waste Water*

Water Resources Association of the Delaware River Basin
P.O. Box 867
Valley Forge, PA 19482
610/917-0090

Western Regional Environmental Education Council
Executive Director
5555 Morningside Drive
Suite 212
Houston, TX 77705
713/520-1936

Wildlife Society
5410 Grosvenor Lane
Bethesda, MD 20814
301/897-9770
Periodicals: *Journal of Wildlife Management/ The Wildlifer/Wildlife Society Bulletin*

World Environment Center
419 Park Avenue S
Suite 1800
New York, NY 10016
212/683-4700
Periodical: *Network News*

World Research Foundation
15300 Ventura Boulevard
Suite 405
Sherman Oaks, CA 91403
818/999-5483

World Resources Institute
1709 New York Avenue NW
Suite 700
Washington, DC 20006
202/638-6300
Periodicals: *World Resources Report*

World Wildlife Fund
1250 24th Street NW
Washington, DC 20037
202/293-4800
Periodical: *Focus*

Worldwatch Institute
1776 Massachusetts Avenue NW
Washington, DC 20036
202/452-1999
Periodicals: *Worldwatch Papers/State of the Worlds*

Glossary

abatement. Removal or the controlled release of contaminants. Includes operations and maintenance (O&M), encapsulation, enclosure, and removal.

above-ground release. Any release of gasoline or other contaminants to the surface of the land or surface water, such as from the above-ground portion of a UST system or overfills.

above-ground tank. A storage reservoir device that is situated above grade so that the entire surface area, including the bottom, can be visually inspected.

ACM. Asbestos containing material.

action level. The concentration of a contaminant that determines the necessity to remediate.

adjacent property. A property that is not contaminated but is located next to or nearby a site that is.

aeration. The introduction of oxygen into a contaminated liquid, which creates gases that are then released.

aerobic. Requiring oxygen.

air and light diminution. The loss of natural sunlight or air space due to the construction of improvements.

air sample clearance test. Air monitoring at the completion of a contamination abatement or remediation project.

air stripping. An in situ groundwater remediation process. Contaminated groundwater is pumped to the surface and processed in an air stripping tower. The water flows over packing materials. The contaminated water comes in contact with air and the contaminants mix with the air. The contaminated air is released or filtered.

amended water. Mixture of water and surfactant.

aquatic flora. Any plant life associated with the aquatic ecosystem, such as algae, seaweed, etc.

aquifer. A subterranean geological formation that is capable of supplying a significant amount of water to a well or spring.

asbestos. Natural mineral mined from rock and used in construction. Properties include noncombustibility, corrosion resistance, high tensile strength, and both thermal and electrical insulating capability.

asbestosis. A chronic lung disease, resulting from the scarring of lung tissues by asbestos fibers.

assemblage. A collection of two or more parcels by one property owner. The buyer may (but not always) pay a premium over the market value because of the buyer's special motivations associated with the buyer's use of the combined parcels.

assessment stage. The first stage of a detrimental condition analysis. It includes all costs and losses of income in this stage.

attainability analysis. A scientific assessment of the use or possible remediation that is proposed.

avalanche. The sudden and swift flow of a mass of ice, snow, soil, rock, or other material down a hillside or mountainside.

backfill. Clean soil replacing excavated contaminated soil.

Bell Chart. An organizational chart used in the real estate professions that delineates 10 classifications of real estate damages and detrimental conditions.

below-ground release. Any release of contaminants to the subsurface or the groundwater, such as from an underground storage tank.

benign condition. Any condition that occurs but has no impact on the real estate associated with the event.

benzene. A fuel additive that is 2% to 4% of gasoline; a known carcinogen.

blast zone. The area impacted by the explosion of a bomb, volcano, or other situation.

blight. A disease or injury of plants resulting in withering, cessation of growth, and death of parts without rotting. Also, a term to describe older neighborhoods with high crime rates.

blowdown. The discharge of recirculating water for the purpose of discharging materials within the system. This eliminates the buildup of materials that could cause damages.

brackish marsh. A marsh, bog, or swamp that receives an influx of both salt and fresh water.

brownfield. A large site that has been contaminated from operations on the site. Upon remediation, it may be referred to as a *greenfield*.

BTEX. Benzene, toluene, ethylbenzene, and xylene—primary toxins of soils and groundwater associated with petroleum products.

building construction condition. Any defective material or workmanship to the improvements.

carcinogen. A cancer-causing substance.

casing. A pipe or tubing lowered into a borehole in order to support the sides of the hole, or to prevent water or gas from entering or exiting the hole.

catastrophic collapse. The disastrous, sudden, and utter failure of support structures or soils.

cementing. The injection of cement slurry into a drilled hole or behind the casing.

CERCLA. Comprehensive Environmental Response, Compensation, and Liability Act of 1980. Often referred to as the Superfund Act.

chlorinated solvents. Cleaning solutions containing chloride.

condemnation. The right, as stated within the U.S. Constitution, of the government to take property for the public good and upon the payment of just compensation to the property owner.

confining bed. A mass of impermeable or less permeable material stratigraphically adjacent to an aquifer.

confining zone. A geological formation that limits the movement of water or other fluids.

connection with identified uses. The association of a property with contaminants or prior uses that lead to contamination.

contaminant. Any physical, chemical, biological, or radiological substance in the soil, water, or air.

contamination. The polluting of air, soils, improvements, or groundwater by the introduction of a hazardous substance into the environment.

continuous discharge. An emission that occurs without interruption except for maintenance or other infrequent activity.

contraction. Expansion of soils.

corrosion inhibitor. A substance that is designed to form a protective film against rust or other corrosion.

cost issues. All costs related to the assessment, repair, and ongoing stages of a detrimental condition analysis.

covenant. A promise to use or not use a property in a specific way.

current or past uses in the surrounding area. The external obsolescence created by a historical or ongoing undesirable use nearby.

current use(s) of the property. The operations or applications to which a property is being put.

current uses of adjoining properties. The operations or applications to which contiguous properties are being put.

cut and fill. The removal (cut) of soil or the addition (fill) of soil.

cyclone. A violent storm with a rotating center of low atmospheric pressure.

daily discharge. The emission or discharge, in terms of mass, of a pollutant in a 24-hour period.

debris compost. The decay of debris and the resulting soils subsidence it causes.

deferred maintenance. Routine property upkeep that has been neglected.

degraded wetlands. Swamps, bogs, marshes, etc., that have been negatively altered by man.

deluge. A sudden flooding or inundation of water.

detrimental condition. Any issue or condition that may cause a diminution in value to real estate.

detrimental condition cost approach. An analysis of a property with and without all costs and losses associated with a detrimental condition.

detrimental condition income approach. An analysis of a property with and without any loss of net operating income resulting from a detrimental condition.

Detrimental Condition Matrix. A matrix that illustrates the three detrimental stages (assessment, repair, and ongoing) and three detrimental condition issues (cost, use, and risk).

Detrimental Condition Model. A graph that illustrates all of the categories of stages and issues that must be considered when studying the effects of a detrimental condition on real estate values—e.g., assessment stage, repair stage, ongoing stage, and market resistance.

detrimental condition sales comparison approach. An analysis of a property through the comparison of market data that is impacted and not impacted by a detrimental condition.

detrimental condition stages. The three stages of a detrimental condition analysis, specifically, the assessment, repair, and ongoing stages.

diatomaceous earth filtration. A water filtering process whereby a coat or "cake" of diatomaceous earth filter media is deposited over a membrane (septum) and water is passed through.

differential settlement. Soils with differing compaction or materials that settle to unequal levels.

diminution in value. The lost value of real estate before (as if impaired) and after (or upon discovery of) a detrimental condition.

direct condemnation. The physical taking of property through the process of eminent domain.

discharge. The spillage, leakage, pouring, emitting, or dumping of hazardous materials into land, air, or water.

disinfectant. Any oxidant, such as chlorine, used to kill microorganisms.

disintermediation. A period when long-term interest rates are lower than short-term interest rates.

disposal. The discharge, deposit, injection, dumping, spilling, leaking, or placing of any solid waste or hazardous waste into the air, water, ground, or groundwater.

disposal system. A system of man-made or natural barriers that isolate spent nuclear fuel or radioactive waste or other contaminants.

distillation. A water purification technique that purifies water by heating the water and condensing the steam. The process reduces salt concentration but is ineffective in removing pesticides and volatile organic contaminants such as benzene or chloroform.

drainage. The sheet water flow and ability of a site to divert and drain excess water.

drought. The prolonged lack of rain or availability of an adequate water supply.

earthquake. The shaking of the ground due to seismic activities. Like some natural disasters, they are unpredictable, unpreventable, and cause indiscriminate damage, so they tend to not cause a diminution in value to a particular property or neighborhood but rather impact a region as a whole.

earthquake fault zone. The area along which the ground or subsurface areas move, creating earthquakes.

earthquake retrofit. Additional structural support added to the improvements to provide the support necessary to withstand earthquake destruction or to bring the property into conformity with current earthquake building regulations.

easement. The non-fee simple estate ownership to utilize a site, or a portion of a site, in some defined manner.

economic depreciation. A decline in the economy that negatively impacts real estate values.

economic disaster. A large-scale event that negatively impacts the overall economy, which in turn impact real estate values.

economic obsolescence. The loss incurred when the depreciated value of the improvements, from a cost perspective, is more than the market value.

ecosystem. The natural community and its environment functioning as a total system.

effluent. Treated liquid waste.

egress diminution. The partial or total loss of the ability to exit or leave a site.

electromagnetic fields (EMFs). The electric forces emitted by power lines or other electrical devices.

eminent domain. The taking of property, as allowed under the U.S. Constitution, for the public good and upon payment of just compensation.

encapsulant. Liquid substances that are applied to contaminants to prevent their escape. *Bridging* encapsulants form a coating over the contaminant's surface. *Penetrating* encapsulants soak into the contaminants to bind its components together. Both types are frequently used together.

encapsulation. A contamination remediation process that encapsulates the contaminants to prevent leaching and surface seepage of contamination into either the air, groundwater, or storm drainage system.

enclosure. Construction of an air or watertight structure that surrounds the contaminant.

encroachment. An improvement that is constructed in such a manner that it crosses the property line or otherwise encroaches upon an adjacent property.

end removal. The removal of contaminants when the property is eventually demolished.

environmental impact report. A study required by governmental agencies to determine the impact that a proposed development will have on the surrounding areas.

environmental lien. A restriction placed on a property for environmental reasons.

environmentally sensitive area. An area where the plant or animal life or their habitat are either rare or particularly vulnerable.

EPA. U.S. Environmental Protection Agency.

equipment decontamination enclosure system. A washroom, holding area, and uncontaminated area for handling materials and equipment.

ex situ. A remediation process that involves excavation.

expansion. The enlargement of soils due to moisture inundation or another natural event.

expansive soil. Soils that expand when moist.

exposure. Contact with a contaminant through skin absorption, inhalation, or ingestion.

external depreciation. Any event or development located off-site that negatively impacts the subject property.

external obsolescence. See *external depreciation*.

feasibility. The capability of a project or development to be accomplished in a successful manner within a reasonable time.

feng shui. An ancient Asian belief, in part relating to the orientation and planning of a property site and the improvement layout.

fill dirt. Soils that are used to fill in low-lying areas.

filtration. Water purification by screening out contaminants using a sediment process, a filter, or a sieve.

flash floods. Sudden-moving flood waters that are generally caused by heavy rains over soils that are not capable of absorbing the moisture.

floodplain. The lowland and flat areas adjoining rivers, canyons, lakes, and ocean waters that are prone to flooding.

formaldehyde. A liquid that is used to preserve woods and other materials and sometimes used in construction processes.

fresh water marshes. Marshes where the water has concentrations of salt less than five parts per 1,000.

friable. Building materials, such as asbestos, that may be crumbled by hand pressure.

functional depreciation. See *functional obsolescence*.

functional obsolescence. All losses to a property's value except for external influences and physical depreciation—e.g., an outdated and undesirable floor plan or design.

general plan. A proposed outline for the overall development of a city or other municipality that is written and issued by that municipality. Also known as a *master plan*.

generator. A site where the hazardous waste is produced.

gentrification economics. Improvement and fixing-up of older neighborhoods.

geotechnical issues. Matters relating to soils or soils engineering.

government incentives. A city's or other governmental entity's enticement to develop or use a property in a particular manner, which may alter the highest and best use of the property.

government mandates. A city's or other governmental entity's decree or order to develop or use a property in a specific manner.

grading. Earth moving for the purposes of property development.

ground lease. The rental of a site for a specified period and at specified terms.

groundwater. Water below the land surface or subsurface soils that are saturated with water.

groundwater contamination. The introduction of hazardous or toxic material into the underground water supply or aquifers.

groundwater seepage. Saturated soils that flow up to the surface.

hazardous substance. A material that is determined by qualified engineers to be poisonous, reactive, flammable, corrosive, toxic, or that has been designed as such by a governmental or regulatory agency.

heavy metal. Uranium, plutonium, or thorium placed in a nuclear reactor.

HEPA. High-efficiency particulate air—e.g., HEPA filter or HEPA vacuum—that filters asbestos fibers.

hurricane. A violent storm that is capable of destroying real estate improvements.

hydric soils. Soils that are saturated with water at or near the surface and are oxygen-deficient long enough to disrupt the growing season.

hydrophytic plants. Plants that grow in or near water, in wet habitats, or in hydric soils.

illegal use. Improvements that have been constructed without the proper building permits.

impaired value. The indicated value of a property upon the application of one or more of the three detrimental conditions to value.

imposed condition. An act or forced event that affects value. Includes long-term and permanent external depreciation.

in situ. In place, referring to an on-site remediation process without excavation.

incurable condition. A detrimental condition that cannot be economically or physically remedied.

indoor air quality problem. A mechanical issue or construction defect that results in inadequate air circulation, or a use within a property that results in a nuisance or health risk to its occupants.

infestation. An invasion of insects, plants, or animals that disrupts a property's use or value.

ingress diminution. The entire or partial loss of the ability to enter or access a site.

in-ground tank. A storage device where any portion is located below grade, thereby preventing a visual inspection of the external bottom surface.

initial removal. The up-front and immediate removal of contaminants.

inner liner. A protective layer of material placed inside a tank or container that helps prevent corrosion.

invasion. See *infestation*.

inverse condemnation. The damages caused by an external issue or use that does not physically impact the property.

kangaroo rat. A rodent that has been designated as endangered by some governmental agencies and thereby may create development constraints.

land disposal. The placement of waste or contaminants on the land, such as a landfill, surface impoundment, waste pile, injection well, land treatment facility, salt dome or salt bed formation, underground mine, cave, bunker, or vault.

landfill. A site that is used for trash disposal. May cause environmental problems or neighborhood nuisances.

landslide. A sudden or creeping movement of earth downslope.

leach. To dissolve contaminants by percolating liquid in order to separate the soluble components.

leachate. A liquid, such as suspended compounds in liquid, that has percolated through or drained from hazardous materials.

lead. A chemical element that is considered environmentally hazardous in some situation where it may be ingested.

lead paint. Paint that has lead added as one of its ingredients. Considered hazardous if ingested.

leak. An unintended seepage of fluids, such as water or gasoline, that requires repairs or remediation.

levees. Embankments to protect flooding along rivers or other bodies of water.

liquefaction. The amalgamation or settlement of soils, such as resulting from a seismic event.

lithology. The description of rocks, based on their physical and chemical characteristics.

lithosphere. The solid part of the earth below the surface, including any groundwater.

littoral zone. The area between the low tide water mark and the high tide water mark.

loading capacity. The maximum level of contaminant discharge that water can receive without violating water quality standards.

LUST. Leaking underground storage tank.

Malibu effect. A slang term used to describe the resilience of many waterfront property values when repeatedly damaged by natural forces.

market conditions. An increase or decrease of real estate value due to general market conditions.

market resistance. The risk, if any, associated with the ongoing stage of a detrimental condition analysis; includes the reluctance on the part of the real estate market to buy a property that has historically been damaged or tainted. Sometimes called *stigma*.

matrix. Hard, non-friable material (e.g., concrete) that contains asbestos.

maximum contaminant level (MCL). The maximum level of contaminant discharge without violating regulatory standards, usually mandated by state requirements and referencing maximum levels of toxins in drinking water.

mesothelioma. A form of chest and abdominal cancer caused by asbestos exposure.

metals. A classification of possible contaminants such as mercury or lead.

monitoring facility. Equipment installed to monitor groundwater below or near an encapsulated site. Used to test if seepage or leaching is occurring on an encapsulated site.

monsoon. A violent storm with the characteristics of heavy rains and strong winds.

MRI release. The escape of magnetic fields from a medical diagnostics device.

MTBE. Methyl tertiary butyl ether, a gasoline additive.

National Marine Fisheries Service. Federal agencies and regulations related to fisheries and aquatic habitat.

natural condition. A detrimental condition that occurs naturally and entirely without the interference of man, such as a volcano, tornado, earthquake, etc.

nature preserve. An area designated by governmental agencies to remain in its natural condition, thereby preventing or restricting its development.

neighborhood blight. Urban decay within a community. May be an imposed condition that is ongoing or may be cured and considered a temporary condition.

neighborhood nuisance. Any annoying or irritating external condition or influence. May be permanent or temporary.

NIOSH. National Institute for Occupational Safety and Health

no discharge of free oil. A discharge that does not cause a film, sheen, or discoloration on the surface of the water or cause a sludge or emulsion beneath the water surface.

nonconforming use. Improvements that are not in line with surrounding uses, such as a jail in the middle of a residential neighborhood.

non-friable. A building material that is not capable of being crumbled by hand pressure.

nonmarket motivation. Any special influence whereby a buyer, seller, or tenant acts in a way that is not typical for the market. For example, a property owner who is in financial distress may sell the property for less that what he or she would have received under normal circumstances.

non-source property. A property that is contaminated, although the discharge of the contaminant occurred on another property—i.e., not the responsible party.

normal property value. The market value of a property in an undamaged condition and without consideration of any detrimental condition.

NPPL. National Priority Pollutants List, a list of common pollutants caused by underground storage tank facilities.

obstruction. The placement of an improvement in such a manner that it interferes with the normal use of a property. A tree planted in front of a gate would be considered an obstruction.

oil seepage. The leakage of oil, possibly from natural underground deposits or from leaking containers or plumbing.

oil spill. The accidental release of oil, often crude oil, into the environment.

ongoing stage. The third stage in a detrimental condition analysis. It includes all costs associated with a damaged property after all repairs or remediation have been completed—e.g., additional financing or insurance costs, use, and market resistance.

operations and maintenance (O&M). An ongoing maintenance program for contaminated properties. For example, for asbestos it could include training, HEPA vacuuming, wet cleaning, and air monitoring. This is also termed *end removal*, as the contaminants remain until the eventual demolition of the building.

OSHA. Occupational Safety and Health Administration, a division of the U.S. Department of Labor.

parts per million (PPM). A unit of concentration. One part per million can be compared to one cent in $10,000.

passive detector. A measurement device that functions without oversight or energy.

PCBs. Polychlorinated biphenyls. Sometimes found in electrical or hydraulic equipment.

PCE. Perchloroethylene or tetrachloroethylene, nicknamed *perk*. A solvent often used for dry cleaning and other uses.

permeability. A measure of a material's ability to transmit water.

pesticide. A substance that controls agricultural pests, such as demeton, guthion, malathion, mirex, methoxychlor, and parathion.

pickleweed. A salt marsh vegetation.

pipeline easement. The right or privilege to install and maintain a pipeline on a property. Can be considered a detrimental condition if the market reacts negatively towards the risks associated with a pipeline explosion or leak.

plume. The areas that are saturated or impacted by underground contaminants.

pollutant. A contaminant, such as dredged soil, solid waste, incinerator residue, filter backwash, sewage, garbage, sewage sludge, munitions, chemical wastes, biological materials, or radioactive materials.

ponding. The puddling of water on a site or its improvements due to improper water sheet flow.

potable water supply. A water supply that is fit for human consumption.

PPB. Parts per billion.

prescriptive easement. The securing of easement rights through adverse possession.

PRG. Nonofficial preliminary risk goals set forth by the U.S. Environmental Protection Agency regarding soil contamination.

process wastes. Any designated pollutant resulting from a manufacturing process.

project incentive. The risk, if any, associated with the repair stage of a detrimental condition analysis.

protected species or vegetation. Any plant or animal that has been designated by a governmental agency to be safeguarded. This designation may limit or restrict development.

puddling. See *ponding*.

quicksand. A soil type that creates a mire whereby a person or animal walking over the area will sink. May both create a hazard and limit the developability of a site.

radioactive. Having unstable atoms that decay or break down to another kind of atom. The process emits high-energy particles. For example, radium decays to form radon. Radiation includes high-energy particles, which include alpha and beta particles and gamma rays.

radon. A colorless and odorless gas that is emitted from decaying uranium deposits. The gas may enter improvements through cracks and create a health hazard if inhaled.

rail easement. The right for the construction, maintenance, and operation of a train on a property.

recharge. Any process whereby water is added to the saturated zone of an aquifer.

reciprocal parking easement. The contractual right of two adjacent parties to share parking with the other.

release. A spill, leak, emission, discharge, escape, leach, or disposal from an underground storage tank into the soils, ground, or surface water.

repair stage. The second stage in detrimental condition analysis. It includes all the costs of repairs or remediation resulting from a detrimental condition, including the repair and incidental costs, contingencies, use issues, and the project incentive.

representative sample. A sample (e.g., groundwater, waste) that can be expected to exhibit the average properties of the whole.

retaining slope. A mound of soil that is designed to hold back the ground behind it.

retaining wall. A wall that is designed to hold back the ground behind it.

retrofit. The renovation of a property to a higher standard. For example, an old brick building may be retrofitted to withstand an earthquake.

reverse osmosis. A water purification process used to remove salts, such as for sea water. The process yields drinking water and salt residues.

riparian habitats. Areas in water courses that are the home of associated animal and plant life.

risk issues. All risks associated with a detrimental condition analysis, specifically within the assessment stage (uncertainty factor), the repair stage (project incentive), and ongoing stage (market resistance).

RP. Responsible party.

salt flat. A site with poor drainage where the water evaporates, leaving salt behind.

Santa Claus factor. A slang term used to describe a situation where the repaired property is better than the improvements that were damaged or destroyed.

saturated zone or zone of saturation. Soils in which all voids are filled with water.

sea water percolation. Underground sea water that passes through soils and seeps to ground level.

sedimentation. A prefiltering process for removal of solids by gravity or separation.

septic system. An on-site system or cesspool to process wastes.

settlement. The sinking of soils, such as those that have not been adequately compacted.

shear strength. An engineering term used to describe a soil or structure to resist applied forces that causes or tends to cause two contiguous parts of a body to slide relative to each other.

sheen. A glistening appearance on the water surface from oil residue.

short-term condition. Any detrimental condition that lasts for a short period of time.

Sick Building Syndrome. See *indoor air quality problem*.

sinkhole. An opening in the earth created by either natural or man-made subterranean activities. For example, if a tunnel fails, it may create a sinkhole.

site grading. The leveling of land for development.

slope creep. A natural landslide that occurs at a very slow rate.

slow sand filtration. A process whereby water is drained through a bed of sand at low velocity, removing particles by physical and biological mechanisms.

sludge. A solid, semisolid, or liquid waste generated from a waste water treatment plant, less the treated effluent.

soft water. Water that contains low levels of dissolved minerals, such as salts, calcium, or magnesium.

soil. All unconsolidated materials naturally found at the surface of the earth, such as clays, silts, sands, and small rocks.

soil compaction. Fill soils that have been pressed to avoid subsidence.

soil contamination. The introduction of a hazardous material into the ground.

soil excavation. A type of remediation process that involves the digging of contaminated soil from the subsurface, where it is treated or disposed of.

soils subsidence. Soils that are unstable and sink.

solder. A metal compound used to seal plumbing joints. Solder compounds containing lead are now banned.

solid waste. Nonliquid trash or other disposed materials.

solvent contamination. The accidental introduction of a cleaning or chemical solution into the soils or groundwater.

source property. Any site that is the source of discharging a pollutant.

staged removal. The staged removal of contaminants over time (i.e., floor-by-floor, one unit at a time).

stigma. See *market resistance*, *project incentive*, or *uncertainty factor*.

storage tanks. Aboveground or underground tanks that are used for storing fluids, such as gasoline or propane.

stratum. A sedimentary bed or layer that generally consists of the same kind of soils or rock material.

stressed vegetation. Plants that have been damaged.

subsidence. The falling or failure of soils.

subsurface construction defect. Any soils-related problem that results from a man-made condition.

sulfates. A potentially corrosive, and naturally forming, substance found within certain soils. May cause concrete foundations to erode.

Superfund site. A property that has been designated under CERCLA to be remedied.

super-surface construction defect. The failure to properly construct some component of the improvements.

supply and demand. The fundamental economic forces that drive real estate prices. Some theorize that the supply of real estate is fixed, and that only demand changes.

surface water. All water that is open to atmosphere.

surfactant. Wetting agent that enhances the penetration of water.

surging soil. Soils that are upheaving.

SVOC. Semi-volatile organic compounds.

TCA. Trichloroethane, a solvent.

TCE. Trichloroethylene, or trichloroethene, a solvent.

temporary condition. A short-term event or one-time situation. Includes temporary external depreciation.

temporary construction easement. The incidental and interim use of a property or a portion of a property, through eminent domain, to use the property while construction is underway.

termites. A small insect that feeds on wood. An infestation of termites can damage or destroy a wood-frame structure.

three detrimental condition approaches to value. The three approaches to valuing a property that has been impacted by a detrimental condition, which are based on the three traditional approaches to value.

tidal influence. An oceanfront area that is affected by tides.

tidal wave. See *tsunami*.

tornado. A violent storm where various natural forces cause a strong circular wind that can reach over 300 miles per hour. Like some natural disasters, they are unpredictable and unpreventable, and they cause indiscriminate damage, so they tend to not cause a diminution in value to a particular property or neighborhood but rather impact a large region.

torrent. A downpour of rain that may cause flooding.

toxic waste. The disposal of a hazardous material in such a way that it threatens plants, animals, or humans.

toxicity. The level to which a substance is toxic.

TPH. Total petroleum hydrocarbons, typically measured by levels of BTXE.

traffic diminution. The loss of vehicular or pedestrian traffic. Can be either a permanent or temporary issue.

treatment zone. A soil area of the unsaturated zone of a land treatment unit within which hazardous constituents are degraded, transformed, or immobilized.

TRPH. Total recoverable petroleum hydrocarbons.

tsunami. A large wave usually caused by an earthquake or an underwater landslide. While unpredictable and unpreventable, they tend to impact certain zones or areas.

tunneling. Drilling or trenching for the placement of underground passages for utility lines, subways, trains, roads, or other uses. Tunnels can cause a diminution in value if the market perceives that they may not be structurally sound or may fail in the event of a seismic event, such as an earthquake.

U.S. Army Corps of Engineers. A governmental agency whose duties include overseeing dredging, salt marsh restoration, and reviewing navigational aspects of projects. Also known as the *Corps of Engineers*.

U.S. Environmental Protection Agency. A federal governmental agency that oversees a variety of environmental issues and regulations.

U.S. Fish and Wildlife Service. A federal governmental agency that oversees wildlife issues and consults with the EPA and the Corps of Engineers under the Clean Water Act and the Fish and Wildlife Coordination Act.

uncertainty factor. The risks, if any, associated with the assessment stage of a detrimental condition analysis.

unchlorinated solvents. Cleaning solutions to which no chlorine has been added.

unidentified substance containers. A drum or other container holding unidentified substances suspected of being hazardous or containing petroleum products.

unimpaired value. The value as if no detrimental condition exists.

unsaturated zone or zone of aeration. The area between the land surface and the groundwater table.

uplands. An area above and adjacent to the high tide level.

urban decay. The deterioration of infrastructure and improvements within a metropolitan area.

use issues. All losses associated with the use of the property during the assessment, repair, and ongoing stages of a detrimental condition analysis.

USDW. Underground source of drinking water.

USEPA. United States Environmental Protection Agency.

UST. Underground storage tank.

utility disruption. The temporary interruption of utilities, such as water, electricity, gas, etc.

utility easement. The rights granted to use a portion of a property for utility lines.

vacuum extraction. A type of remediation process that removes the majority of contaminants through the use of one or more suction wells, or a series of air injection and suction wells. The method is typically less disruptive than soil excavation and may be less expensive than other techniques involving excavation.

variance. The right granted by a city or municipality to develop or use a property in a way that varies from the typical or stated requirements.

view diminution. The partial or entire loss of a view amenity.

VOC. Volatile organic compounds.

volcano. A mountain that historically has erupted, or can erupt in the future, and can cause landslides or other destruction. Like some natural disasters, they are unpredictable, unpreventable, and cause indiscriminate damage, so they tend to not cause a diminution in value to a particular property or neighborhood but rather impact a large region.

waste water. A liquid (including storm water) that discharges into a tunnel, drain, ditch, or stream.

water intrusion. The undesired influx of water onto a site or into improvements.

water table. The upper level of the saturated zone of groundwater.

worker decontamination enclosure system. A series of three temporary rooms for entering or exiting a contaminated work site. They are the clean room (adjacent to the outside or uncontaminated area), the shower room, and the equipment room (dirty room).

wetlands. Areas that are inundated or saturated by surface or groundwater, such as lakes, swamps, marshes, bogs, sloughs, quagmire, wet meadows, river overflows, mud flats, lagoons, and ponds.

woodrot. A situation where a wood structure has become moist and decayed.

x-ray release. The undesired discharge of radiograms.

Bibliography

Adams, Victoria, and Bill Mundy. "The Valuation of High-Amenity Natural Land." *The Appraisal Journal* (January 1992): 48.

Adler, Jerry. "Magma Force." *Newsweek* (May 5, 1997): 67–68.

"All About Hurricanes." In Yatcom Communications, Inc. [electronic bulletin board] 1995 - [cited February 2, 1998]. Available: http://www.yatcom.com/neworl/weather /whatis.html.

American Council on Science and Health. *Health Effects of Low-Level Radiation*. New York: American Council on Science and Health, 1989.

American Institute of Real Estate Appraisers. *Asbestos: Basic Information for Appraisers*. 2d ed. Chicago: American Institute of Real Estate Appraisers, 1990.

___. *Real Estate Valuing, Counseling, Forecasting: Selected Writings of John Robert White*. Chicago: American Institute of Real Estate Appraisers, 1984.

Appraisal Institute. *Guide Notes to The Standards of Professional Appraisal Practice, Guide Note 6 - Reliance on Reports Prepared by Others*. Chicago: Appraisal Institute, 1991.

___. *Guide Notes to The Standards of Professional Appraisal Practice, Guide Note 8 - The Consideration of Hazardous Substances in the Appraisal Process*. Chicago: Appraisal Institute, 1991.

Armstrong, Betsy, and Knox Williams. *The Avalanche Book*. Colorado: Fulcrum, Inc., 1986.

Associated Press. "Ex-Asbestos Giant Faces New Court Challenges." *The Los Angeles Times* (January 19, 1993): Business Section, 1.

Ayre, Robert S. *Earthquake and Tsunami Hazards in the United States: A Research Assessment*. Boulder, Colo.: University of Colorado Institute of Behavioral Science, 1995.

Bell, Randall. "The Impact of Asbestos on Real Estate Values." *Right of Way* (October 1994): 10–21.

___. "Quantifying Diminution In Value Due To Detrimental Conditions: An Application to Environmentally Contaminated Properties." *Environmental Claims Journal* (October 1996): 135.

___. "The Ten Standard Categories of Detrimental Conditions." *Right of Way* (July 1996): 14–16.

Black, Harry Campbell, *Black's Law Dictionary*. 6th ed. Edited by Joseph R. Nolan, et al. St. Paul, Minn.: West Publishing Co., 1990.

Brindze, Ruth. *Hurricanes: Monster Storms from the Sea*. New York: Atheneum, 1973.

Brittendall, Gerald. "Identifying and Resolving Asbestos Problems." *Journal of Property Management*, Bulletin 371 (May/June 1985): 41.

Bullard, Fred M. *Volcanoes of the Earth*. Austin, Texas: University of Texas Press, 1984.

Bunkley, William, and Charles P. Edmonds III, PhD. "Appraising Wetlands." *The Appraisal Journal* (January 1992): 110.

California Energy Commission. *High-Voltage Transmission Lines*: July 1992.

Campbell, Don. *Drought: Causes, Effects, Solutions*. Melbourne, Australia: F.W. Cheshire, 1968.

Chalmers, James A., and Scott A. Roehr. "Issues in the Valuation of Contaminated Property." *The Appraisal Journal* (January 1993): 33.

Criscuola v. New York Power Auth., 621 N.E. 2d 1195, 1197 (N.Y. Ct. App. 1993).

Eaton, J. D. *Real Estate Valuation In Litigation*. 2d ed. Chicago: Appraisal Institute, 1995.

Encyclopedia Americana, vol. 9, s.v. "drought."

Encyclopedia Americana International Edition, vol. 14, s.v. "hurricane."

___. vol. 14, s.v. "tsunami."

___. vol. 14, s.v. "volcano."

Encyclopedia Britannica, vol. 15, s.v. "electromagnetic field."

Evans, S.G. "Landslides and Snow Avalanches in Canada" in *Geological Survey of Canada*, Ottawa [electronic bulletin board] October 1995 - [cited January 20, 1998]. Available: http://sts.gsc.emr.ca/page1/geoh/slide.htm.

"Fiberboard, Insurers Settle Asbestos Suit for Record $3 Billion." *Los Angeles Times* (August 31, 1993): Business Section, 1.

Frankel, Marvin. "Airport Noise and Residential Property Values: Results of a Survey Study." *The Appraisal Journal* (January 1991): 96–110.

Helm, Thomas. *Hurricanes: Weather at Its Worst*. New York: Dodd, Mead & Company, 1967.

Hunter, Malcolm L., Jr. *Fundamentals of Conservation Biology*. Cambridge, Mass.: Blackwell Science, 1995.

"Impacts of Drought" in *National Drought Mitigation Center* [electronic bulletin board] November 15, 1995 - [cited February 2, 1998]. Available: http://enso.unl.edu/ndmc /enigma/impacts.htm.

KC. "Hurricanes: In the Path of Destruction." *Worldwise* (August 1997): 12.

Keating, David Michael. *The Valuation of Wetlands* Chicago: Appraisal Institute, 1995.

Keating, David Michael, Charles P. Edmonds, and Sarah W. Stanwick. "A Conceptual Framework for Appraising Wetland Mitigation Banks." *The Appraisal Journal* (April 1997): 168.

Kluger, Jeffrey. "Volcanoes With An Attitude." *Time* (February 24, 1997): 58–59.

Kung, Hsiang-te, and Charles F. Seagle. "Impact of Power Transmission Lines on Property Values: A Case Study." *The Appraisal Journal* (July 1992): 413.

Latimer, Doug. "Avalanche Information" in *Rocky Mountain Hiking 1997* [electronic bulletin board] 1997 - [cited January 20, 1998]. Available: http://www.discovertherockies.com/Articles/AvalancheInformation/B-36.html.

Lentz, George H. "Asbestos and the Value of Commercial Real Estate." *The MGIC Newsletter* (March/April 1989): 2.

Little, Sheila A. "Effects of Violent Crimes on Residential Property Values." *The Appraisal Journal* (July 1988): 342.

Mansfield, Richard H. III. "Disclosure of Asbestos, Who Is Responsible?" *Legal Line* (April 1992): 36–37.

Marsh, Lindell L., Douglas R. Porter, and David Salvesen. *Mitigation Banking: Theory and Practice.* Washington, D.C.: Island Press, 1996.

McKenzie-Smith, Robert H. "Endangered Species Habitat and Urban Development." *The Appraisal Journal* (January 1994): 129–137.

Mitchell, John G. "Our Disappearing Wetlands." *National Geographic*, vol. 192, no. 4: 40–45.

Mundy, Bill. "Stigma and Value." *The Appraisal Journal* (January 1992): 7–13.

Neustein, Richard A. "Estimating Value Diminution by the Income Approach." *The Appraisal Journal* (April 1992): 283–287.

Oakeshott, Gordon B. *Volcanoes & Earthquakes: Geologic Violence.* New York: McGraw-Hill, 1976.

Odum, Eugene P. *Ecology and Our Endangered Life-Support Systems.* Sunderland, Mass.: Sinauer Associates, 1993.

Olsen, Ralph K. "Hazardous Waste Sites." *The Appraisal Journal* (April 1989): 233–236.

Overbeck, Wayne. "Electromagnetic Fields and Your Health" in *ARRL 1998 Handbook for Radio Amateurs* [electronic bulletin board] April 1994 - [cited January 15, 1998]. Available from http://www.arrl.org/news/rfsafety/wo9404.html.

Pacific Tsunami Museum [electronic bulletin board]. [cited December 29, 1997]. Available: www.planet-hawaii.com/tsunami/faq.htm.

Patchin, Peter J. "Contaminated Properties and the Sales Comparison Approach." *The Appraisal Journal* (July 1994): 402–409.

Pease, Craig M., and James J. Bull. "Do Electromagnetic Fields Cause Cancer?" in the University of Texas Biology 301C [electronic bulletin board] 1996 - [cited January 15, 1998]. Available: http://www.utexas.edu/courses/bio301c/Topics/EMF/Text.html

Perla, Ronald I., and M. Martinelli, Jr. *Avalanche Handbook*. U.S. Department of Agriculture Forest Service, 1976.

Pielke, Roger A. *The Hurricane*. New York: Routledge, 1990.

Porter, Douglas R., and David A. Salvesen. *Collaborative Planning for Wetlands and Wildlife*. Washington, D.C.: Island Press, 1995.

Ramsland, Maxwell O., Jr. "An Asbestos Abatement Model: A Valuation Methodology for Appraisers." *Environmental Watch* (Spring 1990): 2–7.

Slutsker, Gary. "Paratoxicology." *Forbes* (January 8, 1990): 303.

Spengler, John D., et al. *Summary of Symposium on Health Aspects of Exposure to Asbestos in Buildings*. Cambridge, Mass.: Harvard University Energy and Environmental Policy Center, August 1989.

Thompson, Donald N. *The Economics of Environmental Protection*. Cambridge, Mass.: Winthrop Publishers, Inc., 1973.

Turner, R. K., Carl Folke, I. M. Gren, and I. J. Bateman. "Wetland Valuation: Three Case Studies" in *Biodiversity Loss: Economic and Ecological Issues*. Edited by Charles Perrings, Karl-Goeran Maeler, Carl Folke, C. S. Holling, and Bengt-Owe Jansson. Cambridge, England: Cambridge University Press, 1995.

Tyler, Charles. "The Arid Earth." *Geographical Magazine* (May 1989): 44–45.

United Press International. "New Attitudes and Litigation Over Asbestos." *The Los Angeles Times* (September 22, 1993): Business Section, 7.

U.S. Department of Energy, National Institute for Occupational Safety and Health, and National Institute of Environmental Health Sciences. *EMF In The Workplace*. Washington, D.C.: U.S. Government Printing Office, 1996.

U.S. Department of the Interior, Fish and Wildlife Service. *Classifications of Wetlands and Deepwater Habitats of the United States*. Washington, D.C.: U.S. Government Printing Office, 1979.

U.S. Environmental Protection Agency. *Administration's Wetlands Plan: A Comprehensive Package of Reform* [electronic bulletin board]. [cited January 2, 1998]. Available: http://www.epa.gov/OWO/wetlands/wetplan5.html.

___. *EPA Study of Asbestos-Containing Materials in Public Buildings*. Washington, D.C.: U.S. Government Printing Office, 1988.

Webster's Ninth New Collegiate Dictionary, s.v. "Avalanche." Springfield, Mass.: Merriam-Webster, Inc., 1991.

"What is a Tsunami?" in *NASA Observatorium Earth Science* [electronic bulletin board]. [cited January 2, 1998]. Available: www.observe.ivv.nasa.gov/nasa/exhibits /tsunami/tsun_whatis.html.

Wilson, Albert R. "Emerging Approaches of Impaired Property Valuation." *The Appraisal Journal* (April 1996): 156–157.

___. "The Environmental Opinion: Basis for an Impaired Value Opinion." *The Appraisal Journal* (July 1994): 441.

___. "Probable Financial Effect of Asbestos Removal on Real Estate." *The Appraisal Journal* (July 1989): 378.

Wilson, Donald C. "Highest and Best Use: Preservation Use of Environmentally Significant Real Estate." *The Appraisal Journal* (January 1996): 76.

World Wildlife Fund. *Statewide Wetlands Strategies: A Guide to Protecting and Managing the Resource.* Washington, D.C.: Island Press, 1992.

Index

above-ground building construction conditions. *See* detrimental conditions, Class VI
absorption loss, 75-78
ACM. *See* asbestos containing material
action level. *See* maximum contaminant level
adjacent property, definition for Superfund purposes, 129
agricultural drought, definition, 170
air and light diminution, case study, 199-202
air sampling. *See* asbestos, testing for
airport noise, 86-88, 243; assessing the human effects of, 88; case study, 98-104, 213-215; measuring, 87; reducing the effects of, 88
Alaskan Good Friday Earthquake, effects on value of, 187-189
appraisal process, 3, 32; analyzing the property and reconciling its value, 3; defining the appraisal problem, 3; describing the subject property, 3
April Fools' Day Tsunami, effects on value of, 190-191

aqueous phase, 129
asbestos containing material, 133-135
asbestos, 133-135; legal limitations on use, 134; testing for, 135; treating for, 135
asbestosis, 135
assemblage, effects on value of, 50
assessment stage, of Detrimental Condition Model, 9-10
avalanche. *See* landslide

Balcones Canyonlands Conservation Plan (BCCP), 182, 184. *See also* wetland mitigation
barrier wars, 174
bathtub effect, 188
BCCP. *See* Balcones Canyonlands Conservation Plan
BCM. *See* building contamination material
before and after rule, 84-85
Bell Chart, 16-17, 33, 42
Benedict Canyon landslide, effects on value of, 194-197
benign condition. *See* detrimental conditions, Class I

benzene, toluene, ethylbenzene, and xylene, as environmental contaminants, 132-133

bioavailability, of a hazardous substance, 130

biodegradation, 140

bioremediation, 140

bioventing, 140

bog, differential settlement in, 113

brownfields, case study, 234-236. *See also* Comprehensive Environmental Response, Compensation, and Liability Act

BTEX. *See* benzene, toluene, ethylbenzene, and xylene

building construction conditions. *See* detrimental conditions, Class VI

building contamination material, 134-135

bundle of rights, 2, 3

buyer's market, 55

caissons or piles, 116-117, 162. *See also* reinforced repair *and* underpinning

capping, 142

carcinogen, 131-132

Carson, Rachel, 122

CERCLA. *See* Comprehensive Environmental Response, Compensation, and Liability Act

Clean Water Act, 125, 175, 177

closure letter. *See* no further action letter

competence of appraiser, in detrimental conditions situations, 43-44

Comprehensive Environmental Response, Compensation, and Liability Act (CERCLA), 124-128, 234-236, 238; steps in Superfund process, 128 (Exhibit 8.5)

COMPS Infosystems, Inc., 33

condemnation. *See* eminent domain

conditions adjustment, for imposed condition, 79

conformity, principle of, 2, 5. *See also* regression, principle of

construction terms, 106 (Exhibit 6.1)

contamination. *See* environmental contamination

control area, in neighborhood comparison approach, 35-37; in paired sales analysis, 19

corrosivity, as characteristic of hazardous substance, 125-126. *See also* sulfates, as environmental contaminants

cost approach, 3; in Detrimental Condition Model, *see* detrimental condition cost approach

cost, as component of Detrimental Condition Model, 8, 10-13, 34

cradle to grave responsibility, for environmental contamination, 125

creep, 159

crime scene, 71-74; case study, 204, 205, 260-261. *See also* detrimental conditions, Class IV

cyclone. *See* hurricane

Dahmer apartment site, effects on value of events at, 260-261

demand, 58-59. *See also* supply

dense non-aqueous phase liquid (DNAPL), 130

detrimental condition cost approach, 16-19

detrimental condition income capitalization approach, 23-27

Detrimental Condition Matrix, 8-10, 42

Detrimental Condition Model, definition, 15-16

detrimental condition sales comparison approach, 19-23

detrimental conditions, Class I, 46-48; case study, 48, 199-202; graph, 47

detrimental conditions, Class II, 49-54; case study, 52-54; further reading, 50; graph, 51

detrimental conditions, Class III, 55-67; case study, 61-67; further reading, 60; graph, 57; versus Class VII detrimental conditions, 119-121

detrimental conditions, Class IV, 68-78; case study, 75-78, 203, 204; further reading, 74; graph, 69 detrimental conditions, Class V, 79-104; case study, 98-104, 206-212, 213-215, 216-217, 218-220; further reading, 89-97; graph, 80

detrimental conditions, Class VI, 105-109; case study, 108-109, 221-224; graph, 107

detrimental conditions, Class VII, 110-121; case study, 119-121, 216-217, 225-227, 228, 229-230; further reading, 118; graph, 138

detrimental conditions, Class VIII, 122-162; case study, 160-162, 231-233, 234-236, 237, 238-241, 242-244; further reading, 150-159; graph, 156

detrimental conditions, Class IX, 155-189; case study, 187-189; further reading, 186; graph, 156

detrimental conditions, Class X, 190-197; case study, 194-197, 238-241, 257, 258-259, 260-261; graph, 193

detrimental conditions, definition, 8; methodologies, 32; stages, 8-9

differential settlement, 112-113; case study, 228

direct capitalization approach, 23-25

discounted cash flow analysis, 25-27

DNAPL. *See* dense non-aqueous phase liquid

drinking water, standards, 130

drought, 170

Durham Woods pipeline explosion, effects on value of, 203

earthflow, 159-160

earthquake, 115, 157-158; as factor in landslide, 160; as factor in tsunami, 162; case study, 187-189

economic recession, 59

electromagnetic fields (EMFs), 32, 88-89

Emergency Wetlands Resources Act, 176

EMFs. *See* electromagnetic fields

eminent domain, 81-86; case study, 206-212

encapsulation, of environmental contaminants, 136

enclosure, of environmental contaminants, 136-137

Endangered Species Act, 178

environmental condition. *See* detrimental conditions, Class VIII

environmental contamination, 122-162; in building improvements, 136-137; in soil and groundwater, 137-142; third-party liability, *see* indemnification, of responsibility for environmental contamination. *See also* environmental remediation

Environmental Protection Agency, 124-125, 135, 177, 234-236. *See also* Clean Water Act; Comprehensive Environmental Response, Compensation, and Liability Act; *and* Resource Conservation and Recovery Act

environmental remediation, 136-142; estimating cost of, 10-12; ex situ remediation methods, 141-142; in situ remediation methods, 141

environmental site assessment, 138-142; Phase I study, 138-139; Phase II study, 139; Phase III study, 139

EPA. *See* Environmental Protection Agency

equilibrium, of market, 58

erosion, 115; as factor in landslide, 160

ethics of appraiser, in detrimental conditions situations, 43-44

ex situ. *See* environmental remediation, ex situ remediation methods

excavation, of environmental contaminants, 141

expansive soils, 114; case study, 225-227, 229-230

Exxon Valdez oil spill, effects on value of, 237

facility, definition for Superfund purposes, 128

Federal Emergency Management Association (FEMA), 169

federal rule. *See* before and after rule

fee simple estate, 2

FEMA. *See* Federal Emergency Management Association

feng shui, as detrimental condition, 52-54
fixation, of environmental contaminants, 142
flood insurance coverage, 169
flooding, 168-169; case study, 245-256; role of wetlands in preventing, 176
formaldehyde, as environmental contamination, 131
friability, of asbestos containing material, 133
Fujita Scale, 166-167

geology, use of, by environmental engineers, 129
geotechnical construction condition. *See* detrimental conditions, Class VII
geotechnics, use of, in analysis of soil and subsurface construction conditions, 112
government agencies. *See specific titles of agencies.*
governmental regulations. *See specific titles of regulations.*
grading, as factor in landslide, 192, 194
Green Book, 135
groundwater, 129, 137-142
groundwater treatment, 141

habitat conservation plan, 181-182
habitat equivalency program, 182
habitat, environmental, 177-178. *See also* wetlands
hazardous substance, characteristics of, 124-127. *See also* maximum contaminant level
Heaven's Gate mansion, effects on value of events at, 70-71
highest and best use, 3; analysis of, of wetlands, 184-185
Hill View development, effects on value of events at, 199-202
Hodge, Sheida, 52
Hollywood Boulevard sinkhole and subsidence, effects on value of, 216-217
hurricane, 171. *See also* flooding
hydrocarbons, as environmental contaminants, 132-133, 234

hydrogeology, use of, by environmental engineers, 129

ignitability, as characteristic of hazardous substance, 125-126
impaired sales comparables, 20-21
impaired value, definition, 2
imposed condition. *See* detrimental conditions, Class V
imposed effects of time, 79, 81-82
imposed loss of access, 218-220
in situ. *See* environmental remediation, in situ remediation methods
income capitalization approach, 7-8; in Detrimental Condition Model, *see* detrimental condition income approach
income-producing property, diminution of property value in, 39-41
incurable conditions. *See* detrimental conditions, Class X
indemnification, of responsibility for environmental contamination, 231-233

Jarrell, Texas, tornado, effects on value of, 166-168
just compensation, 81-85; calculations, 84-85

land use regulations. *See* Clean Water Act, Endangered Species Act, wetlands, *and* zoning. *See also* detrimental conditions, Class V
landfill, proximity to, 86
landslide, 114, 159-162, 192; as factor in tsunami, 162; case study, 194-197
lava flow. *See* landslide *and* volcanic eruption
lead, as environmental contaminant, 130-131; testing for, 130
leaking underground storage tank (LUST), 137-138; case study, 152-154
Leaning Tower of Pisa, 113
leasehold value, imposed effects of time on, 79, 81-82
liability, for contamination, 125-126; for costs, 14-15

light non-aqueous phase liquid (LNAPL), 129-130
linear regression, use in value calculations, 102-103
liquefaction, 115
LNAPL. *See* light non-aqueous phase liquid
Love Canal, effects on value of events at, 238-241
Luby's Cafeteria, effects on value of events at, 205
LUST. *See* leaking underground storage tank

Manoa landslides, effects on value of, 161-162
Manson Family murder site, effects on value of events at, 71-72
market data, example of, 56 (Exhibit 3.1); sources of, 33; use of, 43
market resistance, 9, 14-15, 62-63; as form of risk, 14-15; case study, 229-230; derivation, 21-22
market surveys, 27-31; broker survey, 28; investor or lender survey, 29-31; structured interviews, 40-41
market trends, influence on value, 55-58
market value, definition, 49
marsh, differential settlement in, 113
maximum contaminant level, 130-131
MCL. *See* maximum contaminant level
Menendez mansion, effects on value of events at, 73
mesothelioma, 134
meteorological drought, 170
Milhaven Mitigation Bank, 181. *See also* wetland mitigation
mitigation bank, 181. *See also* wetland mitigation
monsoon. *See* hurricane
Moorpark Wetlands, 182-183
Mount St. Helens, effects on value of events at, 172-174
mudslide. *See* landslide
multiple listing service (MLS), as source of market data, 33

NAPL. *See* non-aqueous phase liquid
National Fire Protection Agency (NFPA), 126
National Priority List (NPL), 126. *See also* brownfields *and* Comprehensive Environmental Response, Compensation, and Liability Act
natural conditions. *See* detrimental conditions, Class IX
neighborhood comparison approach, 35-37
neighborhood nuisance, 61, 86-89; case study, 213-215
NFA letter. *See* no further action letter
NFPA Hazard Identification System, 127 (Exhibit 8.4)
no further action letter, 142. *See also* indemnification, of responsibility for environmental contamination *and* site closure
non-aqueous phase liquid (NAPL), 129
non-friable. *See* friability, of asbestos containing material
nonmarket motivations. *See* detrimental conditions, Class II
non-source property, definition for Superfund purposes, 129
Northridge Earthquake, effects on value of, 158
"Nothing Down" avalanche, effects on value of, 164-165
NPL. *See* National Priority List

Occupational Safety and Health Administration, 135
oil spill, case study, 237
Oklahoma Federal Building, effects on value of events at, 257
ongoing stage, of Detrimental Condition Model, 10
on-site low temperature thermal desorption. *See* environmental remediation, ex situ remediation methods
operations and management program, 137
OSHA. *See* Occupational Safety and Health Administration
ownership rights, 2

Pacific Motel, effects on value of partial taking of, 206-212
Pacific Tsunami Warning System, 163
paired sales analysis, 19-20; example, 63
piles. *See* caissons or piles
plume, of environmental spill, 129 (Exhibit 8.6), 130-131
potentially responsible party, for environmental contamination, 126
power lines, proximity to, 88-89
preliminary site assessment. *See* environmental site assessment, Phase I study
project incentive, 9; as form of risk, 13-14
proximity approach, 37-38
proximity to neighborhood nuisance. *See* neighborhood nuisance

radioactivity, as environmental contamination, 131-132; case study, 242-243
radon, as environmental contamination, 132
RCRA. *See* Resource Conservation and Recovery Act
reactivity, as characteristic of hazardous material, 125-127
real estate economics, 58-59
recession. *See* economic recession
regression, principle of, 2, 4. *See also* conformity, principle of
reinforced repair, 116-117. *See also* caissons or piles *and* underpinning
remedial action plan, 139. *See also* environmental remediation
remedial investigation. *See* environmental site assessment, Phase III study
remediation. *See* environmental remediation
removal of contaminants, 137
repair stage, of Detrimental Condition Model, 10
residential property, diminution of property value in, 33-38; interpreting market data, 34-38
Resource Conservation and Recovery Act (RCRA), 124-126

responsible party, for environmental contamination, 126
restrictions on use. *See* use, as component of Detrimental Condition Model
retrospective appraisal, 15-16, 34
Richter Scale, 157
risk, as component of Detrimental Condition Model, 8-9, 13-15, 43; quantification of, 40. *See also* market resistance, project incentive, *and* uncertainty factor

SACM. *See* Superfund Accelerated Cleanup Model
sale/resale analysis, 22-23
sales comparison approach, 7; in Detrimental Condition Model, *see* detrimental condition sales comparison approach
scoop and haul, of environmental contaminants, 141
seller's market, 55
Silent Spring, 122-124
Simpson condominium, effects on value of events at, 204
sinkhole, 194; case study, 216-217, 258-259
site closure, 142. *See also* no further action letter
slope creep, 114
slope failure, 160
slope movement. *See* landslide.
slump, 159-160
snow avalanche, 163-165. *See also* landslide
soil conditions. *See* detrimental conditions, Class VII
soil contamination, 137-142
soil vapor extraction, of environmental contaminants, 141
solvents, as environmental contaminants, 135
source property, definition for Superfund purposes, 128
species habitat mitigation, 181-184. *See also* wetland mitigation
state rule. *See* value plus damage rule
stigma. *See* market resistance

structured interviews, use in detrimental condition sales comparison approach, 40

subsidence, 114; case study, 216-217, 225-227

subsurface construction condition. *See* detrimental conditions, Class VII

subsurface study. *See* environmental site assessment, Phase II study

sulfates, as environmental contaminants, 115

Superfund Accelerated Cleanup Model (SACM), 235

Superfund. *See* Comprehensive Environmental Response, Compensation, and Liability Act

supply, 58-59. *See also* demand *and* market trends

surveys. *See* market surveys

swamp, differential settlement in, 113

temporary condition. *See* detrimental conditions, Class IV

terrorism, influence on property value, 73-74, 257

test area, in neighborhood comparison approach, 35-37; in paired sales analysis, 19

Three Mile Island, effects on value of events at, 242-244

tidal wave. *See* tsunami

tornado, 165-168

toxicity, as characteristic of hazardous substance, 125-126

toxicology, use of, by environment engineers, 130

tropical cyclone. *See* hurricane

tsunami, 162-163; case study, 187-189. *See also* flooding, earthquake

tunneling, 110; case study, 216-217

U.S. Army Corps of Engineers, 177, 184

U.S. Constitution, provisions for just compensation, 81

U.S. Geological Survey, 161

uncertainty factor, as form of risk, 13-14

underground storage tank (UST), 152-154

underpinning, 116-117. *See also* caissons or piles *and* reinforced repairs

Uniform Standards of Professional Appraisal Practice (USPAP), 44

unimpaired value, 38; definition, 2; derivation, 8

use, as component of Detrimental Condition Model, 8, 13, 34

USPAP. *See* Uniform Standards of Professional Appraisal Practice

UST. *See* underground storage tank

value plus damage rule, 85-86

view diminution, case study, 61-67

volcanic eruption, 115, 172-174, 191; as factor in landslide, 160; as factor in tsunami, 162

Walker Ranch, 181. *See also* wetland mitigation

water damage, case study, 221-224

wetland mitigation, 180-181, 183-184. *See also* species habitat mitigation

wetlands, 174-186; current trends in development, 179; definition, 176; highest and best use analysis, 184-185; legal issues, 177; past trends in development, 178-179; value patterns, 183-184. *See also* habitat, environmental

white-collar crime, case study, 48

World Trade Center, effects on value of events at, 73-74

x-ray fluorescence, as test for lead paint, 130

Yuba River floods, effects on value of, 245-256